D0024750

Manufacturing Citizenship

In recent years, citizenship has emerged as an important topic in the social sciences with much of the literature focusing on explicitly political methods nation-states use to create concepts of nationalism. In contrast, *Manufacturing Citizenship* concentrates on the ways in which educational agendas impact on national, cultural and individual identities.

This volume brings together contributors from the social sciences, including anthropologists, historians, sociologists and philosophers such as Etienne Balibar, to explore how educational institutions manufacture concepts of citizenship. By comparing cases in Europe, South Asia and China (including Taiwan) this book discusses the ways in which nation-states and their state education systems convey ideas and teach forms of citizenship. Crucially, *Manufacturing Citizenship* also highlights the constitutive political part played by ordinary social actors, including teachers and parents, in negotiating and shaping ideas and practices of citizenship.

Véronique Bénéï is Senior Research Fellow in Anthropology at the Centre National de la Recherche Scientifique (Laboratoire d'Anthropologie des Institutions et des Organisations Sociales, Paris) and at the London School of Economics. She has conducted extensive fieldwork in India on marriage, education and nationalism. She authored *La dot en Inde: un fléau social? Socio-anthropologie du mariage au Maharashtra* (1996) and co-edited four volumes, including *The Everyday State and Society in Modern India* (2000), *At Home in Diaspora. South Asian Scholars and the West* (2003), and *Remapping Knowledge. The Making of South Asian Studies in India, Europe and America (19th–20th centuries)* (2005). She is currently visiting the Princeton Institute for International and Regional Studies and teaching at the Anthropology Department, Princeton University.

Routledge research in education

Manufacturing Citizenship

Education and nationalism in
Europe, South Asia and China

Edited by Véronique Bénéï

Routledge
Taylor & Francis Group

LONDON AND NEW YORK

First published 2005
by Routledge
2 Park Square, Milton Park, Abingdon, Oxon OX14 4RN

Simultaneously published in the USA and Canada
by Routledge
270 Madison Ave, New York, NY 10016

Routledge is an imprint of the Taylor & Francis Group

© 2005 Véronique Bénéï

Typeset in Garamond by Wearset Ltd, Boldon, Tyne and Wear
Printed and bound in Great Britain by MPG Books Ltd, Bodmin

All rights reserved. No part of this book may be reprinted or
reproduced or utilized in any form or by any electronic, mechanical,
or other means, now known or hereafter invented, including
photocopying and recording, or in any information storage or
retrieval system, without permission in writing from the publishers.

British Library Cataloguing in Publication Data
A catalogue record for this book is available from the British Library

Library of Congress Cataloging in Publication Data
A catalog record for this book has been requested

ISBN 0-415-36488-4

22.06.05

To Miguel,
With thanks.
Veronique

To Vasco, Palolem and Dr Tabell

Contents

Contributors

Etienne Balibar is Professor of Philosophy at the University of Nanterre-Paris X, France and at the University of Irvine, California, USA.

Laura Bear is Lecturer in Anthropology at the London School of Economics, UK.

Véronique Bénéï (volume editor) is Senior Research Fellow in Anthropology at the Centre National de la Recherche Scientifique (Laboratoire d'Anthropologie des Institutions et des Organisations Sociales, Paris) and at the London School of Economics. She has conducted extensive fieldwork in India. She authored *La dot en Inde: un fléau social? Socio-anthropologie du mariage au Maharashtra* (1996) and co-edited four volumes, amongst which *The Everyday State and Society in Modern India* (2000) and *At Home in Diaspora. South Asian Scholars and the West* (2003).

Naran Bilik is Professor at the Institute of Ethnology and Anthropology, Chinese Academy of Social Sciences, Beijing, China, and Bernstein Visiting Professor of Anthropology and East Asian Studies at Carleton College, Minnesota, USA.

Rebecca Bryant is Assistant Professor of Anthropology at George Mason University, USA.

Martha Caddell is Lecturer in Development Studies at The Open University, Milton Keynes, UK.

Allen Chun is Senior Research Fellow in Anthropology at the Academia Sinica, Taiwan.

Rana Mitter is Lecturer in History at the University of Oxford and a member of the Institute for Chinese Studies, UK.

Aminah Mohammad-Arif is Research Fellow in Anthropology at the Centre National de la Recherche Scientifique (Centre for Indian and South Asian Studies, Paris/EHESS), France.

Audrey Osler is Research Professor and Director of the Centre for Citizenship and Human Rights Education within the School of Education at the University of Leeds, UK.

Jane Schneider is Professor of Anthropology at the City University of New York, USA.

Peter Schneider is Professor of Sociology at the Department of Sociology, Fordham University, New York, USA.

Acknowledgements

This volume is partly derived from an international conference organized by me at the Maison Française, Oxford on 6 and 7 July 2001 on 'Manufacturing Citizenship: Europe, South Asia, China'. This conference was made possible thanks to the generous support of the French National Centre for Scientific Research (CNRS), Section 38, under the auspices of Raymond Jamous and Gérard Lenclud; that of the Programme for International Scientific Co-operation (PICS 740/CNRS): 'Locality, the nation and transnational developments seen from South Asia. Critical perspectives on "globalization" ', run by Jackie Assayag in collaboration with the Department of Anthropology of the London School of Economics and Political Science, at that time convened by Chris Fuller; as well as, in Oxford, that of Steve Tsang, then director of the Asian Studies Centre, and David Washbrook, of St Antony's College. My heartfelt thanks are due to all of them for their financial, institutional and intellectual support throughout the project, as well as to Jennifer Griffiths of the Asian Studies Centre and Paola Belloni, Claire Stevenson and Carol Johnson of the Maison Française in Oxford, at that time under the direction of Jean-Claude Sergeant, for facilitating the smooth running of the conference. Thanks are also due to the current director of the Maison Française, Alexis Tadié, for allowing the project to come to fruition. Here in Princeton, the invaluable institutional support of Miguel Centeno, director of the Princeton Institute for International and Regional Studies, and of Carol Greenhouse and Carol Zanca, acting chair and manager of the department of anthropology respectively, has seen me through the last stages of the publication. Many cheerful thanks to all three of them.

In addition to making the conference possible, many other people expressed an interest in this project, whether as discussants at the conference or as concerned, committed, and to some extent interactive readers, throughout the various stages this book went through. They are Marianne Bastid-Bruguière, Marion Demossier, David Faure, Stephan Feuchtwang, Thomas Hansen, Deborah James, Sudipta Kaviraj, Sunil Khilnani, Steven Lukes, Adrian Mayer, Francoise Mengin, Brendan O'Leary, Sherry Ortner, Peter Robb, Robert Tombs and Denis Vidal. My gratitude goes to them for their lively contributions to the debate. Last but not least, special thanks are due to the two anonymous reviewers for their supportive comments and, most importantly, to David Phelps, whose patience and rigour in copy-editing have helped this book come into full shape.

In addition to the authors represented in this volume, Keith Brown, Stephan Feuchtwang, Cris Shore, Helen Siu, Anne-Marie Thiesse and David Washbrook also presented papers at the conference. While the conference addressed issues surrounding the process of the making of citizenship in general, the book itself now focuses more specifically on citizenship in relation to education and nationalism. For this reason, only four out of the ten chapters of the present volume are revised versions of papers presented at the time of the conference (those by Bear, Bryant, Chun and Mitter). The remaining six chapters have been especially written for this volume.

Véronique Bénéï
Princeton, February 2005

Introduction

Manufacturing citizenship – Confronting public spheres and education in contemporary worlds

Véronique Bénéï

> Which is the best government? That which teaches us to govern ourselves.
> (Johann Wolfgang von Goethe)

Hyde Park, London, 15 February 2003. Between one and two million demonstrators gathered to express publicly their protest against the impending war on Iraq by the British–American-led alliance. At about the same time, protesters also invaded public spaces in 600 towns, cities and capitals around the world, from Tasmania to Iceland, in the US, the Middle East, Latin America, South and Southeast Asia, and Africa. All in all, up to 30 million people demonstrated worldwide that weekend, making it by far the most important public protest since the Vietnam War. All the social and political actors who took part in this large-scale event were neither thereby complying with any electoral process; nor were they attending any formally institutionalized political event. Yet, they were acting as informed and concerned citizens, appropriating other arenas of political life for themselves. If anything, such a large-scale concern on the part of the citizenry of so many nation-states suggests a need for political analysts to rethink their conclusions about a crisis in participatory democracy.[1] It has become commonplace to lament a crisis in participatory democracy evidenced by falling levels of electoral participation. Such falling levels purportedly testify to a lack of citizenship awareness, which in its turn is seen as calling for remedies. Most prominent among these proposed remedies is citizenship education by means of a specially designed curriculum. Whether the sense of 'civic zeal' underpinning such a project is a long-standing sentiment, periodically renewed, or whether it is a more recent phenomenon, formal education is expected to tackle a general apathy or lack of interest in civic and political life among ordinary members of the various national publics. Interestingly, what in so-called 'established nations' is bemoaned as apathy is denounced as 'ignorance' and 'backwardness' in others, whose history of democracy is a more recent one. The contrasting experiences reflected by these different terms have significance for a comparison of nation-state formations and an understanding of experiences of citizenship, not only within the Euro-American traditions of political philosophy, but also across the world at large.

To be sure, there is a real difficulty in identifying the various layers of meaning and the realities encompassed by the notion of citizenship in different contexts.[2] The nature and the scope of the rights and obligations encompassed by the concept of citizenship vary widely from country to country (Butenschon 2000). Nonetheless, the existence of over 200 nation-states in the world today, as against a mere 40 at the end of the Second World War, suggests that over the last 50 years a vocabulary of political institutions largely derived from a 'Western experience' has increasingly been shared across the globe. Yet this very notion of 'sharing' is itself problematic. First, the generalization of the nation-state model to the rest of the planet has entailed, at best, accommodation to local contexts, and, at worst, misunderstandings, misinterpretation, mistranslation, even resistance on all sides. Consequently, there may be considerable disagreement on the nature of what, if anything, is actually shared. Second, the notion of 'sharing' obscures the possible existence of indigenous notions of political organization comparable to or competing with those of citizenship 'in the West'. Third, it glosses over the multiplicity of experiences of citizenship among different sections of the population that may also be extant *within* a given country. Documenting these experiences among individuals and groups is a prerequisite for comprehending the diversity of the lived realities of citizenship. If, for some official observers and scholars, the terms 'ignorance' and 'backwardness' aptly describe citizens' understanding of and involvement in the life of the political community, they are highly contested by ordinary social actors' very ideas, representations and practices. These, indeed, suggest a much richer field, whose analysis has only recently begun and has led to a renewed discourse on citizenship. Such a discourse has engaged with the comparative paucity of studies of 'new' nation-states' political institutions as against the heavy preponderance of work produced on the earlier exemplars of nation-states. Much European and American scholarship had indeed focused on 'old Western' nations in discussing citizenship in the nineteenth and twentieth centuries. By contrast, so-called 'non-Western' nations attracted far less scholarly attention. At best, they were considered as incomplete, faulty replicas of the French or German models; at worst, as national(ist) anomies. Long-held assumptions about 'Western' categories of political understanding and their implementation have however had to be reconsidered over the last two decades in view of the international redistribution of the geopolitical world order, wherein the issues of democracy, civil society and citizenship have acquired particular salience.

Anthropologists and the 'new discourse on citizenship': the public sphere contested

Studies of citizenship regained ground in the 1990s owing to the exacerbation of ethnic conflicts, the fall of communism and the development of the notion of human rights as a separate category in international law.[3] In contrast to earlier and more highly theoretical debates, the new discourse on citizenship draws especially on feminist (see Rubinstein 1996) and postcolonial critiques, and crucially starts 'from a recognition that citizenship is neither a pure realm of ideas nor simply an area of political advocacy' (Werbner 1998: 2). Central to these new studies has been the questioning of the claim to universalism often associated with notions of citizenship.[4] The moment of so-called 'universal emancipation' indeed coincided with one of female, racial and class subordination and exclusion. The idea that nationalist claims were 'primarily linked to democratization, to claims for the equality and liberty of all citizens and even to the notion of a "community of free and equal citizens" as a source of political legitimacy' (Schnapper 2002: 2) completely ignores the fact that the beginnings of citizenship in nation-states were far from egalitarian, even within European countries. As was highlighted by the recent re-evaluation (Calhoun 1997a; Eley 1997; Fraser 1997) of Habermas's discussion of the notion of civil society as public opinion and culture (largely the fact of the emerging bourgeoisie) and his extension of this to a politicized notion of it following the French Revolution, dispute and contestation were central to the 'public sphere'. It was from the very outset an arena of contested meanings in two ways: contestation and competition from different groups within this arena, and the exclusion of others (women, subordinate nationalities, slaves, colonial subjects, the urban poor, the working class and the peasantry) altogether. As Wallerstein recently reminded us, '[c]itizenship always excluded as much as it included' (2003: 674). Membership in the national political community of many a European country was defined by a limited right granted exclusively to male members of the propertied classes.[5] Such a membership was also predicated upon an urban–rural divide also found in later colonial and postcolonial situations whereby a 'limbo class' belonging neither to rural areas nor to urban civil society, 'in civil society but not of it' (e.g. the working classes in Europe, migrant labour in Africa, the peasantry in South Asia) played a major part in the struggle for emancipation (from the bourgeoisie-led state and employers and colonialists respectively). It is both the need to address the conflictual dimension inherent in the public sphere and the necessity of apprehending processes of civil society formation and citizenship manufacturing in the context of a set of dialectical relations between nations, empires and their colonies that have prompted new studies of citizenship examining both the theory and practice of heretofore neglected issues. Prominent among these issues have been multiculturalism,[6] consumption,[7] religion,[8] gender[9] and transnationalism.[10]

Anthropologists have only recently entered this field (see in particular Butenschon *et al.* 2000; Comaroff and Comaroff 1999; Hann 1996; Joseph 2001; Werbner 1998; Yuval-Davis and Werbner 1999). Indeed, anthropologists working in 'developing nations' for a long time rightfully rejected the assumption of a universal vocabulary of political institutions. Yet this rejection was problematic on two counts. First, it had as its consequence a lasting neglect of modern nation-states and related issues, in spite of an increasingly shared vocabulary of political institutions across the globe (see also Spencer 1997). Second, such a rejection did not provide any deep understanding of how the ideas of citizenship and democracy do motivate political struggles in some of the newer nation-states as well as in the older ones. A need was gradually felt by some anthropologists to embark on an exploration of political modernity and consequently to elaborate a 'theory of citizenship that addresses the complex realities of post-colonial societies' (Werbner 1998: 3). This entails 'exoticizing' the very notion of citizenship, thanks to the 'distant gaze' so dear to anthropology's practitioners collecting first-hand accounts in the field. Postcolonial anthropology is particularly well placed to contribute to the new discourse on citizenship for several reasons. The discipline's theoretical subject-matter has long been 'difference' and 'identity', the dynamics of inclusion and exclusion, but also the particular in the universal, as much as the reverse. Political anthropology in its heyday was, notwithstanding much meandering, concerned with defining a new conceptual vocabulary for politics which would also integrate non-Euro-American forms and practices of 'the political'. Furthermore, anthropology also seeks to reconcile the pragmatics of moral discourses (Bourdieu 1977) with a focus on the power of culture in shaping political institutions (D. Gupta 2000; Spencer 1997; Steinmetz 1999; Werbner 1998). Anthropologists are therefore well equipped to analyse the claims, representations and practices of citizenship as well as the dialogical, relational and interdependent dimensions that enter into citizenship manufacturing.

Yet the students of these processes need to practise disciplinary interaction: anthropologists must engage in a critical dialogue with other disciplines. It is by acknowledging the significance of the work achieved by other disciplines in the analysis of concepts of European political thought, and actively entering into intellectual exchange with other practitioners of the social sciences, that anthropology can both renew itself in its ancient domain of predilection (in this case, political anthropology) and make a significant contribution to the field of 'modern politics'. This volume aims to take a first step in this direction by bringing a majority of anthropologists together with scholars of sociology, political science, philosophy and history.

It focuses on the multidimensional aspects of citizenship that go beyond mere ascription. The coldly constitutional view of citizenship as only entailing a rational, contractual relationship ideally premised on rights and duties and sustained by all citizens with their nation-state has led to an overemphasizing of the study of explicitly political sites of the manufacturing of citizenship such as electoral and other institutionalized processes. Furthermore, even outside of explicitly political sites, attention has often – and understandably so – been paid more to exceptional and spectacular events in the ordinary making of nationality and citizenship (see for instance Nora 1996–8; Pandey 2001; Skocpol 1979). By contrast, this volume purposefully gives pre-eminence to the ordinary and mundane by depicting instances of the 'banality of citizenship' (to echo Billig's (1995) formulation of 'banal nationalism', itself borrowed from Arendt on the 'banality of evil'), whether in Europe, China or South Asia. The volume focuses on the ordinary daily life processes involving cultural, historical and political memories that feed into the educational dimension of the 'manufacturing' of citizenship. By means of various case studies, ranging from the curricular 'strengthening' of citizenship in Britain, through attempts at fostering European citizenship, to Indian and Pakistani textbooks, and the implementation of Chinese state projects, to name but a few, the volume seeks to contribute to an understanding of the part played by educational institutions at various levels (from local, to regional and national). It pays special attention to the role of the Other and the importance of ethnicity and language in creating a homogeneous, dominant citizen, as well as the tensions that may arise between taught ideals of citizenship and various political, religious or ethnic affiliations, and the ways in which states and social actors negotiate them.

To be sure, such dimensions can be explored in *all* nation-states. Yet the scope of the comparison is here deliberately confined to Europe, South Asia and China – including Taiwan. Although India and China have given rise at different periods to much Orientalist fantasizing, not least in matters political, they were the sites of two of the earliest successful nationalist movements in the 'non-Western' world – movements that greatly influenced subsequent independence struggles elsewhere. In spite of this, they have seldom been taken as points for comparison by 'Western' studies of 'Western' nationalism; and only rarely have they been compared with each other. Yet they offer valuable comparative perspectives on the study of the manufacturing of citizenship in relation to education and nationalism, particularly since China, unlike India, was never fully colonized. Furthermore, at first sight, the three regions appear to offer radically different conditions for the production of citizenship, conditions often hastily summarized under the rubrics of a China dominated by political parties (though different parties on the mainland and in Taiwan), an India dominated by culture(s), and a liberal individualist Europe. Yet what the present essays demonstrate is that, on closer inspection, these differences may come to appear less dominant at certain levels of analysis, and other similarities may emerge: France and both China and Taiwan, for instance, appear to have much in common in terms of the relatively high degree of centralization of their educational systems at all levels, whereas India and Britain share educational systems in which there is a considerable degree of plurality and variability particularly at the upper levels that has historically deep and heterogeneous roots – differences that perhaps hark back to a system of state institution and control in the former case, and of state regulation and inspection of systems of mixed public/private origin in the latter. Culture, in all three regions, plays out to varying degrees depending on the period and the issue under consideration. By comparing South Asia, China and Europe, this volume therefore wants to go against the grain of the classicizing pictures of Oriental despotism and political chaos that seem so persistent in contemporary European and North American eyes. True, recent events in Central Asia and the Middle East may have done little to modify such negative views of 'non-Western' governance (though yet more recent events may have reinforced doubts about the allegedly greater abilities of some of the older nation-states to present convincing practical examples of their supposedly greater wisdom in governance in action either). Yet hopefully the social sciences may be able to supply some rather more vivid and contemporary representations to overlay these tired but lingering afterimages.

Manufacturing citizenship

Of course, the use of the word 'manufacture' is a – barely – veiled reference to Noam Chomsky's film *Manufacturing Consent*. In this film, as is well known, the linguist-*cum*-social and political activist documents the various ways in which political consensus is effected in US civil society by withholding or distorting or otherwise concealing disturbing information from the American public. Such a kind of 'manufacturing' corresponds to the more recent, derogatory meaning of 'producing by mere mechanical labour rather than by intellect or imagination' and does not do justice to ordinary social actors' capacity for action and 'cunning intelligence' (see de Certeau 1998; Détienne and Vernant 1974).[11] So that although Chomsky's demonstration at first sight appears persuasive, current international events also forcefully demonstrate that the kind of consensus thus reached is far from stable, thereby confirming the much greater semantic wealth of the term and the relevance of its use in the present context. To 'manufacture' is also to 'bring into a form suitable for use', to 'make or fabricate from material'. Here, the material thus manufactured, which may be fictitious in part, is that of memories, imaginaries, emotions and practices of citizenship in their various dimensions – political, judicial, cultural, social, historical; all materials which are part of a continuous bricolage which may produce even deviant assemblages. In exploring these dimensions comparatively, the book unravels some of the ways in which national identities and modes of citizenship have been elaborated, negotiated and transmitted in different cultural and historical contexts.

States and citizens

The state has obviously played a central role in this quotidian manufacturing, whether in Europe or in most parts of the non-European world. National states have, until recently, penetrated down to the minutest details of everyday life in order to instil a sense of loyalty in their citizens.[12] More recently, however, congruently with theories of globalization emphasizing the demise of the state, the ability of the state to retain its exclusive feature of sovereignty has been questioned. States are said to have been declining in power since the 1970s owing to economic globalization and market liberalism. A consequence of such liberalization is that the power of the national state may seem less effective and relevant owing to the state's having lost some of its earlier capacity to control the movement of capital across its own borders. Thus, according to Habermas, the globalization of information, of economic production, and of financial flows, technologies and armament, together with that of ecological and military risks, has given rise to problems that can no longer find a solution through the mediation of the nation-state (2000: 90–7).[13]

Yet the fact that the state may appear in some domains to no longer be a relevant entity for analysing some of the ongoing economic, financial, cultural and technological processes today should not obfuscate its still inescapable role in a variety of realms impacting on the lives of its citizens. Indeed, state power at times seems even more visible and encroaching (Fuller and Bénéï 2001; Trouillot 2001). The state – and its government – remains essential for the citizens living within its borders. Not only does it still control movement of people across its borders in a majority of cases, but also the definition and production of citizens and citizenship as well as the control and production of violence, towards minorities in particular. The facts that citizens still need a passport for travelling beyond the frontiers of their own nation-states, and that asylum seekers still apply for residence to nation-states' bureaucracies, should alert us both to the wide range of other domains in which the state is still sovereign, and to the consequent need for further studying state institutions, especially schooling. As has been shown by Audrey Osler (this volume, Chapter 8), especially international agencies such as UNESCO recognize nation-states as key players for bringing about awareness, through their educational systems, of various issues such as the necessity of maintaining national and international peace and of furthering respect for equality. Hence the need felt in this volume to focus on education and citizenship *within* the context of nation-states.

To be sure, taking the role of international agencies into consideration remains crucial. But this role has to be envisaged in relation to the Gellnerian perspective (1983) premised on a universalist sociological model of modernization, so oft-encountered at the levels of *both* international aid agencies and state apparatuses. Such a perspective, as is well known, associates modernization with industrialization and secular nationalism. In such a context, industrial division of labour is required, as well as a shared culture of nation-alism that would hold together a society rendered atomized by the very processes associated with industrialization. This homogeneous culture is aimed at being produced through schooling, especially at the primary level. In keeping with such a theoretical premise, all nation-states, whether 'older' or 'newer', have developed and implemented policies and programmes of 'universalisation of elementary education' to varying extents (Lê Thành Khôi 2001).

Such developments have raised the question of the impact of uniform education practices on diverse national populations. In most 'newer' states (although not exclusively), this has often been accompanied by international aid programmes, thus generating questioning of the presence and objectives of these international aid agencies (see Caddell, Chapter 3). In this respect, the role of agendas of citizenship development vis-à-vis those of producing a 'global', uniformly literate labour force have been matters of acrimonious contention in education agendas, *both* in older and newer nation-states. Whether in Britain or in India, to take but these two examples, the issue of racial and ethnic diversity has occupied many public debates about school-ing in recent years. If, in the first instance, these have revolved around the recomposition of British society in regards to the more recent flows of migration, in the latter, they have focused on the implications of religious affiliation (particularly Hindu and Muslim) for defining citizenship.

Regardless of their specificities, these succinct examples confirm the need for comparatively engaging with the all too often taken-for-granted Gellner-ian perspective mentioned above. Not only is this perspective highly prob-lematic in view of its ethnocentrism inasmuch as it precludes any alternative model of modernity (see for instance Van der Veer 2001). It also leaves out *ordinary* social agency. The perception of citizenship and education (school-ing in particular) as state-centred strategies of social control and state-led projects serving the hierarchical structures of social reproduction (Bourdieu and Passeron 1990) and of capitalist inequality does not do justice to the crucial role played by ordinary citizens. Indeed, if citizenship comprises the modern nation-state's range of attempts to define and produce 'ideal, loyal and dutiful citizens', no less does it also comprehend social actors' negoti-ated responses to these. The view that states manufacture identities and cit-izenship at will (Bourdieu 1999) is far too monolithic: it obfuscates social actors' intervention in the public sphere at different levels of mediation – whether state institutions, voluntary organizations or even communalist outfits. Civic movements such as that of the *sans papiers* in France (Balibar 1998, 2001; Fassin 2001), conscientious objection in Israel (Helman 2000), Chinese 'passively resistant' movements such as that of the Falungong sect, secularist mobilizations of Indian citizens protesting against recent upsurges of communal violence in Gujarat (or even the Hindu right-wing activism instrumental in the latter); all are evidence of ordinary social actors' active contribution to the (un-)making of citizenship, whether premised on universalist values, secularism or religious principles. Such processes are constitutive of citizenship, contributing to its continuous redefinition and reshaping, and thus denote congruence with yet another meaning – often neglected today – of 'manufacture': to 'produce by natural *agency*'. And thus it also means how, by 'manufacturing citizenship', one becomes a citizen. In other words, rather than a nation-state project aimed at producing a culturally and nationally homogeneous labour force, education may also be seen as a means for promoting active democracy premised on the building of autonomous, critical citizens, much in congruence with American philosopher and educationalist John Dewey's project.[14]

Educational processes

Although T. H. Marshall's (1950) path-breaking discussion of the evolution of citizenship in modern nation-states (from the formation and democratization of civil citizenship to political citizenship followed by social citizenship) has been criticized as teleological rather than contingent, its undeniable interest is to present a historical process, a movement, rather than a mere status, as in the liberal tradition. Instead of furthering a complacent picture of citizenship as the indication of an unquestioned status bestowal, Marshall stressed that citizenship is nowhere a given, whether at the level of the wider national community or at that of an individual. Rather, citizenship is a process in two different ways. At the national level, it is the ongoing product of a historical process. At an individual one, it involves a Foucauldian notion of subjectification of individuals – principally by means of 'surveillance mechanisms' such as schooling – as well as the naturalization of a civil identification with the national political community over time (see Helman 2000). This secondary identity transcends primary identities in what becomes a *banal* citizenship.

Education obviously plays a crucial role in this naturalization of a civil identification. To be sure, the notion of education encompasses a wide range of processes, from informal learning taking place in a variety of contexts (family, media, cultural activities or events and so on) and at many levels of society through to formal schooling – the systematic instruction and training of children and young people, and by extension, of adults. The term may also refer to the development of mental or physical powers, the moulding of (some aspect of) character, in addition to the public policy of providing formal instruction. Owing to the wide definitional scope of the term 'education', some scholars have aptly interrogated the nature of the relationship between citizenship and education. Schuller (2001), for instance, has questioned the oft-assumed crucial role played by expansive formal education, including that of a specially designed 'civics' curriculum. Indeed, citizenship education is often part of a wider body of cultural knowledge encompassing history, art and the humanities. It is also relayed by cultural and social institutions that lie beyond the scope of formal education.

Yet however differently education is defined, educational institutions are key organizations associated with the promotion of the rights and responsibilities of citizenship (Marshall 1950). School in particular, has often been a privileged site for testing, even implementing projects – however utopian – of citizenship. Today, education often connotes the naturalization of a civil identification that is deemed the mark of an indisputable 'modernity'. Pedagogical missions lay at the very core of modernity projects both in 'Western' and 'non-Western' situations. Educational projects have since the eighteenth and nineteenth centuries been sites for the expression of competing and conflicting visions of modernity. These were promoted by either colonial administrators and missionaries, or by indigenous educationalists and political and social leaders, at the level of public fora, newspapers or other media participating in the construction of a public sphere.[15] Governments, too, particularly envisaged pedagogical missions as crucial tools for safeguarding the viability of the state by producing 'responsible citizens'. Hence the formal educational projects concocted in the nineteenth century by state officials and administrators, whether in Australia, with the establishment of school systems for the 'preparation of the young for their future responsibilities as citizens' (Macintyre 1996: 229), or in India, with the creation of separate schools for separate communities in order to secure the latter's allegiance to the colonial state (Bear, this volume, Chapter 10).

Because the state undeniably plays a major part in the manufacturing of citizenship, many of the contributors have chosen to focus on examples of formal schooling. Schools are indeed privileged sites of observation for the manufacturing of what followers of a communitarian perspective call 'the kinds of social bonds, commitment, and education, maybe even molding, necessary to create and maintain [. . .] a national community' (Shafir 1998: 11) and of the educational initiatives promoting particular visions of citizenship. Yet, in order to highlight the multiplicity of levels at which citizenship is manufactured, most authors in this volume have adopted varied perspectives and levels of analysis; not only top-down views of state projects, but also bottom-up views of social actors' engagement and negotiation with the institutions of their nation-state (from schools to parents or associations involved in educational processes). In so doing, they provide heuristic elements for a contribution to a comparison between 'new' and 'old' nation-states

'New' and 'old' nation-states: towards a comparison

Western modernity and colonial experiences

Many debates have centred on the specificity of (Christian) Western modernity and the issue of its reproducibility in 'non-Western' contexts, that is, whether modernity entails universal adoption of Western forms of political institutions such as democracy, civil society and citizenship.[16] If, such ideas embody the epic of Western modernity, the question is also whether the historical experience of Western politics is meaningful to other societies that have different cultural and historical logics, yet that have historically been affected by the Western model (Khilnani 2001: 14). In this respect, it is important to remember that whether in Europe or elsewhere, citizenship is hardly the product of consistent, homogeneous cultural influences. Just like ideas about the nation-state (Anderson 1991) and 'civil society' (Kaviraj and Khilnani 2001), 'Western' ideas about citizenship are not a new thing linked to a form of unprecedented (political) globalization.[17] On the contrary, they have been circulating around the world since the nineteenth century. European discourses of 'civil society' made their historical entry into non-Western political discourse through entering the political literature of European colonies as early as the nineteenth century (Kaviraj and Khilnani 2001). The ideas of 'civil society' and 'citizenship' are therefore not as recent for new nation-states as they are often purported to be. Yet, if the cross-circulation of models and borrowings for the construction of nationalism (Anderson 1991; Hobsbawm 1997; Thiesse 1999) and civil society (Castro Leiva and Pagden 2001; Goody 2001; Metzger 2001), both across Europe and elsewhere, has been largely documented, this task remains to be fulfilled in the field of citizenship. Such a task requires an appraisal of the problems posed by the debates about political modernity in relation to colonial experiences.

To begin with, these debates have been dominated by a particularly elitist conception of modernity in non-Western and postcolonial contexts: such as in Europe until the mid-twentieth century, only members of *the elite* are seen as possessing an understanding of democracy and of the workings of the state. By contrast, ordinary social actors are deemed powerless agents disconnected from the world of bureaucratic and rational modernity. This position has been challenged over the last decade, especially with regard to notions of the state (see for instance A. Gupta 1995; Fuller and Bénéï 2001; and Hansen and Stepputat 2001). As regards civil society, however, a disjunction is still felt between the reaching out of the state's legal-bureaucratic apparatus to virtually the entire population inhabiting its territory on the one hand, and the still restricted access of 'citizens' to civil social institutions on the other (Chatterjee 2001: 172), with the result that the overwhelming majority of ordinary social actors is still untouched by ideas and notions of civil society. In sum, the theoretical hiatus deemed to exist between members of the *elite* and the rest of the population regarding matters of the state has been reproduced in the domain of civil society. Such a hiatus, Chatterjee argues, is 'the mark of non-Western modernity as an always incomplete project of "modernization"' (ibid.).

There are several difficulties with such a statement. First, there is the suggestion that modernity, whether 'Western' or 'non-Western', can ever be anything other than an 'incomplete project of modernization'. The point here is that the West is also engaged in a project of modernization that by its very nature is incomplete and ever beyond reach: in fact, this incomplete-ness is itself the very *telos* of modernity. Second, the terms of the comparison between the (ever so arbitrary) categories of 'Western' and 'Eastern' forms of modernity are grossly and unfairly flawed: what is actually compared is a Western theoretical position stemming from a specific historical and polit-ical philosophy (political forms of governance as they should be) with an empirical observation pertaining to 'Eastern' political and civil life (political forms of governance as they actually are). As was said above, such incom-plete and ineffective modernity is by no means characteristic of 'Eastern' societies: surveys of citizenship conducted in so-called 'Western' nation-states (see for instance Crick 2001a; Macintyre 1996: 239) have highlighted that – even in these exemplary sites of modernity – most ordinary social actors have little understanding of and connection with issues pertaining to civil society. Furthermore, the incompleteness of civil society and cit-izenship in 'the West' is also highly debated (see for instance Pandey and Geschiere 2003: 11), not least in this volume (see Balibar, Chapter 1 and Schneider and Schneider, Chapter 7 in particular). Therefore, to argue that the hiatus between members of the *elite* and ordinary people is a feature of *non-Western* modernity as an always incomplete project of modernization is a gross exaggeration. The sites of 'non-Western' modernity are not the only ones where the existence of an *elite* political culture has neither done away with 'lower, mass political cultures' nor gained any legitimacy because it has failed to provide a framework of intelligibility for popular expectations and has been unable to live up to them. Theorists of modernity need to allow for the existence of other trajectories than those recognized and charted by Western political theory. And, as Hann argues, '[t]he narrow, western liberal-individualist idea of civil society has long been in need of [. . .] ethnographic investigation' (1996: 22). Especially so that, to paraphrase Comaroff and Comaroff, this idea 'has proven impossibly difficult to pin down' (1999: 5).

Furthermore, if the notion of civility, understood as the development of restraint and 'manners' accompanying the Enlightenment and rationality, became central to the development of civil society and citizenship, it is however not specific to Western Europe. The problem with this kind of 'moral evaluation' attached to the concepts of 'civility', 'rationality' and 'enlightenment' is that these are seen as a Western preserve (Goody 2001: 153). So in order to understand these trajectories – especially in relation to civil society, democracy and citizenship – the colonial experiences of non-European histories need to be explored, along with the individual legal, con-ceptual and political languages that each society has developed; and then also they need to be compared and contrasted with those shaped by the European historical experience. In this respect, it should be emphasized that because there was never any uniform or homogeneous colonial situation (see for instance Cooper and Stoler 1997; Stocking 1991; Thomas 1994), the variety of experiences of political modernity brought about by the colonial encounter in non-European societies is profoundly diverse. Consequently, colonial sovereignty gave rise to some early ideas of 'civil society' and 'citizenship' in a variety of ways. Whether '[a]ctual processes in the Third World are mostly very different from political life in the West' or not (Kaviraj and Khilnani 2001: 4) requires, at the very least, investigation.

Nationality, ethnicity and nationalism

At stake in the notion of citizenship in modern nation-states is the production of individual citizens who will not only enjoy civil, social and political (or even, lately, cultural) *rights*, but also abide by the law and fulfil a number of *duties* related to the pursuit of the common good and coterminous with full granting of membership in the nation-state's political community. Primary among these duties is loyalty to the national community. This places citizenship, nationality and nationalism on extremely intimate terms, to the extent that studies of European nationalism have long assumed a close (even if variable) overlap of these categories. The relationship of nationality and citizenship is a blurred one. A quasi-equation between citizenship (belonging in a political sense, the entitlement to civic, political and social rights and duties) and nationality (belonging to a national historic community) has existed in many languages and institutions of modern states. In English-speaking countries, the two are often seen as synonymous. Yet this equation should not be taken for granted. At least as regards Europe, it was made possible thanks to a 'powerful element of internal democracy, a productive tension between the idea of "people" as community (*ein Volk*) and the idea of "people" as a principle of equality and social justice (*das Volk*)', which was violently shaken by both class struggles throughout the nineteenth century and the two World Wars that tore the continent apart in the twentieth century (Balibar 1998: 104).

If the idea of a fit between citizenship and nationality cuts across the diversity of nation-states, it has also acquired renewed salience in postcolonial times, even if in contrast to studies of European citizenship, those of 'non-Western' nationalism have stressed both the contingency and the extreme variability of such a fit. That such contingency and variability appear salient in the postnational project of European citizenship today has rendered the comparison with the ways in which the categories of nationality and citizenship operate elsewhere more compelling than ever. Yet, such a comparison can only be achieved both by decentring the usual 'Western'-centred perspective and by analysing the ways in which local and idiosyncratic formats and models of citizenship have developed since the beginning of the postcolonial era.

The need for decentring the Western perspective is especially pressing given that citizenship in the 'newer' nation-states has so far been largely overlooked by scholars and political analysts, owing to the doubts held about their ability to build truly democratic regimes. More often than not, these nation-states have been used as counter-examples to the problematic notion of 'good governance' that has acquired dominance in the discursive modes extant among international organizations; in these discourses, the models for 'good governance' have so far been generally European or North American. At issue here are many political observers' expectations that the advent of independence would usher in a democratic regime. Independence was expected to effect more than just a transfer of power from foreign hands to native ones; it was meant to achieve a transformation of the whole pattern of political life. In addition to the creation of a public sphere in which various segments of civil society could express themselves and interact with the state, new nation-states were expected to metamorphose subjects into citizens (Geertz 1973, 2000). Thus, contrary to a theoretical perspective wherein the people as community must be both sovereign and subject (the citizen, by submitting to the law, ultimately submits to himself only), the distinction between subject and citizen has been at the heart of many debates about citizenship in new nation-states today. If, in the political science inherited from French post-revolutionary public law, the logical dichotomy refers to the opposition 'subjection'/'autonomy', it has more recently come to integrate the opposition between 'primordial ties' and 'civic ties'. Whereas subjects were deemed to have been held back by their 'primordial ties', citizens would be freed from such ethnic, cultural or religious bonds, at last bound together by a common sense of universal civic virtue.

Such conceptions are unsatisfactory on many counts. To begin with, the citizen/subject distinction is largely the product of colonial history, although its relevance for the constitution of a political, sovereign community – whether in formerly colonized countries or not – is debatable.[18] True, in many of the cases presented here, the distinction between citizen and subject is often a tenuous one. Yet the fact that, for instance, in India citizens' associations have also been demonstrating against the invasion of the public sphere by Hindu nationalist propaganda suggests alert and reactive practices of citizenship. Education has been in the eye of the storm following recent attempts by the then central Hindu nationalist government to instil their invidious propaganda by redesigning curricula, syllabuses and textbooks to fit their purposes. In this battle over contended meanings of nationality and citizenship, public protest – as well as public support on the other side – does indeed testify to a 'live and kicking practice of citizenship'. Furthermore, these conceptions obliterate an essential interrogation about citizenship, namely whether citizenship does and should represent the deepest layers of cultural identity or only 'proclaim the surface layers of political life' (Shafir 1998: 17–19). To what extent individuals' social and national identities are fixed, and what degree of agency ordinary social actors have in the manufacturing of citizenship, are central questions.

The notions of 'citizenship', 'civic ties' and 'ethnic ties' are not devoid of difficulties either. They need to be both historically and culturally situated rather than hastily posited as universal categories abstracted from their original milieu. To be sure, the fact that very different histories and contexts across the globe have led to nation-state models of political organization suggests the relevance of such a model for peoples recently achieving political sovereignty (Savidan 2001: 19), quite apart from international pressure (Burghart 1996; Butenschon 2000). Yet, rather than the nation-state's enabling the social integration that the old hierarchical relations supposedly no longer undergirded, more often than not these old hierarchical relations did not simply vanish but became redeployed and transformed, playing a part in the new political process (see for instance S. Bayly 1999; Dirks 2001). Drawing attention to the persistence of old ties – whether religious, ethnic or other – both within 'Euro-American' and 'non-Euro-American' contexts enables one to pinpoint heretofore ignored similarities between these contexts.

Indeed, much has been said about a universalist conception of citizenship as a product of the transcendence of ethnic particularisms at the supra-level of the nation (Schnapper 1994). Such a conception is often presented as the brainchild of philosophers such as Rousseau, seen as the promoter of the inalienability of sovereignty and the ethnocultural neutrality of the nation-state. Yet even at the heart of the Rousseauist conception of the nation is an intricate nexus between politics and an ethnically defined nation: in his *Considérations sur le gouvernement de Pologne*, for instance, the philosopher envisaged political freedom as mediated by the preservation of national character, with education playing a crucial role in promoting citizenship consubstantially to nationality (Savidan 2001: 15). The thesis of the political decline of the nation-state internally torn by too many nationalities is thus untenable: the salience of these nationalities and their claims for recognition highlights the mythical and ideological character of the thesis of 'State ethnocultural neutrality'.[19] In other words, the nation is always an ethnocultural one. Even Rousseau defended the idea that, rather than an obstacle to political freedom, culture can be a vehicle enabling the exercise of citizenship (Savidan 2001: 12). This obviously has capital implications for a comparison between older and newer nation-states today, and calls for a more extensive reflection on the statuses of 'subject' and 'citizen', and particularly on their oft-presented mutual exclusivity. It also re-opens the debate regarding the existence (especially in precolonial times) of 'native' socio-political modes of organization competing with European or American models of 'good governance'.

Furthermore, if nationalism is an important feature in any discussion of the legacy of European colonial political structures, the immense power of postcolonial nation-states nevertheless does not lie in their being inherited from colonialism but from their nationalist mobilization (Kaviraj 2001: 314). In societies formerly under colonial rule, the emergence of nationalist consciousness and mobilization against colonial rulers were concomitant processes. There, citizenship and nationalism were closely associated, inasmuch as the struggle for independence was intricately linked to fighting for basic rights. The consciousness of being a free national was thus forged in relation to the establishment of citizens' rights (and duties). This raises the question of the extent to which nationality today can be disentangled from citizenship. The question obtains as much in mainland China or in Taiwan, where the implementation of 'Three Principles Education' systematically engendered a nationalist vision of citizenship and personhood (Chun, this volume, Chapter 2), as in South Asia, or in Europe, both in its old and its newer nation-states (see Bryant, this volume, Chapter 4 for the British colonial context of Cyprus, where citizens' rights were closely tied up either with Greek or with Turkish nationalist claims). In this respect, the attempts currently being made by some South Asian nation-states at making nationality and citizenship fit (in an unprecedented way based on an essentialist religious definition) offer a vivid contrast to the European postnational construction: the latter is currently groping in search of a new model reconsidering the relationship between citizenship and nationality (Balibar 1996, and this volume, Chapter 1).

Lastly, far from non-European models being the products of passive colonial legacies, the volume also highlights the multiple influences that have been at work in the elaboration of different modes of citizenship at one given moment and within one given society.[20] Rana Mitter and Naran Bilik on the one hand and Allen Chun on the other provide instances from mainland China and Taiwan, respectively: in mainland China, Western and Japanese features of political thought have been redeployed in an interesting triangular relationship with Han and Mongolian perspectives. The notion of Western civil society has also led to conflicting visions – some of them as counter-reactions to Western notions – among minorities and majority Chinese citizens. In Taiwan, European and American borrowings occurred together with the inherited Japanese and Chinese ethical ideals of early Republican China (the nationalist ideology of Sun Yat Sen). Interestingly, the international ideology of communism, which was later and until quite recently to reign supreme, is not so much relevant to the manufacturing of interactive citizenship in the Chinese context as it is in places where such an ideology was never implemented, for instance in the Sicily of the 1960s: Schneider and Schneider show that this ideology, together with the 'universalizing rational culture of the French Enlightenment', has been a major influence in the redefinition of citizens' involvement in the life of the *polis*. Furthermore, colonial legacies and international ideologies do not exhaust the potential for borrowing. As is documented by Mohammad-Arif, not only has the British legacy been an enduring one in the formation of India and Pakistan, but also, since their creation, mutual cross-borrowings have occurred between these two rival nation-states in South Asia (for example, the notion of a 'Hindu *umma*'). So the political processes and features of citizenship that are documented in the volume are the products of complex, multi-layered and multi-sited circulatory developments that have taken place over at least two centuries.

Contents of this volume

Because education is not limited to schooling, although schooling accounts for an increasingly large part of it today, the contributors have chosen to vary their sites of observation as well as their perspectives and levels of analysis: from museums (Mitter) to schools (Caddell, Chun and Schneider and Schneider) and textbooks (Mohammad-Arif and Schneider and Schneider); some have more specifically addressed the relationship of schools to public space (Bryant) and society at large (Balibar and Bilik), as well as the community in relation to the nation (Bear), or even to national and international governments (Osler); and contributions vary from top-down views of state projects, to bottom-up views of various levels of social actors' engagement and negotiation with the institutions of their nation-state (from schools to parents to associations involved in educational processes).

Disciplining citizens

In an introductory chapter, drawing on his experience as a French academic and intellectual, Etienne Balibar reflects on the conditions for the possibility of the democratization of the schooling process (involving the effective participation of the *demos*) in relation to the construction of European citizenship. Balibar sees a general 'exercise in education' (*effort d'éducation*) as a prerequisite for even thinking about the possibility of creating any form of European citizenship. Such an exercise is required at every level of each national community within Europe. In order to attain a postnational citizenship, a European system of education would also have to be put into place, rather than nation-states separately devising their own citizenship education studies and having special European citizenship studies programmes concocted for them by Brussels bureaucrats, as in the late 1990s (Shore 2001).

There are ideological tensions at play in the construction of citizenship through educational processes generally: between individual and collective education; between ideals of (post)national construction and the dangers of an essentialist identity; and between primary and secondary identities. Through the examination of these various dialectical relationships, Balibar poses the question of the ideological correlation between various types of educational projects and different modes of citizenship: is education to be conceived of as a liberating, emancipating force conducive to the advent of 'enlightened' (European) citizens living on a territory relatively open to the world lying beyond its sovereignty, or is it rather to become a conditioning force put at the service of manufacturing docile inward-looking citizens living within the closed frontiers of their sovereign space, whether national or postnational? Obviously, there is no straightforward answer to such a crucial question: there exists a vast continuum of possibilities ranging across these two extremes, as is testified by the next three examples discussed in this section.

In his school ethnography of the highly centralized Taiwanese educational system, Allen Chun documents hardly any space to manoeuvre left for negotiation. Education in Taiwan is 'less an autonomous process of knowledge dissemination' and more an 'integral part of the state project of nation-building'. The state's organizational structures and bureaucratic features are replicated within schools, ensuring effective state supervision, control and surveillance in each institution, by means of discipline and militarization. The curriculum is an important framework for the dissemination of social values, cultural identity and political notions of citizenship. Of special import is the influence of the early Republican Chinese ideals of Sun Yat-Sen's philosophy and the political ideology of 'Three Principles Education', encompassing the teaching of etiquette and health, ethics and morality, and citizenship and political thought. Principles of morality and citizenship are intricately linked, and both are rooted in a blend of Confucian ethics and modern political values.[21] Hence a fully-fledged citizenship is expected to mature into the proper ethical behaviour of a proper citizen acting as a 'proper person' (*zuoren*).

Through the daily routine, Chun also emphasizes the materiality of the manufacturing of citizenship, in which bodily procedures inscribe the first stages of citizenship on to the future citizens' bodies, and the spatial representation of hierarchies of state power is effected within the school. Schools are also part of a wider network of social, cultural and political life, mirrored not only by the schools' internal administrative structure, but also by the conduct of extracurricular activities, which promote spiritual education and 'cultural enlightenment' through civic service for the local community. In this citizenship geared towards serving both the Taiwanese state and Taiwanese society, little leeway seems to be left for negotiation, whether on the part of the teachers or the parents, let alone the children.

By contrast, Martha Caddell provides an example of how citizenship is negotiated and expressed in Nepal today by different social agents and groups – in particular aid agencies and Maoist organizations – and their engaging with the state's projects. Interestingly, the modern 'Western' concept of the nation-state has been gradually indigenized over the last two and a half centuries (Burghart 1996). By the same token, today's national project of education is formulated in native terms, whilst also being foreign-oriented, owing to international funding. The agencies promoting development (*bikas*) are central to the processes of Nepali nation-building and manufacturing of citizenship inasmuch as citizens are ideally conceived of as agents of development (although the term *bikas* does not have any connotation of personal development similar to that comprised in the Greek notion of *paideia*; see below). The Nepali case is also a brilliant example of indigenous modernity, whose narrative is associated with official national Hinduism and against which alternative, Christian-inspired visions are being proffered by some development agencies. To be sure, this alternative Christian vision of modernity is a powerful one in the international world order today. Yet this case not only underscores the contingency of Christian modernity, but also the need for generally reassessing the relationship between modernity and religion.

Caddell further highlights the possibility of 'deviance', 'undiscipline' or non-conformity with the proposed national and international models of citizenship and participation. (Interestingly, the Maoists engage with their 'enemies' in the latter's terms of debate, i.e. 'development'.) This is partly due to the fact that schools remain *loci* of the promotion of inequality, even when this is undertaken in the name of development and inclusion, and even when notions of the 'good citizen' are not determined by locality or ethnicity.

If ethnicity does not appear to play all that crucial a part in the definition of citizenship in Nepal, it does play a determinative role in the conflict opposing Greek Orthodox Cypriots and Turkish Muslim Cypriots. As debates are still raging about whether the inhabitants of Cyprus should be (re)united in a common citizenship within a single, unified nation-state accommodating ethnic and religious differences, Rebecca Bryant goes back to earlier phases of the conflict and analyses the value placed in colonial times upon education and educated persons in Cyprus, and how this articulates with notions of nationality conditioning the possibility of any project of citizenship on the island.

By looking at both communities, Bryant demonstrates that the problem in Cyprus has been the inextricability of citizenship from ethnonationalisms. In the Greek case, citizenship was premised on a 'Humanity' defined in the archetypal Ancient Greek sense. *Paideia*, as the foundational pedagogy of the Ancient Greek citizen, encompassed as its ultimate goal the achieving of mastery in personal development, and formed the basis for a citizen's persona. Eloquence, in particular, was deemed conducive to proper thinking and proper living, in accordance with a nationalist self whose development also relied in part on emotions, a fact testified to by teachers' and leaders' impassioned speeches about fulfilling one's duty towards the fatherland and its sacred flag. By contrast with the classic European vision of a universality enabling the creation of a citizenship and a nation in which ethnic particularisms would be transcended, this case reveals a culturally defined notion of universality, which hence becomes a matter of acrimonious contention between competing ethnic communities. In contradistinction, Bryant argues, Turkish Muslim Cypriots were weighed down by a sense of the impossibility of creating a true citizenship, in spite of an already existing conception of rights and duties among the Muslim leaders.

National history and memory

Citizenship is always manufactured locally, and the main material that is drawn on in the process is national history and memory, which feature largely in educational programmes. The next three chapters explore the prominent place history and social memory occupy in the elaboration of national curricula and the ways in which nation-states and citizens appropriate and negotiate them.[22]

Rana Mitter first examines the transformations that have occurred in the meaning of citizenship in China over the last century. The changing nature of these debates is reflected in attempts to reform education, particularly that part of it that inculcates civics. As was said above, Mitter highlights the circulation and borrowings of models across vast geographic and cultural spaces. The result of such cross-borrowings is that today the Chinese political idiom has embedded in it the Western concepts of 'citizen' and 'nation', to some extent as these were revisited in Japan.

In China today, as in many other nation-states, the inculcation of patriotism is an essential element in the construction of citizenship. This is effected through the construction of a 'national' memory in a variety of forms, the most spectacular among which are historical museums. These museums are among the impressive educational tools that have been promoted in the reform era. Diorama historical reconstructions of battles and other memorable events have occupied the centre stage of many museums in recent decades, and are meant to facilitate public identification. These technologies also lend themselves particularly well to the reinterpretation of national history that takes place in the course of attempts to create a consensual national memory. In some ways, the historical dioramas are a means for 'visually re-writing national history'.

The issue of history-writing is also addressed by Aminah Mohammad-Arif, although this time in relation to 'communalization' on the South Asian subcontinent. This term is predicated on that of 'communalism', and denotes the process whereby religion becomes the main component in the definition both of social and political communities, and of nationhood. In such a context, the numerically dominant community seeks to impose its own ethnic or religious identity on the very definition of nationhood and citizenship. Other comparable instances have been documented whereby citizenship – defined as membership in the national political community – was gradually defined in an exclusivist fashion, and in which the implication for citizenship is the exclusion from access to the fully-fledged status of citizen of residents who do not comply with the majoritarian ethnic or religious definition of citizenship (see for instance Pandey and Geschiere 2003 for illustrations in Africa, Asia and Latin America).[23]

Looking at the continuous process that has been taking place since Partition in 1947 and the subsequent creation of the nation-states of India and Pakistan (and later, in 1971, that of Bangladesh), Mohammad-Arif explores how education systems of both countries have turned history textbooks into vital ideological instruments, according a central place to the traumatic events related to Partition. Furthermore, if communalization was a distinctive mark of Pakistani nationality and citizenship as reflected in the emphasis put on Islamic definitions, knowledge and practices in the official curriculum since that nation-state's inception, the continuing implementation of a Hindu nationalist policy over recent years (and until May 2004) in India has now blurred the distinctions between these two rival nation-states' political agendas: in both countries, secular forces have increasingly been marginalized.[24] This has called into question the viability of the notion of citizenship enshrined in the Constitutions and theoretically granted to all residents within the territorial limits of both nation-states, regardless of the painful and traumatic social and historical memories shared by the citizens of both since their creation.

Jane Schneider and Peter Schneider mobilize an altogether different kind of history and social memory in their discussion of the antimafia movement in Sicily: one that is negatively connoted and targeted in a project geared towards educating for legality and citizenship. Interestingly, a conception akin to those often used in non-European contexts is to be found in the common rhetoric applied to southern Italy (and particularly Sicily): a conception akin to 'Mediterranean Orientalism'. Whereas northern Italy is deemed heir to a 'civic tradition' related to city-states dating back to the Middle Ages, the south passes off as steeped in 'feudal, bureaucratic, and absolutist rule'. Schneider and Schneider seek to invalidate such a commonplace opposition by exploring citizens' initiatives in Sicily since the 1980s.

Following major outbursts of *mafia* violence, members of the Leftist sections of society engaged in initiatives that were largely educational and primarily focused on 'middle schools' (the teenage group). Middle schools have thus become the major *loci* for civic action integrated within civic life at large. In contrast to Allen Chun's Taiwanese case, where participation in civic life through schools also occurs, but as the result of the state's designs rather than as the outcome of more autonomous grassroots-level citizens' initiatives, here the emphasis is no more on fulfilling one's duties (observance of the law and collaboration with justice) than on claiming one's rights (to the vote and to fair educational assessment rather than educational opportunities conferred as a matter of personal favour), as exemplified by new didactic materials and antimafia events conflicting with the dominant cultural codes (*omertà* in particular). In accounting for the conflicting views of middle-class (initiators) and working-class Sicilians (dependent on the mafia's economic activities), this case vividly exemplifies how citizenship is not a given but a process involving the negotiation of different social memories and political and cultural allegiances.

Ethnic frontiers and cultural diversity

The issue of the activity of a multiplicity of social actors and interests in the manufacturing of citizenship in relation to minorities is the object of further study in this section. How states and citizens negotiate cultural diversity and members of ethnic minorities themselves envisage their place within the nation-state are among the central questions addressed by the next three contributors.

Discussing the recent strengthening of educational policy on citizenship studies in Britain, Audrey Osler offers a testimony to how the paradox of the crisis in democracy is dealt with in the British context: at a time when ordinary social actors increasingly feel that their views matter little to their elected representatives, citizenship education is further introduced in schools to counter a lack of participatory democracy manifested by electoral absenteeism. The notion of a frontier, both physically and metaphorically, underlies Osler's chapter in two ways. By documenting how a specific nation-state's concerns articulate with international ones in the field of education, Osler shows how nation-states' ideological frontiers are permeable, especially in terms of matters of international security. Since the 1990s and, more recently, the terrorist attacks of 2001, the issues of peace and human rights have attracted renewed attention on the part of international agencies. UNESCO, for one, has devised a framework promoting 'education for greater democracy and human rights internationally', thus bringing pressure to bear upon *every* nation-state to include these issues in its educational agenda.

In addition to external ideological frontiers, states also negotiate their own internal ones. Notwithstanding their oft-made claims to neutrality, they devise all sorts of boundaries between various communities and categories of citizens living within their administrative boundaries.[25] It is to tackle one of these frontiers, following the publication of a report in 1999 in Britain that identified institutional racism as a major cause of social exclusion, that citizenship education has recently been introduced with renewed vigour in schools by the Government. Through citizenship education, schools are expected to help prevent racism from developing by encouraging young people to value cultural diversity.

In a converse movement, cultural diversity has become officially devalued in China since the Cultural Revolution, as is shown by Naran Bilik's discussion of Chinese educational policies with regard to minorities. Bilik reconsiders the notion of the frontier in the light of the issue of ethnicity and citizenship in China, and offers a different reading of its metaphorical and physical dimensions as these are usually imposed by a centralized state. The history of the coming about of ethnic and cultural (Han) dominance in China until the early twentieth century reveals how the state did not initially attempt to trace frontiers; rather, the margins tended to dominate the centre, and enforced geophysical frontiers. Furthermore, following the 1911 revolution, the redistribution of the balance of ethnic power gave preponderance to and shaped discourses of ethnicity. In keeping with this awareness of the issue of ethnicity, the state that resulted from the communist takeover in 1949 paid great attention to ethno-national identities, encouraging 'ethno-national education' for the next few decades. So that, far from transcending ethnic particularisms, national unity and citizenship were to be premised on the cultivation of ethnic pluralism.

The period that followed the Cultural Revolution nevertheless saw a radical change in views about ethnicity and educational policies, with a renewal of Han dominance in national matters. Citizenship and nationality were consequently constructed on the basis of Han ethnicity, relegating other ethnicities beyond the acceptable realm of Chinese citizenship. A metaphorical frontier was thus created by the Chinese nation-state through the rhetoric of (non-Han, other) ethnic backwardness.[26] By looking at the Inner Mongolian and the Xinjiang Uygur Autonomous Regions, Bilik documents how such a metaphorical frontier has been internalized by some minority communities, but also how some members – including teachers – negotiate the state's imposed version of their own ethnic identities and sense of citizenship.

It is also to the negotiation of ethnic identities and senses of membership in the national community that Laura Bear devotes her attention in the last chapter. Yet, rather than concentrating on the links between projects of mass education and citizenship through the study of schools, textbooks or pedagogy, she focuses on the aftermath of schooling through school histories. Narratives of schooling and education provide a way for social actors to discuss how as citizens they negotiate a sense of belonging to various communities, whether their ethnic community or the nation. Bear looks at the specific case of the Anglo-Indians in India. Here, the notion of frontier does not only capture 'the hierarchies of degrees of belonging to the national community', it also 'conveys a sense of nationalism as an existential project at the level of the individual citizen'. Bear argues that 'the existential project of being a citizen-subject is often framed in relation to people's experience of schooling'.

A historical overview of educational projects directed at Anglo-Indians first highlights how the funding of education was intimately connected with the idea of securing loyalty to the state by means of personal and moral transformations. Despite the claims to secularity made by many British administrators and historians alike, the moral reform underlying imperial educational policies – particularly in India – was largely premised on Christian religious ethics – mostly Protestant.[27] A second section is devoted to contemporary school stories as told by Anglo-Indian adults today. These stories enable members of this community to reappropriate both colonial and postcolonial projects of education and to recover a sense of autonomy and agency in the very process of schooling. Bear reveals how the colonial creation of separate schools for Anglo-Indians initially conceived as a state project has today become a community right conducive to producing the internalized frontiers of this 'minority community'.

Epilogue

In sum, far from an analysis built upon measured levels of electoral participation, the purpose of these essays is threefold; first, in contrast to the commonplace according to which the role of nation-states has been reduced to a minimum owing to economic and financial globalization, these chapters aim to highlight the still powerful role that nation-states play, especially in conveying ideas about citizenship and manufacturing citizens. Such a view is also congruent with the more recent works that have underscored the role of agent of the state played by civil society, especially in times of globalization (see in particular Aretxaga 2003; Hardt and Negri 2000; Trouillot 2001; Bayart 2004 also refers to this aspect, although without making it central to his argument). Of course, the definition of 'civil society' as primarily consisting of NGOs working at the interface of private and public corporate partnership does not do justice to the variability of the notion across both time and space (see Comaroff and Comaroff 1999; Hann 1996; Harris 2004).

Yet second, regardless of the definitional difficulty posed by the notion, by focusing on 'civil society', these recent works have sometimes left out of their purview the heuristic potential of the notion of citizenship, evidenced by the significant political part played by ordinary social actors, including teachers and parents, be it in Europe, South Asia or China (mainland and other). Some of the present essays indeed suggest a way out of the conundrum of 'civil society' in postcolonial times by attracting more attention towards the heterogeneity of actors as well as the multiplicity of forms of organization of, and participation in, and expression of belonging to a national political community (what Callon *et al.* 2001 call 'hybrid fora') that citizens experience and manufacture in their educational environment. The critical inventory resting on these case studies brings into relief the high variability of the definition, discourse and practices of citizenship, in the process highlighting the contingency of citizenship as much as its arbitrariness and exclusive character, thus inviting analysts to think of 'citizenship' together with 'non-citizenship', or the denial thereof to some individuals and groups, whether in 'the East' or in 'the West'.

Third, and consequently, this critical inventory also forcefully confirms the need for a dialogical exercise of democracy (*démocratie dialogique*, see Callon *et al.* 2001) to be combined with the more classical forms of delegatory democracy. No less importantly, these essays demonstrate that such a dialogical exercise, involving the participation of social actors of all categories, does not require them to shed their 'cluttered' social and cultural selves and break out from the shackles of their bonds – ethnic, religious or other – prior to entering the political arena of rational debate, as a Habermasian, an Arendtian or even a Rawlsian view of formal democracy would have it. Rather, the educational processes that take place at a variety of levels within a given society are themselves imbued with these particularisms and feed on the emotions and memories – individual and social – entailed by them. Yet, rather than these very particularities and bonds being a hindrance to an active exercise of democracy, what an anthropological approach demonstrates is that it is with them, as they are both shaped through the very manufacturing of citizenship, and contribute to it, that social actors can best actively participate in and enrich the political life not only of their own nation-states, but also of the 'global civil society', as shown by the anti-war demonstrations with which we opened this chapter, as well as by the further events deriving therefrom that have continued to mobilize the citizens of many nation-states. Nevertheless, the present contributions also suggest how long and arduous the path towards the realization and materialization of this thesis still is, both everywhere in general, and in China, South Asia *and* Europe in particular.

At any rate, salvaging the notion of citizenship from what is often conceived as its prerequisite, namely civil society, reveals the dynamic quality and potentiality of political participation by various fora of actors in both 'Western' and 'non-Western' contexts, thereby highlighting heretofore unsuspected similarities, not least in matters of ethnic particularisms and nationalist construction. In the process, citizenship, whether in 'the West' or in 'the East', emerges as a feature of an ever-evolving and incomplete modernity, yet also as one of its elective affinities, real or imagined.

Notes

1 If we accept – granted, in a somewhat Schmittian conception – that mass manifestations can be considered as part of participatory democracy. Thanks are due to Jackie Assayag, John Charvet, Leo Coleman, Stephan Feuchtwang, Chris Fuller, Thomas Hansen, Deborah James and Jean Leca for their worthwhile criticisms and comments on several stages of this Introduction.

2 For a detailed and informative account of the various traditions of citizenship that have existed from Greek to Roman to medieval to modern and contemporary times and the debates they have generated, see Shafir (1998). On the various notions of civil, political, and more recently cultural, global and even ecological citizenship, see Butenschon (2000).

3 See Jelin and Hershberg (1996) on human rights and citizenship with particular reference to Latin America; also on the issue of democratizing institutions as the condition for the advent of a citizenship premised on the recognition of the rights of social actors (both individual and collective). On the latter topic and the relationship of national models of citizenship to new conceptions of human rights, see also Delanty (2000).

4 Furthermore, this claim to universalization raises the question of the 'location' of the scholarship relating to this topic (see Assayag and Bénéï 2003, and Prakash 2003 for a problematization of this notion).

5 From this perspective, citizenship certainly represents an 'aspirational politics', a 'politics of desire' oriented towards the future (Werbner 1998: 2). Yet, unlike Werbner, I argue that this aspirational politics does not stand in stark contrast with nationalism: nationalism may be grounded in a mythical past, but it also looks towards an ideal. Both political projects are grounded in specific traditions, whether of a mythical national past or of a political philosophy. By the same token, both projects look towards the future and are animated by a sense of loss and desire at the same time, a *telos*.

6 On discussions of citizenship in relation to the issue of multiculturalism and the necessity of a theory of minority rights as distinct from human rights, see Kymlicka (1996 [1995]) and Kymlicka and Norman (2000). On the critique of the notion of 'multicultural citizenship', see Joppke (2001).

7 Daunton and Hilton (2001) look at consumption and analyse the triadic relationship between consumer, citizenship and the state, discussing whether consumption has been conducive to the production of an integrated nation or has subverted
   social order. Not only do they study how states have anchored types of consumption in notions of citizenship, but also the ways in which shoppers may extend
   their economic purchasing decisions into political acts or moral statements.

8 On the issues of citizenship, discrimination and religious schooling, see Callan
   (2000) and Spinner-Halev (2000) with reference to Canada and the USA, respectively.

9 See for instance Yuval-Davis and Werbner (1999) and Rajan (2003) on a theoretical perspective, and Joseph (2001) on the Middle East, where she discusses
   the ways in which the linkage woman/mother to nation and man to the state has
   reinforced the reproduction of a gendered hierarchy conducive to the institu-
   tionalization of gendered citizenship in state-building projects.

10 On transnationalism and social actors' accommodation to different notions of
   citizenship according to varying contexts, as well as their embeddedness in networks of relationships that connect them simultaneously to two or more nation-
   states, see Ong (1999) on the Chinese diaspora and Basch *et al.* (1997) on the
   Caribbean and the USA. These works emphasize the fluidity involved in
   simultaneously belonging to several nation-states, and reflect on the problematic
   notion of a nation-state exclusively encapsulating forms of territorial allegiance
   even in a so-called postmodern world.

11 On other types of opinion manufacturing, see Loïc Blondiaux (1998).

12 See also an illustration of this in contemporary France and Germany with
   respect to state teachings on the subject of taste in furniture (Auslander 2001).

13 To Habermas, the solution lies in the acceptance of a 'postnational society', that
   is, a political society whose limits are no longer determined by the nation. Ironically, however, the very model upon which he predicates the construction of a
   postnational society is still that of the nation-state. (This broadly corresponds to
   the concept and political project of the European union [Ferry 2000]. See also
   Delanty [2000] on European postnational and cosmopolitan citizenship and
   global civil society.)

14 See Zask (2001). Note that such a project was in tune with its own times, the
   early twentieth century, since Dewey looked at educational methods and the
   growth of democracy in connection with the then prevalent development of
   experimental methods in the sciences, evolutionary ideas in biological sciences
   and industrial reorganization.

15 See Bayly (1997) for an account of the transformation of what he identifies as an
   'indigenous public sphere' in India prior to the advent of British colonial
   powers. In contrast, see Chatterjee, who argues that social leaders saw their role
   as one of 'guiding [the then emerging] public to maturity' (2001: 167–8).

16 For a broader discussion of other modernities, see Eisenstadt (2000).

17 Even though in recent years, the emergence of notions such as that of global
   justice have probably furthered the scope and extent of penetration of these
   idea(l)s across the world.

18 It was forged – or at least summarized – by Lord Hailey as a distinction between
   different forms of colonial rule subsumed by 'the doctrine of identity' and the
   'doctrine of differentiation', respectively (Mamdani 1996: 7). Such a doctrine of
   differentiation, better known as institutional segregation or British 'indirect
   rule' and French 'association', culminated in the notion of apartheid. See also
   Metcalf (1995).

19 'Dans la formule "Etat-nation", le terme *nation* renvoie directement à une réalité
   ethnoculturelle particulière' (Savidan 2001: 3).

20 Other instances of 'cross-pollination' can be found in other parts of the globe. See for instance Castro Leiva and Pagden (2001) for early nineteenth-century Latin American conceptions of republicanism premised on the 'Ancient World' (Athens, Sparta, Thebes and Rome). On the Middle East, see Butenschon (2000); on Africa, see Mamdani (1996) and Bayart (2004).

21 Confucian-based moral education became a 'spiritual weapon' against socialism and Communist China's values. There is an interesting parallel here with Gandhi's use of the Jain principle of non-violence (*ahimsa*) (see Fox 2002), both being instances of turning 'traditional principles' into modern weapons geared towards resisting colonial or other external powers.

22 For a comparison of the cases of the former German Democratic Republic and Japan, respectively, see Noiriel (2001), and in particular Dierkes (2001).

23 This is certainly on the verge of becoming true in the Indian case, as the Hindu right-wing extremist parties in power in some states and, until recently, in central government explicitly assert that Hindus and others assimilable into the Hindu fold are the 'primary citizens' of India, while the rest are relegated to the status of non-Indians and should be given second-class citizenship (Raman 2003).

24 Following state elections in May 2004, which reinstated the Congress Party back into power, however, there have been constant debates over how best to reverse the stream, especially in matters educational. Yet for the moment, most measures have been deemed insufficient.

25 As was seen above, members of minority communities may implicitly be considered as 'less equal' citizens; they may also be asked to prove their allegiance to the nation-state and relinquish all claims to collective representation (see Asad 1990). By the same token, recent immigrants regularly stand at the centre of discussions about special programmes of citizenship education.

26 Ironically, such a frontier is further strengthened by the very discourse that is aimed at promoting the integration of all citizens by means of assimilation under the banner of Han-dominated citizenship. Furthermore, as in many nation-states across Europe and South Asia, here, a correspondence between race, minority and backwardness is created by the Chinese nation-state.

27 See also Viswanathan (1998) and Bénéï (2002) for a similar claim.

Bibliography

Anderson, B. (1991[1983]), *Imagined Communities: Reflections on the Origin And Spread of Nationalism*, revised edition, London: Verso.

Appadurai, Arjun (1990), 'Topographies of the Self: Praise and Emotion in Hindu India', in C. A. Lutz and L. Abu-Lughod (eds), *Language and the Politics of Emotion*, pp. 92–112, Cambridge: Cambridge University Press.

Appadurai, Arjun (1997), *Modernity at Large. Cultural Dimension of Globalisation*, Minneapolis, MN: University of Minnesota Press.

Aretxaga, Begoña (2003), 'Maddening States', *Annual Review of Anthropology* October 32: 393–410.

Asad, Talal (1990), 'Multi-cultural and British Ideology', *Politics and Society* 18: 445–80.

Assayag, Jackie (2001), *L'Inde. Désir de nation*, Paris: Odile Jacob.

Assayag, Jackie and Véronique Bénéï (eds) (2003), *At Home in Diaspora. South Asian Scholars and the West*, Delhi/Bloomington, IN: Permanent Black/Indiana University.

Auslander, Leora (2001), 'National Taste? Citizenship Law, State Form, and Every-day Aesthetics in Modern France and Germany, 1920–1940', in Martin Daunton and Matthew Hilton (eds) *The Politics of Consumption: Material Culture and Citizenship in Europe and America*, pp. 109–28, Oxford: Berg.

Balibar, Etienne (1984), 'Sujets ou citoyens? (Pour l'égalité)', *Temps modernes* 2: 1726–53.

Balibar, Etienne (1992), *Les frontières de la démocratie*, Paris: La Découverte.

Balibar, Etienne (1996), 'European Citizenship', *Public Culture* 8: 2, 355–76.

Balibar, Etienne (1998), *Droit de cité*, Paris: Editions de l'Aube.

Balibar, Etienne (2001), *Nous, citoyens d'Europe? Les frontières, l'État, le peuple*, Paris: La Découverte.

Balibar, Etienne and Immanuel Wallerstein (eds) (1988), *Race, nation, classe: Les identités ambiguës*, Paris: La Découverte.

Basch, Linda, Nina Glick Schiller and Cristina Szanton Blanc (1997[1994]), *Nations Unbound. Transnational Projects, Postcolonial Predicaments, and Deterritorialized Nation-states*, Amsterdam: Gordon and Breach Publishers.

Bayart, Jean-François (2004), *Le gouvernement du monde: Une Critique politique de la globalisation*, Paris: Fayard. (In press.)

Bayly, C. A. (1997), *Empire and Information: Intelligence Gathering and Social Communication in India, 1780–1880*, Cambridge: Cambridge University Press.

Bayly, C. A. (1998), *Origins of Nationality in South Asia: Patriotism and Ethical Government in the Making of Modern India*, Delhi: Oxford University Press.

Bayly, Susan (1999), *Caste, Society and Politics in India: From the Eighteenth Century to the Modern Age*, Cambridge: Cambridge University Press.

Bellier, Irene and Thomas M. Wilson (eds) (2000), *An Anthropology of the European Union: Building, Imagining and Experiencing the New Europe*, New York: NYU Press.

Bénéï, Véronique (2000), 'Teaching Nationalism in Maharashtra Schools', in C. J. Fuller and Véronique Bénéï (eds) *The Everyday State and Society in Modern India*, pp. 194–221, London: Hurst and Co.

Bénéï, Véronique (2002), 'Missing Indigenous Bodies: Educational Enterprise and Victorian Morality in the Mid-Nineteenth Century Bombay Presidency', *Economic and Political Weekly* 37: 17, 1647–54.

Billig, Michael (1995), *Banal Nationalism*, London: Sage.

Blondiaux, Loïc (1998), *La fabrique de l'opinion: une histoire sociale des sondages*, Paris: Éd. du Seuil.

Bourdieu, Pierre (1977), *Outline of a Theory of Practice* (trans. R. Nice), Cambridge: Cambridge University Press.

Bourdieu, Pierre (1999), 'Rethinking the State: Genesis and Structure of the Bureaucratic Field', in G. Steinmetz (ed.) *Culture/State: State-Formation After the Cultural Turn*, pp. 53–75, Ithaca, NY: Cornell University Press.

Bourdieu, Pierre and Jean-Claude Passeron (1990[1977]), *Reproduction in Education, Society and Culture*, London: Sage.

Brubaker, Rogers (1992), *Citizenship and Nationhood in France and Germany*, Cambridge, MA: Harvard University Press.

Brubaker, Rogers (1996), *Nationalism Reframed. Nationhood and the National Question in the New Europe*, Cambridge: Cambridge University Press.

Brunson, Michael (2001), 'The Media', in Bernard Crick (ed.) *Citizens: Towards a Citizenship Culture*, pp. 74–80, Oxford: Blackwell.

Burghart, Richard (1996), *The Conditions of Listening. Essays on Religion, History and Politics in South Asia*, Delhi: Oxford University Press.

Butenschon, Nils A. (2000), 'State, Power, and Citizenship in the Middle East', in Nils A. Butenschon, Uri Davis and Manuel Hassassian (eds) *Citizenship and the State in the Middle East. Approaches and Applications*, pp. 3–27, Syracuse, NY: Syracuse University Press.

Butenschon, Nils A., Uri Davis and Manuel Hassassian (eds) (2000), *Citizenship and the State in the Middle East. Approaches and Applications*, Syracuse, NY: Syracuse University Press.

Calhoun, Craig (1997[1992]a), 'Introduction: Habermas and the Public Sphere', in Craig Calhoun (ed.) *Habermas and the Public Sphere*, pp. 1–47, Cambridge, MA: MIT Press.

Calhoun, Craig (ed.) (1997[1992]b), *Habermas and the Public Sphere*, Cambridge, MA: MIT Press.

Callan, Eamonn (2000), 'Discrimination and Religious Schooling', in Will Kymlicka and Wayne Norman (eds) *Citizenship in Diverse Societies*, pp. 45–67, Oxford: Oxford University Press.

Callon, Michel, Pierre Lascoumes and Yannick Barthe (2001), *Agir dans un monde incertain. Essai sur la démocratie technique*, Paris: Seuil.

Castro Leiva, Luis and Anthony Pagden (2001), 'Civil Society and the Fate of the Modern Republics of Latin America', in Sudipta Kaviraj and Sunil Khilnani (eds) *Civil Society. History and Possibilities*, pp. 179–203, Cambridge: Cambridge University Press.

Certeau de, Michel (1998), *The Practice of Everyday Life*, Minneapolis: University of Minnesota Press. [Original (French) edition 1990.]

Chatterjee, Partha (2001), 'On Civil and Political Society in Postcolonial Democracies', in Sudipta Kaviraj and Sunil Khilnani (eds) *Civil Society. History and Possibilities*, pp. 165–78, Cambridge: Cambridge University Press.

Coles, Robert (1986), *The Political Life of Children*, New York: Atlantic Monthly Press.

Comaroff, John L. and Jean Comaroff (eds) (1999), *Civil Society and the Political Imagination in Africa: Critical Perspectives*, Chicago: University of Chicago Press.

Cooper, Frederick and Ann Laura Stoler (eds) (1997), *Tensions of Empire: Colonial Cultures in a Bourgeois World*, Berkeley, CA: University of California Press.

Crick, Bernard (2001a), 'Introduction', in *Citizens: Towards a Citizenship Culture*, pp. 1–9, Oxford: Blackwell.

Crick, Bernard (ed.) (2001b), *Citizens: Towards a Citizenship Culture*, Oxford: Blackwell.

Daunton, Martin and Matthew Hilton (eds) (2001), *The Politics of Consumption: Material Culture and Citizenship in Europe and America*, Oxford: Berg.

Davis, S. Rufus (ed.) (1996), *Citizenship in Australia. Democracy, Law and Society*, Carlton: Constitutional Centenary Foundation.

Davis, Uri (2000), 'Conceptions of Citizenship in the Middle East', in Nils A. Butenschon, Uri Davis and Manuel Hassassian (eds) *Citizenship and the State in the Middle East. Approaches and Applications*, pp. 49–69, Syracuse, NY: Syracuse University Press.

Delanty, Gerard (2000), *Citizenship in a Global Age. Society, Culture, Politics*, Buckingham: Open University Press.

Détienne, Marcel and Jean-Pierre Vernant (1974), *Les Ruses de l'intelligence. La metis des Grecs*, Paris: Flammarion.

Dierkes, Julian (2001), 'Absence, déclin ou essor de la nation: manuels d'histoire d'après-guerre au Japon et dans les deux Allemagnes', *Genèses – Sciences sociales et histoire*, Special issue, 44 'Enseigner la nation': 30–49.

Dirks, Nicholas, (2001), *Castes of Mind: Colonialism and the Making of Modern India*, Princeton, NJ: Princeton University Press.

Eisenstadt, Shmuel (ed.) 2000, Special issue on *'Multiple modernities'*, *Daedalus*, Winter.

Eley, Geoff (1997), 'Nations, Publics, and Political Cultures: Placing Habermas in the Nineteenth Century', in Craig Calhoun (ed.) *Habermas and the Public Sphere*, pp. 289–339, Cambridge, MA: MIT Press.

Fassin, Didier (2001), 'The Biopolitics of Otherness: Undocumented Foreigners and Racial Discrimination in the French Public Debate', *Anthropology Today* 17: 1, 3–7.

Ferry, Jean-Marc (2000), 'Avatars du sentiment national en Europe à la lumière du rapport à la culture et à l'histoire', in Will Kymlicka and Sylvie Mesure (eds) *Comprendre n° 1: Les identités culturelles*, pp. 359–80, Paris: PUF.

Firth, Raymond (1973), *Symbols. Public and Private*, London: George Allen and Unwin Ltd.

Foucault, Michel (1991), 'Governmentality', in G. Burchell, C. Gordon and P. Miller (eds) *The Foucault Effect: Studies in Governmentality*, pp. 87–104, London: Harvester Wheatsheaf; Chicago: University of Chicago Press.

Fox, Richard G. (2002), 'East of Said', in Joan Vincent (ed.) *The Anthropology of Politics: A Reader in Ethnography, Theory and Critique*, pp. 143–52, Oxford: Blackwell Publishers. (First published in M. Spinkler (ed.) *Edward Said: A Critical Reader* (Oxford, Blackwell Publishers, 1992), pp. 144–56.)

Fraser, Nancy (1997[1992]), 'Rethinking the Public Sphere: A Contribution to the Critique of Actually Existing Democracy', in Craig Calhoun (ed.) *Habermas and the Public Sphere*, pp. 109–42, Cambridge, MA: MIT Press.

Fuller, C. J. and Véronique Bénéï (eds) (2001), *The Everyday State and Society in Modern India*, London: Hurst and Co.

Geertz, Clifford (1973), 'The Integrative Revolution: Primordial Sentiments and Civil Politics in the New States', and 'The Politics of Meaning', both in *The Interpretation of Cultures. Selected Essays*, pp. 255–326, New York: Basic Books.

Geertz, Clifford (1980), *Negara. The Theatre State in 19th Century Bali*, Princeton, NJ: Princeton University Press.

Geertz, Clifford (2000), *Available Light. Anthropological Reflections on Philosophical Topics*, esp. Ch. 11 'The World in Pieces: Culture and Politics at the End of the Century', pp. 218–63, Princeton, NJ: Princeton University Press.

Gellner, Ernest (1983), *Nations and Nationalism*, Ithaca, NY: Cornell University Press.

Gilbert, M. Joseph and Daniel Nugent (1994), 'Popular Culture and State Formation in Revolutionary Mexico', in *Everyday Forms of State Formation: Revolution and the Negotiation of Rule in Modern Mexico*, Durham, NC: Duke University Press.

Goody, Jack (2001), 'Civil Society in an Extra-European Perspective', in Sudipta Kaviraj and Sunil Khilnani (eds) *Civil Society. History and Possibilities*, pp. 149–64, Cambridge: Cambridge University Press.

Gupta, Akhil (1995), 'Blurred Boundaries: The Discourse of Corruption, the Culture of Politics and the Imagined State', *American Ethnologist* 22: 375–402.

Gupta, Dipankar (2000), *Culture, Space and the Nation-State: From Sentiment to Structure*, New Delhi: Sage.

Habermas, Jürgen (1989), *The Structural Transformation of the Public Sphere: An Inquiry into a Category of Bourgeois Society*, Cambridge, MA: MIT Press.

Habermas, Jürgen (1997[1992]), 'Further Reflections on the Public Sphere', in Craig Calhoun (ed.) *Habermas and the Public Sphere*, pp. 421–61, Cambridge, MA: MIT Press.

Habermas, Jürgen (2000), *Après l'État-nation. Une nouvelle constellation politique*, Paris: Fayard (German original 1998).

Hann, Chris (1996), 'Introduction: Political Society and Civil Anthropology', in Chris Hann and Elizabeth Dunn (eds) *Civil Society: Challenging Western Models*, London: Routledge.

Hansen, Thomas and Finn Stepputat (eds) (2001), *States of Imagination: Ethnographic Explorations of the Postcolonial State*, Durham, NC: Duke University Press.

Hardt, Michael and Antonio Negri (2000), *Empire*, Cambridge, MA: Harvard University Press.

Harris, José (ed.) (2004), *Civil Society in British History: Ideas, Identities, Institutions*, Oxford: Oxford University Press.

Hayes, Carlton J. H. (1937[1926]), *Essays on Nationalism*, New York: Macmillan.

Helman, Sara (2000), 'Rights and Duties, Citizens and Soldiers', in Nils A. Butenschon, Uri Davis and Manuel Hassassian (eds) *Citizenship and the State in the Middle East. Approaches and Applications*, pp. 316–37, Syracuse, NY: Syracuse University Press.

Hobsbawm, E. J. (1997[1990]), *Nations and Nationalisms Since 1780: Programme, Myth, Reality*, Cambridge: Cambridge University Press.

Jeffery, P. and A. Basu (eds) (1998), *Appropriating Gender: Women's Activism and Politicized Religion in South Asia*, New York: Routledge.

Jelin, Elisabeth and Eric Hershberg (eds) (1996), *Constructing Democracy. Human Rights, Citizenship, and Society in Latin America*, Boulder, CO: Westview Press.

Joppke, Christian (2001), 'Multicultural Citizenship: A Critique', *Archives européennes de sociologie* 42: 2, 431–47.

Joseph, Suad (ed.) (2001), *Gender and Citizenship in the Middle East*, Syracuse, NY: Syracuse University Press.

Judt, Tony (1996), *A Grand Illusion? An Essay on Europe*, New York: Hill and Wang.

Kaviraj, Sudipta (1997), 'Filth and the Public Sphere: Concepts and Practices About Space in Calcutta', *Public Culture* 10: 1, 83–113.

Kaviraj, Sudipta (2001), 'In Search of Civil Society', in Sudipta Kaviraj and Sunil Khilnani (eds) *Civil Society. History and Possibilities*, pp. 287–323, Cambridge: Cambridge University Press.

Kaviraj, Sudipta and Sunil Khilnani (eds) (2001), *Civil Society. History and Possibilities*, Cambridge: Cambridge University Press.

Khilnani, Sunil (2001), 'The Development of Civil Society', in Sudipta Kaviraj and Sunil Khilnani (eds) *Civil Society. History and Possibilities*, pp. 11–32, Cambridge: Cambridge University Press.

Kymlicka, Will (1996[1995]), *Multicultural Citizenship. A Liberal Theory of Minority Rights*, Oxford: Clarendon Press.

Kymlicka, Will and Wayne Norman (eds) (2000), *Citizenship in Diverse Societies*, Oxford: Oxford University Press.

Lê Thành Khôi (2001), *Éducation et civilisations: Genèse du monde contemporain*, Paris: Bruno Leprince, UNESCO/Horizons du Monde.

Levinson, Bradley A. (1999), 'Resituating the Place of Educational Discourse in Anthropology', *American Anthropologist* 101: 3, 594–604.

Lutz, C. A. and G. M. White (1986), 'The Anthropology of Emotions', *Annual Review of Anthropology* 15: 405–36.

Lutz, C. A. and L. Abu-Lughod (eds) (1990), *Language and the Politics of Emotion*, Cambridge: Cambridge University Press.

Macintyre, Stuart (1996), 'Citizenship and Education', in S. Rufus Davis (ed.) *Citizenship in Australia. Democracy, Law and Society*, pp. 225–40, Carlton: Constitutional Centenary Foundation.

Mamdani, Mahmood (1996), *Citizen and Subject: Contemporary Africa and the Legacy of Late Colonialism*, Princeton, NJ: Princeton University Press.

Marshall, Thomas Humphrey (1950), *Citizenship and Social Class and Other Essays*, Cambridge: Cambridge University Press.

Marshall, Thomas Humphrey and Tom Bottomore (1996[1992]), *Citizenship and Social Class*, Chicago: Pluto Press.

Metcalf, Thomas (1995), *Ideologies of the Raj*, Cambridge: Cambridge University Press.

Metzger, Thomas A. (2001), 'The Western Concept of Civil Society in the Context of Chinese History', in Sudipta Kaviraj and Sunil Khilnani (eds) *Civil Society. History and Possibilities*, pp. 204–31, Cambridge: Cambridge University Press.

Neveu, Catherine (2000), 'European Citizenship, Citizens of Europe and European Citizens', in I. Bellier and T. M. Wilson (eds) *An Anthropology of the European Union: Building, Imagining and Experiencing the New Europe*, pp. 119–36, Oxford: Berg Publications.

Noiriel, Gérard (1991), *La tyrannie du national. Le droit d'asile en Europe 1793–1993*, Paris: Calmann-Lévy.

Noiriel, Gérard (ed.) (2001), 'Enseigner la nation', *Genèses – Sciences sociales et histoire*, Special issue 44 'Enseigner la nation': 2–75.

Nora, Pierre (ed.) (1996–8), *Realms of Memory: Rethinking the French Past*, English language edition edited and with a foreword by Lawrence D. Kritzman; translated by Arthur Goldhammer, New York: Columbia University Press.

Ong, Aihwa (1999), *Flexible Citizenship: The Cultural Logics of Transnationality*, Durham, NC: Duke University Press.

Pandey, Gyanendra (2001), *Remembering Partition: Violence, Nationalism, and History in India*, Cambridge: Cambridge University Press.

Pandey, Gyanendra and Peter Geschiere (eds) (2003), *The Forging of Nationhood*, New Delhi: Manohar.

Parekh, B. (2000), *The Future of Multi-Ethnic Britain. Report of the Commission on the Future of Multi-Ethnic Britain*, London: Runnymede Trust.

Prakash, Gyan (2003), 'The Location of Scholarship', in Jackie Assayag and Véronique Bénéï (eds) *At Home in Diaspora. South Asian Scholars and the West*, pp. 115–26. Delhi/Bloomington, IN: Permanent Black/Indiana University Press.

Pring, Richard (2001), 'Citizenship and Schools', in Bernard Crick (ed.) *Citizens: Towards a Citizenship Culture*, pp. 81–9, London: Blackwell.

Putnam, Robert (2000), *Bowling Alone*, New York: Simon and Schuster.

Rajan, Rajeswari Sunder (2003), *The Scandal of the State. Women, Law and Citizenship in Postcolonial India*, Durham, NC: Duke University Press.

Raman, J. Sri (2003), 'Hum Hindustani: "Non-Indian" Minorities', *The Daily Times*, 29 April.

Robb, Peter (ed.) (1997), *South Asia and the Concept of Race*, Delhi: Oxford University Press.

Rubinstein, Kim (1996), 'Citizenship, Membership and Civic Virtue: Similar But Not Quite the Same', in S. Rufus Davis (ed.) *Citizenship in Australia. Democracy, Law and Society*, pp. 69–88, Carlton: Constitutional Centenary Foundation.

Sarkar, T. and U. Butalia (eds) (1995), *Women and Right-Wing Movements*, London: Zed Books.

Savidan, Patrick (2001), 'La constellation post-nationale et l'avenir de l'Etat libéral', paper presented at the conference on *Nationalisme, libéralisme et pluralisme*, CERI, Paris, 5–6 February.

Schnapper, Dominique (1994), *La communauté des citoyens. Sur l'idée moderne de Nation*, Paris: Gallimard.

Schnapper, Dominique (2000), in Will Kymlicka and Sylvie Mesure (eds) *Comprendre n° 1: Les identités culturelles*, Paris: PUF.

Schnapper, Dominique (2002), 'Citizenship and National Identity in Europe', *Nations and Nationalism* 8: 1, 1–14.

Schuller, Tom (2001), 'The Need for Lifelong Learning', in Bernard Crick (ed.) *Citizens: Towards a Citizenship Culture*, pp. 90–9, Oxford: Blackwell.

Scott, David (1995), 'Colonial Governmentality', *Social Text* 43: 191–201.

Seyd, Patrick, Paul Whiteley and Charles Pattie (2001), 'Citizenship in Britain: Attitudes and Behaviour', in Bernard Crick (ed.) *Citizens: Towards a Citizenship Culture*, pp. 141–8, Oxford: Blackwell.

Shafir, Gershon (ed.) (1998), *The Citizenship Debates. A Reader*. Minneapolis, MN: University of Minnesota Press.

Shore, Cris (2001), 'Manufacturing European Citizens: The Europeanisation of School Children in Britain', paper presented at the international conference on *Manufacturing citizenship: Europe, South Asia, China*, Maison française, Oxford, 6–7 July.

Skocpol, Theda (1979), *States and Social Revolutions: a Comparative Analysis of France, Russia, and China*, Cambridge: Cambridge University Press.

Spencer, Jonathan (1997), 'Post-Colonialism and the Political Imagination', *Journal of the Royal Anthropology Institute* 3: 1, 1–20.

Spinner-Halev, Jeff (2000), 'Extending Diversity: Religion in Public and Private Education', in Will Kymlicka and Wayne Norman (eds) *Citizenship in Diverse Societies*, pp. 68–95, Oxford: Oxford University Press.

Steinmetz, George (ed.) (1999), *State/Culture: State-Formation After the Cultural Turn*, Ithaca, NY: Cornell University Press.

Stocking, George W. Jr (ed.) (1991), *Colonial Situations: Essays on the Contextualization of Ethnographic Knowledge*, Madison, WI: University of Wisconsin Press.

Subrahmanian, Ramya, Yusuf Sayed, Sarada Balagopalan and Crain Soudien (eds) (2003), *Education Inclusion and Exclusion: Indian and South African Perspectives*, IDS *Bulletin* 34(1), Institute of Development Studies, University of Sussex, Brighton.

Taylor, Charles (1992), *Multiculturalism and the Politics of Multiculturalism*, Princeton, NJ: Princeton University Press.

Thiesse, A.-M. (1999), *La création des identités nationales: Europe XVIIIè–XXè siècle*, Paris: Seuil.

Thomas, Nick (1994), *Colonialism's Culture: Anthropology, Travel and Government*, Cambridge: Polity Press.

Trouillot, Michel-Rolph (2001), 'The Anthropology of the State in the Age of

Globalization: Close Encounters of the Deceptive Kind', *Current Anthropology* 42: 1, 125–38.

Van der Veer, Peter (2001), *Imperial Encounters. Religion and Modernity in India and Britain*, Princeton, NJ: Princeton University Press.

Vasavi, A. R. (2003), 'Schooling for a New Society? The Social and Political Bases of Education Deprivation in India', in Ramya Subrahmanian, Yusuf Sayed, Sarada Balagopalan and Crain Soudien (eds) *Education Inclusion and Exclusion: Indian and South African Perspectives*, pp. 72–80 (*IDS Bulletin* 34(1), Institute of Development Studies, University of Sussex, Brighton).

Viswanathan, Gauri (1998[1989]), *Masks of Conquest. Literary Study and British Rule in India*, Delhi/New York: Oxford University Press/Columbia University Press.

Wallerstein, Immanuel (2003), 'Citizens All? Citizens Some! The Making of the Citizen', *Comparative Studies in Society and History* 45: 4, 650–79.

Werbner, Pnina (1998), 'Exoticising citizenship: Anthropology and the New Citizenship Debate', *Canberra Anthropology* 21: 2, 1–27.

Yuval-Davis, Nira and Pnina Werbner (eds) (1999), *Women, Citizenship and Difference*, London: Zed.

Zask, Joëlle (2001), 'L'élève et le citoyen, d'après John Dewey', in *Le Télémaque. Philosophie, Éducation, Société* 20: 53–64.

Part I
Disciplining citizens

1 Educating towards a European citizenship: to discipline or to emancipate?

Reflections from France[1]

Etienne Balibar

The idea of the European project needs to become something other than a cumbersome contraption uncertainly steered by embarrassed European governments. Clearly, there can be no question of going back. And for this reason, governments constantly explain to their respective electorates, on the one hand, that they must not meddle with it (especially since they have practically no means of influencing it); and, on the other hand, that they must accept its necessity, since it will eventually be for their own good. It is a truism that the constitution of a Europe where the issues of the democratization of culture and its opening up to the world – as well as of resistance to capitalist globalization – could be reformulated can barely be conceived of. And it will indeed remain unthinkable without an enormous concomitant exercise in education (*effort d'éducation*). To be sure, such a statement makes no claims to originality. Yet it is one of the key issues that should be kept constantly at the forefront of any consistent political project for a 'European community'. Because the word 'education' itself has several meanings, it is however necessary to specify what is meant by an exercise in education. The phrase 'an exercise in education' implies that the idea of such a Europe should not be taken for granted: such an objective is confronted with ideological obstacles, traditions and resistances, some of which may be considered as prejudices or as cultural heritage. Consequently, an exercise in education or a pedagogic effort is required in order to open up alternative perspectives.

Although, like many French academics, I come from a family of teachers, this has not led me to worship schooling and university institutions. Nor has it led me to sacralize them to the extent of reacting violently whenever their monopoly is called into question. Yet my teaching experience has led me to think that there is something not only precious but also irreplaceable in the schooling process. Consequently, I cannot imagine that some great collective transitional movement on the European scale towards a regime of transnational and plurilingual communication could be achieved without each national educational establishment's being thoroughly mobilized. Each educational establishment must also put all its resources at the service of this project, and must necessarily give it pride of place. Conversely, if any such establishment were not able to take responsibility for this project and consequently to transform itself, that is, to open its frontiers and reform its methods, it would *ipso facto* itself come to represent a tremendous obstacle to the project.

From this there follows the question: who will perform this educational task? The risk is of stumbling into the pitfalls of, at worst, churning out reactionary clichés about 'the education of the masses'; or at best, dwelling on solemn cogitations about the task of European intellectual and political elites. To put it rather negatively: 'Education is not the same as communication'. Educating involves something different from the complacent resort to communications, propaganda and media hype that is commonly seen today. The nature of obstacles must be looked into, and consequential questions must be asked. The overall issue concerns the type of knowledge or culture whose creation would facilitate the surmounting of the obstacles identified. This, however, is a Catch 22: the construction of Europe is probably not possible without such an educational effort, together with one of mass intellectual and moral reform, as Gramsci would have said (borrowing from Ernest Renan, thus indicating how specific the history of such a phrase is).[2] To be sure, education is not all-powerful. It does not stem simply from the will or the illumination of the elites; there must be a collective, if not a popular, movement underlying the project of a European constitution, so as to put some sort of impetus behind this educational effort. This is what the Catch 22 is about.

In some ways, the issue is about 'democratizing the institution of frontiers' in the realm of education. Whether in linguistic matters or in wider cultural and political issues, the educational system arguably represents an absolutely inescapable aspect and a constitutive element of any such project. Indeed, if such an educational and political project is to escape from communication overkill, that is to say from a representation of collective education dominated by the stock formulae of technology and media culture, then it must rely on – and even transform as necessary – another type of educational process, that precisely which is developed in schools and at university. The issues must therefore be tackled at both ends, and the contradictions entailed must be taken into consideration.

That said, it is agreed that school is not everything; nor was it ever. As Bourdieu (1996) showed, the characteristic of the regime of education in the bourgeois period was the synergy of school and social – especially familial – milieux, which were at the same time cultural milieux, wherein specific types of knowledge were transmitted. And this is true even today, although that does not mean that the bourgeois classes always still have the upper hand.[3] Education, right from the very beginning, must increasingly be thought of as a process of permanent education. And the sites of permanent education are not exclusively schools. Indeed, one could very well imagine the existence of associations that would be active in the learning of languages, or of citizenship, working alongside – and in addition to – the schools. All of these sites must explore possibilities for going beyond national identities, and therefore help in rethinking the constitution of secondary identities.

Primary and secondary identities in a postnational Europe

Recently, the philosopher and sociologist Ulrich Bielefeld (of the Institut für Sozialforschung in Hamburg) published a book (2003) comparing French and German conceptions of the 'ideal' nation, which help in explaining the transition from inclusive to exclusive representations of the community. Although he does not phrase it in terms of primary and secondary identities,[4] his central notion is somewhat similar to that which I developed in *Race, Nation, Class* on the relationship of nationalism to racism and cultural exclusivism. Bielefeld adopts a less extremist position in so far as he defends the importance of national identity against some too glibly cosmopolitan discourses often heard in Germany (Habermas and so on). His perspective is obviously not a chauvinist one. He explains that a certain national republican tradition necessarily rests on the institutional recognition of differences, that is to say on the fact that we simultaneously have several identities, from political to ideological, ethnic, cultural and so on. The phases of ethnic cleansing, nationalist hysteria and institutional racism conducive to processes of extermination are phases in which national identity is amputated from this capacity to integrate primary identities and is in turn itself conceived as a primary identity.

In some ways, it is this process that I sought to expose by arguing that it is not only cultural communitarianism that needs to be fought, but also republican communitarianism, as in French national communitarianism. In some contexts, a national political identity comes to be conceived of as exclusive. In this respect, the construction of Europe represents a possibility of creating another level of secondary identity, thereby underscoring its constructed, institutional character and consequently avoiding its being reduced to essentialist representations of a communitarian 'We'. What is needed is a conception of a community of European peoples that is not accompanied by the representation of a 'European essence', just as there is nothing such as a 'French' or a 'British essence'. As is shown by the chapters of past history, the construction of essentialist images of this type was an intensive and deliberate process. This was the case in Germany, as much as in France.[5] It was also true of England, as is suggested by the fascinating works of Linda Colley (1992) on the history of England and the making of Britishness.

Education is also about constructing a secondary identity. By definition, education fashions a secondary identity. How and which one can be fashioned in a postnational European context is what is at issue here. First, let us go back further in time. There is an analogy, rather than a clear and simple identity, between the distinction between primary and secondary identities and the distinction between 'nature' and 'second nature'.[6] Obviously, the notion of 'second nature' is a paradoxical one. Yet what the philosophical tradition strove to do by resorting to it was to suggest that there is an acquired training (*formation acquise*), which the Greeks called *paideia* and which we have translated by 'education' – what nineteenth-century Germans called *Bildung* – although one is aware of some important connotations being lost in the translation process.[7] The paradox that the philosophical tradition has constantly worked on is the idea that in some ways what comes second is more authentic (*originaire*) or fundamental than what exists in the first place. In other words, one does not *originate from* one's nature, but 'one *evolves towards* it'. Now, a certain educational tradition has made this idea its own. Put simply in the language of sociology or political science, the task of education is principally to relativize primary identities, thus calling into question any essentialist adherence to the notion or feeling – and perhaps the illusion – that by moving away or distancing oneself from them one must necessarily *ipso facto* become 'de-natured' and radically alienated (which is not however to be seen as tantamount to ruling out any conscious, voluntary and implicitly conditional election of such a primary identity as expressive of a significant element of one's own nature). Obviously, such a questioning is possible in the idealist philosophical tradition on the condition that there should be some goal, a *telos* that is sufficiently self-consistent (*consistant*) and essential: primary identities can be deconstructed only if something else substantial is constructed. This is what the great educational philosophies strive to do, even if they explain it in rather abstract terms: they construct 'culture', 'humanity', 'patria', 'citizenship', and so on.

Second, the idea of education has constantly been torn between an individualist pole and a collective, communitarian one. A large number of canonic classic philosophies, such as those of Aristotle, Cicero and Kant, have attempted to explain how one can at the same time conceive of an education's both enabling the achievement and perfecting (*accomplissement*, 'finishing') of an individual and fulfilling a community objective, originally that of the *polis* (the city-state) and later on that of the nation. Hence the idea of a 'national education', born in the French Revolution. There is something ineluctable in all these perspectives. The phrase 'a European education' conjures up the idea that in earlier times the training of an elite of 'finished', 'accomplished' and 'civilized' individuals required them to leave their native places, travelling beyond their national boundaries across the continent of Europe (the 'Grand Tour'). Yet at present, precisely because Europe has become our collective horizon, a concern not only of the aristocratic or the bourgeois elites, but of all classes, and above all of ordinary people, the idea of a European education needs to acquire another, and a less narrowly individualistic, meaning. It must be informed by a more collective and more substantial content in order effectively to fulfil this role of creating a measure of critical distancing from which to consider one's adherence to primary identities. This leads to an apparently paradoxical conclusion. European identity must be strong enough to constitute in itself a *telos*, an end, a horizon within which a collective process of education can develop, rather than leading to a mere administrative framework for university exchange programmes, important though these are. But it should not become an essence, a fiction of uniqueness and superiority leading to inventing or labelling 'Others' in order to exclude them. Substantial or consistent, but not essentialist; this is the paradox on which we should reflect and work.

Towards the construction of Europe: beyond the nation-state form

The idea of a European education (*Education à l'Europe*) must have a content. This content will be more or less difficult to imagine depending on one's initial standpoint. It may be easier to imagine for those at the margins of Europe: for instance, a Turkish student of mine who is in favour of Turkey's accession to the European Community is specifically looking at the role played by human rights clauses in the current European debate on Turkey. Surely the issue of the politics of human rights occupies an important place in the moral and ideal core of a European identity. Such an identity needs to be given existence in both discourses and deeds, so that European education renders possible the acquisition of a 'true second nature'. Yet, again, the idea of a European construction needs to be sufficiently strong to feed an educational process that is replacing other earlier, worn-out collective horizons. But it should not assume the force of an identity myth or an education in 'Europeanism' seen in the sense of a fortress besieged by the barbarians, the underdeveloped, Easterners, Americans and other categories of people who have become the objects of popular phobias. So that, here again, there is a unity of contraries (*unité de contraires*). What is a power (*puissance*) that is not an essence? What is a power that is not premised on the internalization of an exclusive myth of collective identity?

To be sure, this question is not the preserve of Europe: it concerns the rest of the world as well, whether Americans, Iraqis, Chinese, Indians or whoever. This confirms that such a problem cannot be solved unilaterally. Rather, it is part of a much vaster context, with not only cultural, but also juridical, military and other aspects. Such a context requires identifying what there is between or beyond the opposition between the form of the nation-state on the one hand and the open, apparently homogeneous market on the other hand. The answer is that there are supranational entities that have inevitably inherited a certain cultural homogeneity from history, but that today – whether in Europe, in America or possibly in the Far East before long – have reached maturity after exploring all the possibilities of creating closed empires. Which also brings us round to the question of Europe's own openness and closure.

'Fortress Europe' or a more open model?

It is true that there is a contradiction inherent in the project of constructing a European citizen within clearly delimited boundaries, in that the frontiers of Europe have long been shifting and labile. To be sure, this contradiction may be seen as radical. Yet it can also be pointed out that endless factitious obstacles are being put in the way of its solution. There is obviously no clear-cut answer to the question of whether Europe must remain open or closed. If it is not closed at all, it cannot exist as an institutional entity. Conversely, if it is not open at all, then it will be seen as striving to throw the engine of history into reverse gear. But as far as the democratization of frontiers and the citizenship of migrants are concerned, there are arguably institutional solutions, even if these inevitably include a dimension of compromise or negotiation. For instance, clandestine or settled illegal immigrants are maintained within all European countries, in France in particular. It is well known that this is due neither to the impossibility of taking a census of them nor to that of establishing relatively satisfactory regimes of residence and visa systems. For one thing, a residual insecurity at the margins of the working class is despicably but critically needed by politicians for their own exploitative ends. Second, a securitarian ideology constitutes a single whole, and if it is brought into question at one end, it will have to be brought into question at the other. The periodical sorting out of these clandestine settlers, the variable extension of political rights throughout all the European countries to categories of foreigners who are more or less permanent residents, or simply the setting up at the European level of some sort of more or less generalized 'Green Card' (i.e. not only for professionals, but also for manual workers), are not insurmountable juridical obstacles, nor would they require unthinkable prodigies of legislation. Such a course would obviously involve negotiations with the countries of origin; and not only with the countries concerned and their state apparatuses, but also with voluntary associations (NGOs) and with the people concerned, so that their demands may be made known and viable compromises may be found between the necessary imperatives of security and procedures aimed at the normalization of the irrepressible international migration that has become a feature of modern civilization. On the one hand, therefore, there is no absolute solution with regard to the enduring principles of open and closed frontiers and the issue of sovereignty. On the other hand, it is also necessary to shed all pretence in order to reach the core of the difficulty. (By 'pretence' I mean the ideological overload that accompanies all these issues, with the result that the simplest problems are stated as insoluble, as if they shook the very foundations of national sovereignty and identity.)

Building an integrated educational system across Europe

Towards a European university system

On the one hand, there is a large measure of agreement among some politicians today on the creation of a European university. Such a creation should involve exchanges of students and a homogenization of programmes of study, that is, a progressive convergence of university institutions on the European level rather than the imposing of a monolithic conformity. These are critical but praiseworthy key objectives of European construction. On the other hand, any academic from a European country is aware of how difficult the task is. In the French instance, it is well known that the democratic character of the university system is undergoing an acute crisis, and that, for the moment, the creation of 'centres of excellence' (*pôles d'excellence*) explicitly designed to fulfil the ideal of constructing a European university system is heightening the crisis. In some universities, this leads to a radical questioning of the purpose and utility of such measures.

The ongoing reform of the university system at the European level seems to negate any ideal republican model. Indeed, this reform may give rise to the development of a geographical zoning mechanism, or to the construction of 'centres of excellence' (*pôles d'excellence*) in which well-off students may be able to concoct and pursue their own elitist degrees. It will undoubtedly be very difficult to solve this double-bind. What is emerging today is a European university as an institution for research and higher studies, allowing students to circulate through several countries and languages, and travel about among different European universities in order to complete their education at various different sites. How to make sure that such a system does not end up being appallingly elitist, not only in the cultural sense of the term – which would be a good thing – but also in the social sense, is a vexing question. It would imply that both the European Community and the community of European nations should reinstate at the centre of their agendas the question of democratization – currently in retreat in every country – at university level just as much as anywhere else. In other words, a large programme of scholarships is needed, set up either locally or from the centre, together with a systematic – even a compulsory – exchange programme. This would guarantee that each and every European student should not be permitted to finish his or her degree without having completed at least one year of study abroad. Obviously, such a scheme would require a lot of money and effort put into it to ensure its harmonization across Europe. Otherwise, the danger is of falling into the trammels of an exaggerated elitism operating through just two or three prestigious institutions in each country.

Such a risk of elitism is more easily conceived in those countries where a tradition of public schools already exists, for instance in England rather than France, Italy or Germany. It is also likely that Eastern European countries that have started developing along the lines of a liberal model will probably also seek to establish some prestigious universities. This may be the case, for instance, in Poland and Hungary, with either private or public (or possibly public–private partnership) institutions imparting an elitist training. In France, at the cost of dire confrontations, there will eventually be 'elitist programmes' (*filières d'excellence*) within universities. But with very few scholarships, especially in the human sciences, such a system will be highly selective in the worst sense of the term, unless each country signs up to these propositions and each of them becomes convinced that Europe needs a dual programme of homogenization and of democratization within its own universities. This certainly represents an enormous challenge – and perhaps also an immense opportunity.

The creation of a European university can therefore not be taken for granted at all. Yet, without espousing any populist thesis, one must acknowledge that the question of reforming the educational process at the European level is not limited to the universities alone: rather, it goes from university all the way down to primary and nursery schools. This idea has been around for quite some time, and not only with reference to the construction of Europe, but more generally: for instance with respect to the question of learning foreign languages from an early age; or that of reforming the history syllabus so that children can envisage their place in time and space not only within national boundaries, but also transnationally. For it should be emphasized that the idea of constructing Europe has meaning only in terms of the invention of a new transnational regime of languages and cultures. This requires awareness of the transformations that will be required of educational institutions right from the beginning. Indeed, the times are – like those of the foundation of the French Third Republic – an epoch of the (re-)invention of the nation-state and of modern national sovereignty, with politics and education figuring as two intricately correlated notions.

Learning languages in a postnational Europe

The issues of language teaching and linguistic regimes are certainly not matters for improvisation. Yet, even if primarily drawing on their subjectivities, philosophers and sociologists can contribute to some of the ongoing debates on this matter. It is true that the issues of linguistic diversity and regional and national languages are construed differently in all countries inasmuch as they feed on varying pedagogic traditions and practices.

This certainly does not mean that some countries are naturally more resistant to social change than others, or that their pedagogic history can be written uniformly. Let me take the example of the French language to illustrate this point. It could be easily surmised that France is a country dominated by massive linguistic centralization, if not linguistic fetishism. For instance, many Breton speakers may take an extremely jaundiced view of the devastating long-term effects of the politics of language during the French Revolution – a view founded upon and well documented by the work of de Certeau, Julia and Revel (1975). These effects are thus currently only ever described in uniformly negative terms. Now, there is no disputing that the socio-political establishment of the position of the French language over a period of two and a half centuries did include a remarkably powerful element of radically destructive violence in France, as it did in other countries. Yet such a unilateral vision misses out on the aspects of democratization of the access to knowledge that the linguistic and educational establishment has had in France. These aspects also have to be taken into historical consideration. And especially so in the light of their particular contribution to that specific form of republican uniformity and secularism that made possible the constitution of a public sphere in which political life became, perhaps more so than elsewhere, a concern shared by a wide range of different social groups.

Be that as it may, and notwithstanding national specificities, Europeans are now being compelled to embark upon a new linguistic regime. They may either embark upon it dragging their feet, or in a more confident and enterprising spirit. Such a new linguistic regime inevitably entails a compromising of the monopolies of the national languages. This is why it requires thorough reflection on its democratizing aspects and, conversely, its anti-democratic aspects of specialization, monopoly, rupture between the elites and the masses, and discrimination, all of which Bourdieu and others have studied very well (Bourdieu and Passeron 1979, 1990). In the long run, what seems to be inevitable, as well as progressive, is that the overwhelming majority of our fellow citizens across Europe will simultaneously use several languages with varying levels of competence, actively or passively. Amongst those languages will certainly be the lingua franca that is currently in the process of universalization, that is to say, English; obviously, the national language; and to varying degrees, other languages. And these last may be European or extra-European, given that some communities that originated elsewhere now form an integral part of the edifice of the modern Europe that is currently under construction.

It is also very likely that this will provide an opportunity for revalorizing regional languages, or at least some fundamental regional languages. In other words, shedding a monolinguistic model, whether real or apparent, enables the shedding of a linguistic monopoly, thereby allowing an opening up of psychological, and probably also intellectual and technical possibilities that may benefit regional languages. The matter is not only a question of law: it is not solely about inscribing the rights of minority languages into a European charter. Rather, it is about culturally and politically imposing the idea that to communicate, to speak, and to learn are not things that may be done only in one single language, or even through a grammar exercise and a unique and laborious process of translation from one tongue into another, at which some are very good and others rather weak. On the contrary, to communicate, speak and learn is something that allows the use of several languages. There is no disputing the difficulty of it for the majority of people. Nor is there any disputing that what Bourdieu called the aspects of 'cultural heritage' or 'pre-existent aptitudes' (*pre-savoirs*, 'pre-skills') that are class-based pre-skills do have a considerable impact on these acquisition processes. But so they already do today in acquiring a mastery over the means of communication.

Furthermore, another type of prejudice needs to be fought, namely that found in many nations that to step outside one's national language is to somehow betray one's national community. This idea is far more widespread than is usually acknowledged. In France, for instance, it gave rise to dia-tribes about the use of non-French linguistic terms in the French public sphere in the early 1980s. At the time of the petition against the 'Toubon law',[8] an internationally acclaimed philosopher, Michel Serres, declared: 'Today, one gets to read more English words on the walls of Paris than one ever did German ones at the time of the Occupation'. In addition, another type of prejudice needs to be worked on with the help of psycho-linguists and teachers. This is the notion that speaking several languages is very diffi-cult or even near-impossible; in particular, that it would be very difficult, or even impossible, to learn more of them. Now, it is undoubtedly false that difficulty is a linear function of the number of linguistic instruments that have to be mastered. There have been times in history, and places in the world even today, in India or Africa for instance, where plurilingualism is a relatively banal, daily thing. But the conditions need to be created for this to happen.

Bringing politics into schools: a case study in France

In order for a viable pedagogical project of citizenship – whether national or postnational – to be sustained, social realities need to be contextualized in school. The issue of contextualization *ipso facto* elicits that of the extent to which political problems concerning society as a whole should be and must be imported into the teaching institution and school practice. In other words, the question is whether politics should be brought into schools – issues, for instance, of immigration and insecurity, cultural, ethnic or reli-gious differences, and so on. This is politics in its most difficult current reality (*actualité*). On the one hand, one might say that there is no way that politics should be brought into schools. Yet, on the other hand, it can be argued that politics already exists in schools. The issue over the wearing of Islamic veils (see Gaspard and Khosrokhavar 1995) testifies to this. Follow-ing repeated controversies on this issue over the last decade, a proposal was made a year ago – its implementation is still currently being debated – to include the teaching of religious 'facts' (*le fait religieux*) in the school curricu-lum (see Debray 2002).

Secularism in question

Although this curricular innovation is undeniably a welcome one, it does not do away with the difficulties posed by some abstract theoretical questions such as those of the definitions of religion, or of religious facts, or whether the societies in which we live are secularized ones, and in what way(s). Defining religion is a very problematic issue. In discussions about racism, for instance, everybody is agreed that nobody knows what race is; yet nobody knows any better what religion is, shocking though such a statement may be to many. What religion is 'known' after a model invented by the Western Islamo-Judaeo-Christian tradition that has no universal value per se. Furthermore, at the core of this questioning lies the crucial issue of the disenchantment of the world: does the evolution of the contemporary world corroborate the great intuition of nineteenth-century Europe according to which religion is on the decline, with the result that this very decline creates a necessity to sacralize other institutions, among them education? This was the dominant idea of French Durkheimian sociology too (Durkheim 1977), and it has thoroughly permeated the French conception of secularism (symbolized by the classic nineteenth-century conflict between the village curé and the village schoolmaster). To be sure, all these difficult questions do not have straightforward answers.

Arguably, what makes the above type of curricular innovation necessary is that the disenchantment of the world is not a historical reality. Secularization in the sense it was given in the positivist era has not become a verified historical reality on the scale that had been predicted. The places where such a conception may have been historically entertained represent only a tiny part of today's world. Such a conception has very little chance of succeeding in imposing its model upon the rest of the world. For instance, de-Christianization is not a reality in the United States. A decline in religious faith is not on the cards in the Middle East either. Besides, there is a great enduring conflict between secular forms of thought and religious ones. The role of politics is somehow to regulate this conflict. In addition, the traditional forms of secularism, which are profoundly grounded in the state, are themselves undergoing a crisis. So that secularism in turn is itself undergoing a crisis, whilst the crisis in religious faith has not gone away. The net result of this is that some religious minds are suffering from doubt, while at the same time some secular minds are suffering from uncertainty.

Teaching 'religious knowledge' (le fait religieux)

Whether the proposal for the teaching of religions and religious facts in schools is likely to contribute to a political transformation of the educational context is open to question. A need has nevertheless been felt for such political transformation in order to avoid insoluble dilemmas, and the aggravation of violent conflicts and confrontations. Somehow, it takes a profound 'mental revolution', whether in France, Germany or Britain – each for specific reasons – to introduce such changes to the curriculum. (Clearly, some countries are ahead of others in this revolution; 'religious studies' have already been introduced in schools in Britain.) Indeed, the implementation of such changes should provide schoolchildren – and through them, adults and parents helping them with their homework – with a means of understanding the nature of the contemporary conflicts in which they are, to a certain extent, the actors. This is undeniably very important. Whether it is sufficient, in the terms set out above, is debatable. There may be a risk of intellectualism: to assume that schools and the transformation of the existing school curricula can solve the 'cultural question', the question of conflicts between cultures and civilizations, is probably as wrong as to have assumed earlier that it could solve the 'social question', that is, that it could do away with class conflict. The enlightened tolerance that schools may be able to promote will not be enough to solve civilizational conflicts, any more than the upward social mobility facilitated by a relatively democratic school system was ever enough to eliminate class conflicts. So the question of knowing how politics should be brought into schools remains an open and a relatively difficult one.

Perhaps the issue of the Islamic veil has the advantage of demonstrating that in order to master these – masterable! – situations, if not to harmonize radically antagonistic views, and to reach a workable 'regime of civility', education alone is not enough. One must not teach theoretical things only; rather, one must 'engage in politics' in school and beyond the schools. This amounts to 'cautiously dismantling the barrier between school and society'. It is known that the reasons why young girls want to wear what is subsumed under the rough category of 'the Islamic veil' inside educational institutions in France are multiple and often radically mutually contradictory. This is a fact that those who, denouncing the custom, demand a change in the law so as to prohibit the wearing of the veil, systematically and probably deliberately ignore. It is no coincidence that all the worthwhile sociological studies on these issues have been conducted by people not favourable to so denunciatory a position. These studies have shown that the reasons for wearing a veil are many: adolescent crises among young girls who are going through phases of mystical identification with their religious traditions, manifestations of obedience towards the family, or of negotiating greater autonomy from familial authority, forms of manipulation by proselytizing religious groups, some of which are dangerous and others not, and so on.

Yet private interests, for instance those of families – Muslim or other – should not be allowed to set the rules within educational institutions. Nor should the French state educational system set itself the political task of educating and reforming the cultural habits of populations of immigrant origin. The problem is therefore especially difficult because, as has been pointed out by some of the most relevant critics of the Islamic veil, the root of the question is not just cultural difference or community belonging; it is not even religion, as it might be or have been in the case of practising Jews and Catholics. Rather, it is the treatment of gender difference. The Islamic veil, rather than being merely a symbol of cultural belonging, and possibly of dissidence from the dominant Western culture, is a mark of gender inequality and, it might even be said, of symbolic slavery. Naturally, it has been understood by all that this idea is liable to manipulation. Those opposing the repressive treatment inflicted on the Islamic veil in schools may be accused of contributing to women's slavery in the Islamic world. Conversely, such repressive treatment feeds into a kind of hysteria among the teaching staff, making them feel that they are fighting for the cause of women when they are actually displaying intolerance towards cultural difference. That said, if one is cautious and explores possible conciliatory forms of civility that straddle the boundary between school and society in order to solve this type of conflict, then one must remain equally inflexible and adamant over issues that constitute the proper province of education. This means that one must include in the teaching of religions (*le fait religieux*), the question of how religions treat gender difference, men and women, and sexuality. This is obviously no easy task. So that the more one attempts to regulate the conflict politically on the one hand, the more one has, on the other hand, to acknowledge the depth of it. And this is the very object of the educational process and the schooling institution: to strive towards the impossible, that is, to sort out social and cultural conflicts that in some ways have irreconcilably antagonistic backgrounds, by giving social actors the means of apprehending their meanings.

Dismantling the school–society barrier

How can the barrier between school and society (the outside world) be dismantled? Obviously, there is no straightforward answer to such a difficult question. It involves a long-term process that bears some analogy to the social question. In the 1950s, in spite of democratization brought about by the Popular Front and the Liberation, the French educational system was still a profoundly class-based system: underneath an apparently systematic institutional integration, there existed watertight divisions between the bourgeois school and the popular, proletarian school. A *lycée* was a bourgeois schooling institution. Yet it cannot be said that the marks of social conflict were to be found in practical or vocational learning centres,[9] or that conversely, the *lycées* could have been seen as the locus of republican universality. Rather, it was one of the very functions of the educational system to contribute towards reproducing class distinction. Whether this situation has yet come to an end is certainly debatable.

Today, in France, it seems that we are headed back to such a system through a repertoire of rather insidious mechanisms – geographical mechanisms, for instance, such as zoning. Mechanisms that appear absolutely outrageous from a democratic perspective are aimed at protecting particular schools attended by the bourgeoisie and the educated classes. In a way, they are an inverted mirror-image of the school segregation mechanisms confining black people to ghettos that have been exposed in the United States. Thus the *lycées* in the centre of Paris siphon off the good pupils, 90 per cent of whom come from well-off and cultured families. Although they too may run up against drugs problems, these *lycées* project themselves as relatively calm and safe havens; whereas the institutions situated in working-class suburbs or areas of serious unemployment come across as sites of relegation and insecurity (sink schools). Nevertheless, there remains an ideal or a project – that of a universal republican educational system. This ideal consists not so much in striving to abolish social stigmas as, rather, in seeking to nourish and enrich the educational experience (*alimenter la formation scolaire*) with memories and social traditions and attitudes that are not the exclusive preserve of the dominating classes. This is where exposure to non-European bodies of knowledge is useful, inasmuch as it contributes to a wider understanding of complex contemporary social and cultural realities.

Decision-making and social actors' participation in the construction of Europe

One might wonder why the recognition of the importance of civil society, of the activities of all kinds of social groupings, and especially of cultural associations – in other words, of an extracurricular form of education – should specifically be linked to the process of European construction and to the emergence of a transnational dimension to social life and public space. And perhaps part of the answer is simply: 'because both these things are happening at the same time'. Indeed, one could envisage the possibility that all of these conditions might have been met at the level of the nation-state; but the fact is that this simply did not happen, or at least not to any significant extent. A postnational construction can therefore be envisaged somewhat differently, that is to say, as a site for working out alternative solutions to these problems at a postnational level.

   To be sure, there is a sort of 'civil societal' vulgate in which all these different dimensions are bought together all too easily and promptly.[10] For some, the negative idea is that 'there was too much state control' and too much state-directed centralization. This may be felt particularly in the field of education, or in the domain of the control of culture in some countries – France passes as the country *par excellence* where culture is thought of as a state matter. Extreme positions in France may go so far as to denounce the 'cultural state' and the Jacobin tradition (see Fumaroli 1991). In such a view, the postnational situation weakens the state, because the state had completely identified itself with the nation. By weakening the state, one at last opens up the possibility of a greater autonomy for civil society. Yet, in defence of the Jacobin stance, it has to be said that this view fails to do justice to the institutional aspect of the process creative of active citizenship, and to the developments in education that are needed to underpin it.

It is agreed, however, that there are opportunities that were never really seized at the national level and that it is time to seize in a postnational state. This does not amount to saying that 'there was too much state control, and, at long last, the national level is over and done with'. It is possible to work at both levels concomitantly. Indeed, one could imagine a national state that would remain strong and on the basis of which something else might be constructed at the supranational level. To envisage the role that associations might play at the supranational level does not necessarily conflict with the idea of a national education policy. Furthermore, not everything can be expected from the state. One gets a feeling that governments do not know how to set about constructing the European enterprise. They do not know how to turn it into a project that would not only be top-down, but would also co-opt other forms of creative association arising from the grassroots level. Unfortunately, there is every reason to believe that great obstacles – social, cultural, international and so on – to the projected European construction will not be overcome unless there is a collective aspiration towards the existence of Europe. At the moment, such a collective aspiration lies in the distant future. Now, this is something that does not happen privately in the seclusion of people's minds alone, but something that also comes into existence within 'civil society' or 'associations' in the broad sense of the term, that is to say, in networks of competition, conflict, resistance, initiative, creation and enterprise. These, by definition, are not controlled by the state. At different levels today – from alternative responses to, and movements towards, globalization to some very elitist forms of cultural activity such as the transnational itineraries of travelling theatre companies – frontiers are progressively dissolving, and associative activity is crossing frontiers. But much remains to be done. Obviously, the issue of decision-making and social actors' participation raises other questions, among them moral ones such as that of civil disobedience.

Civil (dis)obedience: learning resistance at school?

The notion of civil disobedience is a profoundly antinomic one. First, the idea of learning civil disobedience is almost a contradiction in terms. Civil disobedience is a necessity that one finds oneself driven to in certain circumstances. This was the case, for instance, in the context of the struggle of the *sans-papiers* and of the support that artists and intellectuals gave them (see Balibar 1998; Fassin 2001). It was especially the case with the declaration – recently renewed – by individual citizens that they were willing to place themselves outside the law immediately as soon as that law should be manipulated by the government against certain fundamental democratic principles. Obviously, this is the kind of collective attitude that one might on grounds of civic morality wish education to prepare its citizens for in a democratic country. To phrase it negatively, one might wish that schools should not prepare or condition their pupils to blind obedience. To what extent it was ever the case that schools prepared or conditioned their pupils to blind obedience, it is difficult to say. But there are extreme historical examples that show that there are degrees of (dis)obedience, and that these degrees matter. There have been times in history, in France and elsewhere, where the idea that schools should be institutions that fundamentally inculcate obedience has been both entertained and theoretically justified.

Let me briefly make a provocative comparison. Take the play by Claudel, *Le soulier de satin*, which was staged again recently in France in its complete 10-hour long version by the director Olivier Py (in Orléans and the Théâtre Sarah Bernhard in Paris). This play was written in 1923 but was performed in 1943, at about the time when Claudel was also writing an ode to Marshal Pétain. This is an admirable play, but one that is partly based on propositions of Catholic theology and ideological propositions drawn from the conservative political Catholic tradition in France. At one point, one of the characters says something like 'the greatest objective of human life is to learn obedience', in the sense of obedience to God. Obviously, obedience to God is not the same as obedience to the state. But sometimes they go well together. And the fact is that under the Vichy regime the following idea was copiously elaborated: that what had caused the misfortunes of the French was to have forgotten the meaning of obedience, and to have become a rebellious, anti-establishment, anti-authority and anarchistic people.

This type of rhetoric has resurfaced recently in the context of the very real crisis that the French educational system is currently undergoing: today, both students and teachers are experiencing a moral crisis and acute distress as they are faced with both material difficulties and the glaring contradictions that have developed at the heart of their social function. Yet it is not the 'image' of the role of the educator (*la fonction enseignante*) that has degenerated, as many would have it; rather, it is the role of the educator in today's society and in its relationship to politics that is being very fundamentally called into question. The minister of education and others keep repeating that the fault is the 'ideas of the sixties' (*la Pensée 68*).[11] According to them, the very idea of authority has been progressively undermined by liberalism, individualism, irrationalism and communitarianism. And as a result of this systematic and deliberate destruction of deference to institutional authority – the authority of knowledge, of the state, and so on – 'there is no more education in citizenship' (*on ne forme plus de citoyens*). Such a statement is false, hypocritical, dangerous and reactionary. Yet it cannot be affirmed either that schools should be schools of disobedience as such; this would be a perverse and embarrassing mirror-image. It is better to demand that schools should not be places where the necessity of disobedience is systematically ruled out. This somehow amounts to demanding that schools should be open to a number of conflicting social realities, which will even include extreme situations in which one may experience the need to raise the standard of revolt.

Towards an emancipated citizen?

There is yet another difficulty with the question of schools as a site where disobedience would not necessarily be ruled out. This lies in the fact that we are dealing with children. Indeed, school does not deal with abstract individuals, but with real children. There is a really profound difficulty, and one that has not merely sociological and historical, but also anthropological, roots. And this concerns the status of the child as a social individual and a citizen. In those societies that invented the notion of citizenship and gave a strictly formal and legal definition of it, that is, the societies of Antiquity, Greece, Rome and so on, the problem was easily solved, at least on the surface. Children – or more precisely some of them, i.e. male children belonging to certain social categories – were straight away put into an educational course fundamentally aimed at turning them into citizens. Such a course indeed provided them with the ways and means, the moral customs and eventually the rights appropriate to exercising what, with specific reference to Rome, Claude Nicolet (1980) very cogently and appositely named the 'profession of a citizen' (*le métier de citoyen*). For some male children, therefore, to be a child was to learn the profession of a citizen. And we know through the work of Foucault (1984) and others that this was accompanied by other aspects of moral education, all of which he subsumed under the expression *souci de soi* (care of the self). And all of this has not completely disappeared. An ideal picture of citizenship even now still feeds on the idea that childhood is the learning of citizenship. One could even add to this the catch-22 proposition of an education for citizenship that would not consist of a downright authoritarian education in obedience. This would imply combining possibly diverging European traditions at the European level.

There remains, however, an intractable difficulty. Modern citizenship over the last two centuries has come no longer to be a closed citizenship, in the sense of Antiquity: it is a virtually open citizenship. The notions of human rights and citizens' rights are premised on the idea that nobody should be excluded from citizenship. In the past, there have been all kinds of excluded people: women, until a relatively late period manual workers or employees, dependants, servants, foreigners, obviously, and different categories of 'incapable persons' or 'minors', as the law calls them: criminals, mental patients, children. The tendency of the democratization of citizenship has been to put an end to exclusionary processes. This has been done to a certain extent, at least a juridical one, for women and employees. As for foreigners, the question is still being debated. Perhaps, at the risk of making a utopian statement, it can be suggested that the construction of Europe provides an opportunity to call into question a strictly national definition of citizenship. Indeed, European construction may allow for not only upgrading to European citizenship but also for 'opening up' European citizenship in order to make it a citizenship based on residence. In this way, the status of citizen would also apply to resident foreigners. But as for other categories, such as criminals and mentally ill people, the question is a rather complex one. And in the case of children, who are neither criminals nor mentally ill, there is a real contradiction.

On the one hand, the movement of modern society seeks to make children aware of their responsibilities as early as possible. Yet the only way to do this is not to treat children as adults, but as citizens. This means that they have both rights and duties. On the other hand, one cannot imagine the total abolition of this frontier. Because one cannot go so far as confusing children with adults. At the core of this, lies the relation to obedience and disobedience. To take this provocatively further, the insoluble question is from what moment, under what conditions and in what contexts, at what age, and so on, will we acknowledge in children the right to disobey in the same way that one is led, for political reasons, to acknowledge that adults may disobey. Here again, conservative phobia is obviously very harmful. One can easily see that our societies today, and perhaps more generally societies across Europe, are going through a regressive phase – for a variety of reasons – in which many institutions and social groups are absolutely terrified by youth and childhood. These fears obviously combine with social fears: young people and children belonging to particular categories are more feared than others. People have discovered that children from poor backgrounds, children of migrants in particular, 'are not children': they are not controlled by their parents, the conditions in which they live are not conducive to educating them towards obedience or respect for the establishment, and so on. This situation, however, is not new: it is almost as old as modern democracies, and in any case is similar to that prevailing in the nineteenth century. Arguably, a constructive critique of such a phobia will have to be undertaken at a European level. This is not a nation-specific issue, exclusive to, say, Britain or France. Rather, it cuts across many European societies.

In conclusion, I would like to insist again on a simple idea. An educational project that combines the opposite aims of allowing European intellectuals to play a leading role, with a common background, in critical debates concerning the functions of global culture, and of giving a renewed impulse to the processes of democratization (equal access to the political sphere, in particular, in spite of its increasingly bureaucratic or 'technical' character) is certainly a prerequisite for any notion of 'European citizenship' that is not purely formal. Whether the current management of the European 'idea' by the European Commission and the various governments sees it as a priority is doubtful. But they should consider it more seriously if they want to avoid destructive 'populist' reactions against their policies, which would not even leave the traditional 'national cultures' immune.

Notes

1 This chapter is derived from an interview of Etienne Balibar by Véronique Bénéï conducted on 24 September 2003.

2 The formula 'Intellectual and moral reform' is an astonishing summary of the history of the national idea in Continental Europe. It became popular after Renan made it the title of his brochure *La Réforme intellectuelle et morale*, Paris 1871, in which he reflected on the reasons for the defeat of France in the Franco-Prussian War, borrowing ideas and formulations from Fichte's *Addresses to the German Nation*, itself written after the Prussian defeat in 1807. In his *Prison Notebooks*, written while he was imprisoned by the Italian Fascist regime, Antonio Gramsci separated it from this purely national context, to make it an instrument of reflection on the conditions of modernization of European societies and the 'popular' role of philosophy in the creation of successive historical 'hegemonies'.

3 Indeed, there are things that one does not learn in bourgeois families or milieux; things that one learns elsewhere and that form part of culture even if they are not fully acknowledged by the schooling institution. Such is the case of some political aspirations, and of certain forms of music or popular culture, sports for instance, that are not learnt in bourgeois families.

4 On this distinction, see in particular Elise Marienstras, *Nous, le peuple. Les origines du nationalisme américain*, Gallimard, Paris, 1988; and Dominique Schnapper, *La relation à l'autre. Au cœur de la pensée sociologique*, Gallimard, Paris, 1998.

5 In the French case, however, what was particularly perverse was the periodic fusion of republican patriotism with the essentialism of French culture. French people, and especially intellectuals, only too often believe that their own political traditions and culture enjoy a privileged 'special relation' to universalistic values (so also indeed do many others, e.g. US intellectuals).

6 This distinction is only an old one that philosophy has never ceased to work on, from the Ancient materialists such as Democritus to Hegel, the line passing via Montaigne and Pascal.

7 See in particular Aleida Assman's illuminating work on the history of the usages of – and the problem with – the notion of *Bildung* in nineteenth-century German universities, which also sheds light on the connection with Nietzsche (Assman 1994). This was also much the same as what the early Victorians, such as the elder Arnold, who established the public school movement, meant by the term 'character-building' in the UK. On Thomas Arnold's role in the 'invention' of the classical myth of Europe, see Martin Bernal, *Black Athena. The Afro-Asiatic Roots of Classical Civilization*, Vol. I: *The Fabrication of Ancient Greece 1785–1985*, Rutgers University Press, New Brunswick, NJ, 1987, pp. 347–50.

8 After the name of the minister in the government, during the cohabitation regime under François Mitterrand's presidency, who initiated a law against use of English terms in the French public sphere.

9 It is also doubtful that the forms of violence and resistance to school discipline that were then predominant are similar to those seen today.

10 I fully agree with the idea that movements and associations that are 'non-governmental' in their origins and juridical status, and that reflect the various – sometimes conflicting – tendencies of society should contribute to the emergence of new, post-national, forms of citizenship and political participation. But I do not believe in the abstract separation of 'society' and 'state', and particularly I believe that an *institutional* moment is always needed in the formation of a concept of the citizen at whatever level. For a recent, and critical, discussion of the uses of the notion of 'civil society', taking into account German, British and French material, see Nasser Etemadi, *Concept de société civile et idée du socialisme*, L'Harmattan, Paris, 2002.

11 After the title of a book published by Luc Ferry, the Minister of Education in France from May 2002 until April 2004, and Alain Renaut (1985).

References

Assman, Aleida (1994), *Construction de la mémoire nationale: une brève histoire de l'idée allemande de Bildung*, Paris: Maison des Sciences de l'Homme.

Balibar, Etienne (1998), *Droit de cité*, La Tour d'Aigues: Editions de l'Aube.

Balibar, Etienne and Immanuel Wallerstein (1991), *Race, Nation, Class: Ambiguous Identities*, London: Verso.

Bernal, Martin (1987), *Black Athena. The Afro-Asiatic Roots of Classical Civilization*, Vol. I: *The Fabrication of Ancient Greece 1785–1985*, New Brunswick, NJ: Rutgers University Press.

Bielefeld, Ulrich (2003), *Nation und Gesellschaft: Selbstthematisierungen in Frankreich und Deutschland*, Hamburg: Hamburger Edition.

Bourdieu, Pierre (1996), *The State Nobility: Elite Schools in the Field of Power*, Oxford: Polity Press.

Bourdieu, Pierre and Jean-Claude Passeron (1979), *The Inheritors: French Students and Their Relation to Culture*, Chicago: University of Chicago Press.

Bourdieu, Pierre and Jean-Claude Passeron (1990[1977]), *Reproduction in Education, Society and Culture*, London: Sage.

de Certeau, Michel, Dominique Julia and Jacques Revel (eds) (1975), *Une politique de la langue: La Révolution française et les patois, l'enquête de Grégoire*, Paris: Gallimard.

Colley, Linda (1992), *Britons: Forging the Nation, 1707–1837*, New Haven, CT: Yale University Press.

Debray, Régis (2002), *Le fait religieux*, Paris: Documentation française.

Durkheim, Emile (1977), *The Evolution of Educational Thought: Lectures on the Formation and Development of Secondary Education in France*, London: Macmillan.

Etemadi, Nasser (2002), *Concept de société civile et idée du socialisme*, Paris: L'Harmattan.

Fassin, D. (2001), 'The Biopolitics of Otherness: Undocumented Foreigners and Racial Discrimination in the French Public Debate', *Anthropology Today* 17: 1, 3–7.

Ferry, Luc and Alain Renaut (1985), *La pensée 68. Essai sur l'anti-humanisme contemporain*, Paris: Gallimard.

Foucault, Michel (1984), *Le souci de soi*, Paris: Gallimard.

Fumaroli, Marc (1991), *L'Etat culturel: une religion moderne*, Paris: Editions de Fallois.

Gaspard, Françoise and Farhad Khosrokhavar (1995), *Le foulard et la République*, Paris: Editions La Découverte.

Marienstras, Elise (1988), *Nous, le peuple. Les origines du nationalisme américain*, Paris: Gallimard.

Nicolet, Claude (1980), *The World of the Citizen in Republican Rome*, Berkeley, CA: University of California Press.

Schnapper, Dominique (1998), *La relation à l'autre. Au cœur de la pensée sociologique*, Paris: Gallimard.

2 The moral cultivation of citizenship in a Taiwan middle school, *c*.1990

Allen Chun

This study is based on an ethnography of everyday practice in a Taiwan middle school. Although ethnographies are useful as descriptions of everyday routine, my goal is less factual description than critical understanding of the acculturation process that is seminal to the moral cultivation of citizenship and identity in Nationalist Taiwan.[1] The study of the school is predicated on the role of education within state formation, but emphasis will be laid upon the ethnography of space as power, i.e. the spaces in which ideas and identities are transformed and disseminated within a pedagogical context. Architectural spaces of the school will be explored in relation to disciplinary aspects of the curricular timetable and activities calendar, as well as social hierarchies between students, pedagogues, administrators and bureaucrats, which form the basis of normative power. Physical spaces, social rhythms and hierarchies at the level of the everyday constitute the life routines in which the normativity of power along with the nationalization of identity – in terms of ideology, institution and behaviour – partake of the construction of a social imaginary.

Education and the normal in the cultural geography of nationalist identity

Education is 'normal' in more ways than one. First of all, modernity is the era of the norm. It not only gave birth to the notion of society (and culture) as the social structural framework upon which various institutions, behaviours, rites and practices were seen as functionally integrative, but was also reinforced by theories of the norm in various incarnations that viewed diverse aspects of social and cultural life as inherently systemic and totalizing. That is to say, the notion that society in everyday practice was – or ought to be – normal rather than imaginative, fantastic or inherently violent was nurtured more importantly by social scientific theories that made the norm sacred (as a mode of thought).[2] In the process of empirical observation, objective description and statistical analysis of various kinds reified the diverse modes and institutions of normal life, as though they represented the result of natural evolution, when they were in fact impositions of political policy, social order and rational epistemology, backed by the naked violence of the state. Within the social 'system', some institutions are deemed more 'normal' than others.

In many modern societies, education epitomizes the realm of the normal. The system of Teachers' Colleges in Taiwan is called, for example, Normal University, following *les écoles normales* of France, where 'normal' in Chinese is rendered by a combination of characters for teaching (*shi*) and example or model (*fan*).[3] Thus, education not only inscribes the normal; the normal itself becomes in turn the very essence of pedagogy. Normal, then, is to pedagogy what the norm is to social scientific theory. It embodies the methodology that puts into practice the rites, routines and behaviours of normal life in ways that complement the ideology of the norm as it is imagined or constructed in the domain of epistemology. It is no accident either that one should see the function of education ultimately as one of socialization, in the sense that socialization necessitates the putting into practice of social rules and norms as the embodiment of society within persons as citizens. Citizenship ultimately involves to some extent socialization, in so far as it invokes some institution that is dedicated to inculcating in ontological terms the morality and ethics of being a proper citizen. In many instances, education performs an important role in this regard. The normal epitomizes the social.

Yet in the final analysis, the normal is not just the imagined aspect of the social; it is a political construction *par excellence*. Its institutional existence and vitality are intertwined with the exercise of political power. It does not rely purely and simply upon discipline as a mode of administrative and social regulation, backed by force and sanction. Rather, education is itself a kind of policing that mirrors and supports the technologies of power that buttress the state. The importance of education in the ideology of the state – and citizenship – differs from place to place. In this sense, it can be seen as a function of changing principles and policies. Furthermore, educational principles and policies are the product of specific cultural and intellectual influences. The moral and ethical nature of the cultural norm is an integral part of both the modern political form that gives it social shape and the institutional process that cultivates it in practice.

In this respect, cultural identity and political citizenship are not just national in Taiwan: they are also nationalist, in so far as they are substantially the products of changing political ideologies and perceptions of social reality premised on ideas about the nation. Within the cultural geography of nationalist identity, citizenship, culture and ethos occupy different yet mutually intertwined niches. As spaces within a social imaginary, they invoke distinct notions of person and personhood that somehow contribute to a social commonality. The person is in the first instance the site of moral regulation (through socialized and ritualized behaviour) as well as the site of mass control over bodies (through regulation of social participation in phys-ical activities and distribution of movement within confined spaces and set temporal regimes). As spaces within a political praxis, they entail an adher-ence to shared values and beliefs that cross-cut the real hierarchy of social rank and political privilege. In other words, national identity aims to be unitary within a world empirically marked by distinctions of class and status. Its discursive fictional nature should be viewed in terms of its ideo-logical substance as well as in terms of its politicizing function in maintain-ing the social order, for instance in maintaining inherent political hierarchies and class divisions.

Identity and citizenship tend to be the language of shared values and mass society, and their relationship to the educational regime has a complex history. In postwar Taiwan, which is in certain fundamental respects the continuation of the nationalist polity in early Republican-era China, nation-alism and nationalist identity have always played an explicitly significant role in defining the nature of the state, even as the state's institutions evolved from feudal warlord structures to centralized bureaucracy. The nationalist state reached a certain degree of institutional maturity in postwar Taiwan. This institutional maturation corresponded to the state's increas-ingly explicit articulation of cultural policy in other respects. The adoption of the calendrical system, capitalistic disciplinary routines and new ontolo-gies of the body were all unconscious features of everyday life that inculcated a modern social regime, and they corresponded with the overt militarization of society and the development of new rules of social etiquette. These were embodied, for example, in Chiang Kai-shek's New Life Movement in the political realm.[4] All these aspects were encoded into what eventually became known as 'Three Principles Education' (*sanmin zhuyi jiaoyu*), following the philosophy of Sun Yat-sen.[5] *Three Principles Education* was not just the teach-ing of Sun's political ideology. It was synonymous with the idea of manda-tory education that formed the content of courses in primary school on etiquette and health, secondary-level courses on ethics and morality, and finally high-school courses on citizenship and political thought. The space of education then became the regime within which citizenship was both taught and practised.

Instead of being the 'pure' product of ongoing cultural influences, as though reflective of a pan-Chinese experience, the discursive-institutional relationship that ties notions of identity and citizenship to the educational system and other regimes of socialization – such as military service, the workplace and bureaus of immigration and customs control – is largely the historical interplay of events and developments that are peculiar to early Republican China (see Rana Mitter, Chapter 5 this volume) and that carried over into postwar Taiwan. The Cold War also served to polarize these devel-opments and politics. Thus if education can be seen as epitomizing the normal in Taiwan, it is primarily because it happens to lie at the complex intersection where both 'unconscious' socializing forces and 'conscious'

political ideologies collude to shape bodily ontologies and socializing routines of institutional and cultural life.

The curriculum as constructed knowledge within the state apparatus

The educational system in contemporary Taiwan is the result of traditional
and modern institutions. The examination-based systems that characterize
the pedagogical framework in other Asian countries such as Japan and Korea
are without doubt a product of the Confucian heritage and the Mandarin
meritocracy (see Yamazumi 1995). As a competitive, achievement-based
regime, the examination system can be viewed as the epitome of the standardized knowledge-based educational system that has served as the framework for modernization and the social dissemination of skills in the postwar
era. Pure reliance on standardized examinations as an evaluative criterion of
the system also tends to give the impression that education in such a regime
puts a high premium on the utilitarian aspects of knowledge acquisition.
While one cannot doubt the purely utilitarian aspects that seem to characterize the institutional backbone of this educational system, one cannot
ignore either the evolution of modern Asian education as part of the process
of nation-building and its socializing functions. The role of the central state
is crucial in defining the content and form of education, as epitomized by
the dominant role of the Ministry of Education and the hegemonic nature of
the standardized curriculum, both of which suggest a direct relationship
between nation-building interests and education in general. The practice of
education as an institutional regime easily shows that the scope of education
is not limited only to the utilitarian dissemination of knowledge and skills
within society. The broadly disciplinary functions of the school in the regulation of everyday thought and behaviour also underscore its seminal role as
an agent of socialization.[6]

In the context of Taiwan, this disciplinary regime, which is a general
feature of everyday life in schools everywhere, not only mimics the spread of
modernity as the basic pattern of routine life but is also intertwined with
militarization and politicization of all kinds. The wearing of uniforms, the
application of uniform codes of social conduct and obeisance to political
authority all make school life a microcosm of the militarized and politicized
polity that is already being played out in society at large.[7] Richard Wilson's
(1970, 1974) work on the political socialization of schoolchildren in Taiwan
has duly emphasized the priority of politicization in the socializing process,
with its stress on allegiance and patriotism. It is clear, however, that socialization is taking place in many areas. This is exemplified by the inculcation
of social values, assimilation to culture, appropriation of a certain kind of
moral conduct, and active involvement in sanctioned institutional activities,
in addition to filial respect for authority – from family to teachers and all
other forms of political authority. The very fact that socialization is part of a

totalizing and systemic process that invokes all kinds of cultural rules and moral behaviour makes it important to analyse in its systemic totality.

In effect, if education in Taiwan is understood not so much as an autonomous process of knowledge dissemination, but instead more as an integral part of the state project of nation-building, it will be easier to understand why or how the curriculum is an important framework for the dissemination of social values, cultural identity and political notions of citizenship. The structure of its content within the sequence of mandatory education, which is known simply as 'Three Principles Education', can be read as a narrative of national knowledge, or what it takes to be a moral person and a citizen in a Nationalist society. Equally importantly, these same values, identities and concepts are inculcated in the process of everyday life and throughout the socializing regime of the school. The school, with its direct ties to state power in the form of regulation by the Ministry of Education, is in turn a microcosm for the nationalist society and its citizenry, given its embodiment of nationalist principles.

So what is so-called 'Three Principles Education'? Initial formulations can be found in policy discussions of the early Republican era beginning in the late 1910s and early 1920s. Although 'Three Principles Education' is related to *The Three Principles* conceived by Dr Sun Yat-sen, the founder of the Chinese Republic, *The Three Principles* was less a systematic body of text than an incomplete and scattered set of lectures and writings compiled after Sun's death. Its incompleteness and ambiguity became a point of departure for its divergent interpretations in mainland China and in Nationalist Taiwan, respectively: whereas it was deemed a bourgeois revolutionary ideology in the former, it served as a blueprint for scientific modernization in the latter. Moreover, it is important to note that, while notions of 'Three Principles Education' had been debated throughout the Republican era until the onset of the Second World War, the Kuomintang (Nationalist Party) government in Taiwan did not seriously implement them until after the war. By that time, it became part of the implementation of Chiang Kai-shek's New Life Movement, which was initiated during the 1930s. In this way, 'Three Principles Education' represented the teaching of Nationalist (Party) ideology.

In the initial policy formulation of 'Three Principles Education' concepts such as citizenship (*gongmin*), morality (*daode*), military training (*junxun*) and health (*weisheng*) were repeatedly touted as basic requisites of this moral education, and early policy debates witnessed different attempts to implement the teaching of such concepts. In the present chapter, I do not wish to focus on details of the various intellectual and political discourses that led to a systematic conceptualization of 'Three Principles Education' but merely to note that, in its implementation as a curriculum in postwar Taiwan, it had systematically engendered a Nationalist vision of citizenship and personhood that mirrored the kind of disciplinary and moral society it attempted to invoke and reproduce in the minds and behaviours of people. As a body of ideas, it was not arbitrary. The emphasis on bodily health in terms of personal hygiene, civilized etiquette and physical training was part of Chiang Kai-shek's New Life ethos that was built into courses at the primary level of education. Military discipline became an explicit concern in courses at middle- and high-school levels, while courses on morality and citizenship, rooted in both Confucian ethics and modern political values, were disseminated through the middle- and high-school curriculum, overlapping with more explicit courses on Sun Yat-sen's thought and political theory. Although minor curricular revisions in the contents and sequence of 'Three Principles Education' took place throughout the postwar era, moral education in all the above senses was clearly a seminal aspect of nation-building that transcended the pure dissemination of knowledge.

In this regard, it is less important to understand the nature of citizenship and morality as concepts per se than how they function in the overall process of socialization or the state's project of moral regulation.[8] In other words, what kind of person (citizen) is being cultivated, both ontologically in the process of education and morally in terms of ethical behaviour? Such notions of citizenship go far beyond the overt pressures of political allegiance and respect for authority that accentuate Wilson's notion of political socialization. Politicization is more precisely part of the socialization-cum-education process than vice versa. A citizen is also a particular kind of thinking, acting and feeling being. Political correctness is only one aspect of being a citizen. More than just having the correct thoughts, it is important to act in a particular way and in the appropriate contexts of public expression. Mentally identifying with a social collectivity also involves appropriate sentiments of a kind that are often invoked in moments of patriotic fervour and national pride. Thus, thoughts, actions and feelings that are ultimately invoked at the political level are really accumulations of ritual behaviours already played out in everyday practice, in social interactions and performance of activities, as will be seen shortly.

In political intent, moral education was inseparable from the ideological war that the Nationalist regime waged against Communist China. Grounded in traditional Confucian values, it nonetheless became mobilized for overt political purposes as a 'spiritual weapon' against socialism. In the context of the 'cultural renaissance movement' (*wenhua fuxing yundong*) of the 1970s that was deployed to counter the Cultural Revolution on mainland China, moral education took on an explicitly anti-Communist tone. Culture was part of the explicit political war against communism, and the school became the major venue for initiating political demonstrations that were part of the cultural renaissance movement. It was also during this time that moral education took on a heightened importance as a curricular activity. As the Cold War waned, moral education continued to play a seminal role in the socializing process. In fact, one might say that the Cold War to capture the people's national soul expanded from the realm of 'Three Principles Education' per se to include extracurricular activities of all kinds, even while the explicit politicization of the cultural renaissance gradually waned.

The transformation of moral education, stretching from its embodiment of Nationalist ethics to its politicization of Chinese culture, underscores in the final analysis the role of the school itself as a constant locus in the construction of identity, the cultivation of moral persons and the socialization of citizens in the making. Its operation as a 'total institution', in Goffman's (1961) terms, makes it an ideal site for understanding the way in which its disciplinary control of time (through regulation of curricular and other activities) and space (through maintenance of social and spatial hierarchies) functions to reproduce the existing sociopolitical order. Its direct relationship to state hegemony ties the school into the political space of the nation per se. In the latter context, the school may be a privileged institution of socialization by virtue of its omnipresence in the public domain, but it is at the same time one of many institutional nodes of socialization regulated by similar disciplinary regimes that reinforce similar notions of cultural identity and moral citizenship. More than defining norms, practices make perfect.

Personhood in practice: everyday etiquette as a modality of acculturation

The school is a moment in time and space. As a social institution, it is partly characterized by its ubiquity. Yet, it is also a product of its times, a creation of modern discipline as well as an agent of state hegemonic control. The middle school in the northern Taiwan city of Hsinchu that I observed during the academic year of 1991–2 had been known locally as a generally high achiever in national school exams, but otherwise seemed to be a typical state school of its type, whose students represented a broad cross-section of city residents. Peiying Middle School was established in 1959. Built on the site of an old primary school with seven classrooms, it went through minor name changes after its transformation from an all girls' school to a mixed school and as its administration passed from the hands of the county government to those of the city government. The number of students expanded from 300, occupying six classrooms initially, to a population of 2,640 at the time of fieldwork, occupying 58 classrooms. The faculty and administrative staff members numbered 139.

Peiying is one of ten state schools in Hsinchu. The then principal of the school, a Mr Xu, had served for three years there, having been appointed directly by the provincial Board of Education (*jiaoyu ting*), where he served prior to being principal. Despite appearances on the surface, the school is anything but an island unto itself. Academic development and school activities are tightly coordinated at three levels of bureaucracy, from the Ministry of Education (*jiaoyu bu*) down to the provincial Board of Education (*jiaoyu ting*) and local Bureaus of Education (*jiaoyu ju*). Even 'education' is not the exclusive domain of the school; rather, the school is one of many and various supporting institutions that include county or municipal cultural centres (*shili wenhua zhongxin*), Anti-Communist Youth Corps (*jiuguo tuan*), the Committee for Cultural Renaissance (*wenhua fuxing weiyanhui*) and student–parent associations (*jiazhang weiyanhui*). The internal administrative structure of the school already mirrors the fact that the school is simply one node within a tightly knit network. To facilitate vertical integration, each administrative unit within the school responds directly to the higher levels of offices within the Education bureaucracy. The provincial Board of Education is composed of 12 divisions (*ke*) that are replicated down to the lowest levels. These include a secretarial division, a military training division, a general administration division, a personnel division, a financial division and an academic supervision division. Educational policy at the county or municipal level is divided into five sections: general academic affairs, national education, social education, physical education and academic personnel affairs. According to these categories of educational policy, the municipal-level bureaus of education then coordinate the activities of various kinds of institutions, such as schools, libraries, social education agencies, youth corps groups, extracurricular activity committees and cultural renaissance movement promotion committees. The Head of the Bureau of Education is the administrator in charge of putting into practice educational policy, with the assistance of various section chiefs.

Vertical integration of the same administrative divisions from the highest levels of the educational bureaucracy to the lowest-level institutions enables official notices to be disseminated seamlessly through the system and uniformity to be implemented at all schools. Not surprisingly then, one would also expect the physical and social organization of the school to conform to generally the same patterns and principles. Within such a system, innovation and individuality are unwelcome elements that actually disrupt the effective flow of daily routine and work.

Perhaps the most significant element about the spatial and temporal organization of the school is its compactness, and an environment that is designed to maximize productivity in movement and work. Its linearity and functionality are obvious, just as people's work lives are structured in a way that deliberately leaves little space for idle time. The main campus is a rectangular enclosure that occupies a total of 39,755 square metres. Its classrooms and various administrative offices, as well as its science laboratories and library, are largely spread across four rows of 2–3-storey concrete buildings. Two long rows of buildings run parallel to each other across the long rectangular body of the campus. Two other short rows of buildings are situated perpendicular to these along the front and side ends of the campus in a way that encloses a rectangular public space in the centre of the campus. The main entrance, which faces a major road and is at the foot of the small incline upon which the campus stands, actually faces north (despite Chinese geomantic beliefs, there is no particular preferred directionality for schools). It is situated to one side of the centre and opens up on one of the short rows of classroom buildings to the right, a large rectangular grass court directly in front, and the auditorium and a large meeting-hall complex to the left. The rectangular grass court, which is the only large public space on campus, is marked by the placement of three statues. The first one to be encountered, which is situated in the middle of the walkway that leads up from the main entrance, is a statue of Confucius. Further up the concrete walkway in the direction of the administrative offices that occupy one end of the first of the long rows of buildings is a bronze statue of Sun Yat-sen, founder of the Republic. In the centre of the rectangular grass court is a statue of Chiang Kai-shek, who moved the Nationalist government to Taiwan after 1945.

Classrooms are clustered according to year. Year One (Grade 7) students' classrooms occupy the front row of buildings closest to the main entrance, and Year Two and Three students' classrooms generally run sequentially along a line within the campus. The administrative wing of offices is some-what centrally located, in that it is the first set of offices one encounters as one walks directly from the main entrance up the concrete walkway. It is composed of the principal's office and the school archival office on the first floor, which is surrounded on the ground floor directly below by a general administration office, the academic affairs office, the extracurricular activities office, the student counselling office and teachers' offices, joined by the personnel office and the financial affairs office in an adjacent wing. Science labs and special-function rooms such as the computer laboratory, the music conservatory and the art room are located on various parts of the campus. The track and field sports ground, which is used for school-wide assemblies, is located on the plateau above the main campus and is enclosed by surrounding hills. According to the school's own assessment, there is a shortage of classrooms and other subject-specialized rooms for students, not to mention specialized sports facilities and technical classrooms.

In short, the spatial organization of the school exudes a certain sense of hierarchy, much of which is expected or obvious. The clearest separation is that between students and school staff. There is also no sense of private space, but rather different levels of public or collective spaces. The politicization of public space, reflected in the ubiquitous presence of statues and pictures of political figures and the open involvement of military officers in the management of everyday life, is a clear sign of the school's integration into the polity-at-large. The internal architectural design on the other hand is functional, maximizing use-value. Teachers have desks in large, collective offices that are arranged in open rows. Students sit in numbered seats that are allocated by the teacher according to one's class rank.

Staff workers also occupy particular niches within this spatial organization, and they can be differentiated according to rank and in terms of the respective trajectories that define the course of the work. Of the 139 full-time staff, 132 are considered permanent employees, including the principal and 118 teaching faculty, among whom 58 concurrently serve as tutorial supervisors, 13 serve as administrators within the school bureaucracy, and 47 are engaged solely in full-time teaching. There are also 13 full-time non-academic clerical staff members, and the remaining seven non-permanent full-time employees are custodians, who may perform a number of miscellaneous duties. Of those involved in administration, in addition to the principal, five hold positions as division heads (*zhuren*), 12 are section chiefs (*zhuzhang*), five are clerks (*ganshi*) and three are categorized as assistants (*zhuliyuan*).

Finally, there is at least one military supervisor (*jiaoguan*), a uniformed officer who is usually appointed directly by the armed forces. Although the role of military supervisors has declined over the years, they have been a permanent fixture in most schools, beginning from the intermediate level, where courses in military training begin to be taught, to the university level, where they may serve also in a civilian capacity as masters of student dormitories and assist in security. In the middle school, they are often called on to serve as school policemen and to act as disciplinary (termed in Chinese *xundao*, 'training and guidance') advisers. Their role is more often than not one of putting juvenile delinquents in their places, rather than offering psychological help. The existence of such military supervisors and the principal, who is appointed by the Board or Bureau of Education and not the school, clearly demonstrates the direct involvement of the government bureaucracy and the military in the operation of the school. While many school principals are themselves former teachers, they have in fact become a class of bureaucrats who rarely go back into teaching. Their periodic training (*shouxun*) actually consists of ensuring that their political correctness (as active members of the KMT Party) conforms to various policy directives handed down from the Ministry of Education.[9]

Of the 13 non-academic clerical staff, the four involved in the personnel and financial accounting divisions were considered specialized, but this is a misnomer that reflects the different routes of specialization that actually mark the work of different kinds of personnel. There is on the one hand a distinct barrier between academic and non-academic staff in terms of their formal training. Academic faculty usually have the appropriate degree that qualifies them for their specific field of teaching, and most gain promotion through years of work performance instead of advanced degree learning. Non-academic clerical staff have their own formal merit criteria, which may suffice as qualifications for certificates, which they can attain by passing clerical civil service examinations (*gaokao*); but the bulk of the non-academic clerical staff rarely pass such exams, and move up the system in the course of their work experience (or by apprenticeship). Especially among those in the older generation, many may have worked up to positions of high administrative responsibility as a result of long years of apprenticeship, beginning from lowly entry-level jobs. In this regard, there is a grey area within the administrative bureaucracy that marks the boundary between administrators who have become division or section heads as a result of full-time clerical work and academics who concurrently serve as heads of administrative units, such as the library or general academic affairs on the basis of their overall leadership quality or expertise.

While the spatial organization of the school largely exudes an atmosphere of total containment and internal separation between different strata of people, the mobility of people within the social system, while based on general distinctions between academic staff, administrative clerks and political appointees, is in fact more fluid. At the lowest level of unskilled labour, custodians are expected to perform all kinds of tasks, depending on need. Curricular and extracurricular activities usually entail coordination and intense cooperation between all categories of people. Most work tends to be based on the principle of functional integration rather than functional specialization. Teachers do not just teach. They actively take part in organizing extracurricular activities, most of which are initiated directly from the Board of Education, and spend much time supervising students and liaising with parents. The military supervisors do not just teach military training courses. They generally serve as campus police, and are present at all school activities, especially when called upon to exert 'authority'. The school principal must also straddle many roles, not only as a figure of the ultimate educator but also in internal administrative functions and as interlocutor with various outside educational and government agencies. Even in school activities and sports contests, government agencies routinely send representatives to 'attend' these events to underscore their role as omnipresent sponsors and promotional cheerleaders. The active participation of all sorts and kinds of people in school activities makes education in its essential nature a basic act of socialization. Education is not just about knowledge. Knowledge must be standardized and officially sanctioned to conform to political correctness. Most extracurricular activities are likewise mandated from above and are used to promote spiritual education (*jingshen jiaoyu*) and cultural enlightenment of all kinds, rather than strict competition and professional sports achievement per se. There is thus literally no school activity that does not entail active participation by diverse agents both inside and outside the school.

The temporal organization of the daily schedule is also tightly regulated and leaves little space for free activity. The time from 7.00 to 7.20 a.m. is when students are expected to come to school, and other 'on-duty' students are seen sweeping the school ground and picking up litter; 7.20 to 7.50 a.m. is homeroom time, during which students are supposed to be reading; and 7.50 to 8.10 a.m. is the flag-raising ceremony, during which all students report to the sports field, standing in class formation, to watch the raising of the flag. At this time, the principal will make a daily speech. The disciplinary adviser (*xundao zhuren*) speaks next, making various official announcements, followed by the academic adviser (*jiaowu zhuren*), if necessary. During the speeches, the military supervisor will check students' dress and hair to pick out students who do not conform to regulations. From 8.10 to 12.00 a.m., there are four periods of class in all, each separated by ten minutes' break. After lunch, which is from 12.00 to 1.00 p.m., there will be another stream of three classes from 1.10 to 4.00 p.m. (with an extra hour for tutorial supervision and mock examinations). On Saturday, another half-day of classes, mostly devoted to extracurricular and tutorial activities, is held. There are generally no free or elective class periods.

In short, spatial containment, social hierarchy and temporal regulation constitute the essential framework against which to understand the ritual behaviour and etiquette that characterize the nature of social relations between teachers and students as well as between staff members and the school. While the educational system makes students the object of socializing discipline, with teachers and staff being agents of the system, the system also disciplines staff members in the process of work through similar regimes of official supervision and evaluation. These disciplinary regimes operate in parallel, but they are largely predicated on similar principles.

The kind of behaviour that epitomizes the relationship of students to teachers and staff in the school can be properly characterized as etiquette. Etiquette is not simply a prescribed set of manners (*limao*) or a ritualized demeanour (*liyi*), but also, in terms perhaps indicative of Norbert Elias (1986), a routinized behaviour whose ritualized restraint is largely the product of social control of the emotions as both phylogenetic and ontogenetic processes. Student–teacher relationships are marked – to say the least – by a certain face-to-face decorum and attitude of veneration that reflects the hierarchical distance between the two parties. Manners dictate that students should greet teachers (*laoshi*), when they encounter each other, face-to-face. This applies not only to teachers one knows personally, but also to teachers in general. Etiquette extends as well to behavioural norms that are the product of disciplinary routines of the system. Etiquette means in this regard knowing when to be silent (*sujing*) and when to speak out (*biaotai*). It means conforming militarily to authority in some public contexts and being religiously supportive in other contexts. A more accurate way to explain the kind of etiquette that is being cultivated here is to say that the end-point of such socialization (ultimately acculturation, through the inculcation of key cultural values) is really one of learning how to 'act as a person' (*zuoren*). In the final analysis, 'acting as a person' is not just a keyword for having proper manners, but, more importantly, for acting appropriately in a way that is consistent with the context of things. In this regard, if citizenship and morality (*gongmin yu daode*) constitute the substance of the moral education imparted in the school, the practice of ethical or moral behaviour *in everyday etiquette* is the immediate goal of this 'sino'-socialization.

The role of and pressures upon teachers and staff in the system must also be understood in the light of the same morally regulative regime of discipline, through enforcement of spatial orders and temporal schedules. The way in which people survive, adapt and move through the system is also a function of the way they perform or are expected to perform. In essence, the same system of domination and vertical integration that puts students in their place can be seen to put other people in their place as well. Their everyday behaviour and ritual demeanour must be seen in the context of – and as a direct product of – a total institutional discipline.

In both processes of socialization, the emphasis is less on work performance in the sense of productive efficiency than on moral reward or spiritual gain (*xinde*). Constant self-evaluation through writing of reports places a premium on making conscious one's personal reflections on work and study. The focus on moral cultivation from within is consistent with the Confucian values invoked in 'Three Principles Education'. However, the focus from above on total regulation is a product of a modern regime of discipline, enhanced by internal militarization and Cold War politicization, the latter which is a function of the Kuomintang's ideological values. Seen together, they constitute the crux of the nationalizing impulses that are characteristic of Taiwan's cultural imagination of a Republic of China.

What is 'Three Principles Education'? Notes toward a critical ethnography

The growing popular rise of cultural indigenization in the form of Taiwanese consciousness that, for many, was epitomized by the recent election of the first President from the (Taiwanese independence-advocating) Democratic Progressive Party (DPP) has had explicit influences on the nature and continuing destiny of 'Three Principles Education', at least in government policy-making circles. 'Three Principles Education' has always been linked with the rule of the Nationalist (KMT) Party, not only for its attempt to memorialize the legacy of Sun Yat-sen and his ideology ('Three Principles Education' was synonymous with mandatory education in the sense that 'the ideology of *Three Principles* is what unifies China' (*sanmin zhuyi tongyi zhongguo*)), but also for the KMT's staunch defence of the Republic of China as against an independent Taiwan. The rise of Taiwanese consciousness is a complex historical phenomenon that had been promoted not only by Taiwanese independence activists but also by a Taiwanese faction-dominated KMT regime headed by the former President Lee Teng-hui. 'Three Principles Education' had already been the subject of criticism for a decade, but was officially reviewed and revised after the election in 2000 of Chen Shuibian, the first DPP President. The major consequence of this review was the addition of a series of courses entitled 'Knowing Taiwan' (*renshi taiwan*).[10] The corpus of existing courses on body and health, citizenship and ethics, military training and Sun Yat-sen's thought did not, however, appear to change substantially.

Changes in the nature of 'Three Principles Education' during this most recent policy phase of indigenization indicate that the discourse of mandatory education has centred mostly on the primacy of defining national identity (either as part of China or of a culturally and historically distinct Taiwan) and focused less on the nation's abstract relationship to citizenship and ethics. Not surprisingly, the unchanged substance of existing courses

also indicates that the new regime's relationship to the nation and the practice of nation-building has remained unchanged for the most part as well.
The role of the school as an agent of socialization remains active as ever, nor-
malizing routines that constitute everyday etiquette and behaviour go on as
usual, and the relationships of power that bind the school to the state and its
satellite apparatuses continue to reinforce each other. The recent political
changes thus do not appear to have affected the routinization of power.
What does this say about forms and practices?

Moral education, as inculcated above all in 'Three Principles Education',
goes well beyond the explicit content of course teachings and everyday etiquette. It is also replicated in various extracurricular activities, which are
organized by the Disciplinary Office (*xundao chu*) and which are subsumed
under the umbrella category of 'honesty education' (*chengshi jiaoyu*).[11] The
Bureau of Education schedules activities pertaining to honesty education at
least once a month. For example, in the academic year 1991–2, it started
with a notice (on 26 September) from the Bureau of Education, citing 'Ministry of Education Special Action Plans to implement the strengthening of
honesty education at all school levels'. This was followed (on 8 October) by
the Disciplinary Office's setting up of an 'Honesty Opinion Box' (*chengshi
yijianxiang*) and the establishment of 'Public Statutes on Honesty' (*chengshi
gongyue*). The Bureau of Education (on 17 October) then issued a register of
names of heads for committees 'to strengthen the promotion of honesty education', as well as a notice from the Board of Education 'detailing matters for
the supervision of honesty education activities by Bureau of Education officers'. Saturday discussion groups (*banhui*) then (on 26 October) organized
forums on honesty education. These activities are carried out uniformly in
every school. Officials from both the Ministry and Board of Education
visited the school on 29 October to view results of the promotion of honesty
education activities. The Office on Social Education (*shejiao guan*) sent a
letter on the same day to organize an 'honest spirit, happy spirit' (*chengshi
xin, kuaile xin*) activity in relation with Ministry of Education directives.
The Disciplinary Office's Bulletin of 2 November then asked tutors to use
3–5 minutes in class to announce honesty education activities. The Disciplinary Office on 3 November set up a column on the corridor bulletin board
to display news of honesty education activities. The Social Education Office
sent a letter on 4 November, planning a forum discussion on honesty education. The Bureau of Education sent a letter on 7 November, announcing that
'honesty education' should be included in the promotional activities of
family education (*jiating jiaoyu*). The Bureau of Education sent a letter on 16
November explaining principles of assessment regarding special action plans
to strengthen honesty education in primary and secondary schools. The Disciplinary Office on 17 November held an art competition in relation to
honesty education. The Bureau of Education sent a letter on 21 November
to announce an 'honest spirit, happy spirit' writing competition. It also sent
on 29 November a letter to announce the fifth theme of Hsinchu's literary

education, i.e. leisure education and honesty education. It then sent on 4 December a timetable and report form for monitoring honesty education activities in all schools. It circulated to all students on 4 December bookmarks printed by the Ministry of Education bearing the word 'honesty' (*chengshi*). The Office of Social Education sent on 24 December a further notice on the 'honest spirit, happy spirit' writing competition, and on the same day the Bureau of Education sent the Ministry of Education guidelines for promoting honesty education. The Bureau of Education sent on 26 December a set of guidelines for implementing honesty education that among other things exhorts the school to take note of the items regarding cheating, observance of traffic rules and respect for teachers. Jianguo Middle School of Taoyuan then on 30 December sent a letter to propose an open forum to exchange ideas and experiences on honesty education.

The frequency, intensity and coordination of activities pertaining to 'honesty education' ultimately illustrate how moral education in a broad sense is used to encompass all manner of actions and behaviour that are nonetheless linked with school life. Its implementation also transcends the work of any one institution, as other schools carry out the same directives.

In addition to defining conditions of modernity, the nation-state has welded the function of the school as a disciplinary regime to the functioning of other parallel institutions.[12] The same kinds of socialization can be seen to take place generally in other countries; but culture plays an important part here in specifying the framework of power in which various social institutions interact and overlap.[13] It has become much of a(n Orientalist) cliché, following Rohlen's (1976) study of Japan's high schools, to characterize Asian educational systems as collectivist, in the way they foster conformity to group consciousness, through deference to authority and peer group pressure, and uniform standards of education, reinforced by an all-determining monolithic exam system.[14] In fact, the Confucian notion of filial piety (*xiao*) is one that encompasses various kinds of social hierarchies between ruler and subject, teacher and student, father and son and employer and employee, as a function of the same essential ethical bonds that mirror or work in conjunction with each other. In this sense, it is not surprising that the state, school, family and workplace function in the same way (as socializing regimes) either by overlapping or by reinforcing each other in a long-term process of cultivation of the same kind of ethos, norms and etiquette.

As has already been epitomized in the case of Japanese schools, harmonious relationships between teacher and student rely heavily on teachers' forming good working relationships with parents, who are viewed as an extension of classroom teaching as well as a first line of communication in matters of student behaviour and performance. Parents are expected to be an active participant in assisting with a child's education. They are thus seen as morally responsible for his/her successes and failures. As also perhaps in Japan, in Taiwan the brunt of this responsibility usually falls upon the mother, especially if she is a housewife in charge of domestic affairs. Her role in actively supervising homework is largely related to the excessive amount of schoolwork that is usually assigned to students, beginning from primary school and accelerating up to the years preceding 'examination hell'. However, the symbiotic relationship between family and the state in this regard is first a function of the fact that these institutions view themselves as being based on the same ethical principles and thus obliged to play supporting roles in the larger social order. Pressure of group conformity or allegiance to political authority is in this sense less relevant than the ethical form of these bonds and their pervasiveness in social practice.

In so far as activities of the school and the Bureau of Social Education overlap (through coordination and direct supervision by the Ministry of Education or its local bureaus), one might say that there is already a strong institutional working relationship between the school and various government institutions regarding education in general. Moreover, the school has explicit functions in promoting citizenship education or 'social education' by taking roles of responsibility in community education or social service in much the same way that families are mobilized as an extension of classroom learning. This includes (1) the advancement of 'citizenship training' and lectures on improving various aspects of national life while making available school facilities to residential groups for certain sports and leisure activities and (2) the offering of advice and assistance on matters pertaining to public health and emergency training, air defence and prevention of epidemics, and dissemination of public information on events and activities. According to policies established by the Executive Yuan on 8 April 1965, explicit themes considered as part of the domain of community services performed by the school include social insurance, employment, social assistance, public housing, welfare services, social education and community development, on which meetings are held between school staff and relevant members of the community. The school thus plays a citizen's collective role in local life whilst actively training good, moral and responsible citizens.

In ontogenetic terms, military service is in many respects a continuation of the socialization process begun in school. In addition to military and physical training, military conscripts spend time in the classroom. In this sense, *shouxun* (literally 'undergo training') means more precisely undergoing the same kinds of spiritual cultivation and political correctness that are pervasive in school. The proportion of classroom training tends to be much higher for officers undertaking military service (graduates of military academies as well as postgraduate degree-holders in general) than for regular recruits, and the term *shouxun* is also used to refer to periodic training that personnel in the workplace undergo, especially after gaining promotion or transfer to new positions. Classroom work in military training includes not only learning of required skills but also producing reports, both written and oral, where one is typically forced to express one's feelings of accomplishment (*baogao xinde*). In a military context, bonds of allegiance are based as much on political correctness as on the substantive sharing of a moral stand-point. But both become intricately intertwined in the end.

Ultimately, the kind of socialization (with its emphasis on moral cultivation in a Taiwan context) seen in the routinization of school life and military service forms the rudiments of a disciplinary regime that is in many ways replicated and expanded upon in various kinds of workplaces. Needless to say, it is impossible to generalize on the nature of the latter, given the diversity of the institutions that characterize any enterprise (civil service, private corporate, family firm, etc.), not to mention urban or rural settings and Chinese, Western and Japanese cultural influences. Yet, in the example of the school, teachers, clerks and administrators are clearly disciplined and socialized in ways that are similar to the way that students are 'subjected' (if not objectified as well). Not only does the work regime reflect the moral regulation of a school as a particular kind of workplace but also the influences of other institutions (the state and various bureaucratic appendages) that constantly control, nurture and interact with it.

In sum, the ethnography of everyday practice and the role of cultural values and behavioural norms in sustaining it are not simply objective descriptions of life, taken for granted as matters of fact. The fact that one cannot really understand the school as a phenomenon apart from the entanglements of power that link it to other forms of social domination forms the only real basis for its critical analysis.

Notes

1 'Nationalist Taiwan' refers to the period of postwar rule of Taiwan by the Nationalist or Kuomintang Party, which installed itself there after the Communist takeover of mainland China in 1949 and continued to be recognized as the Republic of China until its expulsion from the United Nations in 1967. Its rule was explicitly characterized by its ongoing attempt to promote a monocultural nationalistic state, and its institutions, the school in particular being one of them, reflected its ethos of staunch cultural nationalism. In recent decades, Taiwan has undergone profound political and social transformation, not the least prominent aspect of this being the emergence of the independence-minded Democratic Progressive Party, which advocated the promotion of Taiwanese culture as an alternative ethos to challenge the cultural policies and institutional practices of the Kuomintang. The present study focuses on work done in 1990, just prior to the large-scale overhaul of the Kuomintang's overt nationalist policies and practices and its subsequent shift in focus to indigenization or Taiwanization, of which the resultant changes are still ongoing. Where I wish to refer specifically to the Kuomintang (literally, the 'Nationalist Party') and its doctrines or policies, I use an upper-case 'N'. Where I wish to refer to 'nationalism' or 'nationalists' in more abstract terms, or in instances where the terms could refer to both the party and a general ideology, I use a lower-case 'n'.
2 Shoko Yoneyama's (1999) critical account of school violence in Japan emphasizes the degree rather than the quality of normative 'rationality' as the inherent source of institutional violence.
3 While the structure of the university system in Taiwan has adopted various features of both European and American models, in so far as nomenclature and

internal divisions of faculties are concerned, one should not necessarily read this to mean that the normal universities mould themselves in any serious way after French or American pedagogical practices and theories.

4 The New Life Movement was a set of ethical principles put into practice by the then President Chiang Kai-Shek in order to instil moral values and orchestrate broad social movements.

5 Sun Yat-sen was the founder of the Republic in 1911 and its first President, after leading the overthrow of the Qing dynasty. The 'Three Principles' was a nationalist ideology attributed to Sun but based on various lectures and essays that were compiled and edited posthumously.

6 Frederick Wiseman's film *High School* suggests that discipline is a staple fact of all schools.

7 Perhaps in some contrast to McVeigh's (2000) description of Japan's cult of school uniforms, students in Taiwan generally wear uniforms with reluctance and disdain the associated state control.

8 Following Corrigan's (1990) use of the term, 'moral regulation' should be understood here in a Durkheimian sense, where the obligatory nature of moral rules necessitates social control.

9 Promotions are the usual occasions on which such training takes place. The Party also sponsors periodic activities at which cardholding members of staff are expected to attend and participate actively.

10 See Hughes and Stone (1999: 985–9) for an overview of policy changes in the curriculum.

11 It is difficult to translate the term *chengshi* except to say that it means honesty in the sense of being sincere (as an attribute of one's moral behaviour) rather than being epistemologically true.

12 The socializing role of schools is what Weber (1976: 303) neatly terms 'civilizing in earnest'.

13 One must distinguish in this regard between the general relationship of culture to the emergence of the nation-state and the specific manifestations of culture that engender different social processes in different societies. See, for example, the case studies in Steinmetz (1999).

14 Japanese scholars, such as Iwama (1995), also reiterate the collectivist ethos of conformity.

References

Corrigan, Philip (1990), *Social Forms/Human Capacities: Essays in Authority and Difference*, London: Routledge.

Elias, Norbert (1986), *The History of Manners*, New York: Norton.

Goffman, Erving (1961), *Asylums*, New York: Anchor.

Hughes, Christopher and Robert Stone (1999), 'Nation-Building and Curriculum Reform in Hong Kong and Taiwan', *The China Quarterly* 159: 977–91.

Iwama, Hiroshi F. (1995), 'Japan's Group Orientation in Secondary Schools', in J. J. Shields, Jr (ed.) *Japanese Schooling: Patterns of Socialization, Equality, and Political Control*, University Park, PA: Pennsylvania State University Press.

McVeigh, Brian J. (2000), *Wearing Ideology: State, Schooling and Self-Presentation in Japan*, Oxford: Berg.

Rohlen, Thomas P. (1976), *Japan's High Schools*, Berkeley, CA: University of California Press.

Steinmetz, George (ed.) (1999), *State/culture: State-formation after the Cultural Turn*, Ithaca, NY: Cornell University Press.

Weber, Eugen (1976), *From Peasants to Frenchmen*, Stanford, CA: Stanford University Press.

Wilson, Richard W. (1970), *The Political Socialization of Children in Taiwan*, Cambridge, MA: MIT Press.

Wilson, Richard W. (1974), *The Moral State: A Study of the Political Socialization of Chinese and American Children*, New York: The Free Press.

Yamazumi, Masami (1995), 'State Control and the Evolution of Ultra-nationalistic Textbooks', in J. J. Shields, Jr. (ed.) *Japanese Schooling: Patterns of Socialization, Equality, and Political Control*, University Park, PA: Pennsylvania State University Press.

Yoneyama, Shoko (1999), *The Japanese High School: Silence and Resistance*, London: Routledge.

3 'Discipline makes the nation great'

Visioning development and the Nepali nation-state through schools[1]

Martha Caddell

Morning assembly was already under way and the rhythmic beating of the drum and the militaristic chanting of 'Attention . . . Stand at ease' could be heard even before I turned the corner of the trail and descended the short, steep path to the flat playground area outside the classroom buildings. Above the doorway to the school office was a brightly painted sign that declared 'Discipline makes the nation great'. In the playground, the students of Arun English Boarding School had formed parallel lines in front of a student holding the Nepali flag.[2] Each class grouping was separated from those on either side by an exact arm's length – a distance meticulously checked by the male teacher conducting the assembly. Their uniforms of white shirts, maroon trousers or skirts, striped belts and leather shoes were checked for cleanliness and those whose clothing or hands did not pass the inspection were pulled to the front of the group and told to crouch down, holding their ears with their hands. The beating of the drum began again. 'Sing the national anthem. Ready. Begin', shouted the Class 5 student given the role of calling instructions. The command was met variously, by the enthusiastic chanting of many of the older boys and by the quiet mumbling of the occasional line by the kindergarten students, who shuffled their feet and stole furtive glances around the assembled crowd when the teacher's attention focused elsewhere. Those who were caught daydreaming or considered not to be singing loudly enough were chastised by the teacher, who pulled their ears or rapped them on the back of the leg with a wooden ruler. A girl from Class 4 was summoned to the front to read from an essay she had written on the topic 'Our Country Nepal'. The piece closely followed the script of the English-medium social studies textbooks used in the school, extolling the merits of Nepal's moves towards development and highlighting the involvement of international agencies such as the United Nations in improving the social and educational conditions in the country. After complying with the barked order to 'Clap!' the girl's efforts, the classes marched out of the playground, row by row, in time to the beat of the drum.

* * *

This scene, describing the daily ritual of morning assembly as conducted in an English-medium private school in eastern Nepal in autumn 2000, graphically depicts the disciplinary dimensions of schooling and the very visible and at times violent way in which students' behaviour is transformed to comply with the norms of the institution.[3] Such a transformation, in Nepal as in many other contexts, is widely associated with a move away from the traditional lifestyle of the locality or village towards that considered modern, developed and more connected with the nation and, indeed, the world beyond. The school is a site where 'children are taught to become citizens' (Wilson 2002: 313) and encouraged to establish a relationship with the nation-state. The school can thus, following Foucault, be considered a paradigmatic disciplinary institution, moulding bodies and minds into particular images through the normalization of particular relationships and forms of interaction (e.g. 1991: 141ff.). The exercise of control and the ordering of lives is achieved both through visible and forceful action by defined individuals and through the more subtle promotion of particular lifestyles and modes of behaviour as more desirable and as garnering greater prestige and opportunity.

The school has emerged as an important social space through which particular representations of Nepal are presented and promoted, a site within which 'the image of the "ideal" citizen for the age of modernity' (Srivastava 1998: 2) is manufactured. Participating in schooling is presented in education policy and, frequently, in school textbooks as a unifying experience. It both provides a space in which to promote a common vision of the nation-state and, in itself, symbolizes a shared engagement in personal and societal transformation and development (Bénéï 2001; Wilson 2002).[4] This perceived link between education and development has, for example, become a widespread basis for justifying the funding of education interventions (e.g. World Bank 1999a). A strong assumption remains that schools offer a route through which to transmit development knowledge to the population and, indeed, participation in schooling is seen as a marker of 'development' in itself (e.g. World Bank 1999b). The girl's assembly speech highlights the intertwining of global and national projects of social transformation and the centrality of the expansion of education as a feature of this, an interconnection further enhanced through the content of textbooks and the wider involvement of donor agencies in schools across the country.

Yet, if the events of the assembly are explored more closely, a further dimension of the experience of schooling becomes apparent. Far from offering a benign vision of citizenship, development and the Nepali state, a highly partial position is presented through schools, which gives only selective recognition of diversity and inequality.[5] The intertwining of visions of the nation and the 'Nepali citizen' with discourses of development and societal progress serves to reinforce and legitimate highly particular constructions of Nepali identity, with the culture and lifestyle of certain groups utilized as the aspirational models for all.

Here the particular meanings embedded in the use of the Nepali term *bikas* (development) require some introduction. *Bikas* has embedded in it a generic 'ideology of modernization' (Pigg 1992: 499), an implicit scale of social progress, which in turn is used by Nepalis to understand their relationships with each other and with the rest of the world. These two dimensions of development are clearly discernible in how people engage with and perceive schooling. First, there is a clear interest in engaging in a process of economic and material transformation. The vision of schooling as a route to improved economic opportunities and enhanced status is common to both the global rhetoric and the popular perception of schooling at the district and village levels. Having a school in the village was regarded by many interviewees as a positive development, as it meant the 'end of the farming life', opening up opportunities for individual advancement through access to education. Second, *bikas* is used as a marker of mobility and, specifically, a basis for differentiating between groups and places. In this form it is a relational concept, understood in terms of the symbols of development associated with each group, individual or place and the relationship each can establish with 'the external'. Schooling, both in terms of content and the actual process of attending class, marks and elaborates such relationships.

The school serves as a new marker of inequality – between the educated and uneducated, the developed and less developed. Yet it also entrenches existing hierarchical relations and differentials in influence and opportunity, including those arising from the valuation of ethnic, gender, class and caste-based differences (Althusser 1972; Bourdieu and Passeron 1977; Bowles and Gintis 1976). Visions of the nation and development become intertwined, both legitimating a particular construction of Nepal and masking the inequalities inherent within it. Consequently, the ostensibly unifying and egalitarian rhetoric of development and the nation-state are, somewhat paradoxically, utilized to advance highly particular interests. The school itself emerges as a site for the promotion of inequality, even 'in the name of development' and inclusion (Shrestha 1999).

As the signboard above the entrance to the school succinctly declares, 'discipline makes the nation great', a motto that further establishes divisions between the ordered, disciplined, modern and 'national' and those practices and people considered 'backward', undisciplined, traditional or confined to the local. The disciplinary practices employed in the school thus attempt to shape and mould students – and indeed teachers and the broader community – into particular versions of modern, developing Nepali citizens. The school is not simply an institution through which the state advocates and delivers development opportunities to the populace, but a site within which what it means to be 'developed', and what constitutes being 'Nepali', are promoted and contested. Stressing the need for 'discipline' also draws attention to the ongoing process of moulding citizens and maintaining order. This in turns implies the possibility of 'deviance', of 'indiscipline' or non-conformance with the model of citizenship and participation presented in schools. Exploring the communication of ideas about citizenship, development and the state through schools as a process of translation may, therefore, offer a useful framework for understanding interactions between actors in and around the education system. Such a move away from a 'transmission' model (Wilson 2002, following Latour 1986) opens the opportunity to explore the agency of teachers, pupils and parents whilst also acknowledging the boundaries and barriers to possible reinterpretation that remain.

Taking the everyday interactions and disciplinary practices of the classroom as a focal point, this chapter explores how discourses of modernity, citizenship and development and the Nepali state intertwine and intersect in the social space of the school. Exploring the experience of school through such a lens allows the complexity and contested nature of visions of development and the Nepali state to be unpacked and opens conceptual space within which to explore the highly political position of schools within contemporary Nepal. It thus opens space for examining the 'banal' construction of citizenship and the Nepali nation-state and the opportunities that exist for groups and individuals to contest and translate existing dominant visions of 'Nepaliness' (Billig 1995). Drawing on research conducted in English-medium private and Nepali-medium government schools in a hill district in east Nepal, the chapter shows how the projects of modernization and development and the promotion of national 'unity amidst diversity' are experienced, understood and contested at the school level. The chapter begins with an exploration of how the everyday practices of the school promote a particular vision of the 'ideal' Nepali citizen. It then turns to an examination of how schools are utilized as key sites for the activities of groups attempting to challenge this hegemonic position. In doing so the chapter highlights how the multiple – and frequently conflicting – discourses of development, the Nepali nation and citizenship are reinterpreted and negotiated through the daily activities of the school.

Education policy and citizenship in Nepal: a historical introduction

Since the establishment of the first academic school in Nepal in 1854, the Durbar School in Kathmandu, the development of education policy has been strongly influenced both by external models of schooling and education reform and by how the ruling elite wish to represent the relationship between the various groups within the Nepali state. The provision of schooling has historically been strongly intertwined with ideas of development, prestige and social status and, as such, is an important site for political interventions aimed at promoting particular visions of the state, both to the Nepali populace and on the international stage. The education system – and specifically primary schooling – has emerged as one of the state institutions with a particularly significant presence throughout the country and, as such, has become a site of political interest for the various post-1950 governments seeking to promote distinct visions of the Nepali nation-state.[6]

Each shift in political regime has been followed by the revision of the education system as the incoming regime attempted to reinforce its vision of the idea of the Nepali nation-state through re-articulating the relationship between the state, schools and 'the people'. The school has been used multifariously by the state. At times education policy has been used to maintain divisions, as under the Rana oligarchy (1846–1950), when formal schooling was explicitly denied to all but the ruling elite. In contrast, the mushrooming of schools in the decade following the overthrow of the oligarchy was presented as emblematic of the new government's openness and more inclusive vision of citizenship (e.g. National Education Planning Commission, NEPC 1955). At other points it has served to promote national unity, as with the introduction of the National Education System Plan (1971) and the nationalization of all schools under the Panchayat system (1962–90).[7] This continual redefining has led to a feeling of 'repeated beginnings' (Onta 1996: 221) as newly formed governments sought to legitimate their position and promote the interests of their supporters by differentiating themselves from the preceding regime.

The relationship between schooling and the state has largely been presented in education policy in terms that secure the position of the predominantly high-caste, urban, Hindu elite within the changed social and political context. In the post-1950 period, this can clearly be seen in the presentation of ideas of the 'nation' and of 'development' that, while portrayed as neutral and inclusive, converge with cultural and social traits associated with the ruling groups (Burghart 1996: 227, 256–9; Pigg 1992). Purportedly 'national education' is thus in practice education that promotes a particular vision of the nation – and benefits a specific group within it. Owing to the considerable donor involvement in the education sector since the early 1950s (e.g. NEPC 1955; Reed and Reed 1968; Sellar 1981; Wood 1965), the construction of a national education system was also strongly influenced by external visions and representations of 'Nepal' and the wider development aid agendas of agencies involved in the reform process. Burghart's assertion that the Panchayat government legitimated itself 'on native terms, but through foreign eyes' (1996: 260) is therefore more widely illuminating in terms of education policy development. Education as a 'national' project thus requires articulation 'on native terms', but the need for foreign funding and support ensures that ideas and forms of organization must be intelligible within an international context. After the return to multi-party democracy in 1990, this assertion does, to some extent, still hold. In this context, however, foreign terms – in particular development discourses – are increasingly being utilized to justify actions, articulate relationships and even challenge existing assumptions of what constitutes Nepali citizenship.

Thus, it is not just the 'goods' associated with development that are sought. A connection with donor agencies and with the rhetoric and practices associated with them has itself emerged as a marker of prestige and a source of legitimacy for the actions of a diverse array of groups within Nepal. It is not, then, simply a vision of development as economic advancement and modernization that is engaged with, but a more complex appropriation of, for example, the languages of 'participation', 'efficiency', 'transparency', 'equality' and 'decentralization' (Robinson-Pant 1997: 162). Discourses of participation, citizenship, equality and development have thus emerged as key aspects of mainstream and oppositional visions of the state and intra-state relations.

Promoting national development and Nepali citizenship through schools

As was the case throughout the Panchayat era (Pigg 1992), so, too, the contemporary formal school curriculum continues to connect the practice of schooling with both national and global projects of development.[8] The school is utilized as an 'extension system' for the promotion of particular messages and the ordering and disciplining of individual and group behaviour, in this case messages that directly link the experience of attending school with a shift in relationship between the individual, the state and processes of development (King 1988: 491). Two distinct, but interlinked, elements of this vision of the relationship between the Nepali state and its citizens are, first, citizens as agents of development and, second, citizens as having a particular relationship with the nation-state.

Citizenship discipline and development in textbooks

Throughout the five primary grades emphasis is placed on the need for personal cleanliness, care of the environment and working with others in the community to improve facilities in the locality and work towards broader national and global development goals, with textbooks presenting images of those ways of life to which the educated, developed Nepali should aspire. The Class 1 social studies book, for example, focuses on personal hygiene, with children encouraged to use a toilet, to brush their teeth and to keep their clothes and other belongings tidy, a point reinforced daily through the inspections that take place during assembly. Exercises at this level focus on distinguishing between what is 'right' and 'wrong' by spotting what is unacceptable behaviour in a series of pictures (*Mero Serophero* ['My Neighbourhood'], Book 1). The distinction is firmly between 'traditional', 'bad' habits and modern, 'good' habits. This position is reinforced in the Class 5 textbook *Mero Desh* ['My Country'], where teachers are encouraged to discuss with the class the disadvantages people will suffer if they follow old customs and superstitions (*rudhibaddi*), as opposed to adopting more scientific or modern approaches to, for example, health care (*Mero Desh* 5 Teachers' Guide).

This vision of appropriate development priorities is extended as the students progress through the school. By Class 4 they are introduced to broader ideas about societal and developmental 'goods', such as the health risks associated with smoking and drinking in the lesson entitled 'Bad Habits Can Take Your Life'. Children are asked to write slogans about the negative effects of alcohol and smoking and are instructed to consider how else the money spent on such vices could be used. The importance of working hard and not wasting money is extended in the lesson 'Our Income and Expenses', with the story advocating that people should not spend more than they earn and, in particular, that large sums should not be spent on festivals and weddings. Rather, students are encouraged to save money in order to be able to afford medicine and to go to school. The frequent use of the word 'Our' throughout the texts is also striking, symbolizing the vision of unity around the project of national development promoted through schools. In addition to discussion of 'our' income and expenditure, Class 4 students also learn of the need to prevent deforestation and respect the protected areas set up by the government in 'Our Forest Resources', and the strong connection between economic development and water resource development in 'Our Water Resources'.

This emphasis on a unified effort to move towards positive change in the local and national context is presented in the apparently neutral terms of 'modern vs. traditional'. But it is also accompanied by a fairly explicit valuation of different lifestyles and locales, reminiscent of the hierarchical presentation of different ethnic groups in the Panchayat era textbooks (Pigg 1992). The curriculum emphasizes progress and linear development, specifically a movement from the rural and agricultural to the urban and industrial. A section of the social studies curriculum on methods of transport, for example, describes for Class 2 the way that 'In early days people walked. Now-a-days we have faster means of transport like helicopters, aeroplanes, cars, buses' (*Our Social Studies* 2: 30).[9] This vision of linear 'progress' is reinforced in Class 3, where children are presented with a view of development that places different lifestyles in a hierarchical relationship to each other, focusing in this case on technological advancement as a marker of 'civilization':

> The invention of the wheel was a wonderful thing indeed. It was one of the most important inventions made by man. It made travelling easier and quicker. It led to many new and more wonderful inventions. The bus which takes you to school is a result of that invention. [. . .] The invention of the wheel set man on the road to progress. He started taking long strides towards a civilized life. He was not a jungle man, a hunter or a food-gatherer now. He could use his thinking power not only to discover things but to invent new things also.
>
> (*Our Social Studies* 3: 24–5)

With much of Nepal still inaccessible by road, this image reinforces the idea that certain areas of the country are more 'backward' than others and maintains a strong spatial dimension to the idea of development. Particular places are considered more developed than others, and the ability to move between places is a marker of development in itself. The urban environment of Kathmandu is presented as the apex of development in the country, the destination of travel and a place where more advanced forms of transport ply the streets, a place where people are 'civilized'.

Engagement in schooling is thus strongly connected with participation in the project of development understood and experienced, to a significant extent, in terms of donor-supported reforms and inputs. Indeed, with school buildings, textbooks and teaching materials largely produced and distributed with external assistance, the vision of the school as a site of connection to something 'other' than 'the local' and distinct from 'traditional' practices is strongly evident. Teachers and students are well aware of which donor agencies have contributed to school building, teacher training and curriculum reform initiatives. The pervasiveness of such a relationship is accompanied by a strong sense that this is a desirable relationship to have, owing to the financial benefits and opportunities for mobility and advancement of status that arise from it. Indeed, this awareness is reflected in how parents discuss their aspirations for their children. Yet, alongside this sense of unity through engagement in schooling and social reform, textbooks and teaching practices also actively promote a particular vision of cultural diversity within Nepal, a particular perspective on what constitutes 'being Nepali' in the post-1990 period.

Visions of national unity and diversity in textbooks

Haami Sabai Ekai Hau ('We Are All One'), the title of a chapter in the Class 5 *Mero Desh* textbook, perhaps best conjures up the image of the Nepali nation conveyed through school activities. The multiethnic, multilingual nature of the population is acknowledged within the text, and the different religious beliefs held by people in Nepal receive consideration, with the colourful cultural diversity of Nepal highlighted. School is seen as a site in which these diverse groups can come together and be treated as equal, with that equality based upon their identification with the projects of modernity and national development. The discourse of unity and participation in the ostensibly irrefutably desirable exercise of 'development' does, however, mask social divisions and limit the possibility for action to be taken to address inequality. The construction of the school as a national institution has a similar impact. It draws students and local communities into a relationship with the state beyond the 'local' and shifts allegiance and emotional affiliation to a broader entity. Yet it also sets up an implicit – and at times even explicit – valuation of the different religious, ethnic and caste groups that make up this apparently unified whole.

The picture accompanying the lesson 'We Are All One' clearly depicts the 'difference' that is to be given discursive space within this dominant vision of the nation (see Figure 3.1). The diversity of the population is highlighted by the different attire of the men and women – the different styles of *sari*, the *dhoti* of the man from the *Terrai*, the Buddhist prayer-wheel carried by the Sherpa, the different styles of jewellery worn by the women and the *topi* of the hill people. While they have come together and appear to be engaging in conversation, they are in effect frozen into their cultural differences. Cultural difference is given recognition at the expense of seeing the inter-relationships among them, and the inequalities experienced by particular groups. The possibility of seeing difference within each group is also diminished as caricatures of particular places and people are built up and extended throughout the various textbooks. These differences are placed firmly in the realm of the cultural and the traditional.

It is also significant that, despite the diversity of the women and men in the picture, two children in the foreground are shown in school uniform, carrying schoolbags and walking away from the group, symbolizing, perhaps, the desired united and modern future of Nepal, with their ethnicity unidentifiable. Attending school is thus presented as a means of transcending cultural differences, of leaving the constraints of the 'local' and the 'traditional' behind, to engage in the modern project of schooling. Indeed, in the exercises associated with this chapter, children are asked to list the different ethnic groups and religions of the people in their class, but are then told that 'Everyone came to fulfil the same objective in class and everyone can do it' (*Mero Desh* 5, Teacher's Guide). Unity as sameness thus becomes

Figure 3.1 'We Are All One' (illustration from *Mero Desh*, Book 4.)

an important component of the school experience, marking a transition from a specifically locally embedded cultural identity to an affinity with a national culture and a national project of modernization and development.

While such representations allow an appreciation of some forms of difference, they do not represent an interest in understanding inequalities between groups such as differentials in status and economic and political power between ethnic and caste groups or the domination of educational and government job opportunities by Brahmin and Chettri elites (Bhattachan 2000; Dixit 2001). Gender inequalities and different economic positions that cross-cut issues of ethnicity are marginalized. Difference is depoliticized, sidelining inequality through a focus on dress, facial features and customs.

Celebrating cultural diversity in such a way is thus somewhat double-edged, enhancing a vision of a culturally rich nation whilst legitimating the hegemonic illusion of Nepal's inclusiveness. Making particular aspects of difference visible in turn casts shadows over other, more pernicious aspects of the relationship between various groups and individuals. Indeed, given the teaching–learning relations that pervade teacher training courses and student–teacher interactions, there is little space for questioning or more critically exploring how these relations are experienced or understood by class members. Difference therefore continues to be selectively acknowledged, with inequalities legitimated through recourse to the rhetoric of development and the vision of opportunities for all who wish to pursue this path.

Promoting unity amidst diversity? Understanding the everyday practices of schools

The disjuncture apparent in school textbooks between the rhetoric of inclusion and the reinforcing of inequality is further highlighted through the everyday practices of the classroom. The valuation of particular places, lifestyles and people over others translates, in the context of teaching, into attempts to mould students into particular forms and the belittling of those who cannot attain this image.

Promoting the 'Language of the Nation'[10]

The valuation of the national over the local is particularly evident in relation to the medium of instruction in government schools. Despite the approval of mother-tongue primary education in the 1990 Constitution, Nepali remains the dominant language of schooling. The shifts heralded by the Constitution allow schools to opt to teach wholly in a local language or provide mother-tongue instruction as an optional subject in Classes 1 to 3. However, without government funding or the production of suitable resources, the only schools able to take up this option are privately funded. Even they are few in number, with limited teaching resources available in such languages and the continued preference expressed by parents for English-medium instruction. Teachers in government schools expressed surprise at the idea that instruction could be provided in a language other than Nepali, citing the lack of teachers who speak the local language and the absence of books in the necessary languages. Consequently, despite recognition of diversity in the Constitution, the everyday practices of the school effectively reinforce the relative valuation of particular languages and language speakers.

For example, teachers display little interest in assisting children who arrive at school speaking only their mother-tongue language. Rather they seek to discipline the students into conforming with the national 'ideal'. Indeed students' inability to speak or understand Nepali in class is frequently ridiculed by teachers, often openly in front of the class. During the 'We Are All One' class I observed, the students were asked if any of them spoke a language other than Nepali. A boy who spoke a Rai language put his hand up and was called to the front of the class by the teacher and asked to say a few words. The teacher started laughing at him and the rest of the students followed suit, calling on him to carry on when he sought to return to his seat. Thus, while teachers often highlighted the language problems faced in the classroom, they generally equated this with the 'backwardness' of the local community. During one interview with a teacher, a boy was summoned out of the classroom to stand in front of me, while the teacher explained that he couldn't understand anything of our conversation (in Nepali) and that he was very stupid.

This valuation of the local has become widely accepted and few parents want their children to be taught in a 'local' language. Most wish them to learn either in Nepali or, preferably, the 'international language' of English as a way of helping them progress and move beyond the perceived constraints of the village – ideally, in many parents' views, towards a job with a development agency. Even in an area inhabited almost solely by people from the Athpariya Rai ethnic group, who use their own language as the dominant medium and where many elderly people do not speak any Nepali, there was no interest in having mother-tongue education. 'Why should we learn in our own language?' asked one woman, 'We can't use it to speak with other Rais, and certainly not with other people'. The relationship between mother-tongue and Nepali language thus reinforces the supremacy of a national affiliation over the local, and has become a significant marker of potential mobility, education and 'development'.

Promoting uniformity in schools

A further, particularly visible, symbol of enforced unity is school uniform, which is the same for all government schools in the country – white shirt and blue trousers or skirt. This moulds children into a particular style that emphasizes the similarity, and hence the apparent equality, of all students.

It acts as a clear symbol that the act of going to school takes them beyond their local affinities and connects them to a wider community of learners. However, private school students, such as the Arun Boarding School pupils, wear slightly different uniforms from their government school counterparts, with ties, belts and shoes compulsory attire and, frequently, a different colour of skirt and trousers used to distinguish students from each school. This difference in clothing very visibly indicates distinctions between children – the non-school-goers, the government school students and those attending private schools – and reinforces the hierarchical relationship between them, with the cleaner, more regimented, more affluent students more distant from the 'tradition' of a 'local', rural lifestyle. In addition, the use of the English language in private schools – even if it is of a very poor level – connects those associated with them to a wider international project, thus highlighting a greater potential for mobility than is offered by the government schools.

It is not just the students who are presented as the 'same' across the nation. Government school buildings are constructed and furnished in a uniform manner, making them instantly recognizable. Schools tend to be one of the most prominent buildings in the village area, a very firm and visible symbol of the presence of the (nation-) state at the local level. The many images of the nation displayed in the school reinforce this idea. Portraits of the King and Queen are placed in prominent positions above the head teacher's desk in all the government schools in the study area. A small Nepali flag is almost always attached to a pen-holder on the desk, and posters from donor organizations and from the education authorities cover the walls. One commonly displayed UNICEF poster features images of a school with rubbish bins, vegetable gardens, children in uniform, girls' and boys' toilets and a female teacher. Another depicts the 'Symbols of the Nation', while others include images of the goddess Saraswati and the kings of Nepal. In contrast, most school classrooms are starkly furnished, often with only a blackboard and a few benches. The equipment and materials in the head teacher's office are rarely used. This is often justified with the explanation that 'only the office has sufficient security to prevent items from being stolen', and the concern that 'if items are placed in classrooms or used by students they will be damaged' (see also Dyer 2001). It results, however, in the symbolic and material resources provided by, and representing, the nation being located spatially near, and controlled by, the most senior person in the school. Attending school is thus seen as offering a step towards the mobility and 'external' connections required of the modern citizen, yet it also establishes further hierarchies, with certain groups and individuals presented as closer to the ideal model of the 'modern, developed Nepali' than others.

Corporal punishment and the school

The motto 'discipline makes the nation great' also explicitly links up the pervasive practice of regimentation and the often violent moulding of children into particular modes of behaviour as part of the project of modernization and development (UNICEF 2001).[11] Hitting children is regarded by teachers as a sign that they are concerned about the children's progress and that they wish them to succeed and move beyond the lifestyle of the 'local' to become educated, developed citizens. Corporal punishment, including the use of sticks, is pervasive in most schools, and children of all ages are frequently exposed to beatings, often of quite a serious nature. In one classroom I visited, a young boy appeared to be having an asthma attack and was unable to breathe. The teacher, who had just arrived in the room, was concerned and considered sending another student to run to the health post in the nearby village. However, other students informed him that the child had misbehaved in the previous class and had been beaten by the teacher, and this had caused the breathing difficulties. The boy was therefore left to recover without any medical assistance. The children, too, appear to have accepted this practice. A British volunteer teacher, who did not use beating to maintain order, recalled how, when a child misbehaved, another student asked 'Should I get Sir from next door to come and hit him?'

Thus, in the few cases where parents did complain about their children being hit, teachers dismissed this as the response of 'illiterate', 'backward' people who did not realize what was best for their children. A quotation from an interview with one Principal highlights an attitude evident in all private schools in the study area:

> There are real differences in terms of the types of parents and their attitudes to the school. Not everyone is literate and those who are illiterate and narrow minded give the school harassment about the discipline in the school and complain that children are hit. They also complain if the children are sent home or if the teachers complain that the standard of cleanliness is not good enough. Each day the children's uniform, hair and nails are checked and if there is a problem they are sent away or their parents are called to the school.
>
> (fieldwork date: 3 March 2000)

Another Principal expressed her belief that 'we don't beat children unnecessarily', and that complaints from parents showed they were not cooperating with the school in the education of their children:

> Parents are very uncooperative. It's time we educated them before we educate the children. There is no cooperation from the parents, and they only complain about the school. Children should be punctual and should be neat and bring their books. Children should enjoy school, but

there is a need for discipline. So we punish the children if they are dirty . . . One parent came to say to me: 'Please don't beat my child.' But the child had not brought his science book for one week, so the teacher thought it was right to beat him. I agreed with him.

(fieldwork date: 18 April 2000)

The values teachers attach to the views and demands of groups and individuals are therefore strongly contingent on their relative degree of education or development. Those considered to be 'backward' are given little chance to express their opinions or have their demands acted upon. Such events clearly do little to encourage students or parents to question the status quo or to attempt to engage with decision-making processes. Indeed, those who do attempt to challenge school practices are likely to be either ignored or further punished. Such daily practices actively reinforce existing hierarchies and relationships of power and influence, as people have to seek out more educated or politically active individuals if they are to push their demands forward.

Contested citizenship: politics and paradoxes in everyday practice

Participating in schooling does not, then, offer a straightforward link with increased 'development' or inclusion in processes of nation-building. Rather, it is a process deeply embedded in relations of inequality, with certain lifestyles, people and places privileged over others. The 'other' to which parents and students aspire is not a generalized 'other', but a highly particular 'other'. The construction of the Nepali nation-state presented in schools is one that takes as its specific referent a particular vision of Nepaliness – urban, educated, Hindu (predominantly high-caste), connected to external processes and engaged in development activities – but is expanded to act as an aspirational model for all; a process referred to by Mohanty (1991) as 'ethnocentric universality'. While the school may, as Wilson notes, be a 'state agent of national culture' (2002: 313), the vision of the nation presented is specific and exclusive. Thus, while the school is heralded as a potential source of advancement and outward mobility, it also, paradoxically, reinforces divisions. It becomes, in itself, a marker of differentiation between the 'educated' and the 'uneducated' person (Skinner and Holland 1996) and between those who are more and less connected to 'development' and the 'nation'.

The precise nature of such distinctions is, however, open to varying interpretations as individuals seek to enhance their own status and access to resources. Clearly, those carrying out the work of the state possess 'some degree of latitude and choice, a capacity to translate – as opposed to transmit – ideas about the state's directives, practices and messages' (Wilson 2002: 317). As the preceding discussion has hinted, attempts to promote a particular vision of citizenship and the Nepali state through schools have been only partially successful. A combination of the inconsistencies within the vision promoted through policy and teaching materials and the layers of individual interests, opinions and approaches to schooling practice played out daily in educational institutions results in the continual contestation and negotiation of messages. While there are boundaries to possible re-interpretation, teachers, parents and students can, and frequently do, act in ways that run counter to the dominant or intended interpretation of intra-state relations as characterized in policy and textbooks.

In other contexts, however, this same rhetoric of development and moder-nity is used by people to reshape their position within the local and national community. Interest in private, English-medium schooling was widespread, owing to its popular association with greater discipline, modernity and the world beyond the village. Indeed, proprietors of such schools frequently play on these concerns with mobility and development, emphasizing that attend-ing their institutions will offer the opportunity to become a 'doctor or engi-neer' and allow children to move away from the village and converse with foreigners. Perhaps not surprisingly, parents from all ethnic and caste back-grounds expressed a wish to send their children to such establishments, with financial constraints the prime reason for not being able to do so. For many, offering their children English-medium instruction was regarded as a way of circumventing inequalities associated with ethnicity or locality, offering a means through which to engage with alternative routes of advancement other than those offered through more traditional pathways of progression by the government schools. Instead of government service or a job in the bureaucracy being presented as the most desirable route to mobility and employment stability, English-medium instruction was seen as proffering the dream of employment with an international aid agency (work with 'a project') or in the tourist industry.

Further, the attempt by the Ministry of Education to maintain a degree of centralized control and top-down management of schooling is continually renegotiated and challenged by everyday practices. The need for central approval of education plans before funds are released, the power that officials have to intervene in recruitment and staff transfer decisions and the develop-ment of textbooks by a team of predominantly high-caste Hindu officials in Kathmandu emphasizes the continuing predominance of a top-down struc-ture. Yet at the interstices of this framework, challenges are made and alternative patterns of influence are asserted.

The contested nature of this relationship between the education adminis-tration and the school is particularly evident during inspection visits made by the Resource Person (RP), a district-level school supervisor based in the District Education Office. Visits are experienced by schools as a sudden swooping down of the authorities into the space of the school, with normal patterns of behaviour disrupted and quick shifts in the form of performance made in order to comply with the type of discipline and order expected by the authorities. No warning is given about proposed visits. Indeed the timing seems to be largely at the whim of the RP, and the frequency of visits is largely dependent on the proximity of the school to the RP's home or to the District Education Office.[12] Yet teachers are also able to use such encounters to their advantage and to use alternative relationships to assert influence and authority in ways not envisaged in the bureaucratic framework.

During my research I accompanied RPs on several visits, observing how they interacted with school staff and how staff changed their behaviour following the arrival of the district official. There was always a strong sense that the RP was there as a representative of a higher authority, there to inspect and report on the conditions in the school. This was interpreted as being both a challenge, requiring a good performance, and an opportunity to communicate any complaints back to the DEO. On one such occasion, we arrived at a school in which none of the classrooms had teachers in them. Many of the children were not in class, but were running around outside:

> In the Head-Sir's room sat two teachers, who looked startled by the intrusion. The female teacher immediately left to tell the children to go into their classrooms. The other teacher produced the school's record and visitor book, which the RP browsed through. There followed a discussion about the whereabouts of the Head-Sir, with the two teachers using the opportunity to voice a range of complaints about the poor management, the poor quality of the children and the need to repair the buildings. The RP then went to inspect the classrooms, only to find that the *peon* [caretaker] and a woman who had been grazing her cattle nearby had been drafted in by the female teacher to maintain order in the classrooms during the visit. When the RP questioned this arrangement, the response came that they thought that she would want to see the children being taught, even if it was by the *peon*. The RP then went into the Class 1 room, where children were crushed into two rows of benches at the front, with the rest of the room packed with broken tables and chairs. After sitting at the back for a few minutes, the RP asked the teacher to use the 'pocket board' and the attendance chart that had been given to the school as part of the Basic and Primary Education Programme (BPEP). Eventually, the RP stood up and taught the class herself for a few minutes, before complaining about the dirt in the classroom and then leaving. Following this, comments were written in the visitor book, focusing again on the need to maintain cleanliness in the school and encouraging the Class 1 teacher to make daily use of the materials given to the school. As we left the school the woman went back to her cattle, the *peon* and the male teacher returned to the school office and the children came back out from the classrooms.
>
> (fieldwork date: 22 October 2000)

This episode highlights the ritualistic nature of the relationship between the school and the district officials, with both parties going through the motions of performing tasks appropriate to the situation. The teachers engaged in classroom activities, using the material that the RP had presented to them, and the RP observed and noted down comments. The teachers demonstrate a clear ability to adapt what could be considered an invasive supervisory visit to their own advantage, giving the appearance of compliance whilst using the forum as a way to have their own opinions voiced.

This complexity of surveillance exercised over schools, and indeed over all layers of the administration, is further emphasized by the broader political context within which decisions are made. Since the return to a multi-party system in 1990, many aspects of everyday life have become imbued with political interests. The transfer of teachers, for example, is influenced strongly by networks of political allegiance and affiliation (e.g. Hacchetu 2000). A decade after the change in the system, the question of teacher transfer and the political appointments of staff at school and district level remain the pre-eminent concerns of many employees. The practice of favouring individuals with personal or political affiliations over those who may have better qualifications or experience continues. As one former District Education Officer explained 'I am just like a football being kicked around . . . I was in [one district] and they didn't like me much so I was kicked to the Regional Office in [another area]'. The hierarchical political party structure, combined with the impact that affiliation and involvement could have on the career of an individual, reinforces inequalities and the concern among teachers to give at least the appearance of complying with instructions given to them.

However, the power of political affiliations does not operate in a strictly top-down manner, but influences actions through more complex networks of relationships. Specifically, political party affiliation opens alternative forms of allegiance and influence to the bureaucratic structure of the education administration. In a number of schools, students and teachers had been recruited into political parties, and these groupings were able to assert influence both within the institution and more widely. Some schools reported that, in the post-1990 period, secondary-level pupils had sought the removal of teachers from opposing political groups from the institution. Such demands were made by the students, in the spirit of 'democracy', with the freedom afforded citizens in the constitution invoked to justify their actions. A decade on, political parties and associated teacher and student unions continue to play an active role in influencing decision-making both within the institutions and within the community more broadly.

Tensions in the intertwining of the rhetorics of citizenship, development and the nation are, therefore, continually negotiated and utilized by those involved in schooling. While the language of opportunity, meritocracy, inclusion and engagement in a global process is used to promote a vision of national 'unity amidst diversity', with people coming together to engage in projects of national development, the lived experience of many contradicts this ideal. However, the dominance that the developed–undeveloped, educated–uneducated divide has assumed (Pigg 1992; Skinner and Holland 1996) ensures that these remain pivotal dimensions of the positions put forward by groups seeking to challenge the dominant visions of the Nepali state. Space is opened for groups and individuals to seek alternative relations with 'the external' and processes of development and consequently to reconfigure and revalue alternative ways of 'being Nepali'.

Alternative disciplinary practices, alternative visions of 'citizenship'?

In this final section of the chapter I wish to highlight more overt challenges being made to the state and the dominant vision of the 'ideal' citizen through schools by a wide spectrum of groups. Groups such as religious organizations, ethnic activists and political movements seek to challenge dominant visions of the Nepali state through challenging or reappropriating aspects of school life and attempting to introduce alternative disciplinary practices. As Covaleskie notes, 'the school becomes a site of resistance and outright rebellion precisely because it is a site of sovereign power' (1993: 4). In highlighting how their actions challenge particular dimensions of the Nepali state I do not, however, argue that they are offering straightforward opposition to the status quo. Indeed, in many respects it is the continuity with the dominant vision and the issues left unchallenged that offer a particularly interesting twist to this story and further help to elucidate the significance of the school in this particular social and historical context.

Challenging the Hindu state through schools

The idea of Nepal as an explicitly Hindu nation-state is a particularly strongly reinforced dimension of the vision of the state presented in schools, with a number of extracurricular activities reinforcing this dimension of 'Nepaliness'. The contradictions inherent in the constitution – the recognition of the multicultural, multiethnic make-up of the Nepali populace, while still preserving the supremacy of the Hindu-based social system, religion and values (Kramer 2000: 2) – are reflected in how visions of Nepal are presented in schools. Only Hindu festivals are celebrated in schools, the use of mother-tongue languages is devalued and ethnic groups are openly dismissed as 'backward' by some school staff. The disjuncture between the inclusive rhetoric and the divisive practices of the school does, however, open space within which previously excluded groups can attempt to challenge the existing order and promote alternative visions of 'Nepaliness'. Discourses of development and connections with the 'external' are utilized to advance the position of previously marginalized or excluded groups. Consequently, schools become a key site through which to promote these interests, a point clearly evident in the current promotion of Christianity in the Hindu Kingdom.

The links to modernity offered by Christianity are expressed in opposition to the practices of Hinduism, which are presented as backward and swathed in superstition, with alternative visions of what constitutes the most appropriate path to modernity, including a 'developed' way of life. For instance, during festivals such as Saraswati Puja Day, during which students and teachers present offerings to the goddess of knowledge, Christian children do not attend school, as they neither wish to worship statues nor eat any food that has been offered to the statues. Superstition is thus contrasted with modernity as a way of establishing Christians in a position of greater discipline and development, thereby promoting and validating the lifestyle of this particular group while directly resisting attempts to mould students into model modern Hindu, Nepali citizens.

Attempts to integrate visions of Christianity with those of development and the Nepali nation were further emphasized through the use of schools as sites through which to promote religious belief. During one school visit, my interview with the Head-Sir was cut short by the arrival of four young American missionaries and their Nepali guide. The group proceeded to gather the children and staff together in the playground and presented a play about the life of Jesus. Bracelets of coloured beads – 'White is for good', we heard one of the men say, 'black is to remind you of evil and red is for sacrifice' – and small food packages were then distributed (fieldwork date: 21 April 2000). In their presentation, the missionaries offered an alternative construction of what it means to be 'backward' or 'developed' that allowed those previously placed in a lower position in this hierarchy to see themselves in a different light. For example, they offered an alternative vision of social hierarchy and modernity, both rejecting the caste structure and then contrasting the 'modernity' and 'equality' of Christianity with the 'backwardness' of Hindu practices such as animal sacrifice. In this respect these missionaries had proved successful since, when I returned to the school five weeks later, many of the students and even the female teacher continued to wear the beaded bracelets, and the Head-Sir discussed the possibility of trying to contact the Americans in order to ask for more financial help.

Similarly, a number of ethnic activist groups in the study district are seeking to promote an alternative valuation of intra-national diversity through attempts to reform school practices. In this case attention focused primarily on the promotion of ethnic language teaching in schools and attempts to change teachers' attitudes towards children from ethnic groups (fieldwork date: 1 December 2000). Scholarship programmes have also been introduced by both the Kirat Rai Yakokkha and Chumlung, mirroring those developed by international NGOs, to help children from the respective ethnic groups to attend school and thus help combat the perception of such peoples as 'backward' and uneducated by increasing their association with the modern institution of the school. Thus, while such groups are challenging homogeneity as a basis for Nepali identity, they maintain a focus on development as a key marker of identity and, significantly, a need for external validation of that identity. Connecting particular interests with concepts that have gained strong support within the community – in this case education and development – makes it possible for groups to engage wider popular interest in their activities. Schooling thus becomes a promotional activity for the wider agenda of the interest group, be that a religious organization or an ethnically based movement.

Promoting political interests in schools

Further, and particularly violent, challenges to the dominant vision of the Nepali nation-state presented in schools are currently being made as part of the 'People's War' declared by the Communist Party of Nepal (Maoist). Since 1990, the CPN (Maoist) has been demanding that the country be declared a republic, a position more vociferously and violently pursued since February 1996, when the party began waging an underground, guerrilla-style war. The scale of attacks and reprisals escalated dramatically following the declaration of a state of emergency by the government in November 2001 (see Maharjan 2000 and Thapa 2002 for a discussion of the movement and government response). The Maoists appear to view schools both as a site for gaining support for their activities and – as a particularly salient symbol of the state and of the abuse of state power – as a legitimate target of insurgency activities. Schools are also considered an important recruiting ground for the movement, a site where disaffected young educated people can be targeted and persuaded of the importance of the Maoists' activities and disciplined into the order and practices of the movement. Indeed, in his pronouncements on education, Comrade Prachanda, one of the key strategists of the movement, recognized students 'as the "reserve force" in a future "mass uprising"' (*Nepali Times* 18 May 2001).

Over the course of my research I was told of a significant number of attacks being made on teachers who refused to give support to the Maoists. Initially, fairly amicable approaches were made. A number of Head-Sirs reported that the Maoists had come to the school to discuss their position, explain their goals and ask for teachers' support. However, in private schools or government schools where fees had been taken from students, demands for financial donations to the Maoists were made, often accompanied by threats of physical violence.[13] Countless examples of such activities have been reported from across the country.

There is, of course, a strong populist dimension to the Maoists' choice of schools as a site for promoting their position and challenging the state, highlighting the movement's ability to pick up on interests of the local community that are not being effectively addressed by other organizations.

This ability to address popular concerns has led to widespread support for many of the Maoist demands, albeit with strong reservations about the violent tactics adopted. For example, demands to end the practice of government schools' collecting additional fees from parents appear designed to gain popular support and to situate the movement firmly on the side of 'the people' in opposition to the elitist 'state'. Similarly, demands to end the teaching of Sanskrit and the reduction of private school charges have also met with broad support. Thus, while the threat of violence is a significant factor in the growing strength of the insurgency movement, consideration must also be given to the support that exists for many of the demands being made. Indeed, as Thapa notes, the potential exists for the Maoists to use the strength of their nationwide organization to significant gain in the domain of above-ground politics, with clear political space 'ready for them in the left-end of the political spectrum' (2002: 96).

A particularly potent symbol of the Maoists' opposition to the existing model of the Nepali nation-state is the concerted effort they are making to end the practice of singing the national anthem as part of school assemblies. As a leader of the All Nepal National Free Students Union (Revolutionary) (ANNFSU(R)) argues, 'It is shameful to have a national anthem which heralds some people like gods and others like devotees, and which has no mention of national pride or the natural beauty of the country' (Parajuli 2000; my translation from the Nepali). They demand instead that the anthem be replaced with patriotic songs that present more appropriate and inclusive visions of 'Nepaliness'. Significantly, school students recruited into the ANNFSU(R) in the study district were encouraged to inform on those teachers who do not comply with such demands, effectively ensuring a high degree of self-regulation by teachers fearful of reprisals.

One of the most effective uses of schools as a tool for expanding understanding of the Maoist agenda and for highlighting the growing power of the movement has been the instigation of a series of school strikes. Some have been focused on specific locales or on specific types of institution, such as the closure of private schools. Others have been country-wide displays of Maoist power and their ability to shape and mould the actions of the population at large, such as the week-long shut down of all schools in December 2000, or the closure of private schools in May 2001. A further shutdown was called in March 2002, to coincide with the School Leaving Certificate exams. The timing of this action demonstrated the growing strength of the Maoists and their ability to disrupt national events, despite a State of Emergency being in place.

In part, shutdowns are a means of highlighting concerns specifically related to schooling and the failure of the government to address the inadequate state of education in the country as well as the wider inadequacies of the state, in particular its inability to provide security to its citizens. During the shutdowns, the government promised to ensure the safety of students and teachers – a claim that did not lessen the widespread fear of violence, and schools remained closed. Indeed, in my research area, parents too were directly threatened and warned not to send their children to school on strike days. This threat was later extended to a more generalized call to stop sending children to private schools, a move that caused a number of private school Principals to reconsider their positions as enrolment and attendance numbers dwindled. This overlapping of school-specific and broader political demands was also evident during the 'indefinite' school *bandh* called by the Maoist-affiliated student union in December 2002. The list of demands ranged from those specifically related to schooling, including the reduction of private school fees, to broader political concerns, including the removal of the 'terrorist' label and the lifting of the ban on the union's activities, which had been in place since October 2001.[14]

Through their activities in and around schools, the Maoists are thus seeking to re-order relations and encourage a shift in allegiances through the promotion of disciplinary practices in line with the movement's interests. Direct challenges to the practices of the state are accompanied by attempts to promote more direct models of participation in decision-making and visions of development and citizenship that reflect an alternative construction of inter- and intra-state relations. The use of connections with the 'external' as a source of legitimacy for actions has taken a further intriguing twist in the current context of the Maoist insurgency. The Maoist movement itself is engaging with the rhetoric of inclusion in development processes, claiming to offer direct opportunities for previously marginalized groups to become involved in development efforts. Here, however, the end vision of development is somewhat different than that presented in the agency texts, involving a more comprehensive overhaul of the political and social landscape of Nepal. Nonetheless, there is an explicit engagement with a discourse of participation and caste and gender equality, with the Maoists presented as more able to deliver on these claims than the existing donor-oriented participatory projects (Marsden 2002).

Concluding remarks: understanding schools as sites of conflict

In the post-Panchayat era, the school has emerged as a space within which disparate groups can attempt to mobilize public support and gain broad-based legitimacy for their viewpoints, providing an opportunity to dominate the state by 'acquiring legitimacy through claiming the focal role in societal progress' (Pfaff-Czarnecka 1999: 49). Certain dimensions of the existing vision of the Nepali nation-state as promoted through schools are challenged. Other dimensions of the hegemonic position – such as its claims to modernity – are utilized and even turned back upon the existing order by those promoting an alternative route to social change. In much the same way as we saw the construction and consolidation of the 'prevailing political culture, shaped by the Hindu elite' (Pfaff-Czarnecka 1999: 81) aided by recourse to ideas of modernity and the use of schools as instruments of social change, schools have also become key sources of legitimacy for groups seeking to advance alternative visions of 'Nepaliness'. Activities in this institution provide a useful 'jumping off' point for populist campaigns to promote particular interests, with groups able to play on the widespread concern of the populace to provide educational opportunities to children. The ability to combine the particular goals of the group with popular interest in modernity and development, as epitomized in the institution of schooling, helps give their cause greater appeal and salience in the current context.

Historically, educational institutions have played a significant role in the political struggles over the shaping of the Nepali state and citizenship. Student groups, for example, influenced the course of events in 1951, 1980 and 1990. This is partly a consequence of the presence of large groups of educated young people in a context where they are able to communicate and mobilize – a situation that continues to make schools and colleges desirable recruiting grounds for support. But the significance of the school goes beyond this. Its political value is integrally linked to the widespread perception of the school as an institution connected to places and ideas considered to be 'developed'. The school thus acts as an arena in which differing models of development and intra-state relations are presented, as groups compete to win the support and confidence of the populace. As Gellner has noted, 'The state's prime method of legitimating itself is through development ... Development involves the state trying to mobilize people and imposing new rules' (Gellner 2001: 7). Here he is referring particularly to development as externally-supported aid, a vision that is used by groups such as the ethnic activists to help legitimate their position. Others, such as the Maoists, also use the ideas of development, but to mean rather different forms of social change from those offered by reform-oriented (as opposed to revolutionary) groups.

The use of schools by groups opposed to particular aspects of the state focuses attention on the complex relationship between those offering 'resistance' and that which they seek to oppose. Even approaches that reject the dominant vision of Nepal and development have to engage directly with the key features that help to define that vision. The ethnic activists and religious organizations therefore emphasize that they are 'not Hindu', an identifier that becomes salient as a 'counter narrative of nationalism' (Bhabha 1990). A dominant cultural form, such as the current vision of the Nepali state, 'at once produces and limits its own forms of counter-culture' (Williams 1977: 114). Groups have to engage with those issues that reinforce the dominant vision in order to offer alternatives. Thus it is very difficult for either reform- or revolutionary-oriented groups to avoid engaging with the dominance of the Nepali language, the centrality of schooling to perceptions of progress, identity and intra-state relations, the connection of the state with development, and the existence of the entity 'Nepal'. Thus, in examining the images of citizenship that are proffered in the space of the school, what emerges is not a straightforward model of transmission of, or resistance to, a dominant vision. A more complex interplay between the different dimensions of the state – political, national and developmentalist – can be observed as groups seek to promote their own vision of 'Nepaliness' and enhance the legitimacy of this perspective. One cannot, then, simply view the school as a site where students – and teachers – are shaped and 'disciplined' into a particular mould of the 'ideal' Nepali citizen. Rather, the school can be considered a 'contradictory resource' (Levinson and Holland 1996: 1) in which groups and individuals seek to assert their influence, enhance their status and gain access to resources through association with an institution that has come to symbolize modernity, development and the geographical and political reach of the Nepali state.

Notes

1 The PhD research this chapter derives from was funded by the Economic and Social Research Council. Further support for writing and dissemination of material was provided through an ESRC Post-Doctoral Fellowship. Fieldwork was conducted between September 1999 and December 2000. Earlier versions of this chapter were presented to the South Asian Anthropologist Group and at the European Modern South Asian Studies Conference in 2002.
2 Names of schools have been changed throughout. The term 'English boarding school' is widely used in Nepal to refer to private, English-medium institutions. In many cases they do not offer boarding facilities for students. In this case, two students lodged with the school Principal during term time. Official statistics on the percentage of students enrolled in non-government schools are rather vague, as they include only officially registered schools. According to the Ministry of Education (MOE) figures, 13 per cent of enrolled students are in private or trust-run schools. The Private and Boarding School Organization Nepal (PABSON) estimates that a third of students are educated in private institutions (as of 21 January 2003).
3 Similar daily assemblies also take place in government schools, with the national anthem, military-style exercises and readings by students common features. In these schools, however, the medium of instruction is Nepali and uniforms are blue and white. Inspections for cleanliness take place, but are less rigorous than in the private schools, and failure does not incur the same level of physical punishment.
4 Indeed, in his classic construction of three elements of citizenship, T. H. Marshall notes that educational institutions are key organizations associated with the promotion of the rights and responsibilities of citizenship (Marshall 1950). He discusses this primarily in relation to 'social' citizenship but, in a way this chapter explores, schools also play a significant role in promoting and contesting civil and political dimensions of citizenship.
5 See Preece (2002) and Jarvis (2002) for discussions of debates relating to citizenship and inequality.
6 Burghart (1996) provides an overview of the development of the Nepali nation-state and the shifts in construction of intra-national relations in the post-1950 period. A process of translation and transformation of the concept of citizenship and the nation-state is evident, particularly during the Panchayat era. A highly particular construction of 'Nepaliness' and of the unity of the Nepali

nation-state emerges, based on a particular construction of the cultural uniqueness of the state. Yet this construction is articulated by the regime in terms that
are intelligible to the wider international community. This in turn offers a
degree of legitimacy and recognition, which in turn reinforces the position of
the ruling elite (1996: 256–9).

7 Under 'Partyless Panchayat Democracy' 'active leadership' was provided by the
King with the assistance of zonal, district and village-level committees (Whelpton 1997: 47).

8 The school system is divided into Primary (Classes 1–5), Lower Secondary
(Classes 7–8), Secondary (Classes 9–10) and Higher Secondary (Classes 11–12).
School-leaving certificate exams are taken at the end of Class 10.

9 The *Our Social Studies* series is utilized in many English-medium schools. Its
content closely follows that of the *Mero Desh/Mero Serophero* books used in
government schools.

10 The Constitution of Nepal (1991) recognizes Nepali as the 'language of the
nation' (*rastra bhasa*) and the official language of the state and government. In
contrast, other languages spoken as mother-tongues were considered to be
'national languages' (*rastriya bhasa*).

11 UNICEF highlights the existence of strong social hierarchies and unequal power
relations as factors contributing to the practice of, and lack of opposition to, corporal punishment in schools (2001: 15–16). In addition, such disciplining is
frequently seen as a necessary part of the schooling process, ensuring students
comply with the norms of the institution.

12 A similar process is documented in relation to monitoring of child-care centres
in Uttar Pradesh (Gupta 2002).

13 In the study district, the life of a school principal was threatened. A gun battle
between police and Maoists was reported in another government secondary
school accused of charging fees. In Hetauda, a large town in the central *terrai*,
rebels threatened to cut off the hand of a head teacher who refused their
demands. In Kathmandu threats turned into direct action, with a school principal being 'black-faced' and cars and buildings set on fire in cases where funds
had not been returned.

14 The strike was postponed after a two-week shut-down as a result of an agreement by the Private and Boarding School Organization Nepal to request
members to reduce their fees to an agreed level. The resumption of the strike
planned for February was cancelled after a ceasefire was declared and the label
'terrorist' was lifted from Maoist groups in late January 2003.

References

Althusser, L. (1972), 'Ideology and Ideological State Apparatus' in B. R. Cosin (ed.)
Education, Structure and Society, pp. 243–80, Penguin: Harmondsworth.

Bénéï, V. (2001), 'Teaching Nationalism in Maharashtra Schools' in C. J. Fuller and
V. Bénéï (eds) *The Everyday State and Society in Modern India*, pp. 194–221,
London: Hurst & Co.

Bhabha, H. K. (ed.) (1990), *Nation and Narration*, London: Routledge.

Bhattachan, K. B. (2000), 'National Governance in Nepal', in South Asia Partnership (ed.) *Nepal Governance in the Doldrums: Who Really Governs Nepal?*, pp. 28–48,
Kathmandu: SAP-N.

Billig, M. (1995), *Banal Nationalism*, London: Sage.

Bourdieu, P. and J.-C. Passeron (1977[1970]), *Reproduction in Education, Society and
Culture*, London: Sage.

Bowles, S. and H. Gintis (1976), *Schooling in Capitalist America*, London: Routledge & Kegan Paul.

Burghart, R. (1996), *The Conditions of Listening: Essays on Religion, History and Politics in South Asia*, Delhi: Oxford University Press.

Covaleskie, J. F. (1993), 'Power Goes to School: Teachers, Students and Discipline', in *Philosophy of Education Yearbook 1993* (www.ed.uiuc.edu/EPS/PESYearbook/93_docs/COVALESK.HTM).

Dixit, K. M. (2001), 'Bahuns and the Nepali State', *Nepali Times* 65, 19 October 2001.

Dyer, C. (2001), 'Operation Blackboard: Policy Implementation in Indian Elementary Education', *Symposium*, Oxford.

Foucault, M. (1991), *Discipline and Punish: The Birth of the Prison* (trans. Alan Sheridan), London: Penguin Books.

Gellner, D. N. (2001), 'Democracy, Resistance and the State in Nepal', Paper presented at South Asian Anthropologists Group Meeting, London, September 2001.

Gupta, A. (2002), 'Governing Population: The Integrated Child Development Services Program in India', in T. B. Hansen and F. Stepputat (eds) *States of Imagination: Ethnographic Explorations of the Postcolonial State*, pp. 65–96, London: Duke University Press.

Hacchetu, K. (2000), 'Nepali Politics: Party–People Interface', Paper presented at the *16th European Modern South Asian Studies Conference*, Edinburgh, 5–9 September 2000.

Jarvis, P. (2002), 'Globalisation, Citizenship and the Education of Adults in Contemporary European Society', *Compare* 32: 1, 5–19.

King, K. J. (1988), 'Primary Schooling and Developmental Knowledge in Africa', in *African Futures: Proceedings of the 25th Anniversary Conference of the Centre for African Studies*, pp. 479–530, Edinburgh: University of Edinburgh.

Kramer, K. H. (2000), 'Resistance and the State in Nepal: How Representative is the Nepali State?', Paper presented at the *16th European Modern South Asian Studies Conference*, Edinburgh, 5–9 September 2000.

Latour, B. (1986), 'The Powers of Association', in J. Law (ed.) *Power, Action and Belief*, London: Routledge.

Levinson, B. A. and D. C. Holland (1996), 'The Cultural Production of the Educated Person: An Introduction', in B. A. Levinson, D. E. Foley and D. C. Holland (eds) *The Cultural Production of the Educated Person: Critical Ethnographies of Schooling and Local Practice*, pp. 1–54, Buffalo, NY: SUNY Press.

Maharjan, P. N. (2000), 'The Maoists' Insurgency and Crisis of Governability in Nepal', in D. Kumar (ed.) *Domestic Conflict and Crisis of Governability in Nepal*, pp. 163–96, Kathmandu: CNAS.

Marsden, R. (2002), 'Participation in Conflict: Development and the Maoists in Nepal', Unpublished MA Dissertation, University of Edinburgh.

Marshall, T. H. (1950), *Citizenship and Social Class and Other Essays*, Cambridge: Cambridge University Press.

Mohanty, C. T. (1991), 'Under Western Eyes', in C. T. Mohanty, A. Russo and L. Torres (eds) *Third World Women and the Politics of Feminism*, pp. 333–58, Indianapolis, IN: Indiana University Press.

NEPC (1955) *Education in Nepal: Report of the National Education Planning Commission*, Kathmandu: Bureau of Publications.

Onta, P. (1996), 'Creating a Brave Nation in British India: The Rhetoric of Jati

Improvement, Rediscovery of Bhanubhakta and the Writing of Bir History', *Studies in Nepali History and Society* 1: 1, 37–76.

Parajuli, D. (2000), 'Why is There a School Strike?' Kantipur 13 December 2000 [Original in Nepali].

Pfaff-Czarnecka J. (1999), 'Debating the State of the Nation: Ethnicization of Politics in Nepal – A Position Paper', in J. Pfaff-Czarnecka *et al.* (eds) *Ethnic Futures: The State and Identity Politics in Asia*, pp. 41–98, London: Sage.

Pigg, S. L. (1992), 'Inventing Social Categories Through Place: Social Representation and Development in Nepal', *Comparative Studies in Society and History* 34: 3, 491–513.

Preece, J. (2002), 'Feminist Perspectives on the Learning of Citizenship and Governance', *Compare* 32: 1, 21–33.

Reed, H. B. and M. J. Reed (1968), *Nepal in Transition: Educational Innovation*, Pittsburgh, PA: University of Pittsburgh Press.

Robinson-Pant, A. (1997), 'The Link Between Women's Literacy and Development', Unpublished D.Phil. thesis, University of Sussex.

Sellar, P. O. (1981), *U.S. Aid to Education in Nepal: A 20 Year Beginning*. A.I.D. Project Impact Evaluation Report No. 19, Arlington, VA: Agency for International Development.

Shrestha, N. R. (1999), *In The Name of Development: A Reflection on Nepal*, Kathmandu: Educational Enterprise.

Skinner, D. and D. C. Holland (1996), 'Schools and the Cultural Production of the Educated Person in a Nepalese Hill Community', in B. A. Levinson, D. E. Foley and D. C. Holland (eds) *The Cultural Production of the Educated Person: Critical Ethnographies of Schooling and Local Practice*, pp. 273–99, Buffalo, NY: SUNY Press.

Srivastava, S. (1998), *Constructing Post-Colonial India: National Character and the Doon School*, London: Routledge.

Thapa, D. (2002), 'The Maobadi of Nepal', in K. M. Dixit and S. Ramachandran (eds) *State of Nepal*, Lalitpur: Himal Books.

UNICEF (2001), *Corporal Punishment in Schools in South Asia*, Kathmandu: UNICEF ROSA.

Whelpton, J. (1997), 'Political Identity in Nepal: State, Nation and Community', in D. N. Gellner, J. Pfaff-Czarnecka and J. Whelpton (eds) *Nationalism and Ethnicity in a Hindu Kingdom: The Politics of Culture in Contemporary Nepal*, pp. 39–78, Harwood: Amsterdam.

Williams, R. (1977), *Marxism and Literature*, London: Oxford University Press.

Wilson, F. (2002), 'In the Name of the State? Schools and Teachers in an Andean Province', in T. B. Hansen and F. Stepputat (eds) *States of Imagination: Ethnographic Explorations of the Postcolonial State*, pp. 313–44, London: Duke University Press.

Wood, H. B. (1965), *The Development of Education in Nepal*, Washington, DC: US Department of Health, Education and Welfare.

World Bank (1999a), *Project Appraisal Document on a Proposed Credit in the Amount of SDR 9.0 Million to the Kingdom of Nepal for the Basic and Primary Education Project*, New Delhi: World Bank SARO.

World Bank (1999b), *World Development Report 1998/99: Knowledge for Development*, New York: Oxford University Press.

School texts referred to

Mero Serophero Social Studies, Books 1–3, Kathmandu: Janak Educational Materials Unit.

Mero Desh Social Studies, Books 4–5, Kathmandu: Janak Educational Materials Unit.

Mero Desh Teachers' Guide, Class 4, Kathmandu: Janak Educational Materials Unit.

Our Social Studies, Books 1–10, Kathmandu: Ekta Books.

4 Disciplining ethnicity and citizenship in colonial Cyprus

Rebecca Bryant

Education provides a particularly good entry point into the study of nationalism, not because – as so many working on this question have assumed – it provides transparent access to the workings of nationalism, but rather because it points most clearly to problems in our attempts to understand the construction of a nationalist self. This chapter takes up the use of education for constructing nationalist selves in Cyprus, where the rights and responsibilities of the citizen have been imagined and ultimately realized in ethnonationalist terms (see Bryant 2001b). In Cyprus, the *polis* has been defined by the *ethnos*, so that the education of citizens has also been an education in ethnicity.

On the surface, the relationship between education and ethnic/nationalist selves appears relatively unproblematic and transparent, since the nationalist self is supposedly created through certain types of curricula and pedagogy – through the imposition of 'high culture'. The Greek and Turkish schools of Cyprus would appear to present a particularly good case for this notion of imposing high culture, since those schools have always been separated and depended throughout the British colonial period (1878–1959) on educating Cypriot students as parts of the larger Greek- and Turkish-speaking worlds. Here I argue, however, that, rather than the inculcation of transparent 'propaganda', becoming an educated person in Cyprus involved a self-cultivation that was also ethnic. Hence the student in Cyprus was not only a product, but also an agent.

Cyprus, like much of Europe, experienced an education boom between about 1880 and 1950, years that coincided with the steady growth of hegemonic nationalist ideologies in communities that had once called themselves Orthodox and Muslim. Not coincidentally, it was the belief of British administrators in Cyprus that much sedition in the island was born in the schools. Colonial administrators frequently accused schoolmasters of instilling nationalist sentiments in the young and of stirring up trouble in the villages, often by political rallying. It is easy to take such accusations at face value, especially since they accord so well with our own 'common-sense' notions about the ways in which education has been used in nationalist projects to disseminate elite-derived nationalist histories and sentiments (see especially Anderson 1992 and Gellner 1983). But when one looks more carefully at the position of schools, pupils and masters within the social structure of the island, contradictions in this thesis immediately become apparent. When such a small proportion of children was receiving an education beyond basic reading and writing, how could nationalism be disseminated through the schools? How did young people who set themselves apart from the community through education manage to become not only leaders but representatives and articulators of the desires and needs of the communities? How could the chaotic and *ad hoc* nature of education result in something as systematic as patriotism?

This chapter takes up these questions by examining the relationship between education and nationalist selves, contending that the relationship was not one based on 'propaganda' but on perceived tradition, and that it relied not on 'inculcation' but on mastery. I have argued elsewhere that education in Cyprus was necessary for nationalism because education already embodied community traditions and represented communal continuity (Bryant 2001a). Both the Greek Orthodox and the Muslim communities of Cyprus were literate in the sense that they considered the best, most representative, and indeed most virtuous aspects of the communities to be embodied in the texts and traditions learned through formal schooling. Education was something that was supposed to create better persons, persons who embodied communal understandings of virtue or worth. In Cyprus, in both the Greek and Turkish communities, it has been common to say that one went to school to 'become a person' (Turkish, *insan olmak*; Greek, *na ghínei ánthropos*). Certainly, students became – in a very fundamental sense – different persons through education.

This chapter, first, examines the value placed upon educated persons in Cyprus, and through doing so suggests why an education whose value was similar for both the Muslim and the Orthodox communities may have been, for that very reason, one of the key elements in the development of nationalisms that would drive them apart. Second, in expanding upon that point, I show how schooling as a form of socialization resulted in considerably different conceptions of what could be seen as a 'master' of those bodies of knowledge. For Greek Cypriots, the intellectual created through the schools was a rabble-rouser, a speechmaker, even a show-off and a poseur. This was the case, I will argue, because persons, in the Greek conception, were always already ethnic beings, and the fuller realization of that through education entailed a comportment that iconically represented the *evocation* of their Greekness. For Turkish Cypriots, on the other hand, the teacher, leader and scholar were to be grave and respectful, iconically representing the seriousness of the traditions of truth that they embodied. This was the case, I will argue, because persons, in the Turkish conception, were bearers of a culture into which one was born, but about the nature of which one needed to be *enlightened*.

Intellectuals, as bearers of long traditions of knowledge, also bore the grave responsibility for knowledge of what constituted the reality or truth of the community. As such, they linked the local community of Cyprus to the imagined communities of the Turkish- and Greek-speaking worlds, worlds that also became the goal of political aspirations and the locus for the patriotism of the citizen.

Production and propaganda

From the high fortress walls of Nicosia, a wide boulevard leads inward to the gates of the archbishopric and to the square that has been and remains the centre for Greek Orthodox life in Cyprus. On many days, the cantors' songs echo in the narrow streets, and the bustle of ecclesiastical business fills the neighbourhood with black-robed priests, marriage applicants and their sponsors, and the cry of children brought to be sanctified. Across the square and shadowed by bristling palms, the columns of the neoclassical Pancyprian Gymnasium stand serene, cerebral and solid. The modern history of Greek Cypriot spiritual and intellectual life is encapsulated in one square block, which today is also graced by a thirty-foot (ten-metre) black marble statue of the late Archbishop Makarios – ethnic father, underground revolutionary and former president of the republic.

The *gymnasium* was built in 1893 with funds from the Cypriot Brotherhood in Egypt, and those who supported its establishment clearly believed that it should be the clean, ordered, disciplined organ of the nascent nationalist movement. The *gymnasium* was staffed with Greek-born 'professors' who were imported to impart a higher, classical education to the best and brightest Christian youths of the island. The central organizing principle of the school was the creation of Hellenic citizens who could parse their ancient Greek verbs, recite Homeric verse, prattle about ancient Greek history, and still be prepared to take an active part in commerce, in the professions and in the intellectual life of the Greek kingdom that it was believed Cyprus would eventually join. This preparation for *enosis*, or union of the island with Greece, was undertaken as preparation for the political actualization of something that was already an imagined reality: namely, the expected unity of the entire *ethnos* under the same *kratos*. In this preparation, the *gymnasium* became important as the training centre for teachers of village schools, soon obviating the need to import Greek teachers or to send young Cypriots to Athens. Along with its much smaller counterpart, the Phaneromeni Girls' School, the *gymnasium* became the site in which Cypriots attuned to peculiarly Cypriot needs – such as comprehension of the Cypriot dialect – could be trained to address those needs while still imparting an Hellenic education. Only in such a way, it was believed, could the movement for union with Greece become a movement of the masses.

Education was the one arena in which the British government, despite its efforts, would never gain full control. British administrators recognized quite early that the education imparted could never be sufficiently described by the documentary evidence that they collected – the books, the analytic programmes, the inspectors' reports. They recognized that the real effects of education were in the teacher's voice, the ephemeral marks on a blackboard, and the near-magical powers attributed to the educated. Even until the middle twentieth century, all the men in a village coffeeshop would rise when the schoolmaster entered. One of the most consistent complaints of British colonial officers was of the involvement of village teachers in local politics, and the ways in which they served as intermediaries between political patrons and their 'constituents' in the villages.

Moreover, resistance to government intervention was always strong, particularly since education in both communities was a sacred rather than a secular practice. The real control of communal education was never among the musty papers of the government offices or the 'native' inspectors with their string ties and impeccable English accents. Rather, it was in the solemn, gilded halls of the archbishopric and in the nearby, smoke-filled chambers of the *mufti*. Within the first three years, British administrators recognized that little could be done in any area of education without the cooperation of the archbishop and the *mufti*, who controlled the priests and imams who – at least in the first years of the administration – were also the teachers of the village schools. Moreover, the financially strapped administration could provide little economic support for what were essentially community projects, and so had no grounds to demand increased control. And even when such control was successfully asserted in, for example, new legislation, it became clear that the system in place was highly resistant to change of the sort that the British wanted.

Moreover, there certainly were overt political, national intents in the content and teaching of education. One governor of the island, Sir Robert Storrs, made lengthy remarks in the late 1920s regarding education and its allegedly seditious character:

> It cannot be said that there is any definitely Anti-British Curriculum in the Schools, but they are all actively Hellenising. All Greek Elementary Schools use the 'Analytical Programme' as published in Greece, definitely adopted by the Board of Education. No reading books are allowed in these schools except those that have been approved by the 'Critical Committee' in Athens. The Gymnasium of each town and the Teachers Training School are recognized by the Greek Ministry of Education, and work under Regulations issued therefrom. Portraits of King Constantine and Queen Sophie, of Venizelos and other worthies adorn the walls of the class-rooms together with elaborate maps of Modern Greece, while that of Cyprus, if to be found at all, is as a rule small, out of date, worn out and frequently thrust behind the black board. I have from the first made a practice of asking one or two questions in each form of the schools in the towns and villages I have visited, and discovered during the first few weeks (until my methods became known through the Press)

a ludicrous difference between the home and abroad knowledge of the best pupils who, always exactly informed as to the distance between Athens and Thebes, and usually as to the capital of Norway or of Japan, would hazard guesses varying from 20 to 1500 miles as to the length or breadth of Cyprus. . . . I am advised, and on the whole believe, that ninety per cent of the population would, if a fair plebiscite were taken, vote for the closest union with Great Britain. But I incline to doubt how far the young generation brought up under the present Pan Hellenic curriculum would continue so to vote. And the curriculum could hardly be modified unless Government were in a position, which it is not, to assume entire financial responsibility.[1]

Storrs's concerns arose from the well-known policy of Greek nationalists within Greece to use the Greek schools of Anatolia and Cyprus to cultivate the *Meghali Idhea*, or the irredentist ideal of uniting all Greek Orthodox in what were seen as historically Greek lands. Educating Greek Orthodox outside Greece into a loyalty to the Greek state invariably entailed teaching them that they were not *Romeii*, or descendants of the Eastern Roman Empire, but *Hellines*, or lineal descendants of the ancient ancestors. This project in turn entailed a purification of the language intended to bring it closer to the ancient language, all wrapped in a romantic nationalism that made appeals to the 'purity' of the Greeks' blood and their direct descent from their glorious ancient ancestors (Herzfeld 1982; Kitromilides 1990).

But I quote Storrs at length for what else his remarks illustrate: namely, the paradox in much British writing on Cypriot education, in which an education that they otherwise viewed as 'useless' nevertheless was presumed to result in patriotism. I have elsewhere commented at length upon these seeming paradoxes of education in Cyprus (Bryant 2001a). British administrators constantly observed that education in Cyprus was an exercise in the useless, in which students memorized details of a distant, cosmopolitan life while learning little that could be put to use in their own lives. This is clearest in repeated discussions of language teaching, which focused on 'high' forms of Turkish and Greek, as well as literary languages, in defiance of British administrators' attempts to include in the curricula instruction in students' 'native' languages. Cypriot resistance to such change worried the administration throughout the colonial period, since it presented a problem – the problem of understanding the apparent emotional efficacy of forms of language that Cypriots did not easily understand. It is well known that the Greek spoken in Cyprus, *Kypriaka*, is different enough from the Greek of Greece to be incomprehensible to other Greek-speakers. It is also common knowledge that a large number of Muslim Cypriots spoke *Kypriaka* as their first language, and that those with Turkish as a first language spoke a form of Turkish highly influenced by their *Kypriaka*-speaking neighbours. But the languages of education were 'high' languages – the reconstructed *katharevousa* Greek taught in the schools of Greece, along with the ancient language; or in Muslim schools the languages were, first, Arabic, as the language of the Qur'an, then Persian, as the language of poetry, and finally Ottoman as the language of bureaucracy. None of these forms resembled the languages spoken in the 'mainlands' of Greece and Anatolia, and certainly they bore little resemblance to the forms of Greek and Turkish spoken in Cyprus.

Not only did Cypriots resist teaching 'debased' vernaculars, but they also resisted British attempts to institute commercial schools and other forms of practical education. What comes across most clearly in such debates is that Cypriot resistance to the banalization of education is the result of a particular aesthetic of the educational ritual, and more significantly of the discipline that education produces. The hidden aesthetic behind the concept of discipline was given its clearest formulation in the German ideology of *Bildung*, or self-formation and cultivation, which was always also a moral discipline. It was preceded, however, by the ancient Greek notion of *paideia*, a word that in ancient Greek was used to denote both education and cultivation. The scholar of Hellenic education, Henri-Irénée Marrou, notes that '[f]or Hellenistic man, the sole aim of human existence was the achievement of the fullest and most perfect development of the personality' (1956: 98). Marrou argues that this was a discipline requiring devotion:

> To make oneself; to produce from the original childish material, and from the imperfectly formed creature one may so easily remain, the man who is fully a man, whose ideal proportions one can just perceive: such is every man's lifework, the one task worthy of a lifetime's devotion.
>
> (1956: 98)

Dumont (1994) notes that it was precisely this notion of self-fashioning that appealed to those German intellectuals who sought to articulate the notion of *Bildung*.

The relevance of this digression to our discussion of education in Cyprus lies in my present attempt to explicate something that to Cypriots of the early twentieth century seemed incredibly clear: namely, that education was more than simple learning; it was the attempt to mould oneself after an ideal cultural type. In other words, in so far as education is seen as 'cultivation', its goals must be aesthetic ones, oriented towards the elaboration and representation of cultural 'truths' that the individual must embody. While our own more theoretical discussions of pedagogy may acknowledge this aspect of education's task, they acknowledge it as a form of 'domination' or 'hegemony', revealing our own inherited biases towards a more individualistic expressivism that leaves little room for ideal cultural types.

As we shall see, those aesthetic goals that colonial observers interpreted as a kind of frivolity can be directly linked to the cultural ideals elaborated in education. But rather than seeing those ideals as either imposed or negotiated in some conscious sense, we shall see them here as an aesthetic —

something that can be consciously theorized but that depends upon the unconscious cultural givens of 'taste'. Any theorization is only a second-order attempt to understand why one form of representation is already preferred over another, and so discipline becomes an aesthetic – a conscious self-moulding in a form that is nevertheless a cultural given. To put it simply, a 'high culture' was not imposed, but was an ideal for which Cypriots strove through education and expected their leaders to embody, while at the same time accepting that, as poor farmers, the immediate concerns of quotidian life would probably prevent them from achieving that goal.

The ethnic fantasy

In early 1912, an article appeared in the *Kypriakos Filaks* that greatly agitated many of the Muslims in the island. The *kadi* wrote a letter of complaint about the presumed writer, Nikolaos Katalanos, and his 'Solution to the Anatolian Question'. The author of the article asserted that the Ottoman Empire – which he calls 'Turkey' (*Tourkia*), following European usage – would have vanished from the face of the earth a long time before if it had not been buttressed by European powers with an interest in its survival. As a solution to the 'Anatolian Question' – the rather presumptuous 'problem' of the division of Anatolia – the writer proposed a Darwinian competition of races, in which the outcome would be determined by 'the racial superiority of the Greeks as they reclaim their paternal inheritance, without injury from neighbouring and utterly enslaved nations'. After a eulogy of the likely benefits to humanity and to Anatolia of Greek rule, the writer concludes that

> the Greek race, if it does not contain its national virtue in the peaceful antagonism towards other races, will find it possible to impose its spiritual nation-state on the thousands of inhabitants of these nations and to enlighten them with faith, and to restore the cross to the dome of Aghia Sophia [in Istanbul] and to return the [Byzantine] Two-Headed Eagle to the battlements of the Empire.[2]

Such was the rhetoric that, by the turn of the century, filled Greek newspapers, was recited by Greek schoolchildren, and flowed from the mouths of Greek politicians. It was a rhetoric of race and regeneration, and one that obviously partook of the familiar, idealized motifs of nationalism at the turn of the century. It was also a rhetoric that by necessity had as its central demand the call for the realization of a dream and an ethnic ideal that, more than any other single idea, would determine the future of the island: *enosis*, or union, which for Greeks meant freedom and for Turks meant fear. The union of Cyprus with Greece was a desire expressed during even the earliest days of British rule, and Greek Cypriot historians usually refer to it as the free expression of a long-cherished hope.[3] Turkish Cypriot historians also find early references to the idea of *enosis*, or union with Greece, though they do so to demonstrate that Turkish Cypriots always reacted immediately against this aspiration.[4] In contrast to both, contemporaneous foreign observers often complained of the trouble-making elites who tried to rouse the contented villagers to fruitless action.

What Greek Cypriots saw as a primordial inheritance, British administrators saw as troublemaking propaganda. What is interesting is that Greek Cypriots, while admitting that much of the inheritance to which they laid claim was learned, appear to have seen no contradiction between a primordial and an articulated identity, or between ethnicity learned and ethnicity lived. In the dispute over the nature of Greek Cypriot education it is obvious that the repeated claim of Greek Cypriots that 'there is no such thing as Greek propaganda in Cyprus' is not only a political one. It reveals, more than anything else, an epistemology in the critical sense, i.e. the articulation of a theoretical mastery of the world. Propaganda – deliberate, second-order and purposeful – could also be a form of enacted ethnic identity.

To put it another way, the fact that teachers overtly attempted to instruct their pupils to nationalist action did not make that instruction any less hegemonic, any less a part of those practices that John and Jean Comaroff remark 'are so habituated, so deeply inscribed in everyday routine, that they may no longer be seen as forms of control' (Comaroff and Comaroff 1991: 25). The dispute over the nature of Greek education hinged, then, on two very different notions of the educational process. In particular, British administrators saw the overt efforts of schoolteachers to 'inflame the minds of the pupils against other races resident in the Island' as a directly political attempt to disturb the status quo. The inspector of schools observed in 1911 that he had found some rather strong expressions in certain schools' books, but the majority of village

> children do not reach to that point (i.e. the higher classes) or they are too young to understand it. I think there is little or no anti-Turkish or anti-English teaching in the *Elementary* schools – what there is is in the secondary schools to pupils who are of an age to take it in – and this does not depend on set lessons or books but on what the teacher *says* on the thousand occasions when he can introduce his sentiments into *any* lesson, without any check.[5]

For their part, Greek Cypriot spokesmen recognized the British fears of nationalist agitation, and often asked, when various educational schemes were offered, 'Will the Government attempt to control the teaching of "Greek national history" in the schools? If so, it were better to repudiate government assistance altogether'.[6]

Moreover, Greek Cypriots agreed that education was explicitly political and believed that it should be. I would argue, in fact, that it is only in arenas in which one attempts to maintain the illusion of non-political objectivity in education that the political is seen as propaganda. Students of the Pancyprian Gymnasium were told, for instance, that they were being prepared to take up their political duties:

> We have had and always have the idea that the Pancyprian Gymnasium excellently fulfilled its purpose, that it not only transmits the light of education throughout the island, but it also prepares young, vibrant youths.... It educates men of wisdom and full of self-denial, true defenders of Faith and Fatherland (*Patridha*). ... To you, noble adolescents of today, tomorrow the fatherland will entrust her future. You will govern her fate, you will be the laborers who will guide her re-establishment, the apostles of the Great Idea.[7]

For Greek Cypriots, then, education was indeed a discipline not unlike that known by their British rulers. The significant difference was in the type of citizen produced: whereas British administrators wished to cultivate in their subjects a pragmatic participation beyond the confines of community, Greek Cypriots aspired to an ethnic belonging.

The use of language is an important key to this. Interestingly, the rhetoric of nationalism was not even fully available to everyone, since it was almost always spoken in *katharevousa* or even in ancient Greek, giving a breath of the Parthenon to each syllable. This was the language of the learned or at least of the literate, the language of 'national' celebrations and political speeches. The villagers to whom such speeches were directed were not expected to understand them, only to have a visceral response of pride. Instead, in speeches given in ancient Greek, the content of such speeches was ontically inseparable from the archaized language; dreams of recapturing Byzantium could only be expressed in the language that was also the historically continuous and consistent spirit of the race. 'Christian Hellenism cannot be fully understood without its original kingly language', explained one newspaper article. 'The new Hellenism is so closely connected with the ancient, that it is not possible to understand how the second can exist without the first, the belief of which is still symbolized by language.'[8] The all-conquering Greek language was the ultimate proof that the Greek spirit was timeless but historical, unchanging but adaptable, continuous but malleable. For these reasons, instruction in the language was much like military training: one did not need to understand the mechanics of the training to understand that the goal was to become a disciplined soldier. The ultimate goal, of course, was to achieve mastery, which would also imply the capacity to command; but until that time unquestioning submission was the rule.

Foucault writes of the 'great book of Man-the-Machine', the modernist project begun by Descartes and finished by those faceless functionaries of the new sort of governmentality that regulated the body (Foucault 1979). The disciplined body of the modern soldier demonstrates in its comportment the ideal regulation of that controllable, manipulable and perfectable machine.

In a strangely similar way, the Greek Cypriot image of 'man the ethnic subject' demanded a discipline that could only be accomplished through the regulation of education, while simultaneously denying the *necessity* of that education for the creation of ethnic subjects. In other words, philosophers of the French Enlightenment would have said that man *is*, by his nature, mechanical, but that education was required to achieve his *telos*. Similarly, Greek Cypriots would have said that man is, by his nature, an ethnic subject, a member of his race, but that education was required to achieve his higher end.

I would suggest, in fact, that much as repetitive military drills train the soldier to respond without thought to commands, so the rote memorization of passages in ancient Greek or the distance from Athens to Sparta was intended to domesticate and control an identity seen as already ethnic. Indeed, articles about education made it abundantly clear that the primary goal was to create ethnic subjects trained in a moral discipline that could best be learned by becoming literate. One 1912 article claimed, for example, that

> Education and the school are foundations and institutions Greek for ages, because first and foremost our nation, in the cultivation of a spiritual and moral man, marks out as special and indispensable the attributes and signs of civilization, of freedom, and of good-citizenship.[9]

Education had begun only within the writer's lifetime to mean more than reading, writing and basic arithmetic, so the writer could have had few illusions regarding any kind of 'higher' education. Moreover, folktales regarding the 'secret schools' that supposedly kept Hellenism alive through the ages never suggest that those schools did more than teach children the basics of their language. Rather, they suggest that the mere fact of linguistic continuity symbolizes a racial continuity.

Benedict Anderson (1992) has suggested that print capitalism created bourgeois communities defined by vernacular languages, and that these first imagined communities would become the basis for nationalist imaginings. The Greek Cypriot case presents a peculiar instance of a local community finding commonalities through a new print network that was written in a nationalist language to which they aspired. In other words, the farmer sitting in the coffee shop listening to the news being read by the teacher or the *muhtar* was simultaneously incorporated into several concentric circles of community – Paphiote, Cypriot, Greek, Greek Orthodox – while finding those identities idealized through a language from which he was excluded. The language was only as 'naturally' his as any other inheritance, and was therefore something that he would have to earn and fight for.

In Marrou's examination of the centrality of rhetoric in the education of antiquity, he makes an important remark about the value of rhetoric that could just as well be applied to our Greek Cypriot villagers:

Learning to speak properly meant learning to think properly, and even to live properly: in the eyes of the Ancients eloquence had a truly human value transcending any practical applications that might develop as a result of historical circumstances; it was the one means for handing on everything that made man man, the whole cultural heritage that distinguished civilized men from barbarians.

(Marrou 1956: 196)

The ideal man was eloquent, but eloquence was also inseparable from ethnicity. To acquire the 'kingly language' and to use it properly was also to become a true Greek, a truly civilized man.

Indeed, it is abundantly clear in discussions of education that the realization of ethnic identity through education was the realization of an unquestionable good, the realization of one's full humanity. This is so much a part of Greek Cypriot discourse that I can pick an example only somewhat at random. It is certainly well expressed in the words of Leontios, Bishop of Paphos during the 1930s, who defended the need for a purely Greek education by saying:

Here, however, it is a question of a historically Greek island, having a history of five thousand years, a history of a glorious civilization, occupied during these times by a population purely Greek, noble, and Christian. . . . For this reason the official and systematic attempt to anglicize the Greek Cypriots is reprehensible . . . [Greek education] consists in its teaching not only of the Greek language, but also of Greek history, the history of the *ethnos*, about which the wise men of all nations have not ceased, and will not cease, their praise . . . It is a truth scientifically proven that the Greeks – the ancestors – became the first creators of education, and in this way they became the educated people of humanity . . . The Greek spirit approaches the universal meaning of 'human', and Greek education (*mórphosis*) means human education.[10]

To deny Greek Cypriots a Greek education was not just to deprive them of their rights but to deny them full humanity, since humanity directly corresponds to Hellenism.

There are a few conclusions that I would like to draw from this. First, Greek Cypriot history is inevitable, unchangeable and irreplaceable. Second, many Greek Cypriots believed that nationalist pedagogy and what might be seen by others as nationalist propaganda were directly successful. However, they were successful because the work of education was a somewhat Platonic evocation of a Greek spirit, a Greek potential, already present in the child. As early as 1916, this was expressed in a eulogy addressed to the first contingent of Boy Scouts in the island:

These youths, by being taught under the liberal status quo of Cyprus their duties towards their motherland, will, when the moment will come that they should be called up to the colours and that they should continue the interrupted work, be the most enthusiastic and most disciplined soldiers of Him. Likewise, when, directly, they will be swearing by this sacred flag of the fatherland, the scouts' oath, a thrill of emotion will run through their bodies, and the whole long and glorious history of the great race to which they belong will, in that moment, pass through their mind, and they will remember, yes, they will remember the sacred oath which, thousands of years ago, the Athenian youths used to swear at the same age, the oath, that is, that they would defend the fatherland both when found by themselves and when found in company with others, that they would not abandon the sacred arms and that they would not hand back the country smaller. They will remember that those who, about a century ago, fell at the Dragatrani as the heroic victims of the Hellenic liberty were, like them, still in their youthful age, in their very boyhood. They will remember all that and how much more will they not remember! The whole history of the race will pass before them as an immaterial power and will strengthen them and will dictate to their souls the creed 'I believe in a great Hellas', and, in a frenzied emotion, they will, with the hand upon this sacred flag and with the soul knelt down, give all of us here the assurance that it will not be they who will disgrace the history of their fatherland, but they will be those who, either as citizens or as soldiers or either here or anywhere else shall be nothing else than the observers of the historical traditions of the nation, and the continuators of a history a more glorious of which no race can shew.[11]

The 'immaterial power' that is the history of their race would be evoked as an orgasmic thrill, an organic shudder, that would leave them spiritually prostrate before the glory contained in the Greek flag. 'They will remember all that and how much more will they not remember!' exclaimed the speaker, arousing in his audience all the ideas of ethnic history already imprinted in the mind.

Third, Greek Cypriots described their own history as the inevitable and inescapable history of humanity, in which their own role was already largely predetermined. Their duty was to be, either as citizens or soldiers, 'nothing else than the observers of the historical traditions of the nation'. That glorious past leads them towards a future in which the *ethnos* will be reunited, and where all members of the *ethnos* will also become citizens. But because the values of ancient Greece also supposedly represent universal values, the ultimate human goal accords with the ultimate national goal, and the good citizen becomes the good human. Citizenship, in this conception, is defined by a willingness to fulfil a historical purpose.

And fourth, this enactment, this self-conscious achievement of an aesthetic ideal, was in fact the achievement of an Hellenic ideal. The movement for *enosis* was a mass movement, its ideals were ones to which one had to aspire. I would insist, however, that this did not make those ideals any less their own, any less of a shared, cultural inheritance. Indeed, education was cultivated precisely because it evoked the inheritance that could be shaped to true humanity. The average villager could only aspire to that ideal, but this did not make it any less *his* ideal. Put simply, the dream of 'progress' through education, of a 'better future' that demanded the moulding of young minds and bodies, was, for Greek Cypriots, the fulfilment of an ethnic fantasy. Man is, prior to cultivation, an ethnic subject, but only through cultivation could he blossom to achieve the aesthetic paradigm that the colonizers saw as propaganda. 'Progress', then, was the fulfilment of an immanent potentiality. Progress becomes predestination, and education becomes evocation.

The dream of enlightenment

Barely a decade after Katalanos asserted the eternal rights of Greeks to 'reclaim' Istanbul, Mustafa Kemal Pasa – also known as Atatürk, or 'father of the Turks' – solved the infamous 'Anatolian Question' by routing the Greek forces then advancing through Anatolia, dissolving the sultanate, and establishing the Turkish nation out of the ruins of the Ottoman Empire. By 1923, Atatürk had firmly consolidated power in the new capital, Ankara, and in the new ideology of Turkish nationalism, of which he was the greatest articulator. By 1937, one year before Atatürk's death, the six founding principles of the republic had been enshrined in the constitution: republicanism, nationalism, populism, revolutionism, secularism and statism (*cumhuriyetçilik, milliyetçilik, halkçilik, inkilâpçilik, layiklik, etatism*).[12] Atatürk himself was both the *gazi*, or religious warrior, and the ethnic father, so highly revered that he could be referred to in writing by a capitalized third-person pronoun, which in English we reserve for reference to God.

Within a matter of a few years, Muslim Cypriots became Turks, taking upon themselves an identity forged in the crucible of nationalism. Atatürk's reforms were adopted with speed and vigour: the Arabic alphabet was discarded and a Roman alphabet instituted in its place; European hats were donned when Atatürk demanded that they be; women appeared in public unveiled at the command of their fathers; and young nationalists opened night schools to teach the new reforms. The entire project was predicated on an orientation towards the future, and a perceived need for self-remaking, indicated both by repeated cries of Turks' backwardness, and by the common understanding of salvation as something that would come from above.

Turkish Cypriots, as the minority, were at a distinct political and economic disadvantage with regards to their Greek neighbours. However, in almost every case the source of this disadvantage was seen not through the lens of political economy, but as a weakness of the self, a weakness internal to the society, and something in need of remaking. In one study of the history of Turkish Cypriot education, the author quotes the remarks of a medical doctor who was educated in the last decades of Ottoman rule, became a member of the Young Turk movement in Istanbul, and escaped exile by fleeing to his native Cyprus, by then under British rule. He also taught French for some years at the *idadi*, or secondary school, published the newspaper *Islam*, and opened his own industrial training school until forced by Nicosia elites to close it. In this teacher's memoirs he explains that:

> because in the villages there were fewer Turks than Greeks; because they spoke Greek, and because without schools, or imams, or mosques, or teachers they were in a pitiable situation, under the influence of clever priests a portion of them were Grecified. He says that in the Ottoman period because not only in the villages but even in the towns not even a speck of importance was given to education, the future of up to forty villages was dark.
>
> (Nesim 1987: 65)

However, thanks to a teacher educated in a *medrese* in Istanbul, 'by founding a large *medrese* in Paphos, and by preaching sermons in the mosques and villages to warn and awaken the people, and thanks to the students that he distributed to the villages, the villager was saved from becoming Greek' (1987). The 'darkness' of custom and ignorance – represented here by the 'Grecified' Muslim villager – was overcome by the 'enlightenment' of civilization represented by the traditionally educated intellectual, who, despite his religious education, was able to 'warn and awaken the people'. This, indeed, was one of the primary responsibilities of those known as the *aydinlar*, a word that literally means 'lights' or 'enlightened ones', but that refers to all those who have 'knowledge'. In this vision, intellectuals would preserve 'the people' from the calamities to which they would otherwise be led by custom and ignorance.

In Cyprus, their own backwardness was clear in comparison with their Greek neighbours, who appeared to succeed at Muslims' expense. Moreover, this self-criticism extended even to the heart of the society, namely to its dealings with women. One Turkish Cypriot teacher whom I interviewed was born in 1919 in a small village in the Paphos area of Cyprus. Both his father and elder brother were teachers, so his family's association with education stretches back into the early Hamidian period. When discussing his own family, he noted that

> although my father was a teacher, he didn't send the girls to school. He said they could go to primary school, but he only sent one sister. My elder brother, oooh, he finished primary school, he finished *rustiye*, he became a teacher. My elder brother. But my father didn't send my sisters who came after him, not even to elementary school.

While this was no doubt a common practice, in actual fact Muslim schools in the island for many decades compared favourably with Greek schools in regard to primary education for girls. One reason for this is indicated in observations regarding girls' education by the first British inspector of schools, Josiah Spencer, who wrote in 1881 that:

> The condition of the Masters of the Christian village schools has gener-ally been hitherto such as to prevent parents from sending their girls, except a few very small ones, to School. The Moslem village Masters being generally older men, and religious Teachers, there is not the same difficulty, and their Schools are usually more mixed than the Christian village schools.[13]

Even as late as 1913, in a report on the state of Cypriot education, Muslim girls constituted 37 per cent of the total of 5,692 Muslim children enrolled in elementary classes, while girls in the Christian schools made up only 30 per cent of the Christian total of 25,854 (Talbot and Cape 1913: 14).

Despite this, however, the same teacher clearly believed that the opposite was the case, and he made a direct association between the perceived back-wardness of Muslim education and the lack of education for girls. In our interview, I had noted that beginning from the early Hamidian period and continuing until Cyprus' independence in 1960 there had been complaints lodged with the British administration about the deficient nature of Muslim/Turkish education, especially in contrast to that of their Greek neighbours. When I asked this retired teacher about the problem, he remarked:

> This was true. Theirs was much better. And in any case they gave much more importance to education than we did. They definitely sent their Greek children to school. It should also be good for the girls. Because with us, boys and girls couldn't ever be together, that is. At twelve years old they [the girls] were completely covering themselves (*carsaf ortusunu giyerlerdi*). The Greeks weren't like that. The Greeks were always in love, always going to the church together, our girls didn't go to the mosque, the women. Of course there were those who went, but they had a separate place. But not like the Greeks, the Greeks on Sunday all went to the church, all together, there was mingling (*kay-nasma vardi*), girl, girl–boy mingling happened. That's why, if a girl goes to school, if a Turkish girl goes to school, and if she learns reading and writing, she writes a letter to her lover. That's why families didn't send them! Greeks weren't like that, the Greeks were different. And they gave much more importance to education, that was the reality.

While my question had concerned the perception of a Turkish backwardness in comparison to Greek education, his answer focused very clearly on the

relationship between that backwardness and traditional practices and perceptions with regard to girls.

Indeed, one of the more puzzling features of Turkish modernity has been
the use of women in Turkish modernizing endeavours.[14] What are often considered to be the 'paradoxes' of Turkish modernity are clearly exhibited in
the early republican demand that women be 'modern yet modest'. Although
Atatürk is, in nationalist discourse, usually credited with freeing women
from the yoke of a slavish religious backwardness, one sees both in family
histories and in writings of the late imperial period a tendency within the
memur, or civil servant, class to educate and 'enlighten' its women. In literature, in memoirs, and in recollections of persons educated in the late
Ottoman and early republican periods, there is a direct association made
between freedom for women and being *medeni*, or civilized.[15]

The association of women with the traditional, the national 'inside', and
hence with an essential identity is a common theme in many nationalist
imaginations.[16] What is fascinating in the Turkish case is the clear popular
association of the traditional with the backward, where the backward is perceived to be a danger within the society, something to be fought, altered or
repressed. It was a danger because it was a weight on the society, something
holding up its progress. For Turkish Cypriots, this was perceived most
clearly in contrast with their Greek neighbours, who both gave more
importance to education and allowed the education of their daughters. And
finally, there was clearly a perception of the possibility of change and self-
remaking.

Correcting the 'backwardness' within the society came to depend, in turn,
on the *aydinlar*, who should teach one the error of one's ways. The concept of
'enlightenment' (*aydinlatmak*) was certainly central to the speed and ease
with which Atatürk's reforms were accepted in Cyprus, where he was often
called the *ikinci peygamber*, or second prophet, and the 'saviour' (*kurtarici*) of
the Turks. He was called the latter certainly because of his military tri-
umphs, but even more importantly because of his renovation of Turkish
society, which supposedly pointed them on the way to 'truth'.

Many Turkish Cypriots felt that while Atatürk had given them an identity, they were in need of their own local 'saviour' to rescue them from their
backwardness as a minority ignored by their Greek neighbours. In the
crucial period following the Turkish War of Independence, for example, an
important Turkish Cypriot doctor and member of the legislative council
wrote of what he saw as the *malaise* of his people. 'In this century of perfec-
tions in which we are living', he wrote, his people are 'obliged to be subject
to its enlightened and civilized currents' at a time 'when nations that have
determined to become holders of word and position' have taken control of
their destinies. In his own country, however, it is different:

Protection of property and family; maintenance of fame and prosperity!
Let a handful of young folk be as much vigilant and cautious as they

can. Let a party of enlightened persons cry out with all their power: this is the way of truth! I wonder in how many hearts and in how many intellects will this cry of truth find an echo.

Indeed, the ideal cultural type to be moulded in Turkish schools was the 'enlightened' individual, and the aesthetic of self-fashioning was one of 'enlightenment'. While the goal of education was *kalkinma* – recovery or progress – pedagogy itself was described by the verb *aydinlatmak* – to illuminate, to clarify, to enlighten. Unlike the European Enlightenment, whose articulators described their task as one of bringing light to the darkness of religious orthodoxy and prejudice, those who called for *aydinlatmak* saw its knowledge as literal clarification. The *aydinlar* – the intellectuals – were presumed to be 'enlightened' and possessed of the clear knowledge necessary for leadership.

Moreover, their fitness to lead could be seen in their possession of certain types of knowledge, and one most often criticized one's political opponents for being 'ignorant' or 'lacking learning'. In 1919, for instance, several young men called together Muslims from throughout the island in an attempt to organize in protest both against Greek agitation for *enosis* and against what they claimed was deprivation of their rights by the colonial administration. A highly admired English teacher, Necmi Potamyalizade – who was a frequent contributor to the magazine *Near East* and an even more frequent correspondent with the government – claimed that the meeting was an attempt to disprove one of his articles, in which he had argued that the British Empire should retain Cyprus in the face of Greek protests precisely because of the loyalty of the Muslim population. Those who organized the meeting, he asseverated, were acting on their own, and 'none of them had the credentials of the people authorizing them to decide and act as their representative'. Furthermore, in the published article that described the meeting, Potamyalizade found evidence of their inability to lead:

Many mistakes in that article, even in the composition of the language, may convince that these persons, whoever they may be, were not of good education, except perhaps in their own businesses, and therefore lacking much both in knowledge and in judgment.

That they were devoid of such standard feelings of nationality and patriotism, which they declare to be their impulse, it is proof enough that they did never show material symptoms of their feelings, even when their duties called upon them. The education and the civilization of the Muslims of Cyprus are in a deplorable condition; they are already in the clutches of the most awful enemies of humanity and civilization, it requires little foresight to see the grim face of Destruction lying in ambush in the way of Muslims a few decades further, and what efforts they made to save these poor men? On the contrary, there are instances that some of them did not hesitate to injure Muslims in different ways.

If they had any feelings of nationality, first of all they would learn their own language, and not display such inability in connecting two passages with each other. [17]

It is clear that Potamyalizade saw a direct relationship between their 'lack of credentials' and their lack of eloquence.

It is the lack of leaders who can show the 'truth' that results, it was believed, in the decadence and despair of the Muslim community. In contrast, they see only unanimity among their Greek compatriots:

> In order to secure their future, they, the Greeks, are unanimously and with one accord doing their best by embracing willingly all sorts of trouble and hardship and sacrificing almost their moneys and lives, and in view of that activity and sacrifice their success is, we are sorry to say, certain and beyond doubt. One envies the Greeks, saying 'would that it were so for the Muslims!', and cannot help crying bitterly for our abasement and lack of proper spirit in face of manliness of the Greeks.
>
> ... There shall come a day when the known persons, who for the decadence of the nation sell their conscience in return for a salary and present of a small amount of money, shall not be allowed to utter untrue words, as they do now in the coffee houses, for the purpose of deceiving the people, and the young men of enlightened ideas will inflict condign punishment upon them, and their benefactor, and they shall be looked upon by the people as 'Traitors of the Country.'[18]

The 'young men of enlightened ideas', the men blessed with the enlightenment of progress, would one day achieve their rightful status and punish those who had led the community astray through 'untrue words'.

Even – perhaps especially – those who slandered each other in their newspapers and in public addresses complained that 'our life is taken up with factions, enmity, revenge'. An article published by the opponents of *Seyf* complained that the two primary problems in the Muslim community were the organization of education, which could not satisfy the needs of the country, and a second disease:

> Our second and most dreadful disease is lack of character. What a great number of important nations that have been sovereigns of the world and masters of arts and knowledge have been buried and lost for lack of character. There is no society, no tribute that has disappeared for anything else but lack of character.[19]

We see, then, that not only is power directly linked to the mastery of arts and knowledge, but also that that mastery is linked in some amorphous sense to 'character', to the unanimity that would bring progress.[20]

There is, then, a linked complex of ideas: the 'young men of enlightened ideas' should possess 'word and power' secured through the unanimity of the community – which unanimity would 'qualify' them for their position. Transparency, clarity and enlightenment were the ideals that continued to be reflected in educational practice. The ideal of transparency helps us, I believe, to understand the links between a school discipline that emphasizes obedience, politeness, self-effacement and replication (see Bryant 2001c), and a mode of political behaviour whose ideal is unanimity. Discipline in the Muslim community taught one to become *as iconic as possible*, not by possessing qualities such as honour but by embodying those qualities – i.e. by becoming honourable. It is, in fact, a rather different notion of agency, defined not by what one *does* but by what one *is*. Hence, identity was always something *to be achieved*, always something to be made through the self-conscious striving for a transparent iconicity. Once one acquired the 'character' of the 'young men of enlightened ideas', this would be reflected in the unanimity of the community.

Moreover, the ideal of 'enlightenment' emphasized education as truth, and becoming educated as an approach to truthfulness. Hence, leaders were educated, and the educated were leaders. But, furthermore, it was precisely the idea of *approaching* truthfulness, of always striving to achieve greater truthfulness, that made the ideal of enlightenment seem immanently progressive. As a result, these same young men would serve as the guides into Atatürk's future.

Conclusion

Briefly, I have attempted to show one possible way of problematizing and rethinking the historical role of education in creating nationalist subjects and citizens. I argue that the status of learning in the Orthodox and Muslim – later Greek and Turkish – communities of Cyprus meant that it was always already a system whereby one transformed the self into a master of those bodies of knowledge. This, I have suggested, might be most easily seen as a form of apprenticeship in which one shapes oneself in the mould of traditional knowledge and thereby becomes the type of person capable of calling upon that knowledge.

Furthermore, I have sketched two alternative ways in which this might be realized. In the Greek Orthodox case, education's task was a cultivation or evocation of a latent potential of the ethnic subject, while in the Muslim case it was a form of enlightenment in which the intellectual occupied the role of the physician whose task it was to guide and heal. I wish to suggest in conclusion that it was these two alternative understandings of the social role of knowledge that in fact proved divisive for the two communities. For as education was, indeed, transformed into a vehicle for nationalism, it acquired force in uniting Turkish- or Greek-speakers across the divides of class, village and genealogy because of the fact that it had always united Muslims and Orthodox in similar ways. Hence, the 'high cultures' of nationalism were not an imposition but an aspiration.

However, as that education united Greek- and Turkish-speakers across previously important divides, it also began to shape notions of citizenship that by necessity excluded the other. In this way, the duties of the citizen also became a source of division.

Notes

1 CO67/228/13, secret dispatch to Amery, secretary of state, from Sir Robert Storrs, governor of Cyprus, 18 January 1928.
2 'Mia lysis tou Anatolikou Zitimatos', *Kypriakos Filaks*, no. 318, 28 April 1912.
3 See, for instance, Alastos (1976: 208) and Pantelis (1990: 7).
4 For instance Gazioglu (1996) and Ismail (1989).
5 SA1/1074/1911, confidential letter from Newham to chief secretary, 18 July 1912.
6 Ibid.
7 'Evghe Neotis', *Foni tis Kyprou*, 2 March 1901.
8 *Foni tis Kyprou*, 21 December 1901.
9 The author continues by noting that 'the ethnic school for these reasons forms the national crucible in which are smelt and opened wide and forged the great and high characters in those advanced persons who accomplish great things': *Kypriakos Filaks*, no. 340, 29 September 1912.
10 AAOCC, no. 500, letter from Leontios, Bishop of Paphos, to Governor Palmer, 18 November 1935.
11 SA1/646/1916/1, extract from *Neon Ethnos*. Although *patridha* translates as 'fatherland', it is 'a feminine word': it is gendered feminine and also has connotations of the feminine.
12 For a succinct explanation of the development of these concepts, see Shaw and Shaw (1977: 340ff).
13 SA1/1314/1881, letter from Spencer to Chief Secretary, 25 July 1881.
14 There is, indeed, a vast literature on this subject alone. See especially Kandiyoti (1991a, b), Arat (1998) and Fleming (1998).
15 Deniz Kandiyoti, while not framing the problem in the same terms, echoes my own observations about the culturally specific nature of Turkish appropriations of Western ideas when she suggests that 'the specificities of the societies in question may have played as determining a role as the history of their encounters with the West. Indeed, it could be argued that, far from being random, the selection of Western sources by local reformers reflected processes of internal negotiation and struggle between factions of political elites with different visions of the "good society"' (1998: 272). For paradigmatic observations of the period in question, see Ziya Gokalp (1978), *Turkculugun Esaslari*, and what is often seen as the prototypical Turkish nationalist novel, Resat Nuri Guntekin's *Calikusu* (1993).
16 Partha Chatterjee, for instance, remarks that in India '[t]he world was where the European power has challenged the non-European peoples and, by virtue of its superior material culture, had subjugated them. But, the nationalists asserted, it had failed to colonize the inner, essential, identity of the East, which lay in its distinctive, and superior, spiritual culture' (Chatterjee 1993: 121).
17 SA1/426/1919, letter from Necmi Potamyalizade to the high commissioner of Cyprus for transmission to the prime minister, 26 December 1919.
18 SA1/465/1912, extract from *Seyf* no. 26 of 25 August 1912.
19 SA1/465/1912, *Dogru Yol*, no. 3.
20 For a very interesting comparison, see Khalid (1998: 135–6).

References

Alastos, Doros (1976), *Cyprus in History: A Survey of 5000 Years*, London: Zeno Publishers.

Anderson, Benedict (1992), *Imagined Communities: Reflections on the Origin and Spread of Nationalism*, London: Verso.

Arat, Zehra F. (1998), 'Educating the Daughters of the Republic', in Z. F. Arat (ed.) *Deconstructing Images of 'The Turkish Woman'*, pp. 157–80, New York: St. Martin's Press.

Bryant, Rebecca (2001a), 'An Aesthetics of Self: Moral Remaking and Cypriot Education', *Comparative Studies in Society and History* 43: 3, 583–614.

Bryant, Rebecca (2001b), 'Justice or Respect? A Comparative Perspective on Nationalisms and Politics in Cyprus', *Ethnic and Racial Studies* 24: 6, 892–924.

Bryant, Rebecca (2001c), 'Pashas and Protests: On Revelation and Enlightenment in Cyprus', *Cultural Dynamics* special issue, 'Epistemologies of Islam' 13: 3, 317–38.

Chatterjee, Partha (1993), *The Nation and Its Fragments: Colonial and Postcolonial Histories*, Princeton, NJ: Princeton University Press.

Comaroff, Jean and John Comaroff (1991), *Of Revelation and Revolution: Christianity, Colonialism, and Consciousness in South Africa, Volume 1*, Chicago: University of Chicago Press.

Dumont, Louis (1994), *German Ideology: From France to Germany and Back*, Chicago: University of Chicago Press.

Fleming, K. E. (1998), 'Women as Preservers of the Past: Ziya Gökalp and Women's Reform', in Z. Arat (ed.) *Deconstructing Images of 'The Turkish Woman'*, pp. 127–38, New York: St. Martin's Press.

Foucault, Michel (1979), *Discipline and Punish: The Birth of the Prison*, New York: Vintage.

Gazioglu, Ahmet C. (1996), *Enosis Cemberinde Turkler: Bugunlere Gelmek Kolay Olmadi*, Nicosia: Cyprus Research and Publishing Center.

Gellner, Ernest (1983), *Nations and Nationalism*, Ithaca, NY: Cornell University Press.

Gokalp, Ziya (1978), *Turkculugun Esaslari*, Istanbul: Inkilap ve Aka Kitabevleri.

Guntekin, Resat Nuri (1993), *Calikusu*, Istanbul: Inkilap Kitabevi.

Herzfeld, Michael (1982), *Ours Once More: Folklore, Ideology, and the Making of Modern Greece*, Austin, TX: University of Texas Press.

Ismail, Sabahattin (1989), *20 July Peace Operation: Reasons, Development and Consequences*, Istanbul: Kastas Publications.

Kandiyoti, Deniz (1991a), 'Identity and Its Discontents: Women and the Nation', *Millennium* 20: 3, 429–43.

Kandiyoti, Deniz (1991b), 'End of Empire: Islam, Nationalism, and Women in Turkey', in D. Kandiyoti (ed.) *Women, Islam, and the State*, pp. 22–47, Philadelphia: Temple University Press.

Kandiyoti, Deniz (1998), 'Some Awkward Questions on Women and Modernity in Turkey', in Z. Arat (ed.) *Deconstructing Images of 'The Turkish Woman'*, p. 272, New York: St. Martin's Press.

Khalid, Adeeb (1998), *The Politics of Muslim Cultural Reform: Jadidism in Central Asia*, Berkeley, CA: University of California Press.

Kitromilides, Paschalis M. (1990), 'Greek Irredentism in Asia Minor and Cyprus', *Middle Eastern Studies* 26: 1, 3–17.

Marrou, Henri-Irénée (1956), *A History of Education in Antiquity*, trans. George Lamb, New York: Sheed and Ward.

Nesim, Ali (1987), *Batmayan Egitim Guneslerimiz: Kibris Turk Egitimi Hakkinda Bir Arastirma*, Nicosia: Milli Egitim ve Kultur Bakanligi Yayinlari.

Pantelis, Stravros (1990), *The Making of Modern Cyprus: From Obscurity to Statehood*, London: Interworld Publications.

Shaw, Stanford J. and E. K. Shaw (1977), *History of the Ottoman Empire and Modern Turkey, Volume II: Reform, Revolution, and Republic: The Rise of Modern Turkey, 1808–1975*, Cambridge: Cambridge University Press.

Talbot, J. W. and C. F. Cape (1913), *Report on Education in Cyprus*, London: HMSO.

Part II
National history and memory

5 Educating citizens through war museums in modern China

Rana Mitter

'This site', reads the notice, 'is an institution for patriotic education'. The sign stands at the front of the Museum of the Nanjing Massacre, the wartime atrocity better known in the 'West' as the 'Rape of Nankin'. The inculcation of patriotism in China, an essential element of the construction of citizenship, is embedded in most of the activities and institutions set up in China as part of the educational regime. The establishment of museums is a significant part of that agenda. Naturally, museums such as the Smithsonian, the British Museum or the Imperial War Museum are surrounded by political agendas. But none of these institutions would place a sign outside declaring openly that it was 'an institution for patriotic education'. To that extent, the Chinese agenda seems a lot clearer and more upfront. Yet even in China, the concepts of 'patriotism' and 'education', not to mention 'citizenship', are all loaded terms that carry a great deal of baggage from the last century or more of Chinese history. In addition, an institution such as a museum is part of a wider agenda of creating a modern form of citizen republic that has been heavily contested over the course of the century.

This chapter surveys the changing debate about what 'citizenship' means in the context of modern China, particularly as refracted through attempts to reform education. It also focuses on one relatively under-studied aspect of public education in contemporary China: museums dedicated to explaining China's role in the war against Japan in the mid-twentieth century.

Public culture, education and citizenship in the early twentieth century

The title of Henrietta Harrison's book *The Making of the Republican Citizen* sums up the immensity of the task facing the Chinese political elites in 1911, the year of the revolution that ended two thousand years of imperial rule in China (Harrison 2000). 'We have made Italy; now we must make Italians' was a saying of the Risorgimento. Likewise, the Chinese revolutionaries had declared a republic; now it was time to make republicans. The history of the early twentieth century is one of a new imagining and reconfiguring of ideas of citizenship, with education an important site of those re-imaginings. 'From the close of the last century,' writes Joshua Fogel, 'a "citizenry" became perceived as one of China's greatest needs' (Fogel 1997: 279). How to create that citizenry became one of the pressing political topics of the following decades, and is an active subject of discussion even today.

However, the establishment of the Republic was not, in itself, the turning-point. Changes had been stirring in China for some decades before 1911. The Opium Wars and the impact both of Western gunboat imperialism and European political thought had led many thinkers of the late Qing dynasty (the last Chinese imperial house, which ruled 1644–1911) to consider alternatives to the traditional Confucian bureaucracy in which the Chinese people were configured as imperial subjects. Among these constitutional thinkers were Kang Youwei and Liang Qichao, who advocated constitutional monarchy as the path for China. Their model was the immensely successful Meiji reforms in Japan, which between 1868 and the turn of the twentieth century had turned Japan from an isolated agrarian country threatened by the Western powers into an industrializing state that had become an imperial power in its own right. At the core of the Meiji project was the top-down push by the ruling elite to force the Japanese people into becoming citizens of a nation-state through socializing institutions such as the army, and most universally, the education system. Meanwhile, many of the old social class distinctions were abolished. These moves were by no means always popular, but they proved highly successful at creating a citizenry.[1] In contrast, China's elite was half-hearted at best about adopting Western political structures such as nation-states and citizenship. However, in 1895, the imperial court had to come to terms with its disastrous defeat in the Sino-Japanese War, and Kang and Liang found a sympathetic ear at court for their ideas of constitutional monarchy along Japanese lines. Shortly afterwards, in 1898, the emperor supported sweeping reforms that might have moved China towards the Japanese model. But within a few months the conservative faction at court, led by the Dowager Empress Cixi, launched a countercoup, imprisoning the emperor, and forcing those of his reformist allies who escaped execution into exile. The reforms were halted. Ironically, though, the aftermath of the 1900 Boxer War[2] saw the Qing court reverse course and begin a new phase of reforms, promoting and developing ideas put forward by the emergent middle classes, such as provincial and even national assemblies, to be set up on an electoral basis (though a restricted one). In particular, educational reform was stressed. 'Officials, scholars and educators after 1900 insisted on the need for a national school system that would train a disciplined and hardworking people who would contribute to national unity and prosperity', notes Paul Bailey (2001: 318).

Yet the reforms came too late. Revolutionaries took the lead and in 1911 succeeded in triggering off a series of provincial revolts that led to the abdication of the Qing boy emperor and the declaration of a Republic. A first, inspiring attempt at a general election in 1912, won by the Nationalist party of Sun Yatsen, was soon waylaid by a strongman militarist, Yuan Shikai, who dissolved parliament and took power in Beijing himself. After his death in 1916, China was split between rival militarist factions, and even the establishment of a 'national' government under Sun's successor as Nationalist leader, Chiang Kaishek, in 1928 did not provide true unity. The period after 1931 was then marked by increasing internal tensions, as the Chinese Communists and some other militarists refused to accept Chiang's authority, and externally, as war with Japan threatened and then broke out in reality. Although the 1937–45 war ended with Japan's defeat, Chiang's government was then defeated in turn in the civil war with the Communists, who took power in 1949.

The catalogue of political events, however, obscures the equally significant and profound change in the political culture of the late Qing and Republican period, when citizenship in particular became an issue for the elites. One of the most prominent forums for the discussion of the new political ideas was the press. The reformer Liang Qichao, in particular, was instrumental in helping to develop a new language that meant that concepts such as 'citizen' and 'nation' were embedded in the Chinese language (usually by the use of classical Chinese lexical compounds which had been exported to Japan centuries before and were now reimported from the Japanese with new meanings) (Judge 1996; Liu 1995). Yet this did not mean a simplistic transfer of European ideas of citizenship to the Chinese context. 'If the republic belongs to its people – the citizens', notes Peter Zarrow (1997: 3), 'the locus of sovereignty must shift away from the ruler'. Yet he goes on to point out that while citizenship as such could only be generated in the context of Western influence, Chinese society had a long tradition of concepts such as mutual social obligation and loyalty to a ruler contingent on his performance, which laid the ground for the acceptance of concepts of citizenship when they emerged. Liang and his allies, in attempting to forge a 'new citizenry' that would serve the emergence of a Chinese nation, believed that 'education was to play a critical role in training the future citizens in public-mindedness, devotion to comrades, and respect for tradition and institutions (Zarrow 1997: 17). As part of this teaching, the new vocabulary of citizenship, particularly the term *guomin* (literally, nation-people), would be at the forefront, though this term was later supplanted by *gongmin* (public-people) (1997: 17–18). The idea that political legitimacy came from the people, rather than the ruler, became widespread in rhetorical terms, even if the term 'citizen' was not always used in that rhetoric. The Communists were most prominent in their discursive links between 'the people' and 'authority', but similar language was embedded in all the modernist political projects of the era.

Education was also a powerful part of that agenda. The Republican era saw attempts to modernize Chinese schools. However, the period after 1916 when China was divided between various militarist leaders held back attempts to introduce reformed education, and even after the establishment of the Nationalist government of Chiang Kaishek in 1928, schools changed only slowly. As Suzanne Pepper has pointed out, by the 1930s, the educational system had been inspected by the League of Nations at the Chinese government's own request and found seriously wanting. It was inconsistent in structure and quality, and ironically, overstaffed and undersupplied with pupils (only about 21 per cent of the elementary school age-group actually attended). Furthermore, the curriculum was unimaginative, and even 'modern' subjects such as civics, as expressed through the teachings of the nationalist leader and icon Sun Yatsen, were taught 'in as formalistic a manner as the teaching of all the sciences' (Pepper 1996: 40). Textbooks might discuss questions such as appropriately modern dress or personal behaviour (such as handshaking) for men and women, yet they could reach only those children from families prosperous enough to be able to afford education (Harrison 2000: 176, 61–5). Various alternatives to the government-sponsored educational system did exist in that period, including missionary schools and schools sponsored by the slowly growing Communist Party. But it was not possible for a large proportion of the population to take part in any project to inculcate citizenship or nationalism via schools, particularly in rural areas.

In urban areas, however, other institutions were set up to create a republican culture. One of the earliest government policies was also one of the most far-reaching, the cutting off of the 'queue', or the long braid of hair worn by Han Chinese men under the Qing dynasty, that was ordered after the Revolution. 'Queue cutting was one of the very few government policies of the early Republic that had an impact at a local level on a national scale', argues Henrietta Harrison. 'Through it men were marked out as citizens of the new state (2000: 40). In urban areas, however, there were other institutions that helped create a new culture of citizenship: among them, the museum. The public museum is a relatively recent addition to the Chinese institutional repertoire, as were other public institutions such as parks. Yet, as Tamara Hamlish shows, the conversion of the Forbidden City into a National Palace Museum was an integral part of the attempt by Republican governments to instil ideas of citizenship among the Chinese people, the establishment of a state museum being seen as an integral part of Western public culture (Hamlish 1995). It is hardly coincidental that one of the priorities of the fleeing Nationalist regime in 1949 was to take the contents of the Palace Museum and display them in a new building in Taipei (where they still are today) as part of their claim to legitimacy. There were even trade-linked museums displaying 'national products' (Gerth 2003). Consequently, although the inculcation of the values of citizenship was patchy before 1949, in urban society there had been a significant internalization of the values that allowed the term 'citizen' to be used meaningfully in the context of Chinese politics.

However, the post-1949 period saw a radical shift in the relationship between the state, education and citizenship. Although much of the teaching material in Republican schools had been propagandist in nature, it also was scattered and unevenly absorbed. The Communist state, however, had enough control and authority to do what its predecessor never could, and to dominate the production and consumption of educational ideology. Yet the dominance of its class-based ideology, and Mao's frequent resort to class war (the Great Leap Forward, the Cultural Revolution, and so forth) meant that the flat, egalitarian model of citizenship that had emerged, albeit mostly at an elite level, in the Republic had little potency during the years of Mao's rule in the People's Republic (PRC). The Mao era had the trappings of citizenship, such as the establishment of a new constitution; but the term *gongmin* was relatively rarely used, not least because the implied equality of status that a truly national citizen body required was necessarily disrupted by the new hierarchies of class created by the PRC. Outside the educational sector itself, public institutions and monuments dedicated to the recent past made the 1946–9 civil war, rather than the Sino-Japanese War, the touchstone of political legitimacy, and the internal, class-based nature of that conflict militated against the propagation of ideas of citizenship. A new attention to citizenship as problematic in its own right would have to wait for the era of Deng Xiaoping, when class war gave way to a new concentration on economism and patriotism.[3]

The changing agenda since 1978: education and citizenship

Deng Xiaoping's reforms, it is now clear, marked a period of sharp deviance from the rule of Mao.[4] Education, both within the formal education sector and outside it, was very much part of those reforms. Ideological education in Marxism–Leninism continued to be a staple of the curriculum through the 1980s and beyond, though the clear lack of interest on the part of the students led to various revisions of the course by the educational authorities, including renaming part of the subject 'citizen knowledge' (Thøgersen 1990: 120). In the 1980s, 'Regulations for Middle School Students' were placed in all schools, including exhortations such as 'Love the motherland, love the people, support the Chinese Communist Party, study diligently and prepare to do your utmost for the socialist modernization' (Thøgersen 1990: 121). In many ways, such exhortations were little different from what had been put out in textbooks of the Republican era. Yet the concept of 'citizenship' that has begun to emerge in China in the 1980s in some ways reflects global trends in this area. The solidarist agenda, which has seen issues such as human rights, environmental concerns, and so on become powerful transnational tools of discursive practice, has also increased the interest of ordinary Chinese in claiming status and rights as citizens; test cases have come up where people have sued for their rights in court, something that was politically and culturally near-impossible in the Mao era.

This puts the state in something of a quandary. As China opens up to the outside world, it does not wish to deny the agendas of citizenship. It has actively encouraged the development of law and the language of rights as part of its agenda to show itself to be a part of the world community, and to take its rightful place in that community as a great power. Yet it is also keen to harness the agenda of citizenship to bolster its people's relationship with the state, rather than challenging it. There are several ways in which it has done this. One is to encourage those ideas of citizenship that are tied up with civics, often bolstered by campaigns using terms such as 'spiritual civilization'. This can often be expressed in seemingly banal forms, such as signs all over cities informing pedestrians: 'Everyone has a responsibility to cherish and preserve green spaces' (*Aihu ludi renren youze*). Yet these efforts are also linked with a more explicit agenda linking citizenship not with class, as was implicitly done under Mao, but with the internally 'flatter' concept of patriotism. The term 'patriotism' (*aiguozhuyi*) was very consciously chosen instead of 'nationalism' (*minzuzhuyi*), as the latter term has ethnic and racial implications that the PRC feels uncomfortable bringing into official discourse. Within schools, textbooks and classes now regularly deal with the importance of patriotism in all sorts of contemporary contexts; perhaps, at the turn of the twenty-first century, the most notable was the concentration on China's attempts to join the World Trade Organization (WTO) and to win the Olympic Games for Beijing (both of which it succeeded in doing). Yet the past, rather than the present, has been one of the most important ways in which patriotism and citizenship have been imagined in tandem with each other. As we shall see, the institution of the museum has been an important part of that imagining.

War museums and patriotic education

History is one of the prime sites in which the re-imagining of Chineseness has taken place in the reform era.[5] Confucius, condemned as a feudal relic as recently as 1973–4 (in the 'Criticize Confucius, Criticize Lin Biao' campaign of the late Cultural Revolution), has in recent years been reborn as a symbol of Chinese civilizational continuity, along with a modernized set of 'Confucian values' that the sage himself would be hard put to recognize. The 'strongmen' of the late Qing, such as the Confucian reformer Zeng Guofan, have also seen a rise in their cultural stock (He and Guo 2000). However, one of the most notable aspects of the new understanding of history is the reassessment of the 1937–45 Sino-Japanese War, the segment of the Second World War that took place on the Chinese mainland.

The war itself was a highly sensitive subject for many years in the People's Republic. The war against Japan was almost immediately followed by the Civil War, won by the Communists in 1949. When constructing a historiography for the newly established state, the PRC had various political priorities on its current agenda. First, it needed to delegitimize the seemingly still-dangerous Nationalist government in exile on Taiwan; thus any

Nationalist contributions to winning the war had to be minimized in the official records. And second, the PRC needed to find ways to woo Japan away from the Cold War embrace of the United States: downplaying Japanese war atrocities was one way to do that. However, the 1980s saw policy change, for a variety of reasons. First, Japan had long since recognized the Beijing government, and Chiang Kaishek had died in the previous decade. Meanwhile, the old class-inflected nationalism of the high Maoist era had less potency in the era of Deng Xiaoping. Instead, economic growth and peaceful reunification with Taiwan became new priorities. Linked to these was the largest political problem of all: the decline of the CCP's legitimacy after the discrediting of Maoist social and economic policies.[6] The Party remained in power, but it needed new sources of symbolic capital to preserve its rule. Clearly, the economic growth that China has shown since 1978 has been in large part responsible for preventing social disorder disrupting the country (although that disorder is by no means absent); but this source of legitimacy is rather contingent on factors outside the CCP's control, such as the world economic climate. In consequence, the Party has been seeking out new sources of political legitimacy. A re-imagining of the experience of the war has been one of the most potent of those sources. During the Mao era, it had been necessary to conceal the reality that the Nationalist government had had a very significant role in winning the war against Japan, and only the role of the Communist armies had been dealt with in historical studies (emphasizing for instance the role of the Yan'an base area). In the 1980s, however, it became apparent that the official narrative of the war had changed, and that a slow, unstated realignment of its history was being placed before the public. The contributions of Chiang Kaishek and the Nationalist government to the war against Japan were now praised, albeit hesitantly, and their role as patriots, rather than as class enemies, was stressed.[7]

Among the most notable of the educational tools that have been promoted in the reform era are the museums that deal with China's re-imagined history of the war. Three of these museums in particular stand out: the Memorial Museum of the People's War of Resistance to Japan, in Beijing; the September Eighteenth Memorial Museum (commemorating the Manchurian crisis of 1931), in Shenyang; and the Memorial Museum of the Nanjing Massacre, in Nanjing. As recently as 1985, Arthur Waldron notes (1996: 949), there was 'no central war memorial: there [was] no cenotaph, no tomb of the unknown soldier, no elite honor guard, no eternal flame'. These museums were a significant contribution to ending that gap in memory, and providing educational institutions that would allow the new historiography to be diffused through society more widely. But what is in these museums, and how do they work?

The three museums share some features in common. First, they are all on sites that are historically connected to the events they deal with: the Beijing museum is in the suburb of Wanping, where the first fighting broke out between Chinese and Japanese troops in 1937; the Shenyang museum is next to the railway tracks blown up by the Japanese when they launched their coup to take over Manchuria in 1931; and the Nanjing museum is on the site of one of the notorious massacres of 1937. Second, they all use a similar combination of display techniques. They lead the viewer on a chronological tour of the events, with copious captioned photographs and artefacts displayed in cases, interspersed with diorama reconstructions of various major events. Most importantly, they all very consciously present themselves as institutions for public education.

The major differences lie in the contents, and the narratives attached to them. The Shenyang museum deals very specifically with the events of 1931 and the consequent 14-year occupation of Manchuria, putting particular emphasis on the role of CCP-organized resistance armies. The Nanjing museum deals with the single most notorious Japanese atrocity of the war and its aftermath. The Beijing museum is the most wide-ranging, perhaps as befits a museum based in the capital, with sections on most of the war nationwide, even devoting small areas to the (actually quite extensive) parts of China under collaborationist control during the war.[8]

In what, then, does the effectiveness of these museums lie? Carol Duncan, speaking of Western 'universal survey museums' such as the Louvre, observes that no museum is neutral, but 'a complex experience involving architecture, programmed displays of art objects, and highly rationalized installation practices'. Noting that even secular cultures are full of rituals, she notes that museums '*work* like temples, shrines, and other such monuments' and can be 'powerful identity-defining machines' (Duncan 1991: 90, 91, 101). Although they are not 'survey museums' like the Louvre, this analysis rings true for the Chinese war museums, not least since they are termed 'memorials' (*jinianguan*) rather than just 'museums' (*bowuguan*). But they fulfil the function of both, and we therefore need to consider both roles.

When judging museums, it is also necessary to decide what the criteria are by which they operate. The literary critic Stephen Greenblatt put forward two attractive models for the 'exhibition of works of art'. One is termed 'resonance', by which he means 'the power of the displayed object to reach out beyond its formal boundaries to the outside world, to evoke in the viewer the complex, dynamic cultural forces from which it has emerged and for which it may be taken by a viewer to stand'. The other is 'wonder', by which he means 'the power of the displayed object . . . to convey an arresting sense of uniqueness, to evoke an exalted attention' (Greenblatt 1991: 42).

However, these points need not be linked exclusively to aesthetics. Rather, for the historical museum, resonance and wonder come from the participation of the museum in the creation and transmission of a wider, in this case a national, narrative. Imaginative reconstruction is clearly not just a Chinese phenomenon: for example, the Imperial War Museum in London features a 'Blitz experience' and mock-ups of the trenches of the First World War. How far can this type of display be reconciled with the traditional purpose of a historical museum, to show the past as it was? Can one dismiss the claim in the Beijing War of Resistance Museum guide that the viewer should feel as if she or he is 'placing [her- or him]self on the battlefield at the time', when it appears that a stylized, romanticized representation of events is being offered for view? Spencer R. Crew and James E. Sims, speaking of historical museums in general, state baldly: 'Authenticity is not about factuality or reality. It is about authority. Objects have no authority; people do. It is people on the exhibition team who must make a judgment about how to tell the past' (Crew and Sims 1991: 163). Bearing this in mind, they suggest that curators can 'break from the concept of object-driven exhibitions and produce presentations controlled by historical themes rather than by available objects', and conclude that 'authenticity is located in the event' (1991: 167, 174).

Certainly the Beijing museum acknowledges a scarcity of artefacts while affirming its own quest for authenticity: 'the storage capacity is not very great' (Zhongguo renmin kang-Ri zhanzheng jinianguan 1997a: 5). However, the dioramas seem to have become tableaux of 'authentic' mood, rather than reconstructions. Elaine Heumann Gurian, in discussing the politics of museum display, states: 'While we may be reluctant to admit it, the production of an exhibition is more akin to the production of a theater piece than any other form' (Gurian 1991: 188). A significant part of the agenda of the Chinese museum, however, is baldly and unashamedly stated as being political, as when the director Zhang Chengyue claimed that it 'has a role for patriotic education for the wider masses' (Zhang 1990: 197). To that extent, the curators of the museums might not be displeased by the comparison with a theatrical performance.

Although the idea of diorama reconstructions comes in part from Western influence (early dioramas were popular with the Victorians, for instance), in some respects the aesthetics of the Museum follow an aesthetic that is recognizably Chinese. For instance, a diorama of a Japanese bacteriological warfare atrocity in the Beijing museum that reproduces a torture act, complete with moving figures, would be considered overblown by the designers of most American and European museums. The same is true of the diorama reconstruction, in the same section, of the Rape of Nanjing, which shows models of corpses covered with blood and a crying baby posed on the dead body of its mother in the foreground, while the skies are darkened by smoke and flames in the background mural. This type of juxtaposition might seem maudlin to a Western curator, or worse still, actually kitsch, fatally undermining its authority. Yet this is a reconstruction of real events that are deeply important in the modern Chinese psyche, and it is clear that the judgements of taste that a Western curator brings to the viewing cannot be the same as those of a Chinese curator, as the point made earlier about aesthetic judgements being rendered difficult by emotional issues comes into play. Similarly, the display of bones of victims at Nanjing would clash with Western taboos about actually showing corpses or body parts. Public education, therefore, takes ideas from the West, but reinterprets them within a recognizably Chinese aesthetic.

The educational message of the museums is reinforced by a range of publications. Most obvious to the ordinary visitor are the guidebooks, which explain the new historiography in detail. In the War of Resistance Museum in Beijing, the main guide, which reproduces many of the explanatory cards by the side of the exhibits, is called the 'Simple Introduction' (*Jianjie*). It contains a preliminary section that explains the establishment of the museum, followed by more detailed descriptions of the four halls. It concludes with statistics on aspects of the War, for instance the numbers of guerrillas led by the CCP from 1937–45, financial contributions by Overseas Chinese to the war effort in 1937–8, and levels of Japanese armaments at various dates. The causes and progress of the War itself are explained in another booklet, the 'Explanation' (*Jiangjieci*).[9] There is also a guidebook in English.[10] The 'Record of Names of the Hall of the Martyrs of the War of Resistance' (*Kangzhan yinglieting minglu*) is a small pamphlet issued by the Museum that also emphasizes the new historiographical narrative. It lists the 296 senior officers (Nationalist and Communist) who are on the Martyrs' Tablet, copying the details of their lives found in the Hall. In addition, the names of the 1,228 junior officers who are listed in the Hall are also recorded in the 'Record of Names'. The introduction to the guide attempts to draw in the visitor's participation by stating that 'The list of names in this hall are not yet complete … and we ask readers to help us come together to do this work.'[11] (Yet it is notable that neither common soldiers nor civilians are mentioned by name in the Hall.) Also designed to stimulate the visitor with connections between the past and the present is the pamphlet 'Today in the History of the War of Resistance' (*Kangzhan shishang de jintian*), which lists one event during the War for each day of the year.[12] The Museum also sponsors an academic publication, the annual 'Essays' (*Wencong*), which combines new research and discussions on the War of Resistance with a section on the latest exhibitions and policy decisions at the Museum itself.[13]

The museum publications very explicitly state that their purpose is to link the lessons of the past to those of the present. In an age of globalization, when outside political and economic forces have great influence in China, the museums serve to remind visitors that China was vulnerable to imperialism and invasion in the past, and in different forms, remains vulnerable in the present. Naturally, the discourse is not purely hostile to the outside world; entry to the WTO and the Olympics, and participation in the UN, show China's face as a responsible, cooperative power, both to its own people and to the outside world. However, both the inward- and the outward-looking parts of the construction of the PRC's identity need to be kept in mind. The museums, in particular, seek to educate the young. The Beijing museum, for instance, calculated that around 60 per cent of its visitors in 1994 were schoolchildren, and has recorded annual visitor numbers of close to a million throughout the 1990s. In addition, special textbooks, publicity campaigns and exhibitions aimed specifically at children have all been promoted by the museum, and, for a selected few hundred, since 1993, there has even been a summer activity camp based at the museum.[14]

Conclusion: educating for citizenship?

To be a Chinese citizen means something different at the start of the twenty-first century than it did at the start of the twentieth. To begin with, until after 1900, the concept of the 'citizen' was not part of official discourse. While the reformers mentioned above had praised the concept, most people would have still thought of themselves, if they problematized the question at all, as imperial subjects. Among the urban and more educated classes, the early Republican period saw the Western-influenced creation of a notion of republican citizenship, although the weakness of the Republican governments prevented those notions taking root more widely. The war against Japan also prevented the strengthening of the Chinese state, and it was only unification under the CCP after 1949 that allowed the state a real grip over the educational and therefore citizenship-building apparatus of the state. While various aspects of the CCP regime did nod toward the citizen ideal (for instance, the implementation of a constitution that granted particular rights to the Chinese as individual citizens), identity became heavily associated with class differentials, culminating in the Cultural Revolution, and thereby disrupting the putative, if often fictive, equality that underlies the classic definitions of citizen status.

The reform era, however, saw a new interest in the emergence of the type of citizenship that had first appeared in the Republic, in which, by contrast with the Mao era, equal citizen status was not complicated by class distinctions. (Perhaps not coincidentally, this recent fading of class rhetoric has happened at the same time that China has developed higher economic inequalities between social groups than at any time since 1949.) It should also be noted that, while class distinctions were once more fading away in the new, flatter, definition of citizenship, other issues that have yet to be worked through are those such as gender and ethnicity. Indeed, while the Communist state has had a much firmer grip than its predecessor regimes on the apparatus of education that can inculcate citizenship, all Chinese regimes over the century have failed to deal adequately with issues such as gender and ethnicity that complicate the notion of what citizenship is. On the former, it is clear that the story of Chinese patriotism and citizenship-building, certainly as told in the museums, is very masculinist and tied up with discourses of wartime heroism on the battlefield. On the latter, it is also clear that it is also a discourse heavily oriented towards Han (ethnic Chinese) identity. Where, for instance, would Tibetan women fit into the discourse that is now being promoted as the legitimate definition of patriotism?[15] The institutions that are promoted by the Chinese state to help create citizenship, such as the museums, may in some respects have remained similar in the journey from the 1920s to the 1990s; but so, in many respects, have the unanswered questions about what that citizenship means.

Notes

1 See, for example, Gluck (1985).
2 Editor's note: The Boxers were members of a nationalist secret society named *yi he quan* – lit. 'righteous harmonious fists' – responsible for a rising in 1900.
3 For an excellent account of education under Mao, see Pepper (1996, Chapters 7–17).
4 For background, see Baum (1994).
5 For more on this, see Unger (1993).
6 See, for instance, Ding (1990).
7 For more on this, see Waldron (1996) and Mitter (2003).
8 For more on the Beijing museum, see Mitter (2000).
9 Zhongguo renmin kang-Ri zhanzheng jinianguan (1997a), *Jianjie* (The Memorial Museum of the Chinese People's War of Resistance to Japan, 'Introduction'); Zhongguo renmin kang-Ri zhanzheng jinianguan (1997b), *Jiangjieci* (The Memorial Museum of the Chinese People's War of Resistance to Japan, 'Explanation'); both: Beijing: Zhongguo renmin kang-Ri zhanzheng jinianguan.
10 The Memorial Museum of the Chinese People's War of Resistance to Japan (1997), *Introduction to the Exhibition of the Memorial Museum of the Chinese People's War of Resistance against Japan*, Beijing: Zhongguo renmin kang-Ri zhanzheng jinianguan.
11 Zhongguo renmin kang-Ri zhanzheng jinianguan (n.d.(a)), *Kangzhan yinglieting minglu* (The Memorial Museum of the Chinese People's War of Resistance to Japan, 'List of names in the Hall of Martyrs of the War of Resistance'), Beijing: Zhongguo renmin kang-Ri zhanzheng jinianguan.
12 Zhongguo renmin kang-Ri zhanzheng jinianguan (n.d.(b)), *Kangzhan shishang de jintian* (The Memorial Museum of the Chinese People's War of Resistance to Japan, 'Today in the history of the War of Resistance'), Beijing: Zhongguo renmin kang-Ri zhanzheng jinianguan.
13 Zhongguo renmin kang-Ri zhanzheng jinianguan (1990–), *Wencong* (The Memorial Museum of the Chinese People's War of Resistance to Japan, 'Essays'), Beijing: Zhongguo renmin kang-Ri zhanzheng jinianguan.
14 Interview with Museum staff (Shenyang, Beijing), September 2000; Mitter (2000: 291–2).
15 A stimulating account of bringing ethnic minorities (in this case Naxi and Dai) into a Chinese-driven curriculum is to be found in Hansen (1999).

References

Bailey, Paul (2001), 'Active Citizen or Efficient Housewife? The Debate over Women's Education in Early Twentieth-Century China', in Glen Peterson (ed.) *Education, Culture, and Identity in Twentieth-Century China*, Ann Arbor, MI: University of Michigan Press.
Baum, Richard (1994), *Burying Mao: Chinese Politics in the Age of Deng Xiaoping*, Princeton, NJ: Princeton University Press.
Crew, Spencer R. and James E. Sims (1991), 'Locating Authenticity: Fragments of a

Dialogue', in Ivan Karp and Steven D. Lavine (eds) *Exhibiting Cultures: The Poetics and Politics of Museum Display*, Washington, DC: Smithsonian Institution Press.

Ding, X. L. (1990), *The Decline of Communism in China*, Cambridge: Cambridge University Press.

Duncan, Carol (1991), 'Art Museums and the Ritual of Citizenship', in Ivan Karp and Steven D. Lavine (eds) *Exhibiting Cultures: The Poetics and Politics of Museum Display*, Washington, DC: Smithsonian Institution Press.

Fogel, Joshua A. (1997), 'Afterword: The People, a Citizenry, Modern China', in Joshua A. Fogel and Peter Zarrow (eds) *Imagining the People: Chinese Intellectuals and the Concept of Citizenship*, Armonk, NY: M. E. Sharpe.

Gerth, Karl (2003), *China Made: Consumer Culture and the Creation of the Nation*, Cambridge, MA: Harvard University Press.

Gluck, Carol (1985), *Japan's Modern Myths: Ideology in the Late Meiji Period*, Princeton, NJ: Princeton University Press.

Greenblatt, Stephen (1991), 'Resonance and Wonder', in Ivan Karp and Steven D. Lavine (eds) *Exhibiting Cultures: The Poetics and Politics of Museum Display*, Washington, DC: Smithsonian Institution Press.

Gurian, Elaine Heumann (1991), 'Noodling Around with Exhibition Opportunities', in Ivan Karp and Steven D. Lavine (eds) *Exhibiting Cultures: The Poetics and Politics of Museum Display*, Washington, DC: Smithsonian Institution Press.

Hamlish, Tamara (1995), 'Preserving the Palace: Museums and the Making of Nationalism(s) in Twentieth-century China', *Museum Anthropology* 19: 2, 22.

Hansen, Mette Halskov (1999), *Lessons in Being Chinese: Minority Education and Ethnic Identity in Southwest China*, Seattle: University of Washington Press.

Harrison, Henrietta (2000), *The Making of the Republican Citizen: Political Ceremonies and Symbols in China, 1911–1929*, Oxford: Oxford University Press.

He, Baogang and Yingjie Guo (2000), *Nationalism, National Identity and Democratization in China*, Aldershot: Ashgate.

Judge, Joan (1996), *Print and Politics: 'Shibao' and the Culture of Reform in Late Qing China*, Stanford, CA: Stanford University Press.

Liu, Lydia (1995), *Translingual Practice: Literature, National Culture, and Translated Modernity – China, 1900–1937*, Stanford, CA: Stanford University Press.

Memorial Museum of the Chinese People's War of Resistance to Japan (1997), *Introduction to the Exhibition of the Memorial Museum of the Chinese People's War of Resistance against Japan*, Beijing: Zhongguo renmin kang-Ri zhanzheng jinianguan.

Mitter, Rana (2000), 'Behind the Scenes at the Museum: Nationalism, History and Memory in the Beijing War of Resistance Museum', *The China Quarterly* (March): 279–93.

Mitter, Rana (2003), 'Old Ghosts, New Memories: China's New War History in the Era of Post-Mao Politics', *Journal of Contemporary History* (January): 117–31.

Pepper, Suzanne (1996), *Radicalism and Education Reform in 20th-Century China*, Cambridge: Cambridge University Press.

Thøgersen, Stig (1990), *Secondary Education in China after Mao: Reform and Social Conflict*, Aarhus: Aarhus University Press.

Unger, Jonathan (ed.) (1993), *Using the Past to Serve the Present: Historiography and Politics in Contemporary China*, Armonk, NY: M. E. Sharpe.

Waldron, Arthur (1996), 'China's New Remembering of World War II: The Case of Zhang Zizhong', *Modern Asian Studies* 30: 4, 869–99.

Zarrow, Peter (1997), 'Introduction: Citizenship in China and the West', in Joshua

A. Fogel and Peter Zarrow (eds) *Imagining the People: Chinese Intellectuals and the Concept of Citizenship*, Armonk, NY: M. E. Sharpe.

Zhang, Chengyue (1990), 'Chongfen fahui jinianguan de aiguozhuyi jiaoyu zhendi zuoyong' ['Fulfilling and giving full rein to the Memorial's position and role in patriotic education'], in Zhongguo renmin kang-Ri zhanzheng jinianguan: *Wencong* [The Memorial Museum of the Chinese People's War of Resistance to Japan, Essays], 1: 197.

Zhongguo renmin kang-Ri zhanzheng jinianguan (1990–), *Wencong* [The Memorial Museum of the Chinese People's War of Resistance to Japan, *Essays*], Beijing: Zhongguo renmin kang-Ri zhanzheng jinianguan.

Zhongguo renmin kang-Ri zhanzheng jinianguan (1997a), *Jianjie* [The Memorial Museum of the Chinese People's War of Resistance to Japan, *Introduction*], Beijing: Zhongguo renmin kang-Ri zhanzheng jinianguan.

Zhongguo renmin kang-Ri zhanzheng jinianguan (1997b), *Jiangjieci* [The Memorial Museum of the Chinese People's War of Resistance to Japan, *Explanation*], Beijing: Zhongguo renmin kang-Ri zhanzheng jinianguan.

Zhongguo renmin kang-Ri zhanzheng jinianguan (n.d.(a)), *Kangzhan yinglieting minglu* [The Memorial Museum of the Chinese People's War of Resistance to Japan, *List of Names in the Hall of Martyrs of the War of Resistance*], Beijing: Zhongguo renmin kang-Ri zhanzheng jinianguan.

Zhongguo renmin kang-Ri zhanzheng jinianguan (n.d.(b)), *Kangzhan shishang de jintian* [The Memorial Museum of the Chinese People's War of Resistance to Japan, *Today in the History of the War of Resistance*], Beijing: Zhongguo renmin kang-Ri zhanzheng jinianguan.

6 Textbooks, nationalism and history writing in India and Pakistan

Aminah Mohammad-Arif

Most states view educational systems as key channels to the manufacturing of national identity and citizenship. Schools in particular are endowed with the task of 'socializing the young into an approved national past, the approving agency being the state' (Kumar 2001: 20). Although this is also true in 'older' nation-states where education often reflects official ideology, it is especially valid in postcolonial societies, where nation-building becomes so crucial that it relegates other concerns into the background. In 'newly-formed' nation-states, the main purpose of education is arguably not to favour the intellectual development of children; it is above all to 'disseminat[e] a view of the nation's past deemed conducive to the strengthening of "national unity" or the furthering of "integration", whether in the present or the future' (Powell 1996: 190). In this process, the teaching of history, as much as its (re)writing, assumes a prominent position.

The cases of India and Pakistan are particularly illuminating in this regard. First, both are newly established nation-states. Present-day India and Pakistan came about as a result of Partition. Although both countries thereby share the same history, they have tended to adopt 'contrasting and conflicting appropriations of the past' (ibid.). After more than 50 years of independence, they still view each other with suspicion, and this affects both their relationships and their respective identity-formation processes. Second, both countries are characterized by internal diversity at various levels: ethnic, religious, sectarian, linguistic and so on. In such a context, history has become a primary tool for national integration and for the production of citizens beyond these multiple identities. However, history can also be (mis)used by governmental authorities to impose their own version of citizenship without necessarily accommodating the internal diversity of the country. This has the effect of relegating some, even large, sections of the population into the background. History then runs the risk of a rewriting whereby historical facts become distorted, falsified and/or (re)invented. In the South Asian context, such a rewriting is intricately linked to religion, which has played a prominent role in the (re)definition of citizenship since the emergence of nationalist movements in the nineteenth century. This chapter explores how history textbooks have emerged as a vital instrument of control over what gets taught and learnt in the expanding system of education.

Religion has in South Asia been considerably instrumentalized in (re)defining nationhood, especially since the emergence of nationalist move-ments in the nineteenth century. The epitome is the two-nation idea, as defended by Muhammad Ali Jinnah. Whether the 'Supreme Guide' (*Qaid-e-Azam*), who was highly anglicized, really had in mind for the future Pakistani state a citizenship based on religious identity is highly debatable. Whatever the case may be, he clearly used Islam as a rallying force to attract the support of his co-religionists in favour of the idea of a separate state for the Muslims. Subsequently, Islam played in Pakistan the role of an ideological cement, even though the question of whether Pakistan should be a country for the Muslims or a Muslim country has never really been resolved. Although the leadership of the early decades seemed to endorse the former view, from the 1970s onwards the latter conception prevailed. At any rate, Pakistan has from its very inception been grappling with the definition of its identity and the attendant implications for the meaning it wishes to give to citizenship.

One concept describes this use of religion in the subcontinent well: 'com-munalism'. Briefly, this notion refers to the elevation of religion as the main component in the definition of nationhood, and carries with it implications of the exclusion of the 'other', who is denied access to the status of (first-class) citizen. I shall however prefer the term 'communalization', which conveys the idea of a continuous process. The process of 'communalization' started in Pakistan almost from the very inception of the country, though, as was stated above, it was not so obvious in the initial years. Indeed, a blatant Islamization of Pakistani society and politics (with all its implications for the issue of citizenship) started from the late 1970s onwards. In contrast, in India, secularism – at least officially – continues to be the dominant ideo-logy. Secularism is defined in India as the equal treatment of all religions (and is thus different from the French model of strict separation between State and Church). This principle allows for the inclusion of all Indians on an equal footing in the definition of a shared citizenship, irrespective of reli-gion. This stands in stark contrast to the *hindutva* (Hinduness) concept, defining nationhood as based on religion,[1] that has been promoted by Hindu nationalists. Their growing influence has been felt in the country since the 1980s as these groups have been working towards the 'communalization' of various arenas of social and political life. In this process, education has also been considerably exploited as a resource – especially history textbooks.

In India as in Pakistan, almost all textbooks are produced by the central or the state governments – a fact that reveals the close link between the government and school history textbooks. These are the primary means through which these governments attempt to foster their own views of Indian or Pakistani history respectively. It should be added that, in both countries, textbooks are extremely influential in schools, this being largely a legacy of the British system. As Krishna Kumar (2001: 63) points out,

> the construction of official knowledge became an important aspect of the colonial enterprise once education was accepted as an administrative need and responsibility. In all subjects, including history, textbooks and examination emerged as the two vital instruments of control on what might be taught and learnt in the expanding system of education.

Since Independence, textbooks have continued to play a major role in the educational process, especially as in both countries large sections of the population are still economically deprived and the rate of illiteracy remains fairly high. Alternative sources of historical information are not easily available, and teachers themselves are often poorly trained, leaving them – as well as the children – heavily dependent on textbooks.

I shall be dealing exclusively with textbooks produced for 'regular' schools, leaving aside the issue of Islamic religious schools (*madrasas*) and of the institutions run by Hindu nationalists. I shall also restrict myself to the study of textbooks written in English. Scrutiny of the Hindi versions of the NCERT-produced textbooks reveals that they are exact translations of the English versions.[2]

The 'communalization' of education in Pakistan: between the search for roots and the quest for legitimacy

Pakistan was created in highly painful circumstances as a result of the Partition of India in 1947 into two sovereign nation-states. The Partition led to the deaths of hundreds of thousands of people and the exile of millions of others. This partly accounts for the structural preoccupation that Pakistan has had with India from the beginning. Since its creation, Pakistan has viewed India as an aggressive and hostile neighbour, seeking to establish its hegemony over the entire subcontinent. The feeling among Pakistanis – particularly the elite – that Partition is to some degree unfinished business (because of the unresolved issue of Kashmir, a highly disputed territory spreading over parts of both Pakistan and India) has further exacerbated their alienation from their neighbour and increased their fear that India will eventually take control over their young nation. These sentiments of fear and obsession have been consciously exploited and perpetuated by the government and other official civil bodies, as well as by the army in a variety of ways. Among other things, this has justified the tremendous share taken up by the defence budget in the national budget of Pakistan. Education is also one of the crucial areas that has been deliberately used by the Pakistani authorities to propagate and utilize this prevailing fear of India. This propaganda makes use of a complex interplay of forces involving Islam, nationalism and militarism (Rahman 2000: 432).

The 'communalization' of education in Pakistan started at an early stage, as part of the nation-building process. It reached its peak from 1979 onwards. Pakistan needed to justify – both nationally and internationally – the relevance and necessity of Partition, that is to say, of its very existence. This need for justification has not subsided today, given the highly volatile political situation and continuing strained relationships with India. Communalization of the Pakistani education system is twofold: it is prevalent both in the place occupied by religion in textbooks and in the way that India and Hindus are portrayed.[3]

First, it should be noted that although education in Pakistan is officially considered as a prerogative of the provinces rather than of the central government, the curriculum system has in effect been highly centralized (since at least the late 1970s), leaving very little leeway for the provinces, either in terms of the medium of instruction, or of syllabus design and textbook writing, or of anything else. The decision as to what should be taught and what should be excluded from the syllabus lies mainly with the federal government. Not only is the system of education centralized, but teachers are also totally bereft of autonomy in terms of curriculum selection and implementation (Saigol 1995). They are expected to follow strictly the goals and objectives of the curriculum as defined in the *Teachers' Guide*. As for students, they 'become passive receivers of official knowledge which is strictly controlled, packaged and transmitted from above' (Saigol 1995: 57). Very little space is left for creativity and innovation, as is testified by the relative lack of exchange in the classroom between teachers and students, the latter not being expected to challenge the authority either of the teacher or of the textbook. The system of examination also contributes to preclude any form of creativity: it requires from the students a faithful reproduction of the knowledge and facts taught throughout the school year. Hence the students are evaluated only on the basis of their memory power and not on their capacity to understand and analyse the material taught to them. This is especially true with respect to the teaching of history. '[I]nterpretation is seen as dangerous as it may vary or deviate from the official one' (Saigol 1995: 61), and a student deviating from the text is penalized. The state in this way aims at constructing its own version of a citizen, whose awareness will be so closely controlled (as in most dictatorships) that knowledge is reduced to a commodity and the citizen to a subject who is merely expected to act and react within a set and well-defined framework.[4]

The use of textbooks for the ideological consolidation of Pakistan started under the regime of General Ayub Khan, who set up an education policy in 1959, imposing the compulsory study of *Islamiyat* (Islamic studies) up to Class VIII. During the same period, the study of history as a separate subject was eliminated from the school system: history was to be included in a new subject called 'Social Studies', also comprising geography and civics. At the undergraduate level, it was diluted into another subject, called 'Pakistan

Studies'. Zulfikar Ali Bhutto took further steps, as he was very keen to align his country with the Muslim world. Pakistan had indeed been 'traumatized' by the partitioning off of its former 'East Wing' in 1971.[5] The image of Islam as the ultimate binding force in the vast mosaic characterizing the Pakistani landscape had at that time been torn to pieces. Bhutto sought the support of Muslim countries in order to reassert Pakistan's Islamic identity, which had been seriously called in question by the establishment of an independent Bangladesh. This policy reached a climax in 1974, when the summit of the Organization of the Islamic Conference was held in Pakistan. At the educational level, Bhutto implemented as early as in 1972 a new education policy, which made *Islamiyat* compulsory up to Class X, paving the way for its heightened importance in the following years. It was however under General Zia ul Haq's regime that the communalization of education reached its peak: the new National Education policy of 1979 clearly showed the State's definite shift towards Islamization. The education policy of 1979 asserts:

> The highest priority would be given to the revision of the curricula with a view to re-organizing the entire content around Islamic thought and giving education an ideological orientation so that Islamic ideology permeates the thinking of the younger generation and helps them with the necessary conviction and ability to refashion society according to Islamic tenets.
>
> (Saigol 1995: 180)

Islamiyat was imposed as a compulsory subject at all levels of the educational system (including the Civil Service Examination), while secular knowledge became islamized as much as possible. During Zia's time, even the hard sciences were so much pervaded with Islamic content that they could hardly be distinguished from *Islamiyat* (Hoodbhoy 1991, cited in Saigol 1995: 182). The Islamization of education also affected teachers, who were no longer appointed solely on the basis of their knowledge of the subject and ability to teach, but were required to know the Quran and the *Sunnah* as well. Textbooks too were thoroughly scrutinized by a committee of religious scholars endowed with the powers of removing any content conflicting with their views of Islam.

As has already been noted, the concept of 'communalization' was coined in relation to the South Asian context: the word 'communal' is specifically used in the subcontinent to refer to the conflicts of opposing religious communities, especially Hindu and Muslim. In the Pakistani context, this translates into typically negative references to India wherein Hindu culture and religion are commonly described as impure and inferior. The Hindu caste system is a particularly favoured target, which the Pakistani textbook writers contrast with Islam, portrayed as an egalitarian religion. Thus the *Social Science* book of 1987 for Class V reads:

The Hindus treated the ancient population of the Indus valley very badly. They forcibly occupied their land. They set fire to their houses and butchered them. Those who escaped were forced to become slaves. After defeating the ancient people of the sub-continent the Hindus started fighting among themselves. They got divided into castes. *They would not intermarry with others or eat with them.* The Hindus did not believe in one God but worshipped the numerous idols in their temples.[6]

Central to the 'communalization' of education in Pakistan has been the two-nation theory, expressed particularly forcefully and in a very essentialist manner during the Bhutto and Zia periods. The whole curriculum and the ideological tenets of social studies are centred around this principle (Saigol 1995: 248), as is evidenced by the following recommendations given by a *Teachers' Guide* for social studies produced in 1975 for Class IV:

Teach the children the history of the Punjab in such a way that the following facts become absolutely clear: 1) The complete difference between the way of life, customs and traditions, beliefs and culture of the Hindus and Muslims. 2) Give special emphasis to those aspects which forced the Muslims to create a separate country for themselves; here especially emphasize the economic, educational and social exploitation of the Muslims at the hands of the Hindus; the favourable and friendly attitude of the British towards Hindus as compared to Muslims; the unequal and discriminatory attitude of the Hindus towards the Muslims.

(Saigol 1995: 248)

Most textbook writers accordingly tend to hammer the idea that Hindus and Muslims have always formed two separate nations, that they were in constant conflict and that this is bound to last for ever. Hindus and Muslims are portrayed as forming an antinomic couple, with 'innate' incompatibilities, while the accommodative trends in the cultural and political fields that characterized the 'Medieval' period are either ignored or belittled. To treat them in any other way would obviously call into question the very validity of the two-nation theory. As has been aptly underlined by Rubina Saigol, a major characteristic of Pakistani textbooks is that:

the sense of history is eliminated by reifying events as natural or eternal. *Things just happened.* The cause, if any, is attributed to individuals or to the group's personality attributes rather than to social, historical, political, economic or ideological factors. Thus there are frequent statements such as 'Muslim women and children were butchered and murdered because Hindus are cruel and heartless', or 'the conquest of the Sind by Muslims occurred because Muslims are brave, valiant and strong'.

(Saigol 1995: 218–19)

The language used is very direct and crude, and replete with 'culturalist', even racist, connotations conveying an essentialization of the opposing political community through the attribution of distinct, opposed and supposedly natural features to Hindus and Muslims. During Zia's era, considerable stress was also laid on the ideology of 'indigenization', a concept that was however extremely vague, and often indistinguishable from Islamization. This indigenization-cum-Islamization policy affected education, the mass media and the judiciary. At the educational level, tremendous importance was given to the teaching of Arabic, so that the reading of the Quran could be better understood, while the revival of traditional teaching institutions, such as the *madrasas*, was also encouraged.[7]

The indigenization and Islamization policy during Zia's period not only made sure that Islamic history and Muslim characters would be given proper coverage and attention, but that non-Muslim characters would no longer be mentioned. This stood in stark contrast with Ayub Khan's era, when the State did not as yet use Islamization as a major tool to assert its ideology, and some non-Muslim historical and mythical figures were still portrayed in a positive light. For instance, figures like Ram and Buddha 'were described as being kind, gentle, just, caring, sympathetic, non-violent and full of mercy and love' (Saigol 1995: 242). Under Zia and even under Zulfikar Ali Bhutto, the mention of prophets of other religions (such as Jesus) was erased and replaced by Muslim religious and nationalistic characters. The first four caliphs of Islam, together with Muhammad bin Qasim and Mahmud of Ghazni, two major conquerors in the history of the subcontinent, took the place of these non-Muslim prophets, while Jinnah and Iqbal replaced Ram and Buddha.

Time too was Islamized, and in two ways. Minimization of the importance, or even uncritical omission, of whole portions of history was common in the 'Pakistan Studies' textbooks. In those taught at the undergraduate level, for instance, history leaps straight from Harappa to the occupation of Sind by Muhammad bin Qasim, thereby totally ignoring the Vedic, Maurya and Gupta eras. And dichotomous categories were also constructed by applying binary operators such as 'before'/'after' or 'pre-'/'post-' to the concept of the *jahiliyya* ('time of ignorance'), referring to the era preceding the coming of Islam, while the period after its advent is regarded as one of enlightenment and knowledge. A typical description of pre-Islamic society as it appeared in a textbook for Class VII produced during the Zia period (1983) reads as follows:

> Prior to the advent of Islam peoples of the world were in a bad state. The rulers were permanently engaged in pleasurable pursuits. Superstition and ignorance were everywhere. Goddesses and Gods were worshipped.
>
> (Saigol 1995: 223)

Space was also refashioned in order to elicit identification with the Muslim world, in keeping with the policy initiated by Z. A. Bhutto of 'reorienting' Pakistan towards the Middle East. The headings in the Class VII Geography textbook are very illuminating in this regard: 'Mountains of the Muslim World', 'the resources of the Muslim World', 'the seas of the Muslim World' and so on. They are aimed at ingraining in the minds of children the idea that they belong to a highly transnational Muslim world, although this notion is in fact fictional, as there is no such entity. The idea of the Muslim *umma* is stressed, presenting all Muslims as united, regardless of territory, culture, language and so on (Saigol 1995: 220). Furthermore, communalization of space is visible through the constant rhetoric of architectural opposition between the mosque and the temple, this referring more directly to the willingness to mark differentiation from the Hindus. The textbook for Social Studies produced in 1988 for Class V states:

> Muslims and Hindus are completely different in their way of life, eating habits and dress. We worship in mosques, open, spacious, clean and well-lit. Hindus worship inside their temples, narrow, enclosed and dark.[8]

The above examples thus show how the Pakistani State has used education to legitimize and root the two-nation concept firmly in people's – and more particularly children's – minds. The military occupied a privileged place in this process, as a major instrument, across time and space, in the construction of the national memory and the manufacturing of citizenship, as was underlined by Etienne Balibar (2001).

In Pakistan, the army has always played a major role in politics – seizing power whenever given the opportunity – and has been in great need of legitimacy. This was especially true after 1971, since the country had not only been 'amputated' but had lost a war against India, whose intervention had proved decisive in helping the Bengalis achieve their independence from West Pakistan. Islamization was one of the major tools used by the military to (re)gain legitimacy and reassert that only Islam could be the binding force in ensuring the unity of Pakistan and in creating citizens who would remain 'loyal' enough not to further undermine the (fragile) national fabric of the country. Congruent with Islamization was the attempt to inculcate in Pakistani citizens the idea that India is the eternal enemy. Textbooks also reflected the importance thus assigned to the army through constant glorification of the military and frequent references to wars, with abundant images of warships, combat aircraft and so on. The several references to the 1965 war against India in particular are interesting, since this conflict had no clear winner. Because Pakistan took the initiative in the war and inflicted severe losses on the Indian Air Force, this conflict was presented in the textbooks as a victory for Pakistan. But in reality the Indian forces were not beaten, as they had crossed the international border and started marching towards

Lahore when the United Nations imposed a ceasefire, under pressure from the 'great powers'.

Other concepts related to the issue of war and the conflictual relations with India pervade Pakistani textbooks: the making of heroes and villains on the one hand, the rhetoric of conspiracy and of treachery on the other. The heroes are typically Muslim conquerors (like Muhammad bin Qasim, the archetypal warrior and martyr) and war heroes, or 'national' figures like Jinnah. As for the villains, they are not only 'Hindu' figures (Shivaji,[9] Nehru, Gandhi) but 'Muslim' traitors as well. In this regard, the example of Mir Jaffer[10] is particularly interesting, in that he is perhaps the only figure about whom both Indians and Pakistanis agree: he is regarded as the archetypical traitor and a villain on either side of the border. But the concept of the traitor is above all used by the Pakistani State to discredit anyone who disagrees with its policies or belongs to minority communities. The definition of citizenship has indeed a very restricted meaning, since a 'good' citizen is necessarily a Muslim. This raises the issue of the status of religious minorities in Pakistan, who are increasingly considered as second-class citizens, notably under the pressure of religious organizations such as the Jama'at-i Islami and the Jamiat-i-Ulama-i-Islam, which have played a growing role in Pakistani political life and the public sphere. This has been the case since the creation of the country, as 'Muslim' has tended to refer to a 'national' group as much as (if not more than) to a 'religious' group; but, the process of denying non-Muslims the right to be first-class citizens has become even more blatant since the policy of Islamization was implemented.

Although Muslims are commonly represented as heroes (as opposed to the 'villainous' Hindus), they can also be represented as victims in the same textbooks: the State can in effect use both notions in its construction of Pakistani citizenship, this being itself reminiscent of Islamic history, where both heroes and victims (seen as martyrs) are celebrated. The use of heroes enables the State to stress its might; that of victims helps it to designate the 'Other' (India) as the ultimate 'villain', this in turn justifying once more the need for Partition and the necessity to create Pakistan. This portrayal of Muslims as victims is particularly perceptible in the way the riots following Partition are presented: they are systematically initiated by Hindus and Sikhs, whereas Muslims are mere helpless victims. The following passage from *Pakistan Studies* (1982) for undergraduate students, describing the killings during Partition, speaks for itself:

> The Hindus and the Sikhs accelerated their pace for Muslim mass killing. So, when Pakistan emerged on the map of the world, communal riots were on the increase: Religion was employed to justify the raging storm of resentment and hatred and to stimulate and glorify the atrocities against the followers of Islam. The pulpit, the press, the temple and the gurudwara, all assaulted with gold and employed to export their followers to expiate their sins by the massacre of Muslims.
>
> (Zafar 1982: 221)

The Zia era ended in the late 1980s, but since then the curriculum has not undergone any drastic modifications or updating, not even after democratic regimes came into power. The negative references to India in particular have remained unchanged. The two-nation theory and the depiction of India as the eternal enemy still constitute the essence of Pakistan's social studies curriculum.[11] This confirms that almost from the beginning to the present day the Pakistani government has looked at textbooks 'as an official propaganda machinery rather than as a means of education' (Aziz 1993: 189), the ultimate aim being the reinforcement of Pakistani nationalism and the manufacturing of a Pakistani identity and citizenship.

As now appears obvious, the textbooks do not inculcate in children respect and tolerance for other faiths. Consequently, the textbooks have made it difficult for children to consider their Indian neighbours rationally. But neither do these textbooks promote pluralism within Pakistan. The country's cultural diversity, far from being considered as enriching, is denounced for being divisive. By failing to infuse tolerance of 'others', the writers of these textbooks have also sown the seeds of the violence that now mars Pakistani society,[12] as can be seen from the violent riots opposing different sectarian groups – Sunnis and Shi'as in particular – and from the attacks against minorities such as the Christians. In present-day Pakistan, even the very definition of 'Muslim' has grown increasingly narrow (Mohammad-Arif 2000: 398).

The communalization of education in India: towards the manufacturing of a 'Hindu' citizen?

The official discourse in India has for a long time favoured the promotion of secularism, one of the founding principles inscribed in the Indian constitution. This secularist policy is reflected in textbooks. As early as in the 1950s, the Indian government headed by the Congress Party was concerned with the influence of religious ideas on the educational system. These ideas were partly a legacy of nineteenth-century colonial historiography, which divided India's past between different 'religious' periods and created stereotypes about various communities (the 'weak' Hindus, the 'violent' Muslims and so on). The National Council of Educational Research and Training (NCERT) was created in 1961 to advise and assist the Ministry of Education in the formulation and implementation of policies in school education. This body released the first series of school textbooks combating communal distortions in the teaching of Indian history (A. Dev 2001: 137–54).

India being a federal state, however, textbooks can be produced both at the central and regional state levels. Edward Vernoff remarks that the central government (especially the leadership of the Congress Party) was not strong enough to prevent regional states from producing their own textbooks. This explains why their contents may vary considerably from the books produced by the NCERT, as well as from one another. At the central level, it is the NCERT that has been entrusted with this task. The NCERT books, which usually represent the views of the Indian government, are used in government schools in New Delhi and in all federally controlled territories, as well as in English-medium 'public' schools and the elite among the state-run schools. At the regional level, textbooks are produced by local bodies. In some states, for instance West Bengal, they can also be privately produced; but they have to conform to the state syllabus. Theoretically, then, 'the Indian system allows for a maximum amount of conflict about the historical legacy of India, each state and the central government being permitted to present its own view of history to Indian students' (Vernoff 1992: 13).

The comparison drawn by Edward Vernoff between the different history textbooks that are produced by the central government on the one hand, and by some state governments, including Maharashtra, Gujarat, West Bengal, Andhra Pradesh, Kerala and Tamil Nadu, on the other reveals interesting findings (ibid.). Analysing the major eras of Indian history that have been the most hotly debated (i.e. notably the Aryan-Dravidian, 'Turkish-Mughal' and colonial periods), the author notes that the texts from these books do not completely represent the views of any one national political party or historical school. Rather, they seem to reflect the particular history and politics of the state where they have been produced. Furthermore, Vernoff identifies the different ways of determining whether a book is communally oriented or not, and concludes on the existence of significant variations across the regional states and the federally administered regions. The textbooks produced (at least until very recently) by the NCERT and by the state of Tamil Nadu are the most secular in their orientation, while the textbooks used in Gujarat are among the most communal.

That the textbooks produced until recently by the NCERT and by the Tamil Nadu government are the least communal is not surprising. Before the recent changes, the political orientation of the NCERT series was modernist and progressive, and aimed at promoting secularism. Scholars at the NCERT were very well-known secular and often leftist historians like Romila Thapar, Satish Chandra, Arjun Dev and Indira Dev, all eager to insist on India's composite past and tradition in order to legitimize the creation of a secular polity and society. Thus the foreword of the NCERT textbook, *Medieval India*, for Class XI stated:

> Promoting an understanding of India's cultural heritage, combating superstition and obscurantism, and fostering a secular, humane and forward-looking outlook are among the major objectives of education which are also the basic objectives of teaching history.[13]

As for Tamil Nadu, apart from the fact that very few Muslims live in this state, it should be kept in mind that politics there has been strongly influenced by the Dravidian movement, for which the conflict between Hindus and Muslims was simply irrelevant. Before Independence, there was even a close relationship between the Dravidian movement and the Muslim League.

Nor is it surprising that the textbooks produced in Gujarat are the least secular given the heavily communal history of this state. As Vernoff underlines, the nationalist movement in Gujarat had been pervaded by Hindu communalism as early as the end of the nineteenth century, when the interpretation of Shivaji as a national leader and a Hindu hero began to be widely accepted.[14] The fact that Gujarat is one of the most prosperous and business-oriented states may be an additional reason: tensions between Hindus and Muslims frequently occur in such places where there is fierce economic competition between the two communities. Others also point out the absence of progressive movements and of a modern intellectual and cultural elite.[15] At any rate, Gujarat has been known at least since the end of the 1960s as a region where the worst communal violence has taken place. The riots that shook several parts of the state in 2002 are the latest (and most tragic) example of a long series.[16] Furthermore, Gujarat has been transformed into a social laboratory by Hindu nationalists who have for years been conducting experiments in communalization and in social polarization along religious lines there. This is particularly visible in the way they have infiltrated all the major official bodies with RSS[17] elements and/or sympathizers and have eliminated Muslims from the State apparatus. The local government, led by the Hindu nationalists since 1998, has in addition taken some measures that violate the Indian constitution, targeting minority communities: the organization of a selective census specially directed at Christians and Muslims in Gujarat, instructions to the state police to investigate every case of inter-religious marriage, and so on (Setalvad 2001). Last but not least, Hindu nationalists have also pursued a very systematic policy (mainly through education and social work) of spreading their hate-ideology in rural areas, in particular among Dalits (untouchables) and tribals. This policy has apparently yielded the 'expected' results, as some members of these communities actively participated in the ghastly riots of 2002.

Indian history textbooks (except perhaps those of the NCERT series) share with the Pakistani textbooks the similarity of heavily focusing on particular characters who are either venerated as icons or reviled as villains. The example of the Mughal emperor, Aurangzeb, is particularly interesting, in that he is probably the character who has been the most hijacked and instrumentalized by communalists from all sides, whether Hindu or Muslim. He has thereby become one of the most 'communalized' rulers. Hindus tend to portray him as a ruthless anti-Hindu emperor, while many Muslims see in him a champion of Islam. Because of these contrasting images, the true character of a secular textbook is discernible through analysis of how Aurangzeb is depicted. As Nita Kumar points out (1999: 145), almost all Indian textbooks regard Aurangzeb as the most fanatical of the Muslim rulers, and the mention of the destruction of any temple by him is bound to be taken as a highly credible fact that is not even worth questioning. Here is an example of the way in which Aurangzeb's religious policy is described in the Class XI textbook, *A New Textbook of History of India*, by D. N. and S. D. Kundra. The presentation of the policy is followed by a list of some 'points to remember':

> 1) The construction of new temples was forbidden; 2) the old temples were demolished; 3) mosques were built at their sites; 4) cows were slaughtered in some temples; 5) opening of new schools was prohibited; 6) *Jaziya* (that is the tax to be paid by non-Muslims that Akbar had abolished) was reimposed in 1679; 7) pilgrims tax was also reimposed; 8) several other obnoxious and illegal taxes were imposed on the Hindus; 9) celebration of Hindu festivals was banned; 10) no government service for Hindus; 11) right of equality was denied to the Hindus; 12) employment of force for winning new converts.
>
> (Kundra and Kundra 1987: 99)

Interestingly enough, in the textbook produced by the NCERT for Class XI[18] (before the current revision policy), Aurangzeb is presented in quite a different light. It goes without saying that the author, Satish Chandra, does not praise Aurangzeb. But he presents a long development of several pages that takes into account the recent writings on Aurangzeb, assessing 'his political and religious policies in the context of social, economic and institutional developments' (Chandra 2001 [1990]: 229). Chandra's attempt at qualifying Aurangzeb's policies can be gauged from the following passage:

> Aurangzeb took a number of measures which have been called puritanical, but many of which were really of an economic and social character, and against superstitious beliefs. Thus, he forbade singing in the court and the official musicians were pensioned off. Instrumental music and *naubat* (the royal band) were, however, continued. It is of some interest to note, as has been mentioned before, that the largest number of Persian works on classical Indian music were written in Aurangzeb's reign and that Aurangzeb himself was proficient in playing the *veena*. Thus the jibe of Aurangzeb to the protesting musicians that they should bury the bier of music they were carrying deep under the earth so 'that no echo of it may rise again' was only an angry remark.
>
> (Chandra 2001 [1990]: 229–30)

In the case of the textbook by D. N. and S. D. Kundra, the 'communal' presentation of Aurangzeb is not necessarily deliberate; but the lack of nuances gives it such a flavour. Generally speaking, notwithstanding the state of Gujarat, where textbooks seem to have 'consciously' accommodated Hindu nationalist ideology for a long time, the existence of communal notions in a large body of textbooks in India has not been until very recently a result of any conscious policy at the central or regional government levels.

156 *Aminah Mohammad-Arif*

This overall secular orientation of the curriculum in India has been jeopardized over the last few years. This phenomenon has become known in India as the 'saffronization' of education, saffron being the colour representing 'militant' Hinduism. Not that this phenomenon is entirely new: a major assault on curriculum policy in history had already occurred during the Janata coalition government in 1977–9, in which the Jan Sangh (the party then representing Hindu nationalists) participated. The attack was at the time quickly defeated, especially since the government itself was short-lived. But the Hindu nationalists had learned the lesson that to carry out their communal programme they must take over all the academic professional bodies controlled by the government. Consequently, since they came back to power in 1999 they have been infiltrating several such major institutions: the Indian Council of Historical Research (ICHR), the Archaeological Survey of India (ASI), the Indian Council for Social Science Research (ICSSR), the Indian Institute of Advanced Studies (IIAS) and so on. This means that even if the Hindu nationalist BJP (Bharatiya Janata Party) currently in power loses the next elections, it will take a long time to reverse the process they have initiated.[19]

The NCERT too has been under vigorous assault: all the leading figures, among them the Director himself, have been replaced by the Hindu nationalists' followers or sympathizers. This was followed in November 2000 by the release of a new National Curriculum Framework (NCF), which was not debated by the Parliament at all, nor by the Central Advisory Board of Education (CABE), which includes among its members the Education Ministers of all States and Union Territories. The new Curriculum Framework, which has therefore not been subjected to any concerted scrutiny, abolishes the teaching of social science subjects up to Class X, replacing them with a course comprising themes drawn from geography, history, civics, economics and sociology. This means that the very teaching of history as a separate subject is now at stake. The NCF also advocates a revision of the existing history textbooks. As a result, the textbooks written by the previous NCERT historians are now being targeted, the reason given being that it is necessary to remove the 'leftist bias' in education policy. New textbooks are now under preparation, a couple of which have already been released in October 2002.

The new policy will lay greater emphasis on religion as a major source of values and on the teaching of religion. The 'unique contributions' of Hindu civilization will also be stressed. As early as 1998, Murli Manohar Joshi, the Minister of Education, who also happens to be one of the hardliners of the BJP, had declared that he was aiming at 'the Indianization, Nationalization, Spiritualization' of school education. In order to achieve this, his goal is to reduce the influence of the 'three Ms', Macaulay (the British figure emblematic of the anglicization of Indian elites), Marx (many of the former historians at the NCERT are leftists) and *Madrasa* (this being both a way of targeting Muslims by insinuating that all *madrasas* breed fundamentalists[20] and of accusing the former NCERT historians of being too 'lenient' with this minority group). Muslims, who represent the largest religious minority in India and who ruled the country for centuries, have also been the prime targets of Hindu nationalists. The latter have developed – in relation to them and to other minorities – a sentiment that has been defined, notably by Christophe Jaffrelot (1996), as the 'minority complex of the majority'. Such a complex is based on the belief that because minorities are being so 'pampered' by the (secular) government, their fertility rate (that of Muslims in particular) is higher than that of Hindus, and their religion promotes proselytism they will eventually overwhelm the Hindu majority. Hindu nationalists have taken advantage in many areas of the public sphere of this feeling of vulnerability that has overtaken many Hindus since the 1980s. This feeling is also largely conveyed by some textbooks at the regional level, notably those produced by the Gujarat Board. Thus in the Class XI *Social Studies* textbook, a chapter titled, 'Problems of the Country and their Solutions' reads thus:

> But apart from the Muslims, even the Christians, Parsees and other foreigners are also recognized as the minority communities. In most of the states the Hindus are in minority and Muslims, Christians and Sikhs are in majority in these respective states [the list of the states is not provided].
>
> (SAHMAT 2001: 125)

The concern of secularists in India is that the 'reformed curriculum' will resemble the texts taught in the RSS-run schools, the *Shishu Mandirs*, or those that have already been revised in the BJP-ruled states. The RSS textbooks teach children that: Aryans are the original inhabitants of India, Indian civilization is essentially Aryan civilization, the ancient period of history when Hindu kings ruled was golden and India made enormous advances during this period. The coming of the Muslims brought darkness, cruelty and backward social practices, and the Mughal kings were cruel tyrants who destroyed the already existing Indian nation. Muslims as a community are traitors, primarily responsible for Partition. Hinduism is synonymous with nationalism. In addition the national movement is one unending struggle of the Hindus against Muslim power and then British power in alliance with the Muslims, continuing into the post-independence period, with the *kar sevaks* presented as heroes in an uninterrupted line of freedom fighters. Muslims, Christians and Parsis are called foreigners, Urdu is referred to as a foreign language, and it is claimed that the first man on earth was born in India (Taneja 2001: 13–14).

So-called 'saffronization' has already taken place in the states where the BJP holds or has held power. Already in the early 1990s, textbooks produced and approved by regional states showed a lack of concern for historical facts.[21] More recently, the NCERT history textbooks have not been spared either. In October 2001, portions of some textbooks were removed without the authors being consulted. Ironically, the deleted passages were said to be offensive to people's religious beliefs. In reality, they contradicted Hindu nationalist ideology, as is shown by the three following examples. The first deleted passage pertains to the eating of beef by Brahmins in ancient India, the second to the role of Brahmanical indoctrination to sustain the caste system, and the third to the use of archaeological evidence instead of sacred texts to historicize the legends of Ram and Krishna:

> For special guests, beef was served as a mark of honour [although in later centuries, Brahmans were forbidden from eating beef]. A man's life was valued as equal to that of a hundred cows. If a man killed another man, he had to give 100 cows to the family of the dead man as a punishment.
> (Romila Thapar, *Ancient India*, NCERT Textbook for Class VI, 2001 [1987])

> The rigid bind of the caste system which started out as a division of labour but was then 'made hereditary by law and religion'. The lower castes worked and toiled in the belief that they 'would deserve a better life in the next world or birth'. What was done by slaves and other producing sections in Greece and Rome under the threat of whip was done by *vaishyas* and *shudras* out of conviction formed through Brahmanical indoctrination and the *varna* system.
> (R. S. Sharma, *Ancient India*, NCERT Textbook for Class XI, 2000 [1999])

> Archaeological evidence should be considered far more important than long family trees in the *Puranas* [Hindu scriptures]. The Puranic tradition could be used to date Rama of Ayodhya around 2000 BC, but extensive excavations in Ayodhya do not show any settlements around that date. Similarly, although Lord Krishna plays an important role in the *Mahabharat*, the earliest inscriptions and sculpture piece found in Mathura between 200 BC and AD 300 do not attest his presence.
> (R. S. Sharma, *Ancient India*, NCERT Textbook for Class IX, 2000 [1999])

The idea that beef could have been eaten by Brahmins in Ancient India is unacceptable to Hindu nationalists, who have elevated the cow[22] to one of the most sacred symbols of Hinduism (this belief is shared by most Hindus). Furthermore, this animal serves in anti-Muslim rhetoric, in which Muslims are accused of sacrificing it on the occasion of *Eid-ul Adha* (the major Muslim festival commemorating the sacrifice of Abraham). It should also be noted that the deletion of this passage, as well as that of the second one, support the views of those who consider the current policy of the BJP as one not only of 'saffronization' but of 'brahmanization' as well. Communal issues are not the only ones at stake here; so are caste issues. Hindu nationalists are mainly upper-caste Hindus and, as such, they represent the interests of those very segments. Thus, in Gujarat, Sanskrit has been made compulsory for the students of Classes X to XII, and the BJP aims at extending this policy to other states. This could well have social implications, since it will give a definite advantage to the upper castes. The third deletion is also interesting, in that this passage completely calls into question the legitimacy of the movement initiated by the BJP in the early 1990s that led to the destruction of the Babri mosque in Ayodhya. The movement was indeed based on the allegation that this mosque had been built (by the Mughal emperor Babur) on the birthplace of the God Ram.

Some of the deleted passages concern religious minorities as well, Sikhs in particular. But because they were announced just a few weeks before the elections in Punjab and Uttar Pradesh it was difficult not to see in them an attempt to attract votes by claiming to protect religious and caste sentiments. More importantly, as is underlined by Mridula Mukherjee and Aditya Mukherjee (2002), 'the larger purpose is clearly to create doubts about the textbooks in people's minds by making allegations that they violate the religious sentiments of different communities, and this diverts attention from the real motive, that is to replace secular history with communal history'.

The first series of revised textbooks has recently been published: *India and the World* (for Class VI) and *Contemporary India* (for Class IX). Although these books have not been radically rewritten, they show a worrying bias coupled with a lack of interest in historical accuracy. Blatant factual errors, such as 'English east India company was established *in India* [*sic*]',[23] or 'Madagascar, an island *in the Arabian Sea* [*sic*]', although they are only the tip of the iceberg, raise doubts about the competence of the authors, who seem to have been selected only on the basis of their close links with Hindu nationalists. In addition to pointing out these errors, qualified Indian historians have raised major objections about chronological and normative issues of special import to the rewriting of a particular kind of history. For instance, the renaming of the Indus Valley civilization as the 'Indus–Saraswati civilization' suggests that the Indus civilization was part of the Vedic civilization, while in reality the latter came much later. Statements such as 'Vedas prescribe a penalty of death or expulsion from the kingdom to those who kill or injure cows' mislead the reader into thinking that the Vedas were normative texts prescribing punishments, which clearly they are not.[24] All these statements are part of attempts by Hindu nationalists to give Indian history a slant towards an exclusively indigenous Hindu Ancient Age.

It is noteworthy that such attempts are also made in respect of more recent historical events. Thus in *Contemporary India* Gandhi's assassination is not mentioned anywhere, presumably because the assassin was a Hindu nationalist. Nevertheless, this particular omission aroused so many protests in India that it is likely to be rectified soon.

These may not be sweeping changes. Yet they raise an alarm as to the extent to which the *hindutva* programme can be further carried out, especially as new subjects of doubtful scientific value (such as Vedic Mathematics, astrology, yoga and consciousness) are to be introduced in some universities, as part of the 'indigenization' of education. This policy conforms to the utopian lines of the past that Hindu nationalists have constructed. It highlights their attempts to portray a Golden Age of Aryan civilization (with the subsequent insinuation that Muslims are uncreative and unoriginal), coupled with an emphasis on the 'unique' contributions of Hindu civilization and glorifying the Vedic period as the era of 'true' Indian culture (as can be seen from the above quotations). If the wealth of knowledge accumulated by India over the centuries cannot be denied, what is an issue for secularists is the lack of space devoted to the contributions of other civilizations in the *hindutva* rhetoric.

The BJP also intends to introduce compulsory 'value education' in all educational institutions. The notion of 'value education', implying ethical education based on Hindu values, is another illustration of the religion-based citizenship and nationhood that the Hindu nationalists are eager to promote. Value education already existed before, but was focused primarily on 'secular' values (honesty, tolerance, compassion and so on). In the *hindutva* rhetoric, this term now essentially refers to Hindu religious instruction.

More generally, Hindu nationalists have started communalizing history by increasingly projecting an image of ancient India as the essential embodiment of Hindu identity and of the history of the nation (defined as several millennia old) as the story of the struggle between Hindus and the 'others'. This is reminiscent of the process taking place in Pakistan. This rewriting of history aims at refashioning collective identity and the very meaning of Indian identity. The goal is essentially oriented towards the redefinition of the nation in Hindu terms. Understanding the past is relegated to the background, Hindu nationalists projecting above all the fabrication of a (new) citizen, whose identity will be based (exclusively) on Hindu religion. Consequently, this 'religious interpretation of the past establishes the right of the nation to the Hindus' (Panikkar 2001). Ironically, as several Indian historians point out,[25] the historiography embraced by the RSS, in complete contradiction to the whole discourse about Indianization (*Bharatiyakaran*), is essentially colonial in so far as it fully endorses James Mill's division of Indian history into a sequence of Hindu, Muslim and British periods.

The whole issue of the communalization of education raises an important question in relation to the central and regional governments with respect to citizenship. Indeed, communalization has implications for regional identities. The various states' very existence challenges the Hindu nationalist claim that there could be one single homogeneous 'Indian' identity by highlighting one of the main features of Indian society, namely its multicultural-ism and composite traditions. The cultures, languages and religions preval-ent in regional states may vary considerably from the 'mainstream' culture. They may also differ greatly from one state and/or region to another. But if these local variations were no longer respected, the very principle of federal-ism could be at stake, the (already) delicate balance maintained between centre and regions would be jeopardized, and this would in return create resentment. This is already the case in Punjabi-dominated Pakistan, where not much space is allowed for regional variation (neither in education nor in most other fields). This in turn provokes periodic resentment, occasionally translated into political unrest (in Sind and Baluchistan in particular, not to mention the 'extreme' case of the former 'East Pakistan'). Interestingly, in India, while the centrally produced history textbooks (by the NCERT) used to be more secularly oriented than those at the regional level, the pressure in favour of a secular education is now coming from the regional states. Thus, in August 2001 the governments of nine states (namely Delhi, West Bengal, Bihar, Rajasthan, Madhya Pradesh, Nagaland, Karnataka, Pondicherry and Chhattisgarh) signed a statement rejecting the National Curriculum Framework, arguing that it was a 'blueprint for lowering the quality of school education and giving it a narrow exclusivist, sectarian and obscurantist orientation'.[26] This reaction of the local governments, which at any rate enables us to qualify the real impact of the *hindutva* policies on the education system, reflects their concern that their local identities might be threatened by these attempts to homogenize culture and education.

Also not without its implications in terms of citizenship is the role played in the communalization of the Indian public sphere by the diaspora. The Indian (Hindu) expatriates, especially those living in the US, tend to be rather influenced by the discourse of Hindu nationalists. Migration and set-tlement in a foreign land usually go together with an enhanced sense of one's own identity. Migration thus engenders an exacerbation of nationalist feeling, a 'long-distance' nationalism as defined by Benedict Anderson (1998). This explains why many of the so-called 'Non-Resident Indians' (NRIs) support and heavily finance the Sangh Parivar, although they may have become citizens of another country. Ironically, the Hindu nationalists in India are not hostile to the idea of granting dual citizenship to the Indian expatriates, whereas all previous governments (under the Congress Party in particular) were opposed to it. In January 2003 a further step was taken in this direction by the present government, which has undertaken to grant dual citizenship to NRIs and PIOs (People of Indian Origin) living in a number of countries (the US, the UK, Australia and New Zealand). This somewhat paradoxical position can be explained by Hindu nationalists' awareness of the influence their politico-cultural programme has on the Indian diaspora, as well as their readiness to take advantage of it. But more fundamentally, this is primarily revealing of the way Hindu nationalists define the nation: all the communities who live within the boundaries of

India are not necessarily part of the nation (Muslims and Christians in particular are excluded from it), whereas all Hindus, whatever their actual nationality or their actual place of birth or residence, are *ipso facto* included in this definition. Interestingly, in such a conception, they form a pan-Hindu community rather similar to that of the Islamic *umma* (Bénéï 1998). Indian expatriates, thanks to globalization and the explosion in the means of communication (the Internet in particular), are in constant touch with their home society and try to some extent to exert an influence on it. This has repercussions too in the field of education. Indian expatriates, as is under-lined by Romila Thapar, show a curious dichotomy in their behaviour: on the one hand they hold highly technical jobs (notably in computer science), but on the other they propagate the most obscurantist views about Indian society and culture, as shown in their publications and websites. Some of the weirdest theories about India's past emanate from Indian computer scientists and astro-physicists working in the United States. These people often repre-sent a role model for the Indian middle classes, and their high qualifications in science give their views legitimacy.[27]

Concluding remarks: a comparison between India and Pakistan

Although India and Pakistan have followed different paths since Independ-ence – India being a democratic country, while Pakistan has had to undergo decades of military rule in its short history – the similarities both in the shortcomings of their respective systems of education and in the ways educa-tion is increasingly becoming 'communalized' are fairly striking.

Some common points could already be noted before the new policy of communalization in India was implemented. Both countries have consider-ably neglected education in general, and the teaching of history in particu-lar, giving it a very low priority. Only a handful of children educated in the elite English-medium schools are given proper teaching beyond factual details, in both India and Pakistan, although the gap between both systems of schooling is apparently wider in Pakistan. Furthermore, in both cases too, textbooks have a strong hold over the system, this being a heritage of the colonial period. Both countries have perpetuated the importance of text-books as the only reliable pedagogical tool after Independence. The con-tentious issues over history textbooks are however different: in India they are centred on the opposition between secularism and communalism, while in Pakistan they focus on the meaning of 'Pakistan ideology' (K. Kumar 2001: 243). This notwithstanding, the methods of teaching are rather similar, especially in non-elite schools: children are requested to learn by rote and rarely encouraged to develop a critical mind or to take an interest in the past. By the same token, most educational institutions in India and Pakistan avoid dealing with issues of current concern, and do not favour any creative discussion, in particular of conflict, or of situations that may generate passionate debates within the classroom. This is supposed to make the task of teaching easier, so that teachers will not have to face 'embarrassing' questions that they cannot answer and that thereby undermine their authority (Kumar 1996).

This obviously raises questions regarding the manufacturing of national identity and citizenship. If children are merely passive receivers of knowledge and information, and if the task of encouraging them to develop a critical mind conducive to curiosity and willingness to shape their own future is evaded, then we may wonder what type of citizens are being manufactured. Can they really be defined as 'citizens'? Or are they educated so as to become mere 'subjects'? It is the latter that is to be feared, since history teaching serves in both countries as a means of ideological indoctrination. The ultimate aim is not to inculcate into students the abilities to develop a critical mind but to instil in them 'a sense of pride in their Indian or Pakistani citizenship'. This is all the more manifest as the concept of freedom in both countries is 'an unfinished or ongoing narrative' (Kumar 2001: 29–30). On both sides, the citizen is moulded in sharp contrast to the other, while the very representation of the other is built in both cases on enmity to such an extent that 'by the time a child becomes a young citizen, he or she is expected to share the inimical mindset that characterizes political relations between the two countries' (2001: 8). The process, however, is an especially delicate one, as the histories and even the societies of both countries are not in reality all that distinct. This also implies that 'each country presents a strong case of dependence on the other for defining itself', as is rightly argued by Krishna Kumar (2001: 32–3).

The tendency to use textbooks for ideological consolidation probably appears stronger in Pakistan, which is particularly preoccupied with the task of state-building owing to the historical circumstances we have already reviewed. In comparison, the identity-building process in India has been less intricate (as the country did not have to be built 'from scratch' and did not undergo more than a single Partition, by contrast with Pakistan). However, in India too, the Education authorities have tended to use education as a propaganda tool serving the purpose of nation-building. This was particularly manifest in the wakes of the 1962 war against China (which India lost) and the 1965 war against Pakistan (whose outcome was ambiguous), as both had shaken the country politically (Kumar 2001: 50).

Another striking common point between the Indian and Pakistani syllabuses is that Pakistan, as a subject of study, is 'taboo' in Indian schools, and the same is observed about India in Pakistani schools. History textbooks in India do not cover the period after 1947, which means that Pakistan is not mentioned after this date; while in Pakistan the syllabus does tackle the post-independence period, but India is mentioned only in reference to the Indo–Pak wars (the last occurring in 1971). This implies that although children of both countries are much aware of the 'other', they hardly hear about one another at school (Kumar 2001: 237). Whenever the 'others' are mentioned in textbooks, they are located in the past and/or in a conflictual context, but never in their contemporary situation, life or culture. Similarly, at the university and academic levels, there are only a very few specialists on Pakistan in India, and even fewer specialists on India in Pakistan. Not only do people in both countries assume that they know the 'other', but the mutual stereotypes acquire such dimensions that they prevent either side seriously trying to develop a deeper knowledge of the other (2001: 3–4). This ultimately raises questions regarding the autonomy of the subject in the subcontinent, as the 'weight' of the (near) past, or at least what is perceived as such, as well as the policies conducted by the two states, prevents individuals' taking the initiative in adopting a more distanced viewpoint and overcoming these stereotypes.

With the ongoing changes made by Hindu nationalists with regard to educational policies, the similarities between both countries have become even more blatant. Just like the Pakistani one, the new educational policy of the BJP promotes the glorification and idealization of the past: each side invents its own Golden Age and constructs the past accordingly. Mythology becomes more important than knowledge, and history is considered through the prism of religion. A confusion is created between science and religion: science is 'Hinduized' in the one case, and 'Islamized' in the other, both sides trying to prove that their own religion has been the most innovative and creative.

Related to this there is in both cases an insistence on the concept of 'indigenization', whose definition remains both obscure and equivocal. In the case of Pakistan in particular, this notion is nebulous given the fact that Pakistan is a newly born nation-state that came into being partly as a result of massive transfers of populations. If 'indigenous' usually means 'opposed to the values and techniques brought by the imperial powers in postcolonial societies', its meaning is also defined in Pakistan in opposition to secularism, as there seems to be a confusion between 'indigenous' and 'Islamic'. Given the history of the creation of Pakistan and the animosity characterizing its relationships with its Indian neighbour, 'indigenous' has increasingly been defined in opposition to 'Indians' and 'Hindus' as well. But in order to promote 'Islamization' and 'indigenization' as defining principles of nationhood, the State has used a concept, that of the *umma*, that goes well beyond the strict borders of the nation-state. This stresses the difficulties of Pakistan both in finding its place on the geopolitical scene and, as already stated before, in defining its identity. If India has not necessarily gone through the same difficulties, the policies of the Hindu nationalists offer striking similarities in the way they view 'indigenization'. This seems to be exactly the other side of the mirror: 'indigenization' is defined not only in opposition to the colonial past of the country but in contrast to its 'Islamic past' as well. Furthermore, although there is no concept of the *umma* in Hinduism, the Hindu nationalists too can extend their vision of the nation beyond the strict borders of the country: they willingly include in their definition the

Hindu expatriates, incorporating even those who lost their Indian citizenship and/or who were born outside India. Associated with indigenization is the trend to eliminate diversity and promote instead homogeneity, thereby endangering the composite culture prevalent in both societies.

Hatred against minorities is equally promoted (riots for instance are always presented as initiated by the 'others'), as is the simplistic opposition between 'heroes' and 'villains'.[28] Hindu/Muslim stereotypes become dominant, and are expressed in a very 'Huntingtonian' style. In this type of rhetoric, the notion of conspiracy and the problematic of the traitor (*Ghaddar*, *desh-drohi*) assume a prominent position, while the fear of the enemy from 'inside' is constantly maintained as a means of targeting and discrediting minorities. On both sides of the border, the ultimate result is that citizenship is defined in increasingly narrower terms. On this interpretation of the nation, all the communities other than Hindu (in the Indian case) and Muslim (in the Pakistani case) are identified as 'foreigners' and therefore enemies of the nation, implying that only Hindus (in India) and Muslims (in Pakistan) have a right to the nation.

The question now is to what extent the BJP will succeed in implementing its policies in a country that can still claim to be democratic and where the space for contestation remains fairly broad. Evidence of the latter lies in the extensive and critical media coverage of revisionism in the field of education, which contrasts with what happened in Pakistan in the 1970s when a similar policy was enforced. Yet, India is also witnessing a worrying 'banalization' of communalist discourse that does not bode well for the future. If the policies of the BJP were to be implemented, they would have tremendous consequences not only for the sheer quality of education in India and the production of future professionals and scientists, but also for minorities. They would thus contribute to reinforcing the existing rift between the citizens of India and Pakistan.

Notes

1 On the issue of Hindu nationalism, see in particular Jaffrelot (1996).
2 A thorough analysis of the non-NCERT textbooks produced in the vernacular languages will be needed, however, as part of an ongoing project, as much of the 'communal literature' is written in those languages.
3 The analysis of history textbooks in Pakistan here borrows largely from Saigol (1995).
4 Although this is less true of the privately run schools meant for the elite, whose creation started in the 1970s and continued well into the 1980s. Their aim was to provide the elite with a high-quality system of education based on 'modern knowledge', so that their children could be turned into future leaders. These elite English-medium schools provide an alternative space where teaching takes on a more dynamic and less authoritarian character (Saigol 1995: 65).
5 During the Partition of India in 1947, East Bengal was incorporated into the newly formed Pakistan and was subsequently known as 'East Pakistan'. The economic exploitation of East Pakistan by West Pakistan, the refusal of the latter to

give to East Pakistan an equal status in the political system, and what was seen as an attempt by West Pakistanis to undermine Bengali culture (its linguistic identity in particular) gave rise to separatist sentiments in East Pakistan, which culminated into a war of independence and the creation of Bangladesh in 1971. East Pakistanis (before they became Bangladeshis) received India's help in their struggle, and this further aggravated the resentment of (West) Pakistanis towards Indians.

6   *Social Studies Textbook for Class V*, 1987, pp. 1–2, quoted in Saigol (1995: 228).

7   On the spectacular proliferation of *madrasas* in Pakistan at that time, see Malik (1996).

8   *Social Studies Textbook for Class V*, 1988, p. 90, quoted in Saigol (1995: 235).

9   Shivaji, the founder of the Maratha Empire, rebelled against Aurangzeb and thereafter came to be seen as a symbol of resistance to Mughal power. He proclaimed on his territories the rule of Hinduism (*Hindu padshahi*) and claimed to be the protector of Gods, Brahmins and cows. See Gaborieau (1994: 128).

10 According to the traditional historiography, Bengal fell into the hands of the British because of the 'betrayal' of Mir Jaffer, who, with their help, plotted against the then nawab, Sirajuddaula, and took over his throne after the battle of Plassey in 1757. This event is considered the starting point of British colonization in India.

11 Zia Mian, 'Making of the Pakistan Mind', *The News*, Sunday, 6 November 1994, quoted in Saigol (1995: 263).

12 'Textbooks and the Jihadi Mindset', *Dawn*, 12 February 2002.

13 K. Gopalan, 'Foreword', in Chandra (2001[1990]).

14 Vernoff 1992: 240–1. It should be noted, however, that earlier in the nineteenth century Gujaratis had much more mixed images of Shivaji, as he was also seen as the plunderer of the city of Surat; but increasingly, they started perceiving him more in the broader context of the history of India, instead of that of the history of Gujarat, and he was subsequently viewed as the Hindu hero who had defeated the Mughals. See Riho Isaka, 'Gujarati Intellectuals and History Writing in the Colonial Period', *Economic and Political Weekly*, 30 November 2002, pp. 4869–70.

15 Bharat Bhushan, 'The Specificities of Gujarat', *The Daily Times*, 21 December 2002.

16 The riots in Gujarat in March 2002 were initiated after a group of Muslims attacked and burnt a train in which Hindu nationalists coming back from Ayodhya (the site of the Babri mosque destroyed by a group of Hindu fanatics in 1992) were travelling. The attack was followed by terrible riots that caused the death of more than two thousand persons (mostly Muslims). The scale of the violence and the blatant collusion of the Gujarat State in this violence have been such that some analysts have used the word 'pogroms' instead of 'riots' to describe the events. At any rate, these events have tragically highlighted the degree of polarization in Gujarati society.

17 The RSS or *Rashtriya Swayam Sevak Sangh* (Association of National Volunteers), created in 1925, is the institutional core of the Hindu nationalist movement. The Bharatiya Janata Party (BJP) is its political branch.

18 Chandra (2001[1990]). The BJP now wants to revise this book.

19 This raises questions on whether an education system should be so much under the control of the government. As has been pointed out by several historians, such as Sanjay Subrahmanyam, a greater variety of textbooks on the market would make the system more independent. Hence the problem would not be raised of the content of textbooks being changed whenever there is a new government: Sanjay Subrahmanyam, 'Legacy from the Past', *Times of India*, 5 January 2002.

20 If the *madrasas* in Pakistan have indeed produced a considerable number of Islamists, the *madrasas* in India do not seem to follow the same orientation. The major failure of most lies above all in the poor quality of the education they impart to their students.

21 For instance, they asserted that the Harappan and Vedic civilizations were the same, attributed child marriage and superstition to 'fear of Muslims', and explained caste in the following way: 'Hindus tried to protect their religion and society by making their caste system': Anjali Modi, 'Tailoring History', *The Hindu*, 21 October 2001.

22 On the cow issue, see in particular Pandey (1983) and Assayag (2001).

23 My italics. See also Basharat Peer, 'Distorting History', *The Rediff Special*, 8 November 2002.

24 Kumkum Roy, 'National Textbooks for the Future', *Economic and Political Weekly*, 21 December 2002.

25 Among them Romila Thapar, 'Vedic Civilization: Learning an Anachronism', a lecture delivered at the SAHMAT convention on the communalization of education in November 2001. Reproduced in Harsh Kapoor, aiindex@mnet.fr.

26 Anjali Modi, 'Tailoring History', *The Hindu*, 21 October 2001.

27 Romila Thapar, 'Vedic Civilization: Learning an Anachronism', a lecture delivered at the SAHMAT convention on the communalization of education in November 2001. Reproduced in Harsh Kapoor, aiindex@mnet.fr.

28 By simplistic opposition between heroes and villains, I mean here in the vision developed by communalists on both sides. This does not imply that heroes in Pakistani textbooks are necessarily considered as villains in Indian textbooks. As Krishna Kumar underlines, historical personalities are given different levels of significance in Indian and Pakistani textbooks, or different parts of their lives may be emphasized. Such is the case with Sayyid Ahmad Khan and Iqbal: Indian textbooks prefer to focus on the earlier part of their lives, whereas Pakistani textbooks insist on the later segment: see K. Kumar (2001: 76).

References

Primary sources

Chandra, Satish (2001[1990]), *Medieval India – History Textbook for Class XI*, Delhi: NCERT.

Kundra, D. N. and S. D. Kundra (1987), *A New Textbook of History of India, for Matric, Pre-University, Higher Secondary and Indian School Certificate Examinations to the Present Day, Part II*, Delhi: Navdeep Publications.

Sharma, Ram Sharan (2000[1999]), *Ancient India – History Textbooks for Class XI*, Delhi: NCERT.

Thapar, Romila (2001[1987]), *Ancient India – History Textbooks for Class VI*, Delhi: NCERT.

Zafar, M. D. (1982), *Pakistan Studies for B.A., B. Com., MBBS, and B.Sc. Engineering*, Lahore: Aziz Publishers.

Secondary sources

Anderson, Benedict (1998), *The Spectre of Comparisons: Nationalism, Southeast Asia and the World*, London: Verso.

Assayag, Jackie (2001), *L'Inde, désir de nation*, Paris: Odile Jacob.

Aziz, K. K. (1993), *The Murder of History in Pakistan*, Lahore: Vanguard Press.

Balibar, Etienne (2001), *Nous, citoyens d'Europe ? Les frontières, l'Etat, le peuple*, Paris: La Découverte.

Bénéï, Véronique (1998), 'Hinduism Today: Inventing A Universal Religion?', *South Asia Research* 18: 2, 117–24.

Dev, Arjun (2001), 'NCERT, "National Curriculum" and "Destruction of History"', in SAHMAT & SABRANG.COM, *Against Communalisation of Education*, New Delhi, SAHMAT, 4–6 August, pp. 137–54.

Gaborieau, Marc (1994), '"La splendeur moghole": les successeurs d'Akbar (1605–1707)', in Claude Markovits (ed.) *Histoire de l'Inde moderne, 1480–1950*, Paris: Fayard.

Hoodbhoy, Pervez (1991), *Muslims and Science: Religious Orthodoxy and the Struggle for Rationality*, Lahore: Vanguard.

Jaffrelot, Christophe (1996), *The Hindu Nationalist Movement in India*, London: Hurst, Columbia University Press.

Kumar, Krishna (1996), *Learning From Conflict*, Hyderabad (India): Orient Longman Ltd.

Kumar, Krishna (2001), *Prejudice and Pride: School Histories of the Freedom Struggle in India and Pakistan*, New Delhi: Viking.

Kumar, Nita (1999), *Lessons from Schools: The History of Education in Banaras*, New Delhi: Sage.

Malik, Jamal (1996), *The Colonisation of Islam: Dissolution of Traditional Institutions of Learning*, Delhi: Manohar.

Mohammad-Arif, Aminah (2000), 'La diversité de l'islam', in Christophe Jaffrelot (ed.) *Le Pakistan*, Paris: Fayard.

Mukherjee, Mridula and Aditya Mukherjee (2002), 'Communalising Education: History Textbook Controversy', *Mainstream* 34: 16, January.

Pandey, Gyanendra (1983), 'Rallying around the Cow: Sectarian Strife in the Bhojpuri Region, c.1888–1917', in Ranajit Guha (ed.) *Subaltern Studies II. Writing on South Asian History and Society*, Delhi: Oxford University Press.

Panikkar, K. N. (2001), 'Whiter Indian Education', in SAHMAT & SABRANG.COM, *Against Communalisation of Education*, New Delhi, SAHMAT, 4–6 August, p. 26.

Powell, Avril (1996), 'Perceptions of the South Asian Past: Ideology, Nationalism and Textbooks', in Nigel Crook (ed.) *The Transmission of Knowledge in South Asia: Essays on Education, Religion, History and Politics*, Delhi: Oxford University Press.

Rahman, Tariq (2000), 'Langues et enseignement', in Christophe Jaffrelot (ed.) *Le Pakistan*, Paris: Fayard.

SAHMAT (2001), 'Demonising Christianity, Islam: How Textbooks Teach Prejudice', in SAHMAT & SABRANG.COM, *Against Communalisation of Education*, New Delhi, SAHMAT, 4–6 August, p. 125.

SAHMAT & SABRANG.COM (2001), *Against Communalisation of Education*, New Delhi, SAHMAT, 4–6 August.

Saigol, Rubina (1995), *Ideology and Identity: Articulation of Gender in Educational Discourses in Pakistan*, Lahore: ASR Publications.

Setalvad, Teesta (2001), 'Gujarat: Situating the Saffronisation of Education', in SAHMAT, *The Saffron Agenda in Education: an Exposé*, New Delhi, SAHMAT, 4–6 August, pp. 75–6.

Taneja, Nalini (2001), 'The Saffron Agenda in Education', in SAHMAT, *The Saffron Agenda in Education: an Exposé*, New Delhi, SAHMAT, 4–6 August, pp. 13–14.

Thapar, Romila (2001), '"Vedic Civilisation": Learning an Anachronism', lecture delivered at a SAHMAT convention on the communalization of education, 23 November.

Vernoff, Edward (1992), *History in Indian Schools: Study of Textbooks Produced by the Central Government and the State Governments of Maharashtra, Gujarat, West Bengal, Andhra Pradesh, Kerala and Tamil Nadu*, UMI Dissertation, New York University.

7 'Educating for legality'

Citizenship and the antimafia movement in Sicily

Jane Schneider and Peter Schneider

In 1860 Sicily, a viceroyalty of the Neapolitan Kingdom of the Two Sicilies became part of the newly unifying state of Italy through a unanimous plebiscite; in recent years, most Italians, including Sicilians, have enthusiastically supported Italy's integration into the European Union. It is often remarked that Italy is a country where, on the one hand, localisms matter intensely as sources of identity, but where, on the other hand, regional nationalisms attuned to ethnic, religious or linguistic differences are unusual. Thus, except for a brief, and easily co-opted, upper-class movement for independence after the Second World War, Sicilian separatism has been noteworthy for its absence. What may be at work, here, is the relative absence, in Italy, of an energetic nationalist push for uniformity in language and culture, the fascist period constituting a brief exception (see Herzfeld n.d.; Levy 1996; Lyttelton 1996).

At the same time, in the decades after Italian unification there emerged a tendency to differentiate Italians strongly along a north–south axis, with northerners defined as 'European', progressive, developed and capable of achieving industrial civilization, and southerners as for ever agrarian, 'Mediterranean' and backward. Summarized as 'the Southern Question', this way of talking and reasoning gathered steam across many fields (from political economy and statistics to literature, journalism and criminology) in the 1870s through to the 1890s, when the Italian state sought to jockey for colonial territories not already claimed by Europe's imperial powers, France and England (J. Schneider 1998). Like classical Orientalism (Said 1979) – indeed, exemplifying what scholars of the Balkans refer to as a kind of 'nested Orientalism' (Bakić-Hayden 1995) – the Southern Question discourse has subsequently had extraordinary staying power, continuing to this day.

Looking at the Question over time, one detects a consistent trickle of minority voices that attribute the south's problems to the capitalist transformation, after Italian Unification, of vast *latifundia*, oriented toward a colonial-style export economy of cereals and pastoral products, and sustaining a highly polarized class system of fabulously wealthy 'prepotent' land-holders and pauperized peasants, with a gallery of rogues and bandits in between. Majority voices conjure up essentializing explanations. Until the Holocaust gave race a bad name, blame was cast on the south's 'Mediter-ranean'-type people, biologically as well as geographically closer to Africa than to Europe and argued to be congenitally deficient – lazy, over-passionate, prone to criminal behaviour in the case of men and to a childlike depend-ency in the case of women (see Gibson 1998). Such racialized images coex-isted with, and eventually yielded to, cultural determinism, anchored, as with so many other 'orientalisms', by a set of binary categories opposing the good and the bad (Moe 1998).

Two American political scientists, Edward Banfield in 1958 and Robert Putnam in 1993, brought the Southern Question discourse to English-speaking audiences concerned with underdevelopment more generally. Ban-field's book, *The Moral Basis of a Backward Society*, argued that industrial capacity, workers' productivity and a decent standard of living were remote goals in Southern Italy because, instead of joining voluntary associations and engaging in collective projects for the common good, southerners pursued an age-old culture of 'amoral familism', each furthering the short-term interests of his or her nuclear family and assuming that fellow citizens were doing the same. Putnam's contribution, *Making Democracy Work: Civic Tra-ditions in Modern Italy*, restates the argument in the more contemporary lan-guage of 'civil society'. Based on a 20-year study of the performance levels of six regional governments distributed over north and south, it documents far better outcomes on a variety of measures for the northern than for the south-ern governments' cases. According to Putnam, this is because the North has enjoyed a 'civic tradition' of communally oriented city-states, stretching from the Alps to Rome and dating back to the Middle Ages, whereas the South has been subjected since medieval times to the corrupt, divide-and-conquer strategies of feudal, bureaucratic and absolutist rule (1993: 123). Two patterns of governance, not to mention ways of life, distinguished the North and the South: 'In the North, people were citizens; in the South they were subjects ... Collaboration, mutual assistance, civic obligation, and even trust ... were the distinguishing features in the North. The chief virtue in the South, by contrast, was the imposition of hierarchy and order on latent anarchy' (1993: 130).

The theme is echoed by the political leader Umberto Bossi, who, in the late 1980s, forged a single 'Northern League' (*Lega Nord*) out of several regionalist movements in the Po Valley. Ridiculing such regional groups as the Venetians for harping on 'folkloric' themes at the expense of a more inclusive political strategy, Bossi shamelessly upended the 'Southern Ques-tion' in order to represent the entire north as an 'internal colony', oppressed by southerners' influence over Rome. Evidence lay, he claimed, in decades of clientelism, Mafia, and corruption at the centre of the Italian state, and in the squandering of the 1950s 'fund for the South' (*Cassa per il Mezzogiorno*) –

a massive advance of investment capital for 'pointless' southern industrial development that had been financed by 'productive' northern taxpayers (Cachafeiro 2002).

It is of more than passing interest that during the 1980s and 1990s, as Putnam, Bossi and the *Lega Nord* were reinventing the North–South dichotomy, a powerful antimafia process was unfolding across the South. Consisting of both a judicial and a police repression of organized crime and a citizens' social movement – the *movimento antimafia* – it advanced the idea of constructing a civil society whose citizens would repulse clientelism and the exchange of favours for votes. Remarkably, given the Southern Question discourse, leaders and followers of this process were themselves southerners, from prosecutors and policemen to social movement activists and civic-minded students, professionals and volunteers. In the pages that follow, we trace but one dimension of this multifaceted intervention in civic life as it unfolded in the city of Palermo from the mid-1980s on, the dimension of bringing schoolchildren into the conversation. As will be seen, an energetic core of Sicilian teachers, principals and volunteers have struggled to make a pedagogical difference in spite of many obstacles (not least a state that has dragged its feet), and with some success. The concluding section of this chapter consists of a reflection on why so many observers, ourselves included, failed, in the past, to anticipate profound challenges to the cultural status quo, emanating from within Sicily.

Mafia and antimafia in the Sicilian context[1]

Thanks to recent antimafia prosecutions in Sicily, there are now over 1,000 *pentiti* – *mafiosi* who have become justice collaborators – and with them, a wealth of new testimony about the inner workings of Sicilian organized crime. Together with the research of a new generation of sociologists and historians, these testimonials point to the 'secret', fraternal quality of the historic mafia *cosca* or 'family'; the boundaries it constructs between inside and outside; and the mafia value of *omertà* or 'silence before the law'.

Historically, mafia families were territorial, each bearing the name of a place. Presumably, it was the prerogative of each to extort a *pizzo* or tax on business activities in its territory, to impose on the territory's employers requirements that they hire particular mafia dependants, and to mediate local conflicts and the return, for a fee, of locally stolen goods. *Mafiosi* have also always pursued geographically deterritorialized activities such as animal rustling and the clandestine butchering and sale of stolen meat. The contraband mediation and sale of tobacco and narcotics, which date from the early twentieth century but flourished after the Second World War, characteristically engaged affiliates of several different *cosche*, not to mention numerous outsiders – a provocation to, and source of tension with, the territorial mode of organization.

Following the Second World War, the Sicilian mafia evolved in tandem with a land reform and agrarian transformation, an expanding state presence, and the explosive growth of cities. Well before the displacement of heroin-refining operations from Marseilles to Palermo in the late 1970s, a Palermo-centred network headed by Gaetano Badalamenti had accumulated substantial profits from drug shipments to America. This provoked the ire of a growing contingent of younger bosses from the provinces, known as the 'Corleonesi' after the rural town of Corleone, birthplace of their most auda-cious leaders. The quest for control over narcotics traffic was an important element in the rise to power of this contingent between 1979 and 1983, when they not only assassinated the leaders of Palermo's principal mafia families, but killed some 15 police officers, magistrates and government offi-cials, labelled 'excellent cadavers' by the press, whom they perceived to be in their way.

This 'mafia war' of the early 1980s involved a level of aggressivity that many *mafiosi* consider a 'betrayal' of mafia; yet it is crucial to analyse the violence that has always been intrinsic to this institution. Here it is helpful to consider the mafia as a *subculture*, structured by the systematic exclusion of women, the rule of secrecy, a clientelistic pattern of recruitment, and the valorization of revenge as a mark of manhood. Although many have argued to the contrary, these practices and values were not a straightforward expres-sion of general Sicilian culture, whose multiple, contradictory aspects will be considered later in this chapter. Nevertheless, as an institution of long standing in Sicily (it dates back to the late 1800s), the mafia penetrated local social, political and cultural life by *provisioning* a host of clients and depen-dants and *conditioning* powerful interlocutors. Attention to such processes helps one appreciate the complexities of 'educating against the mafia'.

The antimafia movement: an overview

The extreme violence of the early 1980s precipitated the prosecution in 1986–7 of some 460 *mafiosi* in a 'maxi-trial' in Palermo. A majority were convicted, and the convictions were sustained on appeal. Throughout this transformation in the mafia–state relation, the prosecution benefited not only from the testimony of the *pentiti*, but also from an antimafia social movement, centred in the regional capital, Palermo. Through a succession of umbrella organizations, activists in this movement staged demonstrations, conferences, book presentations and commemorative events in support of the judicial effort, at the same time changing their island's symbolic landscape.

Activist groups with which we are especially familiar include a network of social centres operating in the poor neighbourhoods of Sicily's major cities, usually with the support of left-wing clergy as well as of lay and Catholic volunteers; a coalition of politicians around Leoluca Orlando, the first antimafia mayor of Palermo, and founder of an antimafia political party (*La Rete*); a coalition of intellectuals keeping watch over the new politicians; and the media-savvy 'Committee of the Sheets' (*Comitato dei Lenzuoli*), traceable to a kinship network of three sisters and their daughters who hung slogan-painted sheets from the balconies of their neighbouring apartments following the funeral of Giovanni Falcone, the pioneering antimafia magistrate who was assassinated in May 1992. We should also note the antimafia administrations of several rural towns in Sicily, which took power after the electoral reform of mayoral voting in 1992.

Having followed the antimafia movement since 1987, we appreciate its resemblance to all social movements, which, as a general rule, are protean and multifaceted, widening and branching in response to crises, and then contracting and fragmenting under the returned weight of 'normalcy' (see, for example, Diani 1995). In Palermo, where the movement has been most evident, activists refer to the mid-1980s – the years of the maxi-trial and Orlando's first election as mayor – as the 'Palermo Spring', but they recall the late 1980s as a time of retreat and backlash. Then came the terrible summer of 1992, when, in addition to Falcone, another antimafia magistrate, Paolo Borsellino, was felled. The burst of energy following these brutal murders transcended any previous mobilization.

As might be expected, the multiple organizations and associations constituting the antimafia movement are not always able to communicate effectively, let alone share meanings or sustain an overarching consistency of purpose. One salient fault line, familiar to many social movements throughout the world in the 1980s and 1990s, derives from the ideologically driven polarization of politics during the Cold War. For Italy, this meant a division between 'Catholics' and 'Communists' – that is, persons whose political socialization was rooted in the historic relationship between the Roman Catholic Church and the Christian Democratic Party, regardless of the intensity of their religious commitment, and persons who grew up with the secular Left, even though they may have been practising Catholics. The resulting 'red–white' dialectic was nowhere more consequential than in Sicily, where, in the decades after the Second World War, most antimafia activists were leftists, whereas most Christian Democrats had to live with the appearance, if not the reality, of mafia conditioning.

Without belabouring the scholarly debates surrounding 'new' social movements, today's antimafia movement clearly belongs to this type, having parted ways with the politics of class struggle characteristic of the postwar era. In part, the transition reflects the emergence of new social groups and generations. Antimafia activists of the 1950s and 1960s, participants in the struggle of Sicilian peasants for land, tended to be male, small-town and not well-schooled, in contrast with the more or less gender-integrated, urban and educated middle-class core of the movement today. This is not to say that the core is homogeneous. Some activists come from comfortable and long-established professional families – the kind of family that is likely to have lived in Palermo for several generations, its various nuclei occupying the same family building, their large and comfortable apartments repositories of heirlooms and antiques. A few, most notably Orlando, hail from the landed elite (Orlando was also a Christian Democrat before founding the *Rete* party). Others are of more plebeian origin, their peasant or labouring parents not having gone beyond elementary school and their living situations being quite modest. Nevertheless, the most engaged activists, women as well as men, have been in their forties or younger and have held degrees from the University of Palermo, where they participated in (left) student politics during the 1960s. The backgrounds of the activist clergy frequently include exposure to the curricular reforms inspired by the Vatican II Council during the same period. On the whole, antimafia leaders constitute a politically experienced intelligentsia – persons with careers or aspirations for careers in social work, teaching, law, government, journalism, health care and the clergy (see Ramella and Trigilia 1997). Dense networks cut across these professions and occupations. It is our impression, in fact, that school ties are salient building-blocks of antimafia organization.

Whatever their background, activists have had to face a daunting set of issues, four of which seem especially important in shaping what they can accomplish: the issue of an ever hovering 'Sicilianist' backlash against the antimafia movement and magistrates, emanating from prior structures of power and earlier cultural practices; the issue of overcoming the Cold War cultures of anti-communism and anti-capitalism so that secular leftists and reformist Catholics can work together; the issue of where to draw the line in suspecting or accusing others of complicity with the mafia; and, finally, the issue of how an essentially middle-class movement can reform the values and behaviours of working-class Sicilians when work in some sectors, above all the construction industry and a great deal of government employment, is widely perceived to have derived from mafia provisioning. It will be important to keep these issues in mind as we review particular educational programmes.

Antimafia education: 'the very school buildings'

In 1963, a conflict between mafia *cosche* rivalling each other for a foothold in Palermo's lucrative construction industry and wholesale fish and produce markets led to the explosion of a car bomb in which several police officers were killed. This provoked mass arrests, a major trial and the formation of a parliamentary Antimafia Commission. A 1971 report of the Commission focused on Sicily's schools – in particular the scandalous condition of their very buildings. Compared with those of Italy as a whole, Sicilian classrooms were severely overcrowded, serving as many as 59 students each. Double and even triple turns were evident in many settings, such as the elementary schools of Palermo, where 20,000 pupils were forced to double up. The reason, it turned out, was not an absence of funds, but corruption. Indeed, the Commission demonstrated a striking parallel between the mafia-infested provinces (the provinces of Western Sicily) and a severe under-utilization or misappropriation of resources available for the construction of new schools.

Whereas in Italy, nearly half the scholastic buildings for which public funds had been approved in the late 1960s were already under contract, in Sicily the percentage was only 16.8 (Attanasio 1983: 60; see also Commissione Parlamentare 1972: 115–18).

Apparently, local administrations in areas of organized crime in Sicily had been ceding properties intended for school construction to mafia-affiliated contractors, who erected high-rise apartment houses on them instead. Nor was this all; the administrators then rented, often from the same contractors, totally inappropriate space for use as classrooms, subjecting children to insanitary and hazardous as well as overcrowded conditions. Following an earthquake in 1968 that damaged buildings in Palermo as well as numerous rural towns of the western provinces, the practice of renting classrooms from the owners of private housing stock (which the Commission called the 'rental industry') intensified. At the time of the report, 110 privately owned buildings or floors of buildings were serving as schools in Palermo alone, 18 of which belonged to the city's most notorious mafia-linked contractor, Vincenzo Vassallo (1983: 66–71).

As the then mayor of Palermo was attacking the Commission for exaggerating the mafia phenomenon, which was, he claimed, 'non-existent' (1983: 71), a dozen or so principals of high schools and technical schools in Palermo and the surrounding communities were preparing, on behalf of 'thousands of teachers', an eloquent letter on the 'crisis' of education in Sicily, which they sent to the Minister of Public Instruction in March 1971. How might the schools contribute to the development of a democratic society if they could not even guarantee the physical and mental health of the students, let alone adequate conditions for learning?

Significantly, new school construction was a priority of the antimafia administration of Orlando in Palermo, which defined the large number of projects that were contracted out after 1985 (according to criteria intended to exclude mafia-compromised firms) as 'the most significant intervention in scholastic construction in the history of the city' (Gruppo Realtà 1990: 53). In the summer of 1992, we were taken to two schools of the old type. One, a middle-class high school, occupied seven high floors of an apartment house, accessible only by stairs and one three-person elevator, the second small elevator having broken down. Not only were its classrooms configured in an awkward way; the provisions for escape in case of fire took no account of the car park in the interior courtyard, there were no facilities for recreation or assemblies, and the plumbing was totally inadequate to its task.

The other, a middle school serving working-class children, was worse. Also situated in a residential building, it shared one of its four dirty and run-down floors (each a warren of yellow-green hallways and tiny, overheated rooms), as well as its littered, dismal and unpatrolled stairwell and elevator, with a bordello. By 1995, however, both of these schools had been moved to spanking new structures that, although far from ideal (teachers complained of flimsy plastic and cardboard doors, noisy hallways, poorly ventilated rooms, unfinished exteriors and playgrounds, and slippery floors), were so much more clearly related to their purpose that they inspired confidence, and even enthusiasm, among the pupils and parents. We believe that new buildings had a similar effect in other locales, particularly where they displaced scandalous rental arrangements.

1980, Act 51

The principals' 1971 letter to the Minister of Public Instruction about the crisis conditions in Sicily's school buildings was but the beginning of an agitation on the part of educators for reform. At the end of the decade, a group co-ordinated by the principal of the middle-class Antonino Ugo middle school in Palermo galvanized the regional 'board of education' and the regional government's Department of Cultural Affairs and Public Instruction to press for legislation promoting 'education for legality'. Regional Act 51, passed in 1980, was the result, to be copied in 1985 in the region of Campania (i.e. Naples) and in 1986 in Calabria. All three laws provide public funds for antimafia projects in elementary, middle and high schools, and for related research and updating at the University level. Significantly, the national ministry, although highly centralized in Italy as in France, had yet to become involved.

Suggested projects include the acquisition by schools of bibliographic, documentary and audiovisual material on organized crime from scholastic and extra-scholastic sources; the creation of special sections on crime and related topics in the school libraries; the opening of the schools to parents, to the neighbourhood and to the city; the hosting or hiring of outside scholars and experts as collaborators or consultants; and the production by the schools, as 'engaged communities', of written, audio-visual, dramatic and other materials related to education for democracy and legality and against crime. Overall, the schools were encouraged to further a civic and democratic consciousness in children beyond what they could read in books or hear from their teachers, experimenting with a combination of research, individual and small-group initiatives, seminars, debates, the production of videos and movies, photographic exhibitions, plays and concerts (see Casarrubea and Blandano 1991: 151–3; Cipolla 1988: 139–43).

Many promoters of Act 51 were disappointed by its lack of teeth: the school projects are not mandated but voluntary: educators have to submit detailed proposals for particular initiatives to the regional ministry, and then await approval and financing before they can begin. Nor does the law oblige the educational bureaucracy (the regional and district 'boards of education') to promote or co-ordinate the activities (Casarrubea and Blandano 1991: 153). According to a survey in 1988–9, only 12.5 per cent of eligible schools had applied for funds under the act. More to the point, the number of proposals increased from 182 in 1980–1 to 331 in 1986–7, the years of the maxi-trial, but then fell off – a rhythm that was consistent with the shift from engagement to 'normalcy' and the backlash to the antimafia movement as a whole. In the context of retreat, teachers who questioned why the subject of the mafia should enter the curriculum, or be the focus of extra-curricular activities and events, and who resented it when others construed their reservations as 'philo-*mafioso*', were able to put the committed teachers – always a minority – on the defensive. A similar isolation befell the activist clergy in the Sicilian Church, and the small group of antimafia journalists on the staff of the main West Sicilian newspaper, the *Giornale di Sicilia*, between 1987 and 1992 (Cipolla 1989: 132; Montemagno 1990; Stabile 1989).

A closer look at responses to Act 51 reveals them to have come dispropor-tionately from the middle (as distinct from the elementary and high) schools. This may reflect the greater openness of schools at the middle level, whose constituents, aged 11 to 14, are neither little children in need of a lot of guidance, nor young men and women in the late stages of preparation for specialized educational or career choices. The middle schools, in other words, stand out for being able to free up 'spaces and times for interdiscipli-nary interventions . . . specifically connected to the themes of antimafia edu-cation' (Casarrubea and Blandano 1991: 157).

According to our interviews with teachers and principals in Palermo and the surrounding region, the extent and enthusiasm of a school's response to the opportunities provided by Act 51 depends, above all, on the climate of the school, as set by the principal and the most experienced teachers. Herein may lie another reason for the concentration of initiatives in the middle schools, which, in 1962, were the object of a major educational reform pro-moted by working-class organizations and the Left political parties. The reform unified, in a single institutional context, the formerly separate tracks of technical and professional education – utilitarian and humanistic instruc-tion – thus overcoming a historic stratifying division in Italian education, which still obtains at the secondary level, where schools are categorized as either *licée* or technical institutes (Barbagli 1982). Because of the reform, and a growing demand for schooling in Sicily, the middle schools were in effect reinvented, often with an infusion of younger teachers and administrators sympathetic to educational democratization, who were hired by the state, rather than by the municipality, as in the past. It is no accident, in other words, that the Scuola Media Antonino Ugo would have co-ordinated the pressure for Act 51. Its principal at the time, Vito Mercadante, was a veteran reformer of the 1960s.

Moreover, in Palermo at least, the most energetic antimafia programmes have unfolded in the middle schools of the city's working-class quarters – neighbourhoods considered to be 'at risk' for violence and crime and often, although not always, for a strong mafia presence as well. Teachers speak of these places as 'frontier zones', making note of the following kinds of every-day challenge: menacing acts on the part of an occasional student; the jailing or murder of a student's father or brother; the beating of a student by an abusive or drunken father; the entry of a student's mother into prostitution; the hidden marriage or pregnancy of a teenage female student; or a family's inability to buy school books, having gone into debt to pay for a First Communion. One has also to consider the sensitivities of students with mafia backgrounds, who feel ostracized from, or compromised by, the antimafia projects. In the light of such difficulties, the principals of the schools 'at risk' view staff solidarity as essential, and attempt to hire, or form, teams of teachers who will collaborate with one another.

Toward a new pedagogy: values, history, gender

Since the early 1980s, Sicilian children have experienced a profound change in the way that crime and mafia are represented – at school, in the media and in public life, even if not necessarily at home. Two sorts of educational intervention encouraged by Act 51, but also by the wider antimafia movement, have influenced this trend: the development of new didactic materials, and the staging of antimafia events at the end of each school year. The didactic materials cover, on the one hand, values, behaviours and comportment; and, on the other hand, 'what the mafia *is*'.

Consistently with the theme of 'educating for legality', the new materials characteristically touch on the principles of citizenship, contrasting them with the clientelism that is perceived to be chronic among Sicilians. Rather than imagining getting through life with the assistance of powerful patrons, students are urged to exercise their civil rights, as outlined in their civics texts, on their own – among them the right to vote, too often understood as what one does in exchange for personal favours. Teachers organize elections for classroom leaders as object lessons in democracy, and arrange for elected leaders to meet to address school problems. In addition they seek to disparage the system of recommendations that in the past permeated all levels of education in Sicily (see Schneider and Schneider 1976: 216–20). Then, for example, it was 'normal' for teachers and school administrators to be deluged with letters and oral representations on behalf of particular students. Now, by contrast, they insist to parents as well as students that assignments and examinations will be evaluated on the basis of merit, and in processes no longer permeable to the intervention of friends and advocates. Once they are judged in this way, students (and their parents) should accept the outcome as fair.

Another cornerstone of the new pedagogy concerns cultural beliefs and practices that are thought to be congruent with the mafia subculture, or to encourage a misplaced respect for that subculture. Authored by antimafia activists among the clergy (see Alajmo 1993; Colotta *et al.* 1972; Santino 1994a, 1994b) as well as by public school teachers, materials in this vein single out a certain pattern of litigiousness, a cluster of attitudes around 'taking offence', harbouring grudges and vindicating wrongs on one's own. Aspects of a long tradition of self-help justice in Sicily, such orientations are held to recall and foster the mafia's valorization of revenge and the code of *omertà* (see Cavadi 1994). In many of the schools we visited, childrens' colourful poster art, decorating the hallways and classrooms, addressed this theme, through both negative depictions of *mafiosi*, of guns and of violence, and positive depictions of symbols of harmony and peace.

Children should learn, it is argued, to conduct themselves in a 'sportsman-like way', to shake the hands of their opponents at the conclusion of a match, to make peace with their enemies after a quarrel, to be tolerant and respectful of the views of others so that talking things through becomes an alternative to fighting. Not that they fight with guns – that is an American problem; but teenage boys often carry knives in their pockets. The antimafia educators devote considerable attention to intervening in and settling disputes, wishing they could convince their young charges not only to turn in these weapons, but also to renounce their many contests and shows of strength. An example of what they condemn, and are likely to introduce as an object lesson in the classroom, is the boy who, upon discovering his peers attempting to steal the carrier pigeons from his father's rooftop, cut off one pigeon's legs, 'showing', he said, 'what would happen to the thieves if they persisted'.

More demanding still, educators 'for legality' propose that, upon witnessing their peers or others break the law or engage in violence, boys and girls should report what they have seen to the relevant authorities, denouncing what they know to be wrong. Such a move runs counter not only to *omertà*, but to what is perceived as a misguided pattern of socialization in traditional Sicilian families. Children are discouraged from being too observant or curious; reaching a certain age, they discover that adults systematically hide things from them, chastise them for being 'nosy', and answer their questions with a trick or a brush-off. The new pedagogy advocates a more open and direct pattern of communication between the generations. In one of the middle schools of Palermo, we observed a group of elected class leaders called together by the antimafia principal to discuss a problem of vandalism in the boys' cloakroom. Although not exhorting the leaders (who, interestingly, were mainly girls) to inform on their fellow students – a request that would certainly have failed – the principal nevertheless got them to explore the idea of posting observers, 'for the sake of all the male students in the school'.

'Educating for legality', citizenship and democracy is a deeply gendered project in the Sicilian context. Many of the producers of the new materials are women, as are, not surprisingly, the majority of teachers at the elementary and middle-school levels. What can be done, they ask, about the long-standing Sicilian practice of defining the male head of household as a *padre padrone*, entitled to keep his wife and children, above all his daughters, in submissive roles? How can democratic values be advanced if half of society is treated as second class? Teachers' concerns with this issue penetrate their classrooms at many points, for example when they encourage their female students to speak up, or chastise lapses of respect for them on the part of the boys. Sports programmes similarly inculcate the message of women's value, whether by integrating the teams, or merely by ensuring that girls particip- ate. What follows are the words of one educator, a male teacher of philo- sophy in one of the middle-class *lycée*, regarding gender as a pedagogic issue:

> In the vision of the mafia world, the male has an intrinsic superiority with respect to the woman. But this *maschilismo* is not presented in a brutal version: the woman, if legally married and thus inserted into the family, has her dignity, is respected ... is not publicly betrayed. Yet this dignity is only in relation to the man to whom she 'belongs'; she merits respect only in so far as she is capable of fidelity to her husband ... The counter proof, should there need to be one ... is expressed in the verbal and practical contempt for homosexuals and the custom of choosing insults that put another's masculinity in doubt. It is obvious that, from a strictly pedagogical angle, we are talking about the need to subvert this *maschilismo*, even when it is purely paternalistic, with all the encouragement possible for a 'feminine' pedagogy (which is not necessarily 'feminist').
>
> (Cavadi 1994: 94)

It is possible that antimafia reformers, who are for the most part middle- class, and among whom women are significant social actors, exaggerate the gender imbalances of working-class Sicilian households. Over the years, we have known of many cases pointing in the contrary direction, in which women stood up to men. Even so, the phenomenon of very young girls choosing marriage as a way to escape a domineering father, and then finding themselves dominated by a husband instead, is well enough documented by social workers in the poorest neighbourhoods of Sicilian cities, as are these neighbourhoods' higher birth-rates and incidences of teenage pregnancy (Zanvito 1989).

It should be noted, finally, that the antimafia values being promoted by teachers were at the same time gaining general public expression through the antimafia movement, in which many teachers participated. From the mid-1980s, Orlando, a politician of considerable charisma and talent, served as a fount of 'civil society' rhetoric, proclaimed at every opportunity, includ- ing visits to social centres and schools. In the mayor's view, the left–right spectrum of party identities was a residue of past conflicts that needed to yield to the values of individual merit and commitment. It is the person and not the label that counts. Ideological badges reminded him of 'tribalism' – the debilitating claims of lineages on the body politic as if it were a 'camp of tents' with nothing going on between them. In another of his favourite metaphors, he likened the typical party affiliate to a stacking Russian doll or Chinese box, in which removing the surface layer only reveals more surface layers, down to a core that is equally superficial. Especially typical of

Orlando's style is a tendency to speak in pairs (binary language put to purposes different from those of the Southern Question). Our experience belies 'economy produces culture' in favour of 'culture produces economy', he told a gathering of United Nations delegates to Palermo in December 2000, on the occasion of the signing of a transnational Treaty on Organized Crime: 'We have built a culture of peace to promote an economy of peace'. Palermo, which once exported the disease of the mafia, now exports the cure: it has become 'an example of the culture of legality for the rest of the world'.

As we have seen, promoting good citizenship goes hand-in-hand with attacking *clientelismo*, and with it the attitude that 'a friend is better than a legal right' (Montalbano 1964). Already in the 1960s, there were antimafia voices, for example the leftist intellectual and lawyer Giuseppe Montalbano, lamenting that 'in Sicily, one does things not because they are just or not, legal or not, but because a friend has asked it'. Not only are the favours 'manifestations of prestige or power because they are obligations to a friend'; clientelism requires *dis*favouring persons who happen to be the friends of one's enemies. A 'civil' relationship between the citizen and the state is thereby hampered. Rather than being able to vindicate their rights, citizens end up submitting to the 'habitus' of the local notables, enduring a long and humiliating mediation in which they may be asked, perhaps by a *mafioso*, to trade their votes for favours (Montalbano 1964).

This theme was forcefully recapitulated in a pamphlet prepared and distributed by the Committee of the Sheets in 1992, entitled 'Nine uncomfortable guidelines for the citizen who would combat the mafia' (Comitato dei Lenzuoli 1992). According to these guidelines, citizens should learn to claim their rights *vis-à-vis* the state, not beg for them as favours. They should educate their children in democracy and respect for the law. Workplace suspicions of bribery, corruption, extortion, favouritism and the waste of public money should be reported to legally constituted authorities. So should irregularities in the delivery and billing of medical, legal and other services, as well as other illegal acts. Before, after and during elections, citizens should refuse any exchange of favours for votes. 'Nothing will change if we continue to vote for parties that have governed us for many decades allowing the mafia to poison public life, consigning pieces of the state to the mafia's hand.'[2]

In addition to addressing values and behaviours that they hope to change, over the last 15 years antimafia intellectuals, researchers and teachers have produced a wealth of materials for teaching history – above all the history of organized crime and its consequences for the society and culture of Sicily. Rather than 'starting with the Greeks', which was the old way of proceeding, it is now possible to begin with the children's own experiences: their families; the monuments in their communities, which they can visit; the events of the last few years. Inserted into the curriculum are subjects such as the nineteenth-century origins of the mafia; the mystifying ideology of 'honour' that *mafiosi* propagate about themselves; the development of the international narcotics traffic and the role of the mafia in it; the *mafiosi* who have turned state's witness and what they have had to say (see Cavadi 1994; Cipolla 1988; Crisantino 1994). Comprehensive bibliographies have been developed for teachers, admittedly a small minority, who want to deepen their knowledge, and there exists, in addition, an experimental manual called *To Teach What the Mafia Is; 6 Didactic Units for the Upper Middle and Lower High School*. Although never widely used, the latter is elaborate, containing numerous 'flashes' – documents, primary sources and summary propositions regarding mafia wars, narcotics traffic, money-laundering and the corrupt relation between mafia firms and politics (Giammarinaro 1989).

Antimafia events

The explosive killings of Giovanni Falcone and Paolo Borsellino in May and July 1992, coinciding as they did with the end of the scholastic year, have reinforced what was becoming a pattern in schools throughout the island: to orient year-end events around themes of the antimafia campaign. Guided by their teachers, schoolchildren prepare vibrant, and often poignant, poster art and photo exhibitions protesting against violence and narcotics; they perform concerts and plays with pro-democracy and pro-peace content for parents and invited guests; they write and recite poems, and submit poetry for contests and publications (see Scuola Media Statale 'Giovanni Meli' di Cinisi 1993; Amurri 1992); and they walk behind their school banners in the marches and 'human chains' that the umbrella antimafia organization, now called *Palermo Anno Uno* (Palermo Year One), co-ordinates each year in honour of the slain. Sometimes they chant slogans like *Palermo è nostra, non è di Cosa Nostra* ('Palermo is ours, not the mafia's'). At the end of the school year in 1992, we witnessed the children of one middle school – the one that still shared its space with a bordello – dramatize some of the words of Bertold Brecht. The occasion was the more moving and interesting for their teacher's conviction that, although Sicilian is spoken in most of the pupils' homes, they are more than capable of performing in Italian, and should not be relegated, as some of her colleagues had argued, to putting on quaint folkloric dramas in dialect.

In Palermo, schoolchildren have been a primary source of the words and pictures that are appended to the 'Falcone Tree', a spontaneous shrine created around the magnolia tree in front of the apartment house of the martyred judge. Since 1995, they have honoured Sicily's antimafia heroes and martyrs with a programme called 'Palermo Opens Its Doors; The School Adopts a Monument', modelled after a similar initiative in Naples, where citizens have also mobilized against organized crime and corruption. Initially, 79 schools – 29 high schools, 32 middle schools and 18 elementary schools – participated, each having identified, studied and taken steps to recuperate a particular historic building or monument in its territory. The number had climbed to 150 schools by 2000 (Lo Dato 2000). Most of the adopted structures had been abandoned, vandalized or closed to the public for decades, perhaps because of *embrogli* or scandals involving *mafiosi*. Learning of their histories, the schoolchildren also became acquainted with this darker side.

The 1996 project that coincided with our fieldwork was jointly sponsored by *Palermo Anno Uno* and the municipal Department of Public Instruction, included well-advertised tours. One weekend a month between January and May, the citizens of Palermo were treated to a different itinerary of ten or so buildings and monuments, each staffed by local schoolchildren, who served as informative guides not only to the structure itself, but to the artwork and explanatory texts prepared by the sponsoring school during the preceding year. Culminating this eye-opening season of itineraries came five days during which all the monuments were open, these days corresponding to the city-wide celebrations for Judge Falcone. (We learned of one student who, although an enthusiastic participant on one of the earlier weekends, did not attend during these five days because his father is a *mafioso*.)

Some year-end commemorations and events revolve around exposing schoolchildren to well-known antimafia politicians and magistrates – persons who appreciate the opportunity to deliver their message to the next generation (but who can sound over-imposing or long-winded to a youthful audience). The assembled students are courteous and quiet, clearly impressed by these endangered figures' need for bodyguards, and by the occasional references in their speeches to child victims of the mafia. But they do not seem engaged, asking only friendly questions carefully penned in advance, obviously with the guidance of their teachers. The 'The School Adopts a Monument' programme has a different tone. Capturing the students' energy and interest, it also provides an occasion for them to think through issues for themselves. Thus a girl guide to the Palazzo Zisa – an Arab pleasure palace built for the medieval Norman kings of Sicily – spontaneously told visitors that the screens behind which women sat while watching the court entertainment back then were 'unfair to women'. Her partner, a boy, added that such separations were 'a kind of racism, I guess'.

Assessing outcomes

It is too early to evaluate the results of 'educating for legality' in Sicily; many will only be realized in the long term. In the short run, however, it is worth considering what teachers are up against. Numerous children – over 40 per cent in some neighbourhoods, according to interviewees – do not attend school or have dropped out before the legal leaving age of 14. Perhaps needless to say, such truants and drop-outs are concentrated in social groups at the greatest risk for involvement in both petty and organized crime. For persons in these groups, the antimafia message is generally an object of ridicule, above all for its emphasis on settling quarrels amicably, eschewing patronage and recommendations, balancing the status of women and men, and reporting illegalities to the State. Beyond this, there are questions to ask about the message's hegemonic potential among working-class Sicilians, whose lives have become increasingly precarious in recent years.

In the spring of 1996, we interviewed 30 sets of working-class parents with at least one child in an 'antimafia' middle school of Palermo. Our goal was to learn how people outside the predominantly middle-class antimafia movement, yet exposed to its efforts at cultural reform, were experiencing Sicily's recent historic shift. Scattered over five 'popular neighbourhoods' of the city, two in or near the centre and four in the outskirts, the families were identified for us, even introduced to us, by the heads of the schools. Although a few interviews took place in a schoolroom, in most cases we were hosted by the interviewees in their homes.

For each couple, we reconstructed the family history of one of them, organizing the interview around the paternal or the maternal genealogy, according to their preference. These family histories suggest that, since the Second World War, Palermo workers have been recruited heavily from rural communities – some of them immediately surrounding the city, others farther afield, still others communities that were swallowed by urban expansion. The pattern was the reciprocal of the exodus of thousands of peasants to the cities following the land reform. Second, in finding city jobs, personal connections and favours were decisive. In many families, we found a string of brothers and cousins hired by the same employer: the post office, the railroad, a restaurant, a bar, a contractor. Moreover, personal recommendations played a role beyond nepotism in most employment profiles.

The interviews reveal the overwhelming impact of one industry – construction – on the livelihoods of postwar working-class Sicilians. A majority of interviewees worked in trades associated with building, as either wage-earners or small-scale contractors, or a combination of both. Moreover, a majority of families had given expression to their 'evolving' urban identity through the handiwork of the man of the household, who proudly told us of having remodelled, expanded or re-built his own and his relatives' apartments, turning roof-top terraces into extra rooms or whole dwellings, embellishing interior archways and windows, and tapping into gas and electrical lines before these services were authorized by an inefficient and inattentive State. Upon completing the family histories, each couple or individual was asked to reflect on a series of issues related to the changes, in Sicily, of the last few years. Staying away from pointed questions about mafia and antimafia, we focused on such topics as the Italianization of the Sicilian dialect, changing gender relations among youth, the image of the city, and the current economic crisis – i.e. Sicily's 20 to 30 per cent rate of unemployment and associated shop-closings, bankruptcies and business failures.

Of these topics, the economic crisis elicited the greatest passion, because it touched on immediate experience: the man of the household was unemployed, his brother was, his close friends were, a storekeeper friend or relative was having to close his shop. Many expressed feeling at the end of an era in which life was becoming less precarious, and at the beginning of an era of great economic insecurity. Several of the households we visited already showed the effects of doubling up. Young people were either postponing marriage because they lacked employment or, having married, were returning to live with one of their parents for lack of affordable housing. Both outcomes violated local norms, on the one hand of youthful marriage and on the other of neo-local residence, because, after all, 'daughters-in-law and mothers-in-law should never be under one roof'.

Several interviewees attributed the crisis to the abrupt and devastating slowdown of construction, in their minds caused by the prosecution of the mafia and the reorientation of the city away from growth toward a mix of preservation and greening. For many, indeed the majority, the 'hysteria about legality' had gone too far. 'The mafia gave us work', said some, 'and now the antimafia has taken this work away'. One man commented that, thanks to the politicians and the mafia, 'there used to be a lifting crane every 20 metres well into the 1980s', but now the cranes have vanished because all their owners are in jail. Another, an ironworker, was experiencing a three-quarters reduction in his work, and claimed the same for any craftsman – woodworker, tile layer, whatever – connected to the building trades. The halt in construction, in the view of still others, was having a giant domino effect; construction was but the first link of a long chain. As a consequence of the chain's being broken, even fishmongers were suffering, as customers stopped frequenting the restaurants that purchase fish. In other words, 'if the masons don't work, neither does anyone else'.

Other arguments filtered in. One woman expressed anger over the TV images of Sicily that draw attention to the mafia, claiming that the new emphasis on legality fosters only negative propaganda. And several commented on the attempt to suppress, and not only that, to criminalize, clientelist behaviour. It used to be possible, they pointed out, citing examples from their own families, *fare entrare qualquno* – to guarantee a dependant's employment by means of a recommendation. Now, if you want to help someone, you might go to jail. Ugly as it is, 'We can't even help our own children any more!' One woman worried that her children would blame her if they failed to get a job. Nor, they said, did all the new legality do that much good. On the contrary, interviewees pointed to an increase of street-level delinquency – purse snatching, for example – this being a problem that derived from unemployment, not from organized crime. 'They have beaten up the mafia and now, with the enterprises finished, crime is on the rise.' After all, 'people have children, they have to eat, they have houses they have to pay for'. Another lament is that the magistrates put too much trust in the *mafiosi* who have turned state's witness, prosecuting too many innocents as a result. If someone uses your phone, one woman told us, quite possibly speaking from a relative's or a friend's experience, and that someone turns out to be suspect, 'you yourself can be put away for six years'.

Although unemployment in Sicily is structural and only superficially related to the new legality, the antimafia movement cannot easily speak to these concerns. Quite literally, the languages diverge. As educated members of the middle class, movement activists' facility with the Sicilian dialect is often minimal, whereas working-class families, although committed to having their children learn Italian, use the national language less easily. These children, meanwhile, even when they attend school regularly and listen to, absorb and participate in the projects of their teachers, return home to a world in which parents declare that if the wheels of justice 'cut the flow of mafia money without replacing it with other money, this only adds to the misery of the people'. As the principal of one of the middle schools put it, 'the external world disqualifies the message of the school'. Another, more optimistic, principal drew a slightly different conclusion: 'Our children are "bilingual"; they live in two worlds and are really good at switching from one to the other'. Down the road, one presumes, it will make a significant difference that many 'at risk' Sicilian children have learned a 'second language'.

Conclusion

Taking for a moment the optimistic view that 20 years of antimafia struggle in Palermo and Sicily have contributed to schoolchildren's acquiring a sense of themselves as 'citizens' – of their city, their nation and the world – it is important to emphasize the extent to which the struggle has been carried on by Sicilians themselves. This flies in the face of the Southern Question discourse, which posits for Sicily an essential 'Mediterranean' culture, widely shared and of great historical depth, that fosters agonistic social relations, generalized distrust and people's dependence on patron–client ties to mediate their relations with the state. Reform is possible, yes, but the impetus would have to come from Northern Italy and beyond – places already steeped in civil society. Moreover, as with Italy's 1950s development fund for the South, according to the discourse the local favour system is bound to trump reformers' good intentions. Our first fieldwork in Sicily was in the mid-1960s, and among other things revolved around answering the cultural essentialism of Edward Banfield (Schneider and Schneider 1976). Nevertheless, when the antimafia process began to unfold in a forceful way in the early 1980s, we were caught by surprise, having never anticipated that such a thing could happen. We conclude with a reflection on various missed cues, these in turn indicating some of Sicily's important inner reservoirs for self-challenge and change.

Our fieldwork of the mid-1960s, which continued off and on through the 1970s, took place in rural towns in Sicily's latifundist interior. There we made note of a cluster of attitudes or dispositions evident in the words and actions of those around us that we glossed over as a preoccupation with honour, following the then-prevalent terminology of anthropologists studying the

Mediterranean littoral. The issue, it seemed, was people's sensitivity to status injury or denials of respect, in which material and emotional considerations were fused. Concern for individual efficacy or potency and a related touchiness in interpersonal relations accompanied this pattern. Among near-equals in the socially stratified communities we studied, status inferiors sought parity, superiors feared envy, and resentment spoiled any number of co-operative endeavours. It was expected that people would closely defend their own interests and take offence at signs of encroachment by others. Self-conscious about equity, persons who improved their positions knew, or anyway believed, that they were the objects of unkind gossip or, at best, grudging admiration. Prophylactic rituals, such as distributing sweets on auspicious occasions and placing amulets on infants, were intended as antidotes to the spiritual danger of a rival's evil eye (1976: 100–2).

Many of the Sicilians whom we met in those days also cared a great deal about reputation, categorizing themselves and each other as *furbo* or *fesso*. The *furbi*, or clever ones, were those who successfully defended their turf and were admired for it whereas the *fessi* let themselves be pushed around. Even trivial slights had to be answered, lest their subject lose face. A related value was that of *fare i fatti suoi* (minding one's own business). Together these dispositions created a moral context in which third parties – those who were neither aggressors nor victims, but merely bystanders to an altercation or an encroachment – felt justified in looking the other way and remaining silent.

Interwoven with these values was the extraordinary warmth and generous hospitality of which Sicilians are rightly proud and at the same time often self-critical. People saw themselves living in a world in which personal connections made the difference between getting ahead and falling behind in life. Going through life, one cultivated a series of quasi-contractual relationships – between patrons and clients, favour-bestowers and favour-seekers, friends and friends of friends, saints and sinners – all of them a mix of instrumentality and affect. Friends were persons whose company one enjoyed but who might, at some hypothetical point, also be 'useful'. Through generosity and hospitality, people invested in people, just in case. Expressions such as *chi non accetta non merita* ('he who does not accept a gift does not deserve it'), and 'with friends one goes a long way' capture the subtle yet palpable power plays that render guests or recipients of favours *'vincolato'* – obligated for the foreseeable future, even if grudgingly. Notwithstanding the warmth and wonderful times, this potentially demanding edge to generosity added a modicum of tension to interpersonal relations.

Most antimafia activists believe that *mafiosi* have benefited from having the remnants of a historical 'honour culture' in their environment. This is nowhere more evident than in the mafia's remarkable ability to condition and provision others. In weaving spider-like webs of patron–client relations, *mafiosi* pick up on the wider cultural significance of generous hospitality and bestowals, expectations of reciprocity, and sensitivity to slight or disrespect, all of which give these relations a compelling edge. Indeed, it is because of these values and orientations that both patrons and clients think twice before dropping the ball in the favour system, the patrons because they fear their clients' enmity and disloyalty; the clients because they fear being abandoned in the future. Apart from self-help justice, no pattern of cultural practice is more anathema to the antimafia struggle than *clientelismo* – the mafia's scaffolding of social and political support.

And yet, other sides to Sicilian cultural practice were evident even in 1965. We knew many people who self-consciously defused interpersonal tensions in various ways. One way was for the parties to a conflict to pronounce themselves *sciarriati* – the dialect word for 'not on speaking terms' – a civil alternative to persistent quarrelling or worse. Disputants also often sought and willingly accepted mediation; informal mediators of all kinds – not necessarily *mafiosi* – were frequently able to negotiate the terms of a settlement between estranged parties. Contrary to the impression of many that peasant politics were necessarily imbued with the sentiment of individual vendetta, in the 1960s we were also greatly impressed by the adherence of thousands of peasants and artisans to a coherent left-wing ideology of class struggle that seemed to transcend their experience of personally humiliating relationships with landlords. Describing the workshops of local artisans as 'little universities', peasants as well as artisans gathered in them in the evenings to hear newspapers read aloud and analyse why the 'system of production' caused suffering and oppression. Armed with this perspective, they seemed to us to stand outside, and self-reflectively to criticize, some of the attitudes outlined above. The same might also be said of the cluster of young idealists, generally from peasant and artisan families, who gathered around Danilo Dolci, the self-styled 'Italian Ghandi', who, in the 1960s, led marches and hunger strikes to draw international attention to Sicilian poverty.

During the 1970s, we undertook research on the 'demographic transition' from a high to a very low birth-rate in rural Sicily. Because different classes experienced this change in different decades, and for different reasons, we became particularly attentive to cultural variation among them. Artisans (shoemakers, tailors, seamstresses, cabinet-makers, stonemasons, blacksmiths and so on) stood out as different. Not only were they the backbone of the local Communist Party; for reasons of their work and travel and way of life, they exhibited a particular affinity for the universalizing rational culture of the French Enlightenment – a culture that many intellectuals of the time felt strongly attracted to but did not think their fellow Sicilians could share. A central question concerned why these artisans were enthusiastic about, and a conduit for the diffusion of, a strikingly rationalized birth-control method, *coitus interruptus*, borrowed from France. Among other reasons, artisans enjoyed companionate marriages, in which, far from any caricatured 'code of honour' with its implied pattern of patriarchy, husbands and wives were partners (Schneider and Schneider 1996).

Looking back now, it seems obvious that yet other possibilities and alternatives would have been evident had we taken account of the cities. Knowing little about urban life except as occasional visitors to Palermo, we were, for example, quite ignorant of the brewing student radicalism at the University of Palermo – this notwithstanding our own backgrounds in the anti-Vietnam War movement in the United States. Yet, as is implied above, some of the seeds of the late twentieth-century struggle against the mafia were planted in the student movements of the 1960s and 1970s. Of course one can argue that these movements 'imported' ideologies from elsewhere – Marxism, Leninism, ultra-radicalism, Vatican II, Liberation Theology. This, however, is beside the point once one explodes the narrow and static understanding of culture implied by the Southern Question. When is any set of values and practices of a wholly internal or external provenance? And when is it not characterized by internal plasticity, contradictions and inconsistencies, such that the raw materials for challenge and change are present and percolating, even if behind the scenes? An understanding of culture as a work in progress, produced and reproduced through tension and conflict, allows us to comprehend why the centre of gravity for the present-day construction of citizenship in Sicily is in Palermo and not in Rome (or Washington, DC).

Notes

1 Additional bibliography and a much more fully developed analysis can be found in Schneider and Schneider (2003).
2 Related values, expressed in a religious idiom, characterize reform Catholicism in Palermo, which counterpoises the gospel of love with what is perceived as its 'opposite' – the vendetta complex, believed to be fostered by popular, or 'folk' Catholicism. The Palermo-based Redemptorist journal *Segno* is an important forum for promoting the evangelical perspective on conflict, frequently publishing documents from around the world on the themes of Christian peace, justice and forgiveness (see Schneider and Schneider 2003: 185, 218, 230–1).

References

Alajmo, Roberto (1993), *Un lenzuolo contro la mafia*, Palermo: Gelka.
Amurri, Sandra (ed.) (1992), *L'Albero Falcone*, Palermo: Fondazione Giovanni e Francesca Falcone.
Attanasio, Maria (1983), *Scuola e sistema mafioso*, Catania: Tringale Editore.
Bakic-Hayden, Milica (1995), 'Nesting Orientalisms: The Case of Former Yugoslavia', *Slavic Studies* 54: 917–31.
Banfield, Edward C. (1958), *The Moral Basis of a Backward Society*, Chicago: The Free Press.
Barbagli, Marzio (1982), *Educating for Unemployment; Politics, Labor Markets, and the School System – Italy, 1859–1973*, trans. Robert H. Ross, New York: Columbia University Press.
Cachafeiro, Margarita Gómez-Reino (2002), *Ethnicity and Nationalism in Italian Politics: Inventing the Padania: Lega Nord and the Northern Question*, Aldershot: Ashgate.

Casarrubea, Giuseppe and Pia Blandano (1991), *L'educazione mafiosa; Strutture sociali e processi di identità*, Palermo: Sellerio Editore.

Cavadi, Augusto (1994), 'Per una pedagogia antimafia', in Augusto Cavadi (ed.) *A scuola di antimafia; Materiali di studio, criteri educativi, esperienze didattiche*, pp. 72–114, Palermo: Centro siciliano di documentazione Giuseppe Impastato.

Cipolla, Giuseppe (1988), *Mafia cultura educazione: Contributi alla didattica antimafia*, Partinico: Centro Jatino di Studi e Promozione Sociale 'Nicolò Barbato'.

Cipolla, Giuseppe (1989), 'Tradizione e innovazione nell'esperienza educativa anti-mafia', in Umberto Santino (ed.) *L'antimafia difficile*, pp. 128–40, Palermo: Centro siciliano di documentazione Giuseppe Impastato.

Colotta, F. *et al.* (eds) (1972), *Sottosviluppo, potere culturale, mafia*, Palermo: Quaderni Universitari Palermitani.

Comitato dei Lenzuoli (1992), *Nove consigli scomodi al cittadino che vuole combattere la mafia*, pamphlet produced by the Comitato dei Lenzuoli.

Commissione Parlamentare d'Inchiesta sul Fenomeno della Mafia in Sicilia (1972), Relazione sui lavore svolti e sullo stato del fenomeno mafioso al termine della V legislatura, Roma: Tipografia Carlo Colombo.

Crisantino, Amelia (1994), 'Mafia: La fabbrica degli stereotipi', in Augusto Cavadi (ed.) *A scuola di antimafia; Materiali di studio, criteri educativi, esperienze didattiche*, pp. 48–57, Palermo: Centro siciliano di documentazione Giuseppe Impastato.

Diani, Mario (1995), *Green Networks: A Structural Analysis of the Italian Environmental Movement*, Edinburgh: Edinburgh University Press.

Giammarinaro, Maria Grazia (1989), *Insegnare che cos'è la mafia*, Cosenza: Luigi Pelle-grini Editore.

Gibson, Mary (1998), 'Biology or Environment? Race and Southern "Deviancy" in the Writings of Italian Criminologists, 1880–1920', in J. Schneider (ed.) *Italy's 'Southern Question': Orientalism in One Country*, pp. 99–117, Oxford: Berg.

Gruppo Realtà (1990), *Dossier Palermo: Le realizzazioni dell'amministrazione comunale di Palermo negli anni 1985–1990*, Palermo: La Sezione Studi Sociali del Gruppo Realtà.

Herzfeld, Michael (n.d.), 'Ethnographic and Epistemological Refractions of Mediter-ranean Identity', unpublished paper.

Levy, Carl (1996), 'Introduction: Italian Regionalism in Context', in Carl Levy (ed.) *Italian Regionalism: History, Identity and Politics*, pp. 1–33, Oxford and Washing-ton, DC: Berg.

Lo Dato, Enzo (2000), 'Palermo's Cultural Revolution and the Renewal Project of the City Administration', *Symposium on the Role of Civil Society: Creating a Culture of Lawfulness: The Palermo, Sicily Renaissance*, Palermo: City of Palermo.

Lyttleton, Adrian (1996), 'Shifting Identities: Nation, Region and City', in Carl Levy (ed.) *Italian Regionalism: History, Identity and Politics*, pp. 33–53, Oxford and Washington, DC: Berg.

Moe, Nelson (1998), 'The Emergence of the Southern Question in Villari, Franchetti, and Sonnino', in J. Schneider (ed.) *Italy's 'Southern Question': Orientalism in One Country*, pp. 51–77, Oxford: Berg.

Montalbano, Giuseppe (1964), 'Natura politica, giuridica e psicologica della mafia', *Homo* 1–8.

Montemagno, Gabriello (1990), *Palermo: La primavera interrotta*, Palermo: Nuova Editrice Meridionale.

Putnam, Robert D. (1993), *Making Democracy Work: Civic Traditions in Modern Italy*, New York: Beacon.

Ramella, F. and C. Trigilia (1997), 'Associazionismo e mobilitazione contro la criminalità organizata nel mezzogiorno', in L. Violante (ed.) *La mafia e societa Itatliana. Rapporto '97*, pp. 24–46, Bari: Laterza.

Said, Edward W. (1979), *Orientalism*, New York: Vintage Books (originally published 1978).

Santino, Umberto (1994a), 'Per una storia sociale della mafia', in Augusto Cavadi (ed.) *A scuola di antimafia; Materiali di studio, criteri educativi, esperienze didattiche*, pp. 36–48, Palermo: Centro siciliano di documentazione Giuseppe Impastato.

Santino, Umberto (1994b), 'Appunti su mafia e pedagogia alternativa', in Augusto Cavadi (ed.) *A scuola di antimafia; Materiali di studio, criteri educativi, esperienze didattiche*, pp. 67–72, Palermo: Centro siciliano di documentazione Giuseppe Impastato.

Schneider, Jane (1998), 'Introduction: The Dynamics of Neo-orientalism in Italy (1848–1995)', in J. Schneider (ed.) *Italy's 'Southern Question': Orientalism in One Country*, pp. 1–23, Oxford: Berg.

Schneider, Jane and Peter Schneider (1976), *Culture and Political Economy in Western Sicily*, New York: Academic Press.

Schneider, Jane and Peter Schneider (1996), *Festival of the Poor: Fertility Decline and the Ideology of Class in Sicily, 1860–1980*, Tucson, AZ: University of Arizona Press.

Schneider, Jane and Peter Schneider (2003), *Reversible Destiny: Mafia, Antimafia, and the Struggle for Palermo*, Berkeley and Los Angeles: University of California Press.

Scuola Media Statale 'Giovanni Meli' di Cinisi (1993), *Le Parole non bastano; I ragazzi di Cinisi ricordano Peppino Impastato*, Monreale: Casa del Sorriso.

Stabile, Francesco M. (1989), 'Chiesa e mafia', in Umberto Santino (ed.) *L'antimafia difficile*, pp. 103–28, Palermo: Centro siciliano di documentazione Giuseppe Impastato.

Zanvito, Giuseppe (1989), Interview with a young social researcher in the Albergheria Quarter, Palermo, 21 August.

Part III
Frontiers of ethnicity

8 Citizenship, diversity and equality in English schools

Audrey Osler

Across Europe and internationally, a number of governments have over the past decade sought to introduce or strengthen citizenship education in schools. Not only those states that are new and developing democracies but also many states that have long traditions of democratic governance are reviewing the position and purpose of citizenship education within their school curricula. This renewed focus on citizenship education is taking place in a changing international context: while a number of developments suggest that the world is becoming more democratic, paradoxically, many states are also experiencing signs of an apparent crisis in democracy.

Citizenship and the crisis of democracy

A number of indicators suggest that the world is becoming more democratic. Between 1980 and 2001, 81 countries took significant steps towards democracy and 30 military regimes were replaced by civilian governments. Now 125 countries, with 62 per cent of the world's population, have a free press. The number of states holding multi-party elections more than doubled over the same period. The number of countries ratifying human rights conventions and covenants has also increased dramatically since 1990. The number of countries ratifying the International Covenant on Economic Social and Cultural Rights (ICESCR) and the International Covenant on Civil and Political Rights (ICCPR) grew from 90 to nearly 150 (UNDP 2002). The UN Convention on the Rights of the Child (1989) is now ratified by all but one country.

Yet the start of the twenty-first century has also seen a crisis of democracy in those states with the longest traditions of democratic governance. The first national elections of the century in the USA, Britain and France were notable for record levels of abstention. The US presidential election in 2000 did not produce an indisputably fair outcome, and the 2002 French presidential election became a referendum on democracy itself when a far-right candidate reached the final round. These electoral developments are not the only threats to democracy. The terrorist attacks of 11 September 2001 were launched by activists who, exploiting modern technology, took advantage of the freedoms of movement, of communication and of association in what has often been identified as 'an attack on the fundamental principles of freedom, democracy, the rule of law and justice' (Held 2001).

Processes of electronic and technological globalization may have brought us closer together than ever before. Yet, the crisis in democracy rests on a feeling among ordinary people that although they can watch what is going on in the world – through the Internet or on television – or wish to make their views heard, they are unable to change the world. They may consequently feel relatively powerless as they watch world events evolve. Recent political events of international import have further strengthened such a feeling. The 'Stop the War' march held in London in February 2003 attracted over a million participants from diverse backgrounds, who shared a broad common agenda. This protest, and other protests across Britain and across the world that took place on the same day, were not only an expression of people's horror of war, but also a reflection of a widespread desire among ordinary citizens to influence the world. The protesters were demanding that political leaders give consideration to their views.

Citizenship education and democracy in Britain

It is in such a context that citizenship education has become statutory required teaching in English secondary (from 2002) and primary schools. All schools will be monitored on how they achieve efficient teaching of citizenship through inspection. Furthermore, citizenship education has been introduced at a time of constitutional reform in Britain, including the introduction of the Human Rights Act 1998; the establishment of a Scottish Parliament and Welsh Assembly; and the development of a new settlement between Britain and Northern Ireland, also involving devolved government. Indications of further devolution to regional level can be seen in the creation of an assembly and an elected mayor for London. These political and constitutional developments are encouraging debate about the meanings of nationality, national identity and citizenship and the extent to which individuals and groups from both majority and minority communities feel a sense of belonging to the nation and the state.

Citizenship studies is being introduced into schools with the explicit aim of strengthening democracy by enabling the greater participation of young people in society. The assumption here is that young people have become wholly uninterested in matters political, least of all citizenship. Yet research evidence suggests that many young people are politically engaged even though they may reject traditional political parties and that they may be learning skills for active citizenship within their local communities (Osler and Starkey 2003; Roker *et al.* 1999). For example, young people may sign petitions opposing building on green-field sites or the closure of a local school. They may write to their MP or local councillors about local, national or international issues. Or, as seen recently, they may also take part in anti-war demonstrations on their own initiative. In these cases they are developing skills for citizenship through political action. Alternatively they may learn through family activities. A young person who accompanies an adult on a visit to a hospital, housing or social security office or in dealings with police or immigration officers will learn about services and procedures. In such a situation, the young person may also be required to support or interpret for an adult, presenting a case or acting as an advocate. Thus home and community are sites for citizenship learning.

Nevertheless, there is a tendency among policy-makers to adopt a deficit view of the young and to characterize them as less politically engaged than their elders. The Report of the Government's Advisory Group on the Teaching of Citizenship in Schools, chaired by Professor Bernard Crick, assumed this deficit model of young people and characterized those young people from minority ethnic communities as having a double deficit (Osler 2000; Osler and Starkey 2002, 2003). Among politicians, there is particular concern about record levels of abstention in elections. This concern is felt particularly for the young, and their apparent apathy is seen as a threat to democracy itself. As the Crick Report asserted:

> There are worrying levels of apathy, ignorance and cynicism about public life. These, unless tackled at every level, could well diminish the hoped-for benefits both of constitutional reform and of the changing nature of the welfare state.
>
> (QCA 1998: 8)

The programme of citizenship education in England thus sets out to engage young people in public life and to promote public service. Its goals are, to say the least, rather ambitious:

> We aim at no less than a change in the political culture of this country both nationally and locally: for people to think of themselves as active citizens, willing, able and equipped to have an influence in public life and with the critical capacities to weigh evidence before speaking and acting; to build upon and to extend radically to young people the best in existing traditions of community involvement and public service, and to make them individually confident in finding new forms of involvement and action among themselves.
>
> (QCA 1998: 7–8)

This statement suggests that citizenship should not be seen as merely another subject in the school curriculum. It will not be enough simply to teach the subject commonly referred to as 'civics' and ensure that students know about the British constitution, the relationship between the two Houses of Parliament, the system of local government, and the role of the monarchy. Young people will also need to experience democracy and develop new skills. Because citizenship education is aimed at constructing participatory and active citizenship among young generations, it entails schools and young people tackling political questions and so-called 'controversial issues'. Citizenship education requires teachers and schools to consider new domains, examining power, young people's rights and responsibilities, and society's problems, such as poverty and inequality, homelessness and injustice – problems that may not be far from students' own experiences. Yet the Crick Report acknowledges the need to tackle controversial issues and suggests young people will need to understand the meaning of human rights, but avoids explicit mention of inequalities between citizens as a result of racism, sexism or homophobia. It presents citizenship as something that has been accomplished, a given rather than as an ongoing struggle, as repeatedly emphasized by new trends in research on citizenship (see for instance Calhoun 1997 [1992], Rubinstein 1996).

The Crick Report also argues in favour of the creation of a stable national identity as follows:

> [A] main aim for the whole community should be to find or restore a sense of common citizenship, including a national identity that is secure enough to find a place in the plurality of nations, cultures, ethnic identities and religions long found in the United Kingdom. Citizenship education creates a common ground between different ethnic and religious identities.
>
> (QCA 1998: 17)

Schools are expected to play a specific role in helping reach the explicit goal of shaping that national identity. Unlike the national programmes of study for citizenship in France, which assume an agreed national identity associated with the Republic, there is no clear sense of existing national identity in the English programme of study. This is presented as something yet to be created (Osler and Starkey 2001). The expectation here is that a sense of national identity will be forged in the context of examining the plurality of nations, cultures and ethnic and religious identities within the UK (Parekh 2000). This implies an examination of culture, 'race' and ethnicity, the role of religion, power relationships, the media, the treatment of refugees and asylum seekers, discrimination and racism. These are topics on which students, their parents and communities are likely to have strong views and emotional reactions (pride, fear, anger, a sense of belonging, feelings of insecurity and injustice) and in connection with which they may well be suspicious of 'political indoctrination'. In order to address these issues teachers will not only require a pedagogy that encourages reflection and permits debate, but they will also need a shared and explicit values framework. Such a values framework can be evolved through focusing on human rights.

Citizenship education, human rights and learning to live together

Governments, across Europe and internationally, recognize the need for education for living together in our increasingly globalized world. Dominant narratives of globalization tend to focus largely or exclusively on economic developments. Yet globalization is also political, technological and cultural, as well as economic. People living on different continents, who may never meet, are nevertheless members of overlapping 'communities of fate' (Held 1996), sharing common concerns or identities. It is increasingly recognized that new mechanisms are needed at both regional and global levels to promote greater accountability and democracy (Held 2001). The terrorist attacks of 11 September have brought these issues into sharper focus, requiring governments and intergovernmental organizations to re-think their global responsibilities and work cooperatively and with moral consistency with regard to human rights, justice and aid. Moreover, as I have previously argued, they have increased the pressure for educational responses to globalization (Osler and Vincent 2002). Thus, UNESCO has provided a framework that promotes education for greater democracy and human rights internationally.

Ministers of Education, meeting at the 44th session of the UNESCO's International Conference on Education in 1994 in Geneva, mindful of their responsibilities in this field, determined:

> to strive resolutely ... to take suitable steps to establish in educational institutions an atmosphere contributing to the success of education for international understanding, so that they become ideal places for the exercise of tolerance, respect for human rights, the practice of democracy and learning about the diversity and wealth of cultural identities.
>
> (UNESCO 1995: 2.2)

The following year, the General Conference of UNESCO approved an *Integrated Framework of Action on Education for Peace, Human Rights and Democracy* at its 28th session in Paris, which identified policies and actions to be taken at institutional, national and international levels to realize such education. It states:

> There must be education for peace, human rights and democracy. It cannot, however, be restricted to specialized subjects and knowledge. The whole of education must transmit this message and the atmosphere of the institution must be in harmony with the application of democratic standards.
>
> (UNESCO 1995: IV. 17)

Education for living together in an interdependent world thus entails education for peace, human rights and democracy. The intention is that this education should be a mainstream concern and part of the entitlement of every learner. Citizenship education has a key role to play within any such programme; but the principles of peace, human rights and democracy need to be addressed across the taught curriculum. Equally importantly, the institutional ethos needs to be one in which democracy is practised. The UNESCO General Conference recognized that any attempt to incorporate these issues into the curriculum will need to be matched by processes of democratization within schools and education authorities. The UNESCO statement thus echoes the sentiment of the Council of Europe Committee of Ministers Recommendation some ten years earlier, on teaching and learning about human rights:

> Democracy is best learned in a democratic setting where participation is encouraged, where views can be expressed openly and discussed, where there is freedom of expression for pupils and teachers, and where there is fairness and justice. An appropriate climate is, therefore, an essential complement to effective learning about human rights.
>
> (Council of Europe 1985, reprinted in Osler and Starkey 1996)

Such a concern with human rights has also been echoed in Britain, as is acknowledged by the Crick Report, which also makes references to the changing constitutional context in which citizenship education is being introduced. In fact, the single most important constitutional development has been the Human Rights Act 1998, which incorporates the European Convention on Human Rights into domestic law. One of the stated aims of the Act is to establish a 'human rights culture' in Britain (Klug 2000). This human rights culture is expected both to qualify and to complement that of national citizenship. Indeed, the focus has so far been on national identity, and on the roles of citizens within the legal and constitutional framework of the nation, with young people being socialized into the 'imagined community' of the nation (Anderson 1991). Furthermore, this imagined community is necessarily diverse, and in most contexts, multicultural. It is thus inappropriate to educate for one single national identity. Instead, one needs to acknowledge the fact that young people will identify with a number of communities. It is important to recognize that there are many ways, for example, of being British. Young people at school in England may identify with their town or city, with their family, and with a local or diasporic community. The emphasis that an individual places on a particular aspect of her or his identity is likely to vary over time and according to the place in which that individual is situated. Diversity needs to be 'given public status and dignity' as well as visibility, and politicians need to work together with other citizens to 'develop a new social and cultural policy capable of nurturing ethnic identities' (Parekh 1991: 197). As Figueroa puts it:

> 'British' must be seen as fully including the ethnic minority communities. But the minority communities being seen as British does not imply their denying their 'ethnic' origins and identity.
>
> (2000: 59–60)

In other words, what is needed is a vision of multiculturalism that recognizes that each individual has multiple identities. This new multiculturalism needs to be founded on human rights and must be inclusive of all, including white communities (Osler and Starkey 2000). It is important that all young people and their parents are able to accept and share the values of the school. For this, the values base needs to be explicit. Within multicultural societies, human rights provide us with a set of internationally agreed principles on which those values can be based. These principles can form the framework of a dialogue between individuals from diverse backgrounds and cultures. To be sure, human rights do not provide clear answers to all problems and differences. Yet they do provide a structure within which issues can be debated and conflicts resolved. By the same token, it is crucial to acknowledge that racism and discrimination in British society are not confined to 'visible' and established minorities, but that other individuals and communities, including refugees and asylum-seekers, Jews, Irish and Gypsies and Travellers may currently experience racism, disadvantage, harassment and violence. A number of these communities may also recall a long history of racism and discrimination. It is therefore crucial to take these variegated histories into account when envisaging the construction of a common values base.

Equality, diversity and English education policy

> Globalisation has caused the transformation of a number of major cities in Britain and elsewhere in Europe, which have become increasingly diverse in their make-up. Many schools have experienced considerable changes in their populations and some which previously perceived themselves to be relatively homogeneous are now having to re-think their approaches as they acknowledge cultural diversity. At the same time, there is evidence of increasing levels of racism and of particular intolerance towards refugees and asylum seekers.
>
> (Thalhammer *et al*. 2001)

In February 1999 the report of the Stephen Lawrence Inquiry (Macpherson *et al*. 1999) identified institutional racism as a major cause of social exclusion in Britain. Senior politicians from a range of political parties went on record to acknowledge institutional racism in British society, and the Government pledged itself to a programme to eradicate racism. The Government's response to the Stephen Lawrence Inquiry's recommendations (Home Office 1999) identified citizenship education as a key means by which schools would address and prevent racism and encourage young people to value cultural diversity. Since 1997 the Labour government has taken a number of steps to promote race equality. In setting up the Stephen Lawrence Inquiry and accepting its finding of institutional racism, it acknowledged the importance of political leadership in challenging racism and in creating a climate in which race equality is seen as the responsibility of all. As then Home Secretary Jack Straw stated, when presenting the report to the House of Commons:

> The report does not place a responsibility on someone else; it places a responsibility on each of us. We must make racial equality a reality. The vision is clear: we must create a society in which every individual, regardless of colour, creed or race, has the same opportunities and respect as his or her neighbour.
>
> (*Hansard*, 24 February 1999)

The report of the Stephen Lawrence Inquiry defined institutional racism as:

> The collective failure of an organisation to provide an appropriate and professional service to people because of their colour, culture, or ethnic origin. It can be detected in processes, attitudes and behaviour which amount to discrimination through unwitting prejudice, ignorance, thoughtlessness and racist stereotyping which disadvantage minority ethnic people. It persists because of the failure of the organisation openly and adequately to recognise and address its existence and causes by policy, example and leadership. Without recognition and action to eliminate such racism, it can prevail as part of the ethos or culture of the organisation. It is a corrosive disease.
>
> (Macpherson *et al.* 1999: para. 6.34)

In responding to the Stephen Lawrence Inquiry report the government recognized institutionalized racism, and ministers pledged themselves to eradicate it. Richardson and Wood (1999) provide a useful working definition of racism in education, exploring how it can become institutionalized:

> In the education system there are laws, customs and practices which systematically reflect and reproduce racial inequalities ... If racist consequences accrue to institutional laws, customs and practices, a school or a local education authority or a national education system is racist whether or not individual teachers, inspectors, officers, civil servants and elected politicians have racist intentions ... Educational institutions may systematically treat or tend to treat pupils and students differently in respect of race, ethnicity or religion. The differential treatment lies within an institution's ethos and organisation rather than in the attitudes, beliefs and intentions of individual members of staff. The production of differential treatment is 'institutionalised' in the way the institution operates.
>
> (Richardson and Wood 1999: 33)

Table 8.1 highlights examples of racial inequality in the education system in Britain, drawing on the research evidence. Despite this overwhelming

Table 8.1 Racial inequality in schools (adapted from Richardson and Wood 1999)

Dimensions of inequality	Examples of inequality in the education system
Outcomes White people receive more benefits than black, and racial inequality is therefore perpetuated	White pupils leave school at 16 or 18 with substantially better paper qualifications than African-Caribbean pupils (Gillborn and Mirza 2000; Richardson and Wood 1999; Tikly *et al.* 2000)
Black people receive negative results more than do white people, and in this way too inequality is perpetuated	African-Caribbean pupils experience punishments, particularly permanent and fixed-term exclusions, more than white pupils (Osler 1997a)
Structure In senior decision-making and policy-making positions there are proportionately more white people than black, and in consequence black interests and perspectives are inadequately represented	There are few black and ethnic minority headteachers or deputy heads, and few black education officers, inspectors, teacher trainers and textbook writers (Osler 1997b)
Culture and attitudes In the occupational culture there are assumptions, expectations and generalizations that are more negative about black people than about white	Black pupils are more likely than white pupils to be seen as trouble-makers, and to be criticized and controlled (Gillborn 1995; Sewell 1997)
Rules and procedures Customary rules, regulations and practices work more to the advantage of white people than black	The national curriculum reflects white interests, concerns and outlooks and neglects or marginalizes black experience (see e.g. Figueroa 1993)
Staff training Staff have not received training on race and racism issues, and on ways they can avoid indirect discrimination	Neither initial nor continuing professional development pays sufficient attention to race and racism issues (Osler 1997b; Siraj-Blatchford 1993)
Face-to-face interaction Staff are less effective in communication with and listening to black people than they are in interaction with white people	Encounters between white staff and black pupils frequently escalate into needless confrontation (Sewell 1997; Wright 1992)

evidence of institutionalized racism in the education system, including the disproportionate exclusion of African-Caribbean children; notable differentials in attainment, with African-Caribbean, Bangladeshi- and Pakistani-heritage children performing, on average, well below their peers; and a national curriculum that marginalizes the cultures and experiences of learners from minority communities, the Department for Education and Skills was slow to respond. The Government named the school inspection agency OFSTED as the body responsible for monitoring how schools were preventing racism and promoting race equality (Home Office 1999). Our research, carried out on behalf of the Commission for Racial Equality (CRE) found that senior inspectors did not accept this brief and that those employed to inspect schools were not adequately prepared to address issues of racial equality. Headteachers, although generally sensitive to the need to ensure racial equality, were not trained to address equality issues, and did not always make the link between the Government's broad policy of raising standards and the need to address inequalities and the underachievement of particular ethnic groups within the education system (Osler and Morrison 2000). As one secondary headteacher expressed it: 'If race equality is a Government priority in education no one has made it clear to me'.

In 1999 the Department for Education and Employment (DfEE) introduced the Ethnic Minority Achievement Grant (EMAG), which replaced the former Section 11 arrangements, administered by the Home Office, as the main funding mechanism for addressing the specific educational needs of children from minority communities. Although the Government promised to evaluate the impact of the EMAG, no proper evaluation has taken place. In 2000 a team from the universities of Bristol and Leicester carried out an analysis of 151 local education authority (LEA) action plans developed in response to EMAG and of performance data returned by the LEAs. Our report provided the first national picture of pupil attainment at the end of primary school (Key Stage 2) by ethnicity, as well as providing a national picture of attainment by ethnicity at the age of 16. It confirms that there are considerable gaps in attainment between ethnic groups. For example, at the end of primary school (Key Stage 2) African-Caribbean children are seven percentage points below the national average, Pakistani-heritage children 13 points and Bangladeshi-heritage children 11 points below in tests in English. At 16 years the gap has widened for African-Caribbean students, who are 21 percentage points below the average in attaining five A*–C grades at GCSE. At GCSE Pakistani-heritage students are 11 percentage points behind, and Bangladeshi-heritage students more than nine percentage points behind their peers (Tikly *et al.* 2000).

The Race Relations (Amendment) Act 2000 marks a key development in government policy. It places a positive duty on schools, universities and other public bodies, including local education authorities, to promote race equality. From 2002 schools and other public bodies are required to take steps to ensure that they fulfil their legal duty to promote race equality in accordance with the Act. Under the Act schools must aim to: eliminate unlawful discrimination; promote equality of opportunity, and promote good relations between people of different racial groups. Most importantly, the CRE has the power to enforce these duties. The law applies to all schools, whether or not they have pupils from minority ethnic communities on roll. Schools are required to prepare a policy for promoting race equality that provides details of how the school will monitor and review the policy's effectiveness. Schools are required to monitor attainment, access to benefits and the impact of disciplinary procedures, including exclusion, by ethnicity. Agencies that carry out statutory inspections and audits of public authorities also have a duty under the Act. OFSTED is required to examine and report on whether schools are meeting their general and specific duties under the Act.

Despite the acceptance of the need for schools to prevent and address racism through their curriculum and ethos, until 2003 no British education minister acknowledged the existence of institutional racism in the education service (Osler 2002). Bernard Crick, the Chair of the Government's Advisory Group on Education for Citizenship and the Teaching of Democracy in Schools, suggests that those Home Office ministers who have endorsed antiracism in schools are 'perhaps not wholly conversant . . . with good practice in actual classroom teaching' (Crick 2000: 134). He argues that Education ministers are wiser in not adopting an explicit antiracist position. A government consultation document *Aiming High* (DfES 2003) is the first official and explicit acknowledgement of institutional racism within the education service. Effectively the document is mainstreaming antiracism, recognizing that efforts to improve the educational opportunities and experiences of young people from minority communities are a mainstream responsibility rather than an extra. Consequently, emphasis is placed on the training of headteachers and other mainstream teachers, not on the work of additional specialist staff. Rather than focus on minority ethnic learners in general, *Aiming High* seeks to focus on those particular groups that schools are currently failing.

Antiracism and political literacy

One of the key strands within the citizenship curriculum in England is the development of political literacy. Political literacy is defined as 'pupils learning about and how to make themselves effective in public life through knowledge, skills and values' (QCA 1998: 41).

A politically literate citizen will require knowledge and understanding of human rights; opportunities to develop confident multiple identities; experience of democratic participation; and skills for social inclusion, for participation and to effect change. Since racism is an anti-democratic force that serves as a barrier to full participation, then a politically literate citizen will need the knowledge and skills to challenge racism.

In Britain antiracism is often simply seen as the opposite of racism, rather than as a set of values or beliefs that is part of a human rights discourse (Lloyd 1998). If multiculturalism and antiracism are to be inclusive of all and to appear relevant to all, then students need to understand the links between various forms of injustice, to recognize the need for solidarity, and to understand how, in practice, racism may combine with other forms of discrimination. It is only through understanding the complex ways in which racism may operate to exclude that it is possible to find effective ways of challenging it. Antiracism requires teachers to consider pedagogy. Our study of education and training projects funded by the European Commission sought to identify the ways in which such projects might contribute to active citizenship. From this study we devised a checklist designed for use by those planning citizenship education projects or curricula. In order to integrate the cognitive and affective elements, projects for citizenship require an appropriate pedagogy based on participation and active learning. An effective project is likely to include the following features: information about democracy and human rights in theory and in practice; a focus on key skills for social and economic inclusion; an equal opportunities dimension addressing the specific needs of women; an antiracist focus and consideration of the specific needs of minority communities; opportunities to explore and reflect upon various identities and cultural attributes; cooperative practice and group or team work; experiential learning; democratic decision-making, including participation in the management of the project; independent reasoning and critical awareness; development of effective communication skills, including those required for transnational and intercultural communication; community involvement; negotiation and participation skills (Osler and Starkey 1999). A number of transnational projects funded by the European Commission have sought to promote active learning for citizenship. A project coordinated by a Belgian high school in partnership with schools in Finland, Greece and Britain did this by encouraging students to discover the realities of social exclusion in their towns. They did this by viewing the work of local voluntary organizations. They were able to see at first hand the work of active citizens and the structures they had put in place to contact and support disadvantaged people. The project put the young people in touch with members of the community who were marginalized, including those with disabilities, the unemployed and victims of violence. The students reported on what they had found by contributing to a newsletter, developing an exhibition and preparing and running workshops for fellow students (Osler and Starkey 1999).

Conclusion

Citizenship education has been introduced into schools in England as a response to a perceived crisis in democracy, in which the young, in particular, are seen to be apathetic and disengaged from political processes. Across

Europe and in Britain racism has been identified as a threat to democracy and as a barrier to participation. Following the publication of the report of the Stephen Lawrence Inquiry, the government proposed that citizenship education be the key means through which racism might be challenged and diversity and equality promoted in schools. Despite this, there was little official recognition of the ways in which schools and the wider education service were themselves institutionally racist. The acknowledgement in 2003, by the Department of Education and Skills, of institutional racism within the education service opens up the way for schools to address current inequalities through their policies, procedures and practices. By acknowledging that schools are part of the problem as well as part of the solution this opens up the way for developing a programme of education for citizenship and democracy that is grounded in human rights and racial justice.

Teaching for citizenship implies not only learning to live together within the nation-state, but also learning to live together within a broader international community. Educating young people as cosmopolitan citizens means constructing learning experiences that draw on their multiple identities and their experiences within and beyond the cosmopolitan communities in which they live. Research with young people in Leicester confirms that they are comfortable with a range of identities and that they are learning the skills for citizenship within their communities (Osler and Starkey 2002, 2003). Education for cosmopolitan citizenship needs to build upon these experiences and extend them. It is only on this condition that it can tackle one of the most pernicious internal frontiers that divide communities within the nation-state.

Lastly, the example of education against racism as part of a more general approach to the teaching of citizenship in Britain is one shared by many other nation-states. This sharing of educational concerns also takes place at the international level and suggests that nation-states' ideological frontiers are much more porous than is often acknowledged.

References

Anderson, B. (1991), *Imagined Communities: Reflections on the Origins and Spread of Nationalism*, London: Verso.

Calhoun, Craig (1997[1992]), 'Introduction: Habermas and the Public Sphere', in Craig Calhoun (ed.) *Habermas and the Public Sphere*, pp. 1–47, Cambridge, MA: MIT Press.

Crick, B. (2000), *Essays on Citizenship*, London: Continuum.

DfES (Department for Education and Skills) (2003), *Aiming High: Raising the Achievement of Minority Ethnic Pupils. A Consultation Document*, London: DfES.

Figueroa, P. (1993), 'History: Policy Issues', in P. D. Pumfrey and G. K. Verma (eds) *Cultural Diversity and the Curriculum*, Vol. 1, London: Falmer.

Figueroa, P. (2000), 'Citizenship Education for a Plural Society', in A. Osler (ed.) *Citizenship and Democracy in Schools: Diversity, Identity, Equality*, Stoke on Trent: Trentham.

Gillborn, D. (1995), *Racism and Antiracism in Real Schools*, Buckingham: Open University Press.

Gillborn, D. and H. S. Mirza (2000), *Educational Inequality: Mapping Race, Class and Gender, a Synthesis of Research Evidence*, London: Office for Standards in Education.

Held, D. (1996), *Models of Democracy*, 2nd edn, Cambridge: Polity Press.

Held, D. (2001), *Violence and Justice in a Global Age*, 14 September. www.open-democracy.net.

Home Office (1999), *Stephen Lawrence Inquiry: Home Secretary's Action Plan*, London: Home Office.

Klug, F. (2000), *Values for a Godless Age: The Story of the United Kingdom's New Bill of Rights*, London: Penguin.

Lloyd, C. (1998), *Discourses of Antiracism in France*, Aldershot: Ashgate.

Macpherson, W. *et al.* (1999), *The Stephen Lawrence Inquiry*, London: The Stationery Office.

Osler, A. (1997a), *Exclusion from School: Research Report*, London: CRE.

Osler, A. (1997b), *The Education and Careers of Black Teachers: Changing Identities, Changing Lives*, Buckingham: Open University Press.

Osler, A. (2000), 'The Crick Report: Difference, Equality and Racial Justice', *Curriculum Journal* 11: 1, 25–37.

Osler, A. (2002), 'Citizenship Education and the Strengthening of Democracy: Is Race in the Agenda?', in D. Scott and H. Lawson (eds) *Citizenship Education and the Curriculum*, Westport, CT: Greenwood.

Osler, A. and M. Morrison (2000), *Inspecting Schools for Race Equality: OFSTED's Strengths and Weaknesses*, Stoke on Trent: Trentham, for the Commission for Racial Equality.

Osler, A. and H. Starkey (1996), *Teacher Education and Human Rights*, London: David Fulton.

Osler, A. and H. Starkey (1999), 'Rights, Identities and Inclusion: European Action Programmes as Political Education', *Oxford Review of Education* 25: 1 and 2, 199–215.

Osler, A. and H. Starkey (2000), 'Citizenship, Human Rights and Cultural Diversity', in A. Osler (ed.) *Citizenship and Democracy in Schools: Diversity, Identity, Equality*, Stoke on Trent: Trentham.

Osler, A. and H. Starkey (2001), 'Citizenship Education and National Identities in France and England: Inclusive or Exclusive?', *Oxford Review of Education* 27: 2, 287–305.

Osler, A. and H. Starkey (2002), 'Learning to Live Together: Young People as Cosmopolitan Citizens', in F. Audigier and N. Bottani (eds) *Education et vivre ensemble. Actes du colloque: la problématique du vivre ensemble dans les curricula*, Geneva: Service de la recherche en éducation (SRED).

Osler, A. and H. Starkey (2003), 'Learning for Cosmopolitan Citizenship: Theoretical Debates and Young People's Experiences, *Educational Review* 55.

Osler, A. and K. Vincent (2002), *Citizenship and the Challenge of Global Education*, Stoke on Trent: Trentham.

Parekh, B. (1991), 'British Citizenship and Cultural Difference', in G. Andrews (ed.) *Citizenship*, London: Lawrence and Wishart.

Parekh, B. (2000), *The Future of Multi-Ethnic Britain. Report of the Commission on the Future of Multi-Ethnic Britain*, London: Runnymede Trust.

QCA (Qualifications and Curriculum Authority) (1998), *Education for Citizenship and the Teaching of Democracy in Schools* (Crick Report), London: QCA.

Richardson, R. and A. Wood (1999), *Inclusive Schools, Inclusive Society: Race and Identity on the Agenda*, Stoke on Trent: Trentham.

Roker, D., K. Player and J. Coleman (1999), 'Young People's Voluntary and Campaigning Activities as Sources of Political Action', *Oxford Review of Education* 25: 1 and 2, 185–98.

Rubinstein, Kim (1996), 'Citizenship, Membership and Civic Virtue: Similar But Not Quite the Same', in S. Rufus Davis (ed.) *Citizenship in Australia. Democracy, Law and Society*, pp. 69–88, Carlton: Constitutional Centenary Foundation.

Sewell, T. (1997), *Black Masculinities and Schooling: How Black Boys Survive Modern Schooling*, Stoke on Trent: Trentham Books.

Siraj-Blatchford, I. (ed.) (1993), *'Race', Gender and the Education of Teachers*, Buckingham: Open University Press.

Thalhammer, E., V. Zucha, E. Enzenhofer, B. Salfinger and G. Ogris (2001), *Attitudes Towards Minority Groups in the European Union: A Special Analysis of the Eurobarometer Survey*, Vienna: European Monitoring Centre on Racism and Xenophobia.

Tikly, L., A. Osler, J. Hill and K. Vincent (2000), *Ethnic Minority Achievement Grant: Analysis of LEA Action Plans. Research Report 371*, London: Department for Education and Skills.

UNDP (United Nations Development Programme) (2002), *Human Development Report 2002: Deepening Democracy in a Fragmented World*, Oxford: Oxford University Press.

UNESCO (United Nations Educational Scientific and Cultural Organization) (1995), *Declaration and Integrated Framework of Action on Education for Peace, Human Rights and Democracy*, Paris: UNESCO.

Wright, C. (1992), *Race Relations in the Primary School*, London: David Fulton.

9 Language, ethnicity and internal frontiers

Schooling civil society among China's minorities

Naran Bilik

While the prototype of the nation-state evolved in the West through a cumulative process, the rest of the world, including China, have had to adopt this model at such short notice that they can hardly experience their accommodation to it as anything other than Procrustean. This is due to a complex of numerous historical, social and other factors. From the very outset, China's nation-building efforts have blended Western individualistic liberalism with a Chinese collectivized version of ethnicity, racism and cultural-centralism, all this being also variously created, reproduced and imagined by the numerous different linguistic communities within the new configurations of China. A concoction of citizenship with collective loyalty to an authoritative leader locates ethnic education on an often controversial stage where there builds up a tension between mainstream homogenizing policies (one nation, one culture, one language) and sidelined ethnic self-development endeavours. It is to be expected that China will soon take another sharp, assimilationist turn in dealing with its national minorities.

I will base my discussion of the findings in Inner Mongolia and Xinjiang on the thesis that a modern Chinese civil society will have to take shape under the influences both of tension between minority efforts to maintain their languages and cultures and the endeavours to civilize national minorities on the part of mainstream society, and of the geopolitical reconfiguration of relationship between China and outside powers. Drawing on the definitions of 'indexicality' and 'frontier', I want to build an argument about 'indexical frontiers' going against the grain of a notion of citizenship seen exclusively from the homogeneous viewpoint of the centre, a notion that is often defined by the state in ethnic terms. I take indexicality to refer to 'the pervasive context-dependency of natural language utterances, including such varied phenomena as regional accent (indexing speaker's identity)...' (Duranti 2001: 119). But here I involve the term more with military-political 'utterances', in an analogical way.[1] My version of military-political utterances reveals the 'uncivilized accents' of physical violence; accents that also carry, however, symbolically understandable messages in such a way that frontiers are defined and redefined by repeated conquests of each other between the Han and the northern non-Hans. My use of 'frontiers' largely, though not entirely, comes from my reading of E. Balibar (1991a). It involves race, class, nationalism and culture; but also geopolitical situation.

China's nation-building efforts: background

The boundaries of China have been changing as a result of interactions and encounters between the centre and the periphery, between the landbound and the seaboard people, (Lattimore 1951; Wittfogel 1957), and between China and foreign countries.[2] Old China constructed itself as the 'Middle Kingdom', condescending towards those barbarians beyond the pale of civilization who were waiting to be 'tamed'. However, most major historical confrontations between the centre and the periphery took place in the north, represented by conflicts and by symbiosis between steppe herders and agricultural farmers. All these landbound groups negotiated and fought their way to and fro across the Great Wall, that gigantic symbolic divide between civilization and barbarism. Both the 'barbarian horde' and 'civilized society', however, looked down on the southerners, on the seaboard groups. In Chinese history the Mongols and the Manchu broke their way through the Great Wall and ruled the whole of China for centuries. Ghengis Khan and Nurhachi, the founding fathers of the Mongols and the Manchu, respectively, both came from the Margin, from peoples who had connections with both the steppe people and the Chinese sphere of civilization. They were middlemen, who knew and seized their chances well (Lattimore 1951: 118–19). As masters at handling the interplay between different cultural systems, their middlemanship invested heavily in their ability to create 'indexical frontiers'[3] in spite of that major watershed between civilization and barbarism, the Han frontier marked out by the Great Wall of China. The 'barbarian' margins dominated the 'civilized' centre and became the centre in a political sense by imposing new geophysical frontiers, even while they still remained culturally marginal in the face of a strong and resilient Han Chinese culture. Such 'conquering dynasties' were finally to be replaced by the modern nation-state builders, who are mostly Han. Modern history saw the Sino-foreign interactive creation of new frontiers, which were measured and drawn both physically and culturally. The new territorial China emerged against a changed landscape of the Western conquest of the world.

The physical confrontations with the Eight-Power Alliance Army have also helped change the discourse of ethnicity in China. New ideas, new objects and new images swarmed in to match and change Chinese reality. People imagined and created what they could not before. Between 1918 and 1919, Dr Sun Yat-sen wrote The International Development of China, which became the second part of Jianguo fanglue ('Nation-building Strategies'), planning to relocate ten million Han people over a period of ten years in

north-west China, especially Inner Mongolia and Xinjiang. This long-term
resettlement plan was designed for those demobilized soldiers who otherwise
might turn into troublemakers (Sun 1998: 175–6). It has been faithfully
carried through both by the current policy of the PRC in Xinjiang, and by its
earlier policy in Inner Mongolia and Heilongjiang (a north-eastern Chinese
province bordering on Russia). Each major confrontation with the Other
would create some new core concepts and a resultant praxis, which would
create new landscapes, and, especially, new indexical frontiers. Before and
after the communist takeover in 1949, the CPC (Communist Party of China,
formerly known as the CCP), armed with Marxist ideology and a long-term
strategic vision of the 'united front', has made and implemented favourable
ethno-national policies encouraging minority-group education. Such policies
were based on the results of the Ethno-national Identification Project, which
classified different ethnic groups (including the Han) in China into 55 officially recognized ethnicities or *minzu*.[4] This grand project, which employed
the labours of thousands of professors, students, officials, and members of the
local elites, lasted for about twenty years, from the 1950s to the 1970s.

Language and ethnicity

Language has been the principal criterion for the identification of such ethnicities, though other 'measurements' were also taken into account following
Stalin's 'four-common' definition of a nation.[5] China's leadership are
inclined to take language as a vital component in the construction of a civil
society. China is generally thought of as equivalent to the Han, both inside
and outside China (Gladney 1998: 11). Therefore, as one component of
building up civil society in China, if we follow this line of logic, education
will become a Han-type education. In order to sinicize education in minority regions, the Han elite and some minority politicians/educators would say
that language is no more than a tool for communication, and so you are
always free to choose the better or the best one to facilitate communication
and the procurement of (intellectual) 'capitals'.

There has long been a prejudice against minority languages in China, a
prejudice well expressed by the view that Mandarin stands at the acme of a
linguistic hierarchy mirroring the vertical structure of power in China
today. In the eyes of many nationalist thinkers and practitioners, Chinese is
the best language, just as China is at the centre of the world. One
representative view in China holds that the speed of building a Chinese civil
society often corresponds to the speed of acculturation on the part of the
national minorities. It follows that the promotion of standard Chinese
among the 55 national minorities has always been a mainstream concern,
although China has not yet designated standard Chinese as the sole official
language.

Yet in the early years of the New China the Communist Party of China
had already adopted a series of preferential policies to guarantee freedom of

language use and language development for the national minorities. Between 20 and 28 September 1951 the Ministry of Education held a national meeting on ethnicity education. The Education Minister M. A. Xulun, in his report to session 112 of the Government Administration Council, stated that, for all those *minzu* such as Mongolians, Koreans, Tibetans, Uygurs and Kazakhs, it was imperative that they should use their own languages and scripts in education. Special funds should be set aside for developing national minority education. Session 112 passed four important documents, namely, Directives on Strengthening National Minority Education, a Resolution on National Minority Educational Administrative Organs, a Working Programme on Training National Minority Teaching Staff, and a Temporary Solution for the Treatment of National Minority Students (Han 1998b: 103–4).

Several instruments are fundamental to putting into practice the CPC ideology of nationality education. First, the guideline on minority education is that the New Democratization should be grounded in education, and specifically in national, scientific and mass education. The training of minority political elites was the focus; the training up of professional personnel for the minorities was secondary. Second, minority education should disseminate CPC nationality policies and the Marxist view on nations and nationalism. It should help to fight off Han chauvinism and minority nationalism. Third, minority education should pay due heed to local customs. Fourth, and more importantly, minority education should honour the CPC's linguistic policies toward minorities. All the nationalities' governmental organs should use the local minority languages, and the cause of minority educational and cultural development should be fostered. Fifth, local governments should build up teams of minority teaching staff. Sixth, minority students should receive preferential treatment. Seventh, local governments should establish minority education offices in the relevant bureaux to strengthen their administration (Wu 2000: 4–9).

Two major setbacks, however, stand out in this whole basically affirmative process: one came during the Cultural Revolution, when all minority education almost came to a halt; and the other is now looming large, at a time when China is trying to embrace the market economy, albeit in a version with 'Chinese characteristics' – a time when homogenization on all fronts is needed to improve economic efficiency and political unity. Facing a common situation of economic (but not political) devolution and a rising Han culturalism (nationalism) adopted in compensation for China's current economic disadvantage compared with the West, hitherto culturally indulged minorities such as the Mongols and the Uygurs gradually found themselves situated on the losing side of the game. The Mongolian elite need to bring about major changes in the format of their education to cope with a losing linguistic situation in which an increasing number of young people have started to learn Chinese and a foreign language, with an eye to better job opportunities and further education. In Xinjiang, concurrently with the mounting of an anti-terrorist campaign, Chinese teaching is on its way to replacing Uygur teaching in higher-level education. The future is not bright for these two languages if the situation does not change.

Case study I: Inner Mongolia

The 1911 Revolution not only enabled the Han to replace the Manchu as rulers of China, but also emancipated 'Outer Mongolia' from Manchu rule. The Republic of China sent troops to reoccupy Mongolia in 1919, but they were driven out in 1921 by Russo-Mongol forces. The new Mongolian government proclaimed its independence on 11 July 1921 (Soucek 2000: 297–8). As part of the Sino-Soviet geopolitical reconfiguration, Inner Mongolia was to remain in China, despite many futile attempts made by Inner Mongolian leaders – attempts that included collaboration with the Japanese and going in person to Ulanbaatar to negotiate for reunification. It was Ulanhu, a sinified Mongolian and a Communist, who finally persuaded most of the Mongolian nationalists to embrace communism, thereby bringing about a temporary suppression of various internal frontiers of class (Mongolian intellectuals, including those who had received a Japanese education, came together with Mongolian peasant-revolutionaries under the flag of communism), language (Mongols who did not speak Mongolian united with Mongols who spoke Mongolian or both Mongolian and Chinese, or even Japanese), ideology (Mongolian nationalism gave way to Chinese-centred Communism), and 'space' (East Mongols united with West Mongols). The CPC was strengthened by the mutual collaboration of all these groups. As part of this deal, Inner Mongolia became a titular autonomous region within China in 1947, two years before the founding of the People's Republic of Communist China. However, 'it is difficult to reconcile the fact that Mongols constitute an absolute minority in China's Inner Mongolia Autonomous Region ... [with their] ... enjoying nominal status as its titular rulers' (Bulag 2002: 3).

Inner Mongolia, a place regarded as beyond the pale of Chinese traditional civilization, was now scheduled to become a communist 'classroom', where a new state-sponsored education full of revolutionary energy would help to draw the boundaries of an emerging nation-state. A multilingual civilizing project came into full force of implementation, and was made concrete by building Mongolian schools, publishing Mongolian books, training Mongolian teaching staff, and recruiting Mongolian students. Much energy was expended to ensure that Mongolian students and the Mongolian populace knew that the CPC, which was mostly Han, could save the Mongolian people, and that Mongolian nationalism and communism could come together as Chinese patriotism (*aiguozhuyi*). Textbooks were largely translated from the Chinese and were full of discourses of *huaxia* (Chinese) 'civilization' and communist propaganda. To carry the messages of nationalist-Marxism through to the minority masses, most of whom did not know a single word of Chinese, in the Region, Mongolian education was badly needed and was fully encouraged, and all this was synchronized with an effort to establish and to naturalize diversity (Balibar 1991b; Bulag 2002: 3). This was and still is a component of the 'civilizing' project. By the time of the founding of the Inner Mongolia Autonomous Region in May 1947, there were only six professional schools and 935 students, including 250 Mongolian students, in the region. By 1953, however, with full support from the central government, the number and variety of schools had dramatically increased, to 1,140 primary schools for 93,166 Mongolian pupils with 3,387 teaching staff; five Mongolian middle schools; 17 Mongolian–Han professional schools with 243 Mongolians among the teaching staff; and two colleges with 125 Mongolian students and 16 Mongolian teachers on campus (Han 1998b: 104, 107–8). Mongolian textbooks were also compiled and published, largely based on translations of Chinese textbooks and teaching materials adapted from the Mongolian Republic. By 1950, 573,150 copies of Mongolian textbooks and reference books in 60 subjects had been published. The subjects included Mongolian, Maths, Elementary Knowledge, History, Geography, Basic Political Knowledge, Nature, Mongolian Grammar, the Lunar Calendar and a 'Textbook for Winter', as well as 'Readings for the Masses' (Han 1998b: 106). By the year 1984 there were six publishing houses that were turning out publications in both Mongolian and Chinese.

While the Cultural Revolution wrought havoc in Mongolian as in other forms of education, the end of it in 1976 helped to restore Mongolian education. From then until 1997, the numbers of on-campus Mongolian students and Mongolian teaching staff saw impressive increases. According to statistics on Mongolian students learning Mongolian as a first or second language during 1985–6, there were 6,691 Mongolian university/college students out of a total of 31,242 minority university/college students; Mongolian university/college students who received education in Mongolian numbered 3,405; and university/college faculty members teaching in Mongolian totalled 638. In the same period, Mongolian technical school students increased to 7,404 out of a total of 40,184 minority technical school students, Mongolian technical school students receiving education in Mongolian numbered 4,662 and technical school teachers who used Mongolian as a teaching medium totalled 700; Mongolian middle-school students numbered 169,070 out of a total of 1,116,646 for all minority middle-school students. Mongolian middle-school students receiving education in Mongolian totalled 92,720, Mongolian middle-school students learning Mongolian as a second language totalled 22,832, and middle-school teachers who taught in Mongolian increased to 6,123. There were 365,336 Mongolian primary-school students out of a total of 2,548,977 minority primary-school students, 3,328 Mongolian primary-school students who received education in Mongolian, 782 Mongolian primary-school students who learned Mongolian as a second language, and 246 primary-school teachers who were teaching in Mongolian. Mongolian children in pre-school education numbered 8,796 out a total of 81,524 minority children in pre-school education. There were 5,027 Mongolian children in pre-school education who were receiving education in Mongolian, and 1,268 were learning Mongolian as a second language, while 403 teachers were teaching in Mongolian in pre-school education. Adding other figures for institutions such as technical schools and adult further education, we have a total of 591,033 Mongolian students out of a total of 4,120,147 minority students, 371,008 Mongolian students who were receiving education in Mongolian, 43,549 Mongolian students who were learning Mongolian as a second language, and 25,953 teachers who were teaching in Mongolian (INS CASS and SNC 1994: 23–4). 'By 1990, the total number of professional tutors [technical instructors] who teach in Mongolian should reach 26,230' (Han 1998b: 152).

But in the cities and towns, even though many teachers have been given posts reserved for minorities in educational institutions, a substantial number of them actually are either sinified Mongols or have only recently turned themselves into Mongols. During the 1980s the Chinese minorities were allowed to 'correct' their ethnic national identities, and a huge number of those who had previously been Han Chinese became members of minorities, largely attracted by the affirmative action programmes available to the minorities (for example, minorities can often have more than one child and can be promoted to higher rankings according to fixed local quotas; and minority children can get in to local schools or universities with lower scores). As some ethno-demographers comment, the sudden jump of the minority population in Inner Mongolia by 1.17 million between the 1982 census and the 1990 census is due to the addition of 524,700 people who switched their identity from 'Han' to a minority identity, and this shift accounts for 44.85 per cent of the general increase in the minority population during this period (Zhang and Huang 1993: 162–3).

However, after half a century a gap appeared between what was meant to be and used to be and what is now the reality. Though there is still an impressive number of Mongolians in Inner Mongolia speaking Mongolian and attending Mongolian schools and universities, the general situation and the trend of development are not promising. The symbolic as well as the practical power of minority languages, including Mongolian, has been seriously challenged. With the ever-widening spread of marketization showing a Han-nationalistic bent and weakening the autonomy mechanism in Inner Mongolia,[6] the Mongolian language is losing ground to Chinese in respect of employment and social promotion and in many other ways. Most Mongolian residents in Hohhot, the capital of Inner Mongolia, send their children to nursery schools, primary schools and middle schools that teach in Chinese, not in Mongolian. The schools the parents send their children to are largely state-sponsored. A similar situation prevails in other cities and towns in Inner Mongolia where the major medium of communication is Chinese. Some Mongolian parents will first send their children to classes taught in Mongolian and then redirect them to those taught in Chinese, where students are prepared to go on to the better middle schools, to colleges or even to renowned universities outside the Autonomous Region. Again, graduates from Chinese-language schools have better chances of finding a job. It is a well-known fact that Chinese as a nationwide, official language has engrossed all the possible 'capitals' for social promotion and economic advancement, a fact that is easily explained, in part by the large presence of the Han majority population in the Autonomous Region (five Han to one Mongol) and in part by the politico-economic advantages communicated by the use of Chinese: those who speak Chinese are more likely than those who do not to be employed and promoted. To the disappointment of the Mongolian older generation, more and more Mongols from the younger generation choose to send their children to Han schools.

According to the analysis of 282 interviews with households of immigrants to Hohhot consisting of 133 minority (largely Mongolian) households and 149 Han Chinese households conducted by Iredale *et al.* (2001), 46.6 per cent of the minority (mostly Mongolian) migrants had a university or technical-school level education, and a much lower proportion of the Han Chinese migrants, that is, 8.7 per cent, had these levels of education, while one-quarter had only primary schooling or none at all. Yet the current employment status shows that 83.9 per cent of the Han Chinese migrants were employed, compared with 48.9 per cent of the minority (Mongolian) migrants, though the employment figures do indicate a high rate of selection of student minority migrant households (Iredale *et al.* 2001: 125–6). Such discrepancy can be partially or even largely explained by the language factor: in Hohhot, where the Han Chinese are in the majority, Chinese is the language for most professional positions. Though most Mongols in Hohhot would prefer to send their children to Mongolian-language classes or schools, they actually send them to receive education in Chinese. The language hierarchy indicates that English or some other major foreign language is at the top, Chinese comes second, and is the means for political promotion and economic advancement, and Mongolian remains at the bottom (Bilik 1998a, 1998b).

Mongolian urbanites use Mongolian as part of their cultural capital (Bourdieu 1973) with their imagined (Anderson 1991) or immediate communities. Many of them embrace their Mongolian identity, despite the fact that they barely speak the language, though they may understand it. The theory goes that the uprightness of Mongolian writing (it is written top-to-bottom) symbolizes the Mongolian value of personhood, and, metaphorically, a 'real' Mongol should speak and write Mongolian. Even one or two phrases or a handful of characters will do the job. In comparison, Mongols in pastoral areas use Mongolian as a habitus (Bourdieu 1990). Ironically, Mongolian pastoralists would not give it the same weight as a part of their social identity as do their urbanized counterparts.[7] Social and economic advancement, which is largely realized through Chinese and in cities, has created a situation that is compounded by ethnic pride versus practical gains.

The Tumed Left-Wing Banner School of Mongolian offers a telling case (interview, 1996). The school was established in the early 1980s with the support of Inner Mongolian leaders who were born and joined the revolution from the area of Tumed, a farming area adjacent to Hohhot. The Tumed Mongolians[8] lost their Mongolian language about two centuries ago and have now started to recover it in a bid to cultivate a satisfactory image for themselves, as they usually take up top political positions in the Autonomous Region. Following a 'closed-door-Mongolian-teaching regime',[9] education was conducted in the Mongolian language only. Once in a while, the pupils were sent to the pastureland to learn 'pure Mongolian' in a way that resembled the 'Study Abroad Program' in the USA. The initial optimism, however, before long gave way to pessimism. The enrolment rate slumped and the dropout rate was high. The fundamental cause for this crisis was that the pupils graduated with a limited knowledge of Chinese, and felt 'inadequate' (*shou yueshu/shou xianzhi*) when they came to large cities such as Hohhot, where most people spoke Chinese. They also felt 'wasted' (*feile/langfei*) when they returned to their original homeland, since nobody there understood Mongolian. Some adjustments were made in view of this situation: both Mongolian and Chinese courses were now to be offered. Some old Mongolian cadres, however, attacked this change by charging that it watered down the original enthusiasm for the Mongolian language (Bilik 1998a).

At the same time, Chinese leaders at all levels are calling for raising the *suzhi* (roughly translated as 'quality', 'qualifications', 'competence' or 'capability' in English) of the national minorities, especially those in the western part of China. Some Han intellectuals, in a nationalistic mood of ressentiment[10] towards the West, are pressurizing and appealing to the central government in Beijing to modify or abandon either pro-minority affirmative actions or the national autonomy system or both, arguing that the national minorities are partly responsible for the backwardness of China, which makes them feel humiliated and impotent. They publish articles, write internal governmental reports, send proposals and deliver speeches. They feel safe in what they are doing, which would not have been the case, say, two decades ago. China's U-turn towards 'a market economy with Chinese characteristics' has drastically increased the perception of an urgent need to 'civilize' the minorities, and any drive for efficiency that is based on one-language-one-nation will predictably remain among the safer forms of politico-academic speculation. Both market economy and nationalistic discourse favour the Han language and Han education, while on many occasions silencing minority-language attempts at cultural revival.[11]

The ending of the Cold War has created a stronger version of Han centralism that feeds into a drive for minority cultural recovery and reconstruction focusing, more often than not, on language. Though the Mongolians are recovering and rebuilding their cultural images in response to the Han endeavour to develop a new cultural symbolism, their resources, in terms of printing, digital technology, finance, political power, administration, etc., are no match for those of their Han counterparts, who can easily muster nationwide spiritual and material 'assets' to assist in the control of social memories and public actions. After the demise of the Soviet Bloc, cultural reconstruction has once again become a grand project throughout the non-Western world. Though the Communist Party of China began by burning the temple of Confucius, now it is eager to engage in or encourage the resuscitation of old Han traditions, including the restoration of the Tomb of the Yellow Emperor, the legendary common ancestor of the Han, and the temple of Confucius itself. The hidden message of 'One Nation, One State, One Culture, and One Language' readily harmonizes with the century-old Chinese efforts at nation-building. The modern usage of the term 'Chinese' (*hua* or *huaxia*) developed as a result of Han efforts to drive out the Manchus and Mongols (*dalu*). After this goal had been realized and a Han-centred republic had been established, however, racial-ethnic differences were to be naturalized in the effort to build a nation-state. By redefining actively or passively external and internal frontiers, that is, by 'territorialization' (Balibar 1991a), China is well advanced down the track of nation-building. This process starts with the *Minzu* Identification, which is a form of 'producing the people'. 'The production of ethnicity is also the racialization of language and the verbalization of race' (ibid.). And it is true that language investigation and *minzu* identification go hand in hand. A diversity of *minzu* is thus produced through a unified organization, by a unified Communist government with a unified power and a unified supply of political, human and material resources, and according to a unified timetable.

It was on 2 September 1992 that the PRC Education Commission announced The Method for Practising HSK[12] in National Minorities Schools. This is a standardized test of linguistic competence in Chinese for non-Chinese-speakers, with certificates provided for those who pass it. The Education Commission also issued an Announcement of Trial Implementation of HSK in National Minorities Schools (1997), stipulating that starting from the year 1998 a two-year trial of the test would take place in Xinjiang, Inner Mongolia, Qinghai and Jilin. HSK offices were established in the Inner Mongolia Normal University, Qinghai Normal University, Yanbian No. 1 Middle School and Xinjiang Finance and Trade College.

The arguments that lie behind the efforts to strengthen Chinese teaching in higher education are manifold. Some believe that since the trend of globalization and integration is unavoidable, it makes little sense to teach class in Mongolian in colleges and universities in places where the Han are the majority; even some Mongolian parents think that majors that are taught in Mongolian are of limited practicality and bring no future benefits; some insist that minority languages as media of instruction are only suitable for basic education and should be given up in higher learning owing to their

lack of any link with modernity; still others think that ethnic-native education only serves for political stability and has not much to do with the cultural development and formation of the relevant communities.[13]

After the Cultural Revolution, which brought disaster to all kinds of education, especially minority education, Uygur education started to recover
under the careful planning and guidance of the educational authorities in
both Beijing and Urumqi, the capital of the Xinjiang Uygur Autonomous
Region. In July 1976 the Autonomous Revolutionary Committee decided to
replace the old Uygur and Kazakh scripts with new Latin systems. Between
1965 and 1982 over 800,000 students and workers, peasants and herdsmen
have been organized to learn the new scripts. In 1979, however, the
Autonomous government had to yield to the demand from the Uygur populace for continued use of the old script. When it came to 1982, the fifth
regional congress passed a decision to restore the old scripts (both Uygur
and Kazakh) (Han 1998a: 386–7).

Case study II: Xinjiang

The Xinjiang Uygur Autonomous Region was established on 1 October
1955, eight years after the Inner Mongolia Autonomous Region. The
Uygurs have always been exposed to a diversified linguistic and cultural
world. Xinjiang, also known as Chinese Turkestan in Western literature, is
an important link between China and Central Asia. Its great Silk Road
through the deserts brought the empires of China and Rome into remote
relation (Lattimore 1962: 184). The land offers a kaleidoscopic, vicissitudi-
nous historical landscape where different peoples, with their different cultures, languages, writings, religions and world views, interact. Xinjiang
used to be an 'outer frontier' to China, 'which less frequently took part in
direct assaults on China, and was less affected [than Mongolia, Manchuria,
etc.] by Chinese control in the periods of reaction' (Lattimore 1962: 183–4).

Since the start of modern history it has been a hotbed of competing inter-
ferences and influences instantiated by agents, many of them double agents,
who provided 'leads' for Russia, China, Britain and other powers. Like the
Mongols, the Uygurs also experienced a period of semi-independence (that
of the Three-Region Government and National Army) with support from
the Third International based in the former Soviet Union, and with the
consent or acquiescence of the CPC. Though its present geographical boundaries and administrative organization follow the lines laid down under the
Qing dynasty (1644–1911), which was established by another minority
group, the Manchu, Xinjiang was developed and cultivated thoroughly
under CPC rule. Minority education has been greatly advanced since 1949,
when the CPC and its army took over Xinjiang.[14] From 1949, when there
were 130,543 on-campus students in primary schools with 4,765 teaching
staff, 678 on-campus students with 33 teaching staff in middle schools, 975
on-campus students with 58 teaching staff in technical secondary schools,

and 150 on-campus students with four teaching staff in higher education, the figures in 1965 had risen to 570,140 students to 17,946 staff, 61,852 to 2,771, 4,355 to 364 and 2,521 to 216 for each of these categories, respectively (Han 1998a: 346).

On the whole, as far as statistics go, Uygur education appears to be advancing in quantity, if not in quality. By 1990, the number of Uygur primary-school students had risen to 993,276, and of primary-school teachers to 42,131; their middle-school students had increased to 267,109, and middle-school teachers to 20,387; the number of Uygur students in technical schools had risen to 10,947, and of teachers to 365; the number of Uygur students in tertiary normal schools had increased to 4,897, and of teachers to 591; and Uygur university students had risen to 13,245, and university teachers to 1,829 (Han 1998a: 388–439).

In terms of minority languages in educational use, there are seven for primary education (Uygur, Kazakh, Kirghiz, Xibe, Mongolian, Russian and Chinese), five for primary to middle-school education (Uygur, Kazakh, Kirghiz, Mongolian and Chinese), and four for primary to higher education (Uygur, Kazakh, Mongolian and Chinese). Since 1990, there have been occasional terrorist attacks launched by a small number of Uygur extremists, who have been met with a firm hand and relentlessly suppressed by the government. After the terrorist attacks of 9/11 in New York, China strengthened its hand in dealing with separatists or 'terrorists'. As one strategic component, Chinese education or education in Chinese is to be emphasized and reinforced and to be institutionalized.[15] HSK (the Chinese TEFAL) is the core of the project. According to an official from the Xinjiang HSK Office, competence in Chinese should be given top priority in the Western Development Project. HSK has 11 grades, with 6–8 as the mid-level and 9–11 as high level. According to the educational authority, teachers, especially those Uygur teachers who used to teach in Uygur, who were born after 1958 should reach the 10th grade in three years starting from 1998. Those who fail will not be promoted. According to the same authority all *minzu* should replace native languages with Chinese in three years, with the exception of majors in national minority languages and literatures (Li *et al.* 1999: 8–12). In 1999 the Xinjiang Autonomous Government and its Education Bureau produced a further training plan and decided that no one would be promoted without obtaining a proper certificate of his or her level in Chinese.

The background theory of these promoters of Chinese is that national minority languages such as Uygur are not as useful as Chinese; while Chinese represents advancement (it is a 'quality' language), the minorities' languages symbolize backwardness. Thus, to be a qualified PRC citizen, one must know Chinese, as the National Common Language Law of the PRC (passed by the 18th Standing Committee Meeting of the 9th People's Congress on 31 October 2000) would have it. Accordingly, the poor educational attainment on the part of the minorities is said to be due to their use of their own languages. It is therefore imperative that Chinese should be used for raising the *suzhi* (quality, competence, capability) of Uygur teaching and students. This position accords with the so-called 'barrel theory', namely that the largest possible capacity of a barrel is determined by the length of the shortest piece of wood used in its construction. In this particular case, it is the Uygur language that is the shortest piece. It is argued that the 'backwardness' of the Uygur language has held up social and economic progress in Xinjiang. According to the Xinjiang HSK Office, the Western development should begin with a change in the language of instruction.[16] The coincidence in timing is symbolically significant. Are we going to bid goodbye to old 'nationality' and to embrace new 'ethnicity'? If we regard language as a tool for communication much as a bowl is a tool for eating, there should be nothing to make a fuss about. But as the saying goes, there is an army behind every language. The matter does not seem that simple. Language is as much cultural and emotional as political.

My interviews with Uygur teachers and students in Urumqi highlighted their bitter opposition to such a racist linguistic strategy. By way of summary, the Uygur interviewees have this to say:

- At least in Normal Colleges and Universities students should continue to receive their education in the Uygur language, since most of them will return to the countryside, where people only understand Uygur; there they will become teachers themselves.
- The Uygur language is not responsible for the poor quality of minority students. These students' lower level of attainment in standard Chinese is a result of the fact that many teachers are themselves incompetent in Chinese, and so produce students like themselves.
- The teaching conditions in minority schools are appalling, and they are sometimes without even desks or stools. The teaching materials are too old, and there is no money to improve the situation. By contrast, Chinese textbooks are updated every year.
- The main obstacle lies with the government: if they really regarded the matter as serious as the translation of Marxist books, which can be done in three months, they could solve it right away.
- Assessment is largely based on Chinese thought-models rather than those of Uygur.
- Uygur is an emotional rallying-point for the people. You can never pay too much respect to it.

Most Uygur teachers and students in universities in Urumqi oppose such a racist linguistic strategy, which holds the Uygur language responsible for local poverty and underdevelopment. Their different phenotypical features have made Uygurs an easy target for racial discrimination, and were used to naturalize their behaviour and 'social affinities'; meanwhile, their 'exotic' culture and language 'can also function like a nature', reconfirming a widely held 'internal racism' (Balibar 1991b). The openness of China economically, if not politically, to the world, and especially to the capitalist world, brings a new 'internationalization of social relations' 'within the framework of a system of nation-states'; rethinking 'the notion of frontier' and 'redistributing its modes of application' has become a necessity, a necessity of 'interiorization of the exterior' and 'exteriorization of the interior' (Balibar 1991b). The Uygurs look different, and their language sounds different, and so their way of thinking must be different (an old Chinese saying goes that if a race is different from us, then their mentality too is bound to be different). Internal frontiers are fixed by externalizing them.

Xinjiang, however, is an integrated part of China in the eyes of the policy-makers: everything above or beneath the ground, every body and soul, belongs to the republic. Hence the externalized internal frontiers have to remain internal. The Shanghai Five and Shanghai Six Summits have also contributed to the rebuilding of external and internal frontiers for the Uygurs. The Muslim brothers have to be kept apart from each other by various frontiers, especially those of the nation-state. The gap in terms of power relationship between the Uygur language and Chinese leads to 'educational inequalities and intellectual hierarchies' (Balibar 1991b) between Uygur speakers and Han speakers. In universities, the Uygur faculty have to pass the HSK test before they get promotion, while their Han counterparts are not subject to any requirement of competence in the Uygur language to gain such promotions. My interviews in Urumqi reveal complaints and even resentment on the part of Uygurs who teach or study in universities or colleges. Actually, many Uygur teachers and students are well aware of the importance of Chinese as a tool for economic gain and social promotion; but they are often afraid of losing their original culture and language, and that this may lead to a final estrangement from their own communities. Uygurs who cannot speak their own language are often despised by their fellows. John Ogbu's notion of 'folk theories of success', as used by Harrell and Ma to explain the success and failure of Yi minority students in school, proves useful here:

> if members of a minority hold the view that they can use education to achieve success, they devise ways to surmount the obstacles posed by cultural divergence. If they hold, on the other hand, that the education system will merely strip them of their own culture and identity without giving them equal opportunity in the wider society, they will respond with resistance.
>
> (Harrell and Ma 1999)

Harrell and Ma try to prove that most involuntary minorities hold the oppositional folk theory of success, and most voluntary minorities hold the positive folk theory (Harrell and Ma 1999). This is the case in Xinjiang now: Chinese education is linked to the Western Development Project, with a heavy backdrop of concerns over borderland stability – concerns that are expressed in an all-out anti-terrorist campaign. What was originally an innocent, voluntary and positive curriculum for teaching Chinese as a second language has become a sensitive, nervous political token.

One of my Uygur interviewees said that it was not a matter of 'whether' to learn Chinese; rather, it was a matter of 'how' to learn: 'We have our own understanding of civil society and literacy'. Living along the Silk Road, the Uygurs know the value of Chinese, but also of English. And they have their own way of creating language frontiers: they would rather choose English as a second language than Chinese, because, they argue, English is an international language, while Chinese is not; English symbolizes American dollars, technology and military power, while Chinese represents stigmatization. The core of the problem is that, rather than as an economic-cultural menu, HSK has been prescribed as a political recipe for redistributing the modes of application of 'the notion of frontier'.

Civil society and the 'civilizing' of minorities in China

After the CPC takeover, the Chinese version of the discourse of Western civil society, which consists of a socialist citizenship of high morality and a merger of individual interests with that of the state, such as we are seriously discussing now, has been built into the 'four modernizations' (modernization of agriculture, industry, national defence and science and technology) and *zonghe guoli* (comprehensive national power). The most influential idea at the historical roots of such discourse can be traced back to Dr Sun Yat-sen, the founding father of the Chinese nation-state. He started with the slogan of 'drive out the Manchu and restore China' (meaning China for the Han only); then this was changed to one of 'co-existence of the five zu' (read: race, ethnic community, people or nationality) of the Han, the Manchu, the Mongols, the Muslims and the Tibetans.

So Ming-ke Wang (Wang 1999), using the 'remembrance model' of Halbwachs (1992) and the 'imagining model' of Hobsbawm (Hobsbawm and Ranger 1983) and Anderson (1991), is able to explore how the geographical and ethnic concepts of the Qiang (a minority people in China) have been redefined by the Han Chinese in demarcating their ethnic boundaries for over 3,000 years, especially during the past century of China's nation-building efforts. By selective remodelling of their history, using information provided by the Han Chinese and foreign missionaries, the mountain people who lived along the upper Min River Valley in the north-western Sichuan province of China have gradually gained their Qiang ethnic identity during the last half-century (Wang 1999). Wang points out that the fact that this occurred during the past century during which China became a nation-state makes such a redefinition even more remarkable (Wang 1999).

Wang's analysis coincides to some degree with that of another, Taiwan-based, author, Chih-yu Shih, who states that before it became a nation-state

China clung to a moral superiority that 'crossed human-made boundaries of all kinds', and did not need definite borders or to draw sharp lines 'to indicate ethnic distinction' (Shih 2002: 1). However, since China had entered the process of nation-state building it had become a process itself, 'a constant reference point'; it 'lives on millions of mini-practices of citizenship'. Hence 'China is a part of minorities rather than minorities a part of China' (Shih 2002: 1). The insights of these authors have shed fresh light on the way we 'read' China, and coincide with Balibar's idea of 'frontiers' that cut across, in repeatedly different ways, class, race and nationalism, unfolding a history of the ways that political arts and military violence have redefined internal frontiers. Since the boundaries of ethnic identities do not agree with the borders of a modernizing China, there are constant tensions and contradictions over how to reconcile a culturally diversified China, a demographically mixed China, with a territorially unified China.

We need, however, to add another useful dimension by not underestimating those 'middlemen', like Ghengis Khan and Nurhachi in their early instantiations of the category, who came from a 'buffer zone' such as the 'Inner Asia Reservoir' (Lattimore 1951: 247–51, 547), who 'knew how to act, because as vassals of vassals they were familiar with different kinds of power and understood how to carry themselves both in the tribal world and in the dynastic world' (Lattimore 1951: 119), and their modern counterparts, who 'are almost Chinese', speaking or not speaking their mother languages, connecting the central government with the locals, and building up high stakes in the process of such manoeuvring. Their becoming or potential to become rulers, either of the whole of China or of 'parts of China' (such as the Autonomous Region) give the relevant minority elite (commoners are included in modern times) the status of majority actors, and they are thus empowered to redefine the internal frontiers through coercion (in the case of Ghengis Khan) or negotiation (in the case of Ulanhu). These 'middlemen' are born into intermediary zones and are adapted to the fluidity of the frontier. While the intermediary zones create their physical being, they are also part of the intermediary zones, which they also help to build up. Here is a good metaphor for the boundaries being built and rebuilt between the 'civilized China' and the barbarian non-China, a process negotiated by these political, 'almost Chinese' brokers.[17]

Minority language and education owe their vitality to confrontations and negotiations between generations of the Han and the non-Han through the thick and thin of history, power and culture. There is no universally accepted model of civil society apart from particular negotiated versions of it (Howland 1996: 7–8).[18] History, power and culture are structurally coupled to produce and reproduce an ongoing version of a civil society (with Chinese characteristics and Chinese characters – 'ideograms'). The Chinese version of civil society, which tends to merge, not without great difficulties, with the earlier notion of *wenming* (civilization), is haunted by a constant majority concern over the minority-populated peripheries where the nation-state was territorially staked out, wars were fought and deals were struck. On the one hand, the traditional Chinese version of civilization, which emphasizes filial piety, devotion to the emperor and literacy in classical literature, has to be reconciled to or even merged with the modern Western version of civilization, which values individualism, freedom, bourgeois civility and the market economy. Military failures in confrontation with foreign powers have proved the necessity of such a reconciliation or merger. It is time to redefine the external and internal frontiers of China, to determine who are civilized, and who are not civilized and should be civilized. The civilizing project goes hand in hand with physically redrawn borders – political sovereignty in relation to foreign powers. In the past, a foreign community could easily join the Greater China by learning the Chinese language and ritual and paying tribute to the central court. Now, the Western industrial-bourgeois revolution has brought a sea change to the landscape of civilization, its interpretation and its implementation. A new vision of civilization that is suited to the Western notion of the nation-state is urgently needed.

For a country like China, which is proud of its ancient civilization, and which used to pay more attention to political-territorial integrity, leaving linguistic-cultural affairs to the local minority leaders, is now more eager to spread the Han language and culture, though its Han population largely lacks experience with the national minorities. According to this view, to build a civil society can also mean to build a Han-centred nation-state, and is synonymous with persuading the national minorities to replace their languages and cultures with Chinese language and culture. According to this view, as far as culture is concerned, a civilization, just as good as Western culture, will make its appearance in the world through the emergence of a new phase of Han-Chinese culture. This will be a force competing with the West in its achievements in the economy, in science and in technology. The value system, the social consciousness and the worldview it relies on, however, will be unique. Despite the Western myth that is created by the West's hegemony, development does not always coincide with Westernization.

The ebbs and flows of 'ethnic events' along the 'Great Wall Frontier' have kept China alert and alive. It is not only a matter of 'China ... [being] ... a part of [the] minorities' (Shih 2002: 235) and 'Marginal China' (Wang 1999); more importantly, it is also a matter of three-dimensional confrontations of landbound people versus seaboard people, nomadic versus sedentary, and China versus the Rest (mostly, the West). A broader perspective with a geopolitical vision can provide us with a more powerful interpretation of China's ethnic history and its civil-society- (nation-) building efforts. Chinese civil society cannot take shape without a 'structural coupling'[19] between minority visions of civil society and mainstream perspectives on the common recognition that education and civil society are tied together by the politics of ethnicity. The Han majority would prefer to externalize minority languages and cultures by creating internal frontiers of 55 minority *minzu*

within the boundary of the Chinese state, the ideal type of which is one language (Chinese), one culture (huaxia culture), and one political system. On
the minority side, however, they would rather maintain their identity of language and culture by playing with the politics of those ethnicities that were
once so freely and liberally imposed by the state.

This reminds us of the striking contrast of attitudes over the reform of
the Chinese writing system between the early twentieth century and more
recent decades. Formerly unchallengeable figures such as Chairman Mao,
Premier Zhou and Lu Xun (a revolutionary writer, and Chairman Mao's
favourite) are now challenged (He *et al.* 1995: 5–11; Liu and Gao 2001).
Books and articles are published in praise of those same Chinese ideograms
that used to be blamed for their difficulty and therefore for holding back the
pace of China's modernization. But this is in fact the result of a nationalistic
backlash of a 'compensatory' nature,[20] rather than a matter of pure cognitive
science, even though such science is now ostensibly being used to prove a
quicker response time for Chinese ideograms than for most other writing
systems. The long-continued existence of Chinese writing cannot be so
simply explained, but only as a result of the interplay of pragmatic factors,
in just the same way as the writing systems of any other languages, minority
languages in China included.

Should this be the way people interpret the current state of affairs, then
such nation-building efforts are creating head-on conflicts with those of the
minorities to maintain and develop their languages and cultures in China.
Chinese nationalists would argue that the language for Chinese civil society
is none other than Chinese; and therefore Chinese education is 'quality' education.[21] One of the major goals for opening up western China is to raise the
'quality' (*suzhi*) of the local minority populations. Most of them do not speak
Chinese and live in the poorest part of China. They should start with the
'advanced' Chinese language. Why not? Modernity means that the political
boundary should agree with that of language! A Han researcher states that
China has entered an age of 'post-autonomy' and that it is time for so-called
'jointnomy' (a word said to have been coined by him) (Zhu 2001). He argues
that China has adopted the French model of the political nation, which is
different from the German–Austrian model of the cultural nation, such as
was exemplified by Dr Sun Yat-sen's 'Five Peoples of China' model. Therefore, nationality or *minzu* in China should, from now on, switch its emphasis
from autonomy to 'jointnomy'. This self-fulfilling recipe denies four vital
elementary facts.

First, it denies the negotiated nature of the history of China – negotiated
between interest groups that are divided by what are called ethnic ties.
Second, it denies the fact that most minority populations still live in the
poorest parts of 'western China', speaking their own ethnic languages to
communicate their cultural traditions. They are the most disadvantaged.
Third, it denies that fact that Dr Sun Yat-sen started his nation-building
efforts by 'driving out the Manchu to restore the Han nation', and that this

racist slogan, which he took over from the Ming emperor Yuanzhang Zhu, who drove out the Mongols under an earlier version of the same slogan, was replaced with the 'Five Peoples of China' policy only after the Han had taken over. Chairman Mao Zedong and his CPC used to recognize the right of self-determination of the national minorities in China, and their right to complete separation from China, and to the formation of an independent state for each minority (Article 14 of the 1931 CPC constitution, MUF 1991: 206–9). The hidden message is that, on the basis of the 'social evolution of the social division of labour', it is up to the Han, the most advanced nationality, to establish a nation-state, and the minorities should join in to 'govern the newly established nation-state', with or without autonomy! As if such guided social amnesia were a remedy for ethno-nationalistic remembrance and consciousness of discrepancies in culture, power and history! Fourth, it denies the fact that the Cultural Revolution has destroyed as many 'ethnic cultural fruits' as had been produced before. The author seems to suggest that twenty-odd years is too long a time for the recovery of minority cultures; they are given too much privilege.

> This will be a glorious new age for Chinese ideographic writing and Chinese culture! By then the Chinese ideographic mentality and Chinese ideographic psychology will have a brand-new content and subjects, and will write a new chapter in the history of the world!
>
> (Quotation from Wang Demai by Yao 2001: 309)

The notion and practice of the nation-state has undergone several 'waves' of historical politico-economic changes. Its prototype, however, has always been built on the Western conception and practice of individual freedom, democracy and the sanctity of private property. For many years China has been in several minds about how and what to model herself on. A typical Marxist view would have it that the nation-state is a product of the bourgeoisie, a container of class violence and a tool for exploitation. There is only one reason for the proletariat to establish its own state: to rid the earth of the state. A stateless, free, and equal society, namely communism, is the goal. What was inherited from the past by the Communist Party of China was a semi-feudal, semi-colonial society, which lacked individual freedom, lacked a working class, lacked democracy and lacked the sense of civil rights. To build a nation-state, the CPC must resort to both political nationalism and cultural nationalism, though the distinction between the two '-isms' is quite ambiguous (see Hutchinson and Smith 1994: 122, 131 for a discussion of the two terms). Learning from (Bolshevik) Russia, the CPC identified 56 different 'nationalities'; learning from the West, China then started to take another turn by diluting ethnicity and strengthening Chinese education.[22]

The conundrum is that, while citizenship should ideally be built on an unbiased language, an unbiased culture, and an unbiased configuration of territory, no language and culture, so far as we know, could fulfil such innocent expectations; all of them are destined to belong to a particular ethnicity or nationality. In China, in the eyes of many of the Han social elite, raising the flag of social modernization, the assimilation of all non-Han groups is shorthand for building a civil society.

There is an increasing gap between the administrative mechanism under a one-party system on the one hand and common practice on the other with regard to the interpretation of the nationalistic version(s) of the market economy. It is true that the government still injects some money, though far from enough, into the previously established institutions that deal with national minority affairs and provide autonomous regions and areas with preferential treatment. But a variety of protests is rising from a more pluralized horizon on the part of the Han. One thing, however, is certain: that the Nationality Policy and the National Autonomy System have long been embedded into the 'history' of the CPC. More than that, the past experience of practising National Autonomy has shown that there are far more minority cadres who are loyal to the Party than those who are not. The senior generation of the Party leadership had a better idea of what they were doing. Ethnic-linguistic education, such as happened in Inner Mongolia and Xinjiang, represents the general situation in which minority communities in China now find themselves. The unending cause of building up a civil society in China, the structural coupling of history, power and culture will build up a contesting stage on which, in response to the 'quality' education strategy imposed by mainstream officials and educators, both the majority Han and the minority *minzu* compete with each other to practise their own preferred definitions and interpretations of frontiers.[23] However, since 'social taxonomies allow for specific forms of violence at specific times' (Stoler and Cooper 1997), and the designer and operator of such social taxonomy in this case is the Han-majority state machine, such episodes of violence will be manifested and directed in the interests of the 'civilizing mission' of the sinification process. The minority voice is too weak to change the 'hierarchies of civility' (Stoler and Cooper 1997), which are defined and superimposed strategically by the majority leadership according to shifting frontiers that alter in response to the geopolitical reconfigurations of the world landscape.

Notes

1 By using 'indexical' (indexicality), I also want to emphasize its negotiating role between 'iconic' (iconicity) ('a relationship between a sign and its object in which the form of the sign recapitulates the object in some way': Duranti 2001: 102) and 'symbolic' (symbolism) ('something that stands for something else').

2 Lattimore (1951, 1962) and Wittfogel (1957), who had experiences in China, provided us with powerful historical accounts of China and her ethnicity. Their works arguably help us examine the creation of ethnicity at the margin of China. A hydraulic organization appeared at the margin of interaction between geography and mankind; a history of ethnicity was created along the marginal divide of the Great Wall of China.

3 Here, 'indexical frontiers' more specifically refers to the situational, shifting borderlines created by the military activities and political manoeuvring of 'frontier middlemen' such as Ghengis Khan.

4 There is no proper translated equivalent for the Chinese word *minzu*. It can mean 'peoples', 'ethnic group', 'nationality' or 'minorities', depending on various contexts, or even 'nation-state'. China's Han-culture centralism and the antiquity of its authoritarianism destined it to embrace a brand of civil society that is also an ideal model for the nation-state, envisioning its linguistic-cultural border in agreement with its newly drawn political border. Interestingly, *minzu* is so polysemous that it often carries conflicting meanings. China is first one *minzu* (nation); second, this *minzu* again contains 56 different *minzu* ('nationalities', or, more recently, 'ethnic groups'). Though scholars in China differ over the English translation of *minzu* (Zhou 1999), I would agree with Kymlicka (1995) and Bulag (2002) that a 'multinational state', which involves 'previously self-governing, territorially concentrated cultures' that were incorporated into 'a large state', with cultural diversity created as a result – of which China is a case in point – is different from a 'polyethnic state', in the case of which 'cultural diversity arises from individual and familial immigration'. Hence, in the former case, the incorporated cultures are 'national minorities', for which I would rather use the Pinyin Chinese *minzu* to avoid complications and conflicting interpretations. Another critical point for further understanding China's *minzu* is that their identification and recognition depends, in the final analysis, on the state's will.

5 'The nation is a historically evolved, stable community of language, territory, economic life, and psychological make-up' (Stalin 1942: 12). This Identification Project, however, sometimes switches to other parameters, either in sum or individually, such as history, ethnic origin, or self–other identities (Gladney 1998; Harrell 1999). For example, the Zhuang and the Buyei, who belong to the same language branch, were classified into separate ethnicities; whereas the Western Yogur, speaking a Turkic language, and the Eastern Yogur, speaking a Mongolian language, were merged into one Yogur ethnicity. Today, China has over 120 different languages and 30 writing systems. Starting from the 1950s, under government organization, linguists in China designed 14 writing systems for ten national minorities.

6 Among the changes the Autonomous Region system in Inner Mongolia has been undergoing, the most serious one happened during the Cultural Revolution when hundreds and thousands of Mongolian cadres were thrown into jail, and many of them were tortured to death. Then, in October 1981, thousands of Mongolian students from Inner Mongolia University and other higher-learning universities and colleges went on demonstrations in protest at the central government's assimilationist policies; as a result, many Mongolian presidents and deans, who were accused of supporting the students, were removed from their posts. Since the latter half of the 1990s, there have been discourses of sinification in support of the Western Development Strategy (China has started in recent years to open up its western region, where most of the national minorities live, owing to an increasing socio-economic gap between East and West China in terms of 'socialist spiritual and material civilization'). In 1998, while touring Xinjiang, the former CPC general secretary Jiang Zemin commented that there was a trend for the languages in the world to decrease in number – a seemingly innocent speech that hinted, in reality, at the projected fate of minority languages in China. Today, few Mongolian local leaders are able or willing to use Mongolian in their formal public speeches. Management, the supply of teaching materials and salaries for those staff who teach in Mongolian are left to the

mercy of the market economy. Economic support for minority education has not increased much, and the teaching budget's deficit has increased by nine digits. A message has also been passed around, at least amongst the researchers: it is time to de-emphasize the *minzu*: the minority should become Han as soon as possible, and join 'civilization' at the earliest possible stage.

7 Once, for example, I interviewed a *suyulin gachaa darag* (a head of a production team, who is responsible for cultural activities), asking him what would happen should the locals lose their native tongue. In answer to my question, he smiled and said: 'We'll just speak Chinese and go on living.'

8 The Tumed Mongols moved to the Hohhotian region during the 1500s. Their leader, Altan Khan, with a mind open to Han immigration and the practice of agriculture, built the city of Hohhot ('Blue City') in the late sixteenth century. In a matter of three hundred years, the Tumed Mongols abandoned their language for Chinese and became agriculturalists. They were the first among the Mongolian tribes to join the Communist revolution, and have raised as important a native leader as Ulanhu (1906–88), who joined the CPC in the 1920s, was present at Yan'an (the 'cradle of the revolution' in the second half of the 1930s and the first half of the 1940s), and became a vice-premier of the PRC in 1954 and a vice-chairman of the PRC after the Cultural Revolution.

9 The local way of referring to an 'immersion programme' for language acquisition. As its basic requirements, pupils are obliged to remain behind closed doors, and no other language other than Mongolian is allowed on the campus.

10 Ressentiment 'refers to a psychological state resulting from suppressed feelings of envy and hatred (existential envy) and the impossibility of satisfying these feelings' (Greenfeld 1992: 14–17). Many Chinese intellectuals envy Western wealth and power, which are typically mediated through English. Returned overseas graduates with PhDs and MAs, who speak English or other foreign languages, are highly respected and well treated, while those with degrees from universities and colleges within China, who cannot speak a major foreign language well, are sidelined. The latter envy and hate the former as well as their Western base. US dollars and British pounds are hard currency, and are easily earned by these foreign-tongued 'imitation foreign devils' (*jiang yangguizi*). These returnees irritate their counterparts not only by their easy professional promotions and good salaries, but also by their Western knowledge, which is embraced by the Central Government.

11 'Ethnic displays' for tourists form an exception, which is allowed and encouraged to flourish under 'a foreign, hunt-for-the-exotic gaze' (Schein 2000).

12 HSK is short for *hanyu shuiping kaoshi*, which is designed for testing non-Chinese speakers, including foreigners, overseas Chinese and minorities, for their competence in Chinese. It was passed as a professional assessment in 1990. HSK is a standardized Chinese test (OSCLEC 1996).

13 Chen Bateer, personal communication, May 2003.

14 Since 1952, a large number of the Han population have been transferred to Xinjiang to build paramilitary state farms, a traditional practice that goes back as far as the Han dynasty. In 1954 the Production and Construction Corps (PCC) was formally established by reorganizing those immigrants. The PCC controlled a population of 2.41 million by 1998 and accounted for 13.78 per cent of the total population in Xinjiang (Zhang and He 1999). It 'has been a major political force in maintaining Chinese control of Xinjiang' (Rudelson 1997: 37). With an independent network of courts, militia, markets, industry, etc., the PCC has the same level of authority as the Xinjiang Autonomous Government, and takes its orders only from Beijing.

15 One suppressed official explanation for failures to give early warnings about

terrorist attacks is: 'They talked in Uygur, and we could not understand'. Thus, according to some officials, strengthening Chinese-language teaching is vital both to the building of Chinese civil society in the long run and to local stability in terms of information security and the early prevention of extremist activities.

16 An official from the Xinjiang HSK Office told me that Chinese should be given the top priority in the Western Development Project, which was designed and promoted by the Central Government in Beijing. The CPC secretary of the Xinjiang Uygur Autonomous Region, Lequan Wang, states that minority languages in Xinjiang contain only limited amounts of information, and cannot express some more advanced knowledge (interview on Western Channel CCTV). It is therefore imperative that Chinese should be used to raise local teaching standards.

17 'Ghengis Khan chose Uygurs to create a Mongol written language and "the beginnings of a civil service". Their service enabled his successors to administer China without immediate surrender to the Chinese scholar-gentry' (Lattimore 1951: 81).

18 If '. . . [t]he changing world order in the nineteenth century presented Chinese with a critical choice: was China to deal with Japan as kin, in terms of tong wen (shared language/civilization), or as an alien of the Western sort? Ultimately, this was a question of rival claims to universality: the Chinese model of Civilization described relation with foreign domains in terms of proximity, and proposed to order the various domains according to principles of hierarchy and unification; the Westerners, by contrast, described foreign relations in terms of an international legality that promised equality and differentiation. In the end [. . .], growing contradictions undermined the Chinese model of Civilization as a viable possibility.' In reality, such a model is not applicable inside China either. The reconstruction of a revolutionary China since Dr Sun Yat-sen's era has helped to add yet more varieties to the pre-existing 'polyphonic voices' of political ethnicity. It is 'evident that no foreign model could fit the Chinese situation, and that many models would be used but none would be adequate, and that the creative Chinese people would have to work out their salvation in their own way' (Fairbank and Goldman 1998: xix).

19 'We speak of structural coupling whenever there is a history of recurrent interactions leading to the structural congruence between two (or more) systems' (Maturana and Varela 1998: 75).

20 A typical Chinese reaction to Western material-technological superiority is to counterbalance it with discourses of Chinese cultural-civilizational superiority for over 5,000 years.

21 The Chinese translations of 'civilization' (*wenming*) and 'culture' (*wenhua*) share the character *wen*, which means 'writing'. By default, to be 'civilized' or 'cultured' means to learn to write (Chinese) characters.

22 Starting from 1959, with the help of the Institute of Minority Language Studies of the Chinese Academy of Sciences, Latinized scripts were designed and implemented and put into trial use. Latinization of scripts, including Chinese, in China followed the guidelines established under the premiership of Zhou Enlai, who presided over an important meeting in Qingdao in Shandong province in 1957 (the Qingdao huiyi or Qingdao Conference). These Latinization efforts can serve two purposes: one is to standardize writing systems to facilitate transcription and language learning (thus also creating a common bond for unity); the other is to distinguish from each other members of the same ethnic groups who have been separated by recent changes of geopolitical configuration (political boundaries should agree with linguistic boundaries). What Zhou did was merely following the line of Chairman Mao, who thought that the Latin system,

which according to him looked better than the Russian and other writing systems, should be the vehicle for Chinese script reform (Liu and Gao 2001).

23 As exercises in the arts of survival, both the Mongolians and the Uygurs have started to test their own educational programmes, including teaching English in Mongolian and in Uygur. In Inner Mongolia, for example, experimental trilingual (Mongolian, Chinese, English) classes were opened in 1992 for the sake of 'training a team of transnational professionals who master the most up-to-date technology'. The trial programme received both support and protests from the Mongolians. To save Mongolian while at the same time empowering Mongolian youngsters in the job market after graduation, Mr Sejo, who was then a headmaster in Hohhot, devised a scheme that would reinforce Chinese teaching and add on English classes at the level of the higher middle schools without losing Mongolian teaching. Now the Inner Mongolian government have issued documents contemplating the wider implementation of such trilingual education. Apparently, their vision of a civil society in China is a trilingual one at least. They are not going to lose the Mongolian language and culture in the course of the 'civilizing drive'. Some Uygur teachers are trying to follow the same path.

References

Anderson, B. (1991), *Imagined Communities*, London: Verso.

Balibar, E. (1991a), 'The Nation Form: History and Ideology', in E. Balibar (ed.) *Race, Nation, Class: Ambiguous Identities*, pp. 86–106, London: Verso.

Balibar, E. (1991b), 'Racism and Nationalism', in E. Balibar (ed.) *Race, Nation, Class: Ambiguous Identities*, pp. 37–67, London: Verso.

Bilik, N. (1998a), 'Language Education, Intellectuals and Symbolic Representation: Being an Urban Mongolian in a New Configuration of Social Evolution', *Nationalism and Ethnic Politics* 4: 47–67.

Bilik, N. (1998b), 'The Mongolian–Han Relations in a New Configuration of Social Evolution', *Central Asian Survey* 17: 69–91.

Bourdieu, P. (1973), *The Field of Cultural Production*, New York: Columbia University Press.

Bourdieu, P. (1990), *The Logic of Practice*, Stanford, CA: Stanford University Press.

Bulag, U. (2002), *The Mongols at China's Edge*, Lanham, MD: Rowman & Littlefield Publishers, Inc.

Duranti, A. (ed.) (2001), *Key Terms in Language and Culture*, Oxford: Blackwell.

Fairbank, John K. and Merle Goldman (eds) (1998), *China*, Cambridge, MA: The Belknap Press of Harvard University Press.

Gladney, Dru C. (1998), *Ethnic Identity in China*, Forth Worth, TX: Harcourt Brace College Publishers.

Greenfeld, L. (1992), *Nationalism: Five Roads to Modernity*, Cambridge, MA: Harvard University Press.

Halbwachs, M. (1992), *On Collective Memory*, Chicago: The University of Chicago Press.

Han, Da (1998a), *Shaoshuminzu jiaoyu shi* (*A History of Minority Education in China*), Vol. I, Guangzhou, Nanning, Kunming: Guangdong Education Press, Guangxi Education Press, Yunnan Education Press.

Han, Da (1998b), *Shaoshuminzu jiaoyu shi* (*A History of Minority Education in China*), Vol. II, Kunming, Nanning, Guangzhou: Yunnan Education Press, Guangxi Education Press, Guangdong Education Press.

Harrell, S. (1999), 'The Role of the Periphery in Chinese Nationalism', in S. M. Huang (ed.) *Imaging China: Regional Division and National Unity*, pp. 133–60, Taipei: Institute of Ethnology Academia Sinica.

Harrell, S. and Erzi Ma (1999), 'Folk Theories of Success', in G. Postiglione (ed.) *China's National Minority Education*, pp. 213–41, New York: Falmer Press.

He, Jiuying, Shuangbao Hu and Meng Zhang (1995), *Zhongguo hanzi daguan* (*The Kaleidoscope of Chinese Ideograms*), Beijing: Beijing University Press.

Hobsbawm, E. and Terence Ranger (eds) (1983), *The Invention of Tradition*, Cambridge: Cambridge University Press.

Howland, D. (1996), *Borders of Chinese Civilization*, Durham, NC: Duke University Press.

Hutchinson, J. and A. Smith (eds) (1994), *Nationalism*, Oxford: Oxford University Press.

INS CASS & SNC (Institute of Nationality Studies of the Chinese Academy of Social Sciences and the State Nationality Affairs Commission) (eds) (1994), *The Use of Minority Languages in China* (*Zhongguo shaoshu minzu yuyan shiyong qingkuang*), Beijing: China Tibetology Press.

Iredale, R., Naran Bilik and Wang Su (eds) (2001), *Contemporary Minority Migration, Education and Ethnicity in China*, Cheltenham: Elgar.

Kymlicka, W. (1995), *Multicultural Citizenship*, Oxford: Clarendon Press.

Lattimore, O. (1951), *Inner Asian Frontiers of China*, New York: Capitol Publishing Co. and Irvington-on-Hudson: American Geographical Society.

Lattimore, O. (1962), *Studies in Frontier History*, Collected Papers 1928–58, London: Oxford University Press.

Li, Ruzhong, Wenyan Ju and Fuqian Fu (eds) (1999) *Shaoshu minzu hanyu jiaoxue yanjiu* (*A Study of Teaching Chinese to Minorities*), Urumqi: Xinjiang Education Press.

Liu, Y. and Hua Gao (2001), *20 shiji 50 niandai guanyu hanzi gaige de zhenglun* (*Debates over Reform of Chinese Writing in the 50s of the Twentieth Century*), *Zhonghua dushu bao*, 10.

Maturana, Humberto R. and Francisco J. Varela (1998), *The Tree of Knowledge*, Boston: Shambhala.

MUF (Ministry of the United Front) (ed.) (1991), *Minzu wenti wenxian huibian* (*A Collection of Documents on the Minzu Problem*), Beijing: CPC Central Party School Press.

OSCLEC (The State HSK Office) (ed.) (1996), *HSK*, Beijing: Xiandai Publishing House.

Rudelson, Justin J. (1997), *Oasis Identities*, New York: Columbia University Press.

Schein, L. (2000), *Minority Rules*, Durham, NC: Duke University Press,

Shih, Chih-yu (2002), *Negotiating Ethnicity in China: Citizenship as a Response to the State*, London: Routledge.

Soucek, S. (2000), *A History of Inner Asia*, Cambridge: Cambridge University Press,

Stalin, J. (1942), *Marxism and the National Question*, New York: International Publishers.

Stoler, Ann Laura and Frederick Cooper (1997), 'Between Metropole and Colony', in F. Cooper and A. L. Stoler (eds) *Tensions of Empire: Colonial Cultures in a Bourgeois World*, pp. 1–56, Berkeley: University of California Press.

Sun, W. (1998), *Strategies for Nation-building* (*Jianguo Fanglue*), Zhengzhou: Zhongzhou Guji Press.

Wang, Ming-ke (1999), 'From the Qiang Barbarians to the Qiang Nationality: The Making of a New Chinese Boundary', in Shu-min Huang (ed.) *Imagining China: Regional Division and National Unity*, pp. 43–80, Taipei: Institute of Ethnology, Academia Sinica.

Wittfogel, K. A. (1957), *Oriental Despotism*, New Haven, Oxford: Yale University Press, Oxford University Press,

Wu, Shimin (2000), *Zhongguo minzu jiaoyu* (*Minority Education in China*), Beijing: Changcheng Publishing House.

Yao, X. M. (2001), *Hanzi xinlixue* (*Psychology of Chinese Ideograms*), Nanning: Guangxi Education Press.

Zhang, Tianlu and Qingrong Huang (1993), *Zhongguo minzu renkou de yanjin* (*The Evolution of the Chinese Ethnic Population*), Beijing: Ocean Publishing House.

Zhang, Y. and Bingyu He (1999), 'Xinjiang bingtuan renkou qianyi yu xinjiang shehui fazhan' ('Population Movement in Xinjiang PCC and the Social Development of Xinjiang'), *Journal of Xinjiang University (Philosophy and Social Sciences Edition)* 27: 4, 30–4.

Zhou, Xufang (1999), '1998 nian "minzu" gainian ji xiangguan lilun wenti zhuanti taolunhui' ('The Discussion of the Minzu Conception and its Relevant Theoretic Issues: An Overview of the 1998 Symposium'), *Shijie minzu (Global Ethno-national Studies)* 1: 77–80.

Zhu, L. (2001), 'Minzu gongzhi lun' ('On Jointnomy'), *Chinese Social Sciences* 4: 95–105.

10 School stories and internal frontiers

Tracing the domestic life of Anglo-Indian citizens

Laura Bear

This chapter is concerned with the emotional afterlife of schooling, or in other words how the experience of education is carried into domestic contexts and through people's lives as a shifting touchstone against which they define their agency. In particular it addresses how narratives of schooling are told by people and within families as part of life histories, as commentaries on present predicaments and as foundations of self-worth. This is an interesting arena for analysis because it joins together issues of education and citizenship in a slightly different manner from studies that centre on the process of instruction itself. It allows us to trace the internal frontiers – both within people's self-fashioning and their homes – of the nation and notions of citizenship conveyed in projects of education.

My use of this idea of an internal frontier builds upon Stoler's (1992) important redeployments of discussions of nationalism by Fichte and Balibar. Stoler suggests that from their work we can derive the notion that the national community has an interior frontier. This concept captures the hierarchies of degrees of belonging to the national community, but more importantly for the discussion here, it conveys a sense of nationalism as an existential project at the level of the individual citizen.[1] She suggests that 'When coupled with the word interior . . . frontier marks the moral predicates by which a subject retains his or her national identity despite location outside the national frontier and despite heterogeneity within the nation-state' (Stoler 1992: 526). This conveys the important ways in which it becomes the duty of every citizen to maintain their morality in order to hold together the 'multiplicity of individual ties' that bind the nation together (Fichte, quoted in Stoler 1992: 526). Since schools are the primary site in which the affective structures of the home are reoriented to transcendent entities such as the state, nation and civil society, in this chapter I argue that the existential project of being a citizen-subject is often framed in relation to the experience people have of schooling. Narratives of education provide a central idiom for expressing individual and intimate identities, for binding or separating yourself from a national project.

It is the tales told by a specific group of people, Anglo-Indians, and the projects of education directed at them that have led me to take school stories seriously.[2] As I carried out research with Anglo-Indian families in Calcutta and in the railway town at Kharagpur, I was struck by how often people returned to accounts of schooling in order to: verify genealogical origins; express moral disorders within families and communities; create reference points for domestic practices; and anchor individual social agency. Education was never described as simply a process of the acquisition of skills and knowledge. It was perceived as a dramatic field for the creation of the moral self and the denial or creation of emotional attachments to families, communities and political entities. Take, for instance, the account given by Mrs Thompson, a 60-year-old widow, whom I met in a charity home in Calcutta. Her only daughter, Clare, had married a Muslim man eight years earlier, somewhat to the consternation of her Catholic mother. This was partly why she was living in a charity home rather than with her daughter. In explaining Clare's decision, Mrs Thompson told the following school story:

> the bringing up is the main thing, a tree must grow straight ... but you get children, you bring them up, then they are gone. See my Clare: I have brought her up, not dragged her up. I'm very fond of her. She was a very good actress in school in all the plays. I remember she took the part of Peter denied Christ at school and how funny that she did that. It was foretold to me in that school play that later she would change and become a Muslim. But in the school they just all clapped and said how attractive. Now the link is broken between us.

In Mrs Thompson's story school becomes the public domain in which her daughter undermines her inherited ties and upbringing. Her performance there heralds her adult decision to transfer her allegiances to another kind of community of Indians, and the sealing off of her future identity from her past domestic life and genealogical inheritance. The particular shock of this event would not be immediately clear to someone unfamiliar with Anglo-Indian ideas about education. For Mrs Thompson it is startling because schools are generally seen by Anglo-Indians as places in which their genealogical family connections and the links of these to Britain are retrospectively confirmed. Often Anglo-Indians are without documentary proof of their lineage histories or of their current claims to be attached to the national entity of Britain, and schooling is liberally used in conversation as an indication of European or British origins (Bear 2001). When people talk about deceased relatives they will almost immediately mention the schools they attended. They frequently add that they were educated by teachers from Britain according to Cambridge Board exams. So for Anglo-Indians the *most intimate* aspects of family origins and domestic life cannot be fully imagined as separate from the public institution of the school. This makes the telling of school stories particularly important to them in their definitions of what it means to be a self-creating citizen-subject. They are, as it were, at one end of an experiential continuum along which all modern subjects of education can be arranged.

The first half of this chapter explores the historical origins of this contemporary Anglo-Indian experience of and disposition towards schooling. The chapter then turns to their current school stories. In these accounts Anglo-Indians attempt to reappropriate the terms of public projects of colonial and postcolonial education in order to fashion themselves as self-determining citizens and members of communities. These tales reveal the anxieties produced by and the fault lines of attempts to manufacture civic emotions and community loyalties in schools. Ultimately they also have implications for how we might think about education and citizenship in both postcolonial and European contexts.

From state project of national moral rearmament to community right: creating internal frontiers in the education of Europeans and Eurasians

Until the 1860s the education of poor Europeans and Eurasians received no concerted government attention. Their schooling was distributed among an eclectic mix of institutions. Some were placed by relatives in the military and civil orphanages set up by charitable organizations (Arnold 1979). Others attended missionary, free or church schools in urban areas. Still others attended Anglo-Vernacular schools in smaller towns alongside other Indians. The East India Company only gave grants to the institutions intended for the children of military men. Under Dalhousie and Wood in 1854 a new comprehensive educational scheme was introduced to India. This aimed to promote general European knowledge through the medium of English and vernacular languages by bringing all educational institutions under the scrutiny of a government department in each presidency. In return for grants-in-aid these would be inspected, and the instructors within them would be increasingly professionalized through central training institutions. As Bayly (1996) puts it, the informational order was being redirected towards the patronage and hierarchy of the East India Company and its institutions, with dramatic effects on the shape of schooling (Shahidullah 1996). European and Eurasian education did not appear as a separate category in this scheme. The wide variety of schools that these groups attended would receive funding and inspection alongside vernacular schools so long as they did not teach religion during or after school hours. It was of no concern to the government who attended which schools, nor was any one form of education seen as more appropriate than any other for certain social groups. Despite later claims to the contrary, it did not seem to be of particular concern either to parents of Eurasians that they should receive separate education from other Indians.

This indifference to the provision of specific institutions began to change in the period from 1860 on. Bishop Cotton of Calcutta, who had an interest in education from his time as headmaster of Marlborough and as a master at Rugby, mounted a campaign to persuade the government to provide schools in the hills for Europeans and Eurasians (Kennedy 1996). These segregated schools would remove the children from Indian influences. Cotton expressed an anxiety that these children were growing up in close association with other Indians, from whom they acquired evil habits (Arnold 1979). He argued that their poverty and ignorance of faith and civilization undermined the claims to authority of both Christianity and Empire in India. Cotton's assertions were not entirely new. Since the beginning of the nineteenth century similar concerns had been raised by clergymen and philanthropists, and had led them to found orphanages and schools. What was new was that Cotton's arguments linked individual habits of life to potential political subversions of Empire and, more importantly, that these arguments found a receptive audience in the upper levels of the administration. The Viceroy, Canning, enthusiastically endorsed Cotton's crusade in his 1860 minute on European and Eurasian education. He recommended that boarding schools should be established in the hills for Europeans. He also added to the ambition of Cotton's scheme by suggesting that cheaper central day and boarding schools should be set up in the plains for Eurasians. All of these new institutions would be provided with government support and the standardization of their teaching, environment and syllabus would be guaranteed by regular inspection by the education department. Canning's minute explicitly made this a matter of the security of the state.

This government interest represented much more than a pragmatic realization that the numbers of Europeans and Eurasians were increasing in India owing to the growth of the administration, industry and the railways. The education of Europeans and Eurasians was now a matter of political importance. This concern signalled a shift in the purpose of education. It was now necessary for it to be directed towards the creation of internal frontiers. These had to be secured within subjects, ensuring their sentimental attachments to the state, race and nation. They also had to be formed hierarchically within the broader entity of the Empire between different kinds of racial and community subjects. This change in the purpose of education certainly reflected in part projects of liberal reform in Britain. Canning was a friend of Gladstone, and shared many of his views on the importance of greater government support for schooling. Yet Canning's scheme predated Gladstone's education act, passed in 1870, which provided primary school education for every English child through state grants to Church and voluntary schools and rate funding for non-denominational schools. And Canning's proposals highlight two elements that remain hidden in this later, metropolitan project. The first is that the funding of education was a matter of securing loyalty to the state and its mechanisms through personal transformations. The second is that the model of the moral reform of subjects through education involved the transference of a Protestant project of reform to the creation of an attachment to the state. Here in Canning's scheme we can see a clear appropriation of religious projects of moral reform in order to manufacture loyal citizens in schools. Significantly, a hidden transcript of the importance of religious sentiment for loyalty to the state was embedded within educational projects in India.

This government interest in European and Eurasian education reflects more than just a shift in educational ideas. It is an indicator of a change in the whole tenor of the post-1857 state in India. In an attempt to prevent a recurrence of rebellion in India Canning and bureaucrats on the India Council aimed to secure loyalty to the state at many levels of society, and attempted to work with what they perceived as the natural differences of Indian communities. For instance, community sentiments were seen as central to the remodelled army. Regiments would be raised from different parts of India, and any two regiments had to be alien enough to each other that they would fire on each other if ordered to do so. This, it was thought, would use the natural antagonism of Indian 'races' to great advantage.

Apart from political measures such as these there was a change in the general structure of feeling among British officials in India that was manifested in and reproduced by changes in material culture and the spatial organization of domestic and public spaces.[3] This structure of feeling linked personal conduct to community identity. It also suggested that behaviour within families and communities had tremendous significance for the perpetuation of British rule. Although theories of ethnoclimatology had been current among medical and military men in India before 1857, they became more widely subscribed to after the rebellion. These naturalized the differences between populations and communities by calculating the different risks posed to them by the same environment. They made personal habits among Europeans central to their moral and physical well-being and their potential to produce offspring. They also gave great impetus to the growth of hill stations in the post-rebellion period, which literally and metaphorically distanced rulers from ruled. Railway colonies were constructed to guarantee the Europeanness, discipline and respectability of working-class Eurasians and Europeans (Bear 1994). Domestic arrangements were increasingly centred around white memsahebs (Stoler 1989). The restructuring of the post-rebellion state therefore involved a concern with personal loyalties and a naturalization of distinct populations. In this reformulation of what the state, nation and Empire were in India it is not surprising that European and Eurasian education became a matter of political import.

Yet in the 1860s the significance of European and Eurasian education remained contested, and the implementation of measures to support it was limited. Canning's minute had only succeeded by 1870 in producing 12 hill schools, whose charges were so high that only the very wealthy could send their children to them. Government officials disagreed about the importance of the education of Eurasians and working-class Europeans. Their parents did not seem particularly interested in sending their children to separate schools either. However, by 1875, when Archbishop Bayly of Calcutta, another clergyman, raised the issue of European education his views received greater government support. By 1875 the idea that it would be advantageous to foster a connection between poorer Eurasians and Indians by their sharing of the same schools was unthinkable.

Archbishop Bayly's scheme, unlike that of Cotton, was targeted towards the provision of education for Eurasians and Europeans of the working classes. He envisaged the establishment of elementary schools at a very low cost for the lower-class Eurasian population in large towns and in railway colonies funded by grants-in-aid and inspected on the model of the new English national schools. Higher-level boarding schools would be provided at the principal towns, which would be funded by government aid and private voluntary contributions. In this system all children would pass on at the age of nine or ten years to a hill boarding school. This was to prevent a 'deterioration in their bodily vigour and mental energy' that would reduce their subsequent productivity and lead them to produce enfeebled children.[4] To this end Bayly suggested that a cheaper range of boarding schools should be created in the hills, since the children of the working classes could not go to the same schools as wealthier Europeans. Railway companies, religious organizations and the government would fund these.

For the Lieutenant Governor of Bengal, Richard Temple, Bayly's scheme was important because it had alerted him to a scandalous situation in which education was not reaching the poorer classes of Europeans and Eurasians. In Calcutta alone he reported with shock that one child out of every three children whose parents earned less than 300 rupees per month was not going to school. As a result they were growing up in ignorance in a manner that was 'detrimental to the public interest and brings discredit on the government'.[5] Now, aware of this failure, Temple asked education officials and civil servants to inquire into educational provision and poorer classes' lack of attendance across Bengal.

The answers received reveal an interesting collision between the ideas of bureaucrats that Europeans and Eurasians constituted a discrete, unified community and the variable practices of families according to class position, which suggested that there was nothing fixed about their identity. Government education officers and clergymen reported that the main reason poorer Europeans and Eurasians did not attend schools was that they did not want their children educated alongside Muslims and Hindus in government secular schools by Bengali teachers. Nor did they want their children to study with Indian Christians in missionary schools. These sentiments were attributed to an essential difference between communities. These assertions were contradicted by commentaries from other officials. The commissioner of the Bhagulpore division reported on the numbers of Europeans and Eurasians in the railway town of Jamalpur.

> There are a few families claiming to be European or Eurasian which are in truth Eurasian or pure native only. As these, however, are accepted at their own estimate both in and outside the workshops and having raised themselves by good behaviour and steady application are found desirous of maintaining their children in a position equally good if not better by giving them the benefit of education they are returned in the tables at their own price. Such persons are all Christians and their children now attend the Jamalpore School.[6]

This evidence of racial identity as related to class position did not lead officials to abandon the project of European and Eurasian education in favour of one that catered to particular class groups. Instead, it led them to assert that it was the parents' fault that children did not live up to their racial essence. They blamed parents for domestic subversions of the natural, invisible bonds that made up the community of Europeans in India across differences of class and religion. These parents provided bad examples to their children by their drunken habits, improvidence, lack of respectability and most of all absence of moral sense. Some of them, such as the Feringhees of Noakally, forgot completely that they were Europeans.[7] They had no concern for their children's education, and left them to the mercy of Indian servants. Their children became degraded versions of the European moral self. As a result it seemed vitally important to remove Europeans and Eurasian children from the influence of their parents. Schooling would now be directed to preventing domestic subversions of the natural ties of national/racial community. Government-funded schools would lift children out from the influence of their families and return them with a new, more appropriate moral sense. Temple concluded by advocating that elementary schools for Europeans and Eurasians under the age of nine should be funded by government grants so that they were affordable and accessible for all. But he also insisted that it was important to follow Bayly's scheme, in which all children at the age of nine or ten years should go to boarding schools in the principal towns or hills. This would create a level of discipline among such children that they would not receive at home.

This new idea that it was the purpose of education to create a moral rearmament of the European community in India involved bureaucrats in a contradictory notion of racial/national community. It was something that existed out there, to be served by particular forms of schooling appropriate to it. It was also constantly under threat, and had to be remade across class boundaries by schooling. Yet class never quite went away in these fantasies of national racial and cultural unity. It troubled them at two levels: in the actual variability of the lives lived by different classes of Europeans and Eurasians, and as an implicit part of the government education schemes themselves. Temple, government civil servants, railway officers and clergymen repeatedly emphasized that children should not be educated above their predestined role in life: that of being the working classes of the Raj.

This new project of education was implemented much more enthusiastically than Canning's scheme. This new idea of education was most fully realized in the new boarding schools set up for the children of railway employees, which were partly funded by the government. From 1875 to 1888 railway companies and churches built 11 hill boarding schools for them in places such as Kurseong, Nainital and Mussorie. Central boarding schools in the plains, for example at Jamalpur, were also constructed. Temple and officials in the education department kept a close watch on these schemes. Pressure would be brought to bear by railway officials and charitable bodies on Europeans and Eurasians to send their children to the schools. The hill schools were mainly intended for European children or children who were 'nearly' European with a father who was British and a mother who was Eurasian. These, according to the ethnoclimatological theories, required the reviving influence of a 'British' climate. To the new Lieutenant Governor of Bengal, Ashley Eden, these schools were particularly vital. He argued that a comparison of the physical appearance of 'even Eurasian boys brought up in the hills with that of boys of a similar class brought up in the towns in the plains' would reveal 'the advantage of the hill climate on the physique of the boys'.[8]

In 1879 the Viceroy Lord Lytton gave his backing to these projects in his minute on the education of Europeans and Eurasians. He argued that the government of India should spare no efforts to give free elementary education to such children, and that they should bear a substantial amount of the cost for the establishment of industrial boarding schools. These institutions were necessary in order to produce 'young Englishmen', 'brought up and educated in India itself', who would be equipped with the right British cultural competency to work in upper subordinate positions in industry, replacing imported European labour.[9] These schools would also provide a similar cultural competency to girls; but these would be trained only to an elementary standard and provided with domestic skills. Yet it is important to note that this apparently unequivocal statement of a class-based educational project was not so transparent in its intentions. This concern with the proper training of European and Eurasian labourers has to be seen against the background of the demand by Indian middle-class organizations that Indians should be employed at all levels of the Raj in greater numbers. In the agitation against income tax in 1870–1 and against the new civil service regulations in 1877–9 these organizations specifically attacked the use of Europeans and Eurasians in supervisory positions. The Indian National Congress continued this. It is in this context that we must see Lytton's concern with European and Eurasian education. Like other government officials, he responded to these challenges to the Raj's racial typology by stepping up efforts to enforce European habits of life and 'higher' moral standards within the national/racial community. Any departure from these standards could potentially be seized upon by Indians as proof of the hollowness of British arguments against the further employment of Indians in the civil service and railways because of their moral unsuitability to lead.

The syllabus and routines of the schools set up during this period in the plains and hills laid down the form and content of European education up to independence. Government inspection standardized routines and forms of instruction. Annual holidays were for Good Friday, Easter Monday, the Queen's birthday, the last week in May and the first in June, with one month's break at Christmas. This tied pupils to a Christian and state-based calendrical year that had nothing to do with the rhythms of Indian weather or festivals. In year one English-language reading, penmanship, simple arithmetic and drawing were emphasized. In year two language work continued with more stress on elocution, which was seen as vital to the cultural competence of children. Geography and British history were introduced in the fifth year, along with geometry and grammar. In the sixth year, along with the composition of letters, the geography and history of India were added. At this point Urdu also began to be taught.[10] Throughout, military drills were carried out by male children. Often as boys grew older their teams were attached to local volunteer or military battalions.

The primary aim of schooling across all these contexts was 'above all to form the character' through exercise and a disciplined British environment.[11] Almost as many girls as boys went to these schools. In 1908, for example, 210 boys and 151 girls attended the East Indian Railway's Oak Grove School at Mussorie. As was typical of many of these schools, at Oakgrove there was an annual prize day at which the railway agent gave awards for 'womanliness' and 'manliness' and the boys performed military drills. So important were these domestic and military elements of education both in the plains and the hill schools that in 1884 the education department in Bengal made the grants provided to schools partly dependent on whether they taught drill, gymnastics and needlework.[12]

This project of the moral reform of citizens was consciously moulded on Christian ethics. Dependence on government grants-in-aid meant that all schools, whether they were Anglican, Catholic or non-denominational, had to be secular. Yet this insistence on secularism went hand in hand with an assertion that the education provided in order to transform children into upright citizens through the inculcation of morals should be Christian in spirit. In 1881, when the education department drew up a specific European schools code and set up a department for European education, this insistence on the practice of a Christian secularism provided the rationale for a separate system of schooling. It was assumed that parents of European extraction and habits of life would not countenance sending their children to government-funded schools for natives where there would be a non-Christian atmosphere. In this project of education the internal frontiers within people and the national community were now marked with the signs of race, habits of life and religion.

Yet schooling also produced a hierarchy within the community of

'Europeans'. This hierarchy wove together differences of class and graded differences of race. One of these distinctions could now not be imagined without the other. Which school you attended not only affected your class position but also retrospectively indicated the degree of your European lineage. By the 1890s a three-tier system of education had developed that continued until independence. Elite hill schools such as St Paul's, Darjeeling provided education for children with solely European parentage and middle-class parents. The newer railway and Protestant hill schools provided for children with lower-middle-class parents and more ambiguous backgrounds. These schools were perhaps the least successful in terms of attracting pupils, and often suffered from financial deficits.[13] There were several reasons for this. Lower-middle-class parents were not so certain that their children needed the distance from their domestic environment and the kind of reform that these schools promised. On the other hand, parents who were in favour of such a form of education periodically panicked about the moral atmosphere of particular schools. They feared especially the influence of other pupils 'of the lower grade subordinates' on their children.[14] This suggests that the aim of the educational project was somewhat deflected by children's agency in the schools. It also reveals just how permeable and fluid, dangerously so in the eyes of colonial officials and some parents, the boundary between social and racial groups was in this system of education. This anxiety about the malleability of children also reflects a muted awareness that education did not just provide a service for already existing segments of European society, but helped to construct the internal boundaries within that society.

Children who were not sent to any of these schools were quite simply assumed to be of non-European background. People who did not participate in the hierarchical system of education that produced the moral frontiers of being European were now inadmissible to the racial/national community. Education now guaranteed both social privileges and a particular kind of lineage identity. It did not simply exist for Europeans; instead, it helped to make them.

Up until independence there was very little alteration in the actual structure of European education. The changing political environment led to some piecemeal alterations. There was some improvement in access to education above the age of 16. Senior Cambridge exams were introduced. These gave access to the seven European colleges (with an enrolment of 722 students) and two professional colleges for teachers that had developed by 1917. Yet there were important alterations in the justification and purpose of European schools. These increasingly had to prove their relevance to a newly imagined Indian nation. This in particular was an issue for the Anglo-Indian Association, who came to be the officially recognized, if elite, political voice of the Europeans and the Eurasian community in India. From the 1930s the Anglo-Indian Association campaigned to make education more relevant to life in India. Gidney, the president of the association argued that

> If we are to be acceptable to the future India, we must at once com-
> pletely reorient our ideas, our outlook and our objects in life, especially
> our education system; so that we may become more sons of India than
> aliens, as we are now regarded by all Indians, thanks to our educational
> system which is entirely alien to Indian nationalism and aspirations.
>
>   (Henry Gidney, quoted in Weston 1938: 130)

Gidney also suggested that the education of Anglo-Indians had been much too concerned to form character and not useful skills. To rectify this situation Gidney set about trying to make Indian vernaculars, in particular Hindi, compulsory in European schools. He also suggested that it should be possible to prepare for exams for the Indian universities at European schools. He felt that preparation for the senior Cambridge exams meant that Anglo-Indians knew little or nothing about either Indian or Anglo-Indian history. This left them 'more as aliens than citizens of their motherland India'.[15] The Interprovincial Education Board took the half-measure of recommending the teaching of a vernacular in European and Anglo-Indian schools. It was not until after independence that schools dropped their connections to the British exam system.

More important in the wider political arena than this campaign to Indianize European education were the attempts by the Anglo-Indian Association to justify the continuing existence of this separate system of schooling. This was done on the grounds that Anglo-Indians were a minority, like Muslims or Parsis, who had a right to education in their own language and moral traditions. Gidney and his successor Frank Anthony sought to make the right to European education a minority community right guaranteed by law. In 1935 at the Round Table Conference, Lord Irwin agreed that special grants should be provided by the government to European schools and that these should receive statutory protection. More importantly, just after independence, Anthony was closely involved in the negotiations that led to the drawing up of sections 29(1) and 30(1) of the constitution. These state the fundamental right of minorities to establish and administer educational institutions of their choice in the following terms:

> Any section of citizens residing in any territory of India or any part
> thereof having a distinct language, script or culture of its own shall have
> the right to conserve the same. This protection extends to its right to
> administer its own schools where the community's Christian heritage is
> fostered and the English mother tongue is reinforced through its use as
> the medium of instruction. . . . All minorities, whether based on religion
> or language, shall have the right to establish and administer educational
> institutions of their choice.[16]

As a result of this campaign a colonial state educational project that aimed to produce loyal citizens by correcting the influence of their domestic life was transformed into the cultural right of a minority to educate its children according to the wishes of their parents beyond the influence of the state. What is forgotten in this change of a state project into a community right is that this colonial project of education in fact helped to produce the internal boundaries of this 'minority community'.

Despite this apparent change of education into a community right there is an important continuity between the colonial past and the present at the level of lived experience. For Anglo-Indians, though not for other Indians, to send your child to an English-medium school is to make a statement about your community origins, domestic life and lineage. The anxieties of grandparents about education are passed on to their grandchildren in the form of assertions about community identity and failures to live up to this. For example, one family I knew in Calcutta were filled with shame when their 16-year-old daughter failed a school exam in English literature. Her parents, her grandparents and the girl herself were all equally outraged because, in the girl's words: 'How could I not pass, it's my mother-tongue?' Her failure showed a perplexing lack of ability to live up to supposedly heritable lineage-based characteristics. It was shaming because it cast doubt on their claims that they were actually an *Anglo*-Indian family.

The changes in Anglo-Indian education have also, despite Gidney and Anthony's aim to make education relevant to the production of Indian citizens, not resolved the status of Anglo-Indians within the Indian nation. They exist as a discrete community protected by the state, but potentially not quite inside the nation. As we will see in the later school stories, their education, as it did in colonial times, continues to disembed them from belonging to India. Now, in cities like Calcutta, the Indian middle and lower middle classes flock to the old Church schools. This popularity increased after the 1980s, when states such as West Bengal made regional languages compulsory as the medium of instruction in government schools. Parents hope that these institutions will equip their children with the correct manners and a facility with English, which will enable them to achieve good positions in the civil service or the corporate sector. Emphasis is still placed on the formation of character, discipline and the acquisition of a cosmopolitan or anglicized demeanour. Debating, elocution, drill and sports are seen as routes to this. The school year is still punctuated by Christian routines, with prize-giving and celebrations often occurring in chapels attached to the schools. Old school songs suffused with Christian symbolism are sung at these events. Yet, interestingly for the understanding of the multiple religious influences on India's contemporary public sphere, parents often suggest that their children have acquired a more secular self from attending these schools. There are reserved places for Anglo-Indian and Christian children at the schools, with some scholarships available. Anglo-Indians and Indian Christians frequently work as teachers, especially in the primary classes of these schools. Church schools also often have heads drawn from these two groups.

When Indians attend these schools, this adds to their range of cultural competences. It makes them 'cosmopolitan', in the popular version in which this means to be liberal and middle-class; but it does not automatically make them any less Indian. Their residual Indianness is grounded in their participation in other community organizations in civil society and in their domestic inheritance and milieu. Yet for lower-middle- and middle-class Indians, Anglo-Indians are not Indian enough, as their *only* cultural competence appears to be that of the cosmopolitan/Anglicized public space of the school. They are not sufficiently embedded in the apparently autochthonous experience of 'being Indian' that is transmitted through religious, regional or domestic inheritances of culture and language. In fact many Bengali middle-class stories about Anglo-Indians emphasize that their essential nature is to be shallow, inauthentic and fickle in their loyalities to countries, religions and professions. Fundamentally they are seen as 'without culture', because they are not anchored in place by domestic and community life. Yet on occasion, of course, it is also true that the competence of Anglo-Indians in being cosmopolitan makes them appear enviably middle-class to working-class Indians.

On the wider national scene public debates about the constitutional right to minority education have suggested also that Anglo-Indians and the schools that exist for them are not quite Indian enough. Politicians, state governments and the central government have periodically sought to impose civic projects or standardized practices on minority institutions, including English-medium schools. In particular in the 1980s state governments attempted to impose regional languages as the medium of instruction. A Supreme Court ruling that English-medium schools must continue to exist in order to protect the rights of parents to choose the medium of education for their children ended these debates. More recently, in 2002, there has been widespread discussion of minority education around the Supreme Court consideration of the validity of Section 30 of the constitution. The court ruled that the right of a minority to establish educational institutions of their choice should be unrestricted, but that the right to administer them is not absolute. The state and the universities could apply regulatory measures in order to maintain educational standards and excellence in institutions. This ruling was based on a particular vision of the Indian nation and the place of the state in securing its unity. As one of the judges put it,

> The essence of secularism in India is the recognition and preservation of the different types of people, with diverse languages and different beliefs, and placing them together so as to form a whole and united India. Articles 9 and 30 do no more than seek to preserve the differences that exist and at the same time unite the people to form one strong nation.[17]

Yet in the wider popular and political debates around this ruling, members of the ruling BJP-led coalition government and the Sangh Parivar have argued that minority educational rights enable the presence of subversive institutions and groups within the body politic. Christian and Muslim schools in particular threaten the cohesion of this national entity. Interestingly, in spite of the attempt of Nehruvian secular socialism to break with the colonial past of education in the debates about minority schooling, we can see a return of old issues in new forms. On the one hand the administrative argument is that education merely exists to serve the needs of various populations and that the government acts as a facilitator of this. On the other hand the nationalist argument claims that citizens should belong to a natural community of sentiment and that educating them is part of a religio-moral project of unification. Both of these perspectives emerged in the post-1857 state approaches to education and as we have seen were present in the debates on European education. They continue to haunt discussions of education in contemporary India. The issue of interior frontiers and the suspicions of disloyalty to the nation that suffused the discussions of European education have not disappeared. In these debates Anglo-Indians often appear as not quite Indian enough in the same way as in the past they were not quite British enough. Colonial projects of education continue to have an influence on public debates at the national level and on the contemporary experience of Anglo-Indians. As we shall see this is expressed in their use of school stories as a site for exploring how to be Indian, how to be Anglo-Indian and how to be true to their own selves.

Uncertain communities, unbounded homes and the national project of education

Colonial projects for the education of Europeans and Eurasians emphasized the importance of the school as a public space that counteracted the influences of the home. The structure of boarding schools and the content of education were designed to extract children from subversive domestic habits and to create moral subjects who would know how to be European citizens. At maturity they would be returned to the private sphere as adults with a proper sense of family habitus that would prevent the degeneration of the next generation and allow the natural recreation of the invisible ties of race/nationality. By independence this project had been transmuted into the apparently uncomplicated task of leaving in place an education system that merely served the private needs of a minority community. From the perspective of the politicians who drew up the Indian constitution and civil servants, domestic practices naturally formed the invisible ties of community, and this community identity was merely expressed in schools and in the wider public sphere of the encompassing nation-state. It was under this administrative assumption that Anglo-Indian, Islamic and Hindu revivalist schools continued to receive some government funding and legal support after independence. But at the level of educational experience this suturing together of schooling, community identity and domestic practice is much more problematic. In the particular case of Anglo-Indian school stories, people puzzle over the ways in which education forms and breaks domestic and community ties. At other points they indicate the ways in which schools enable immoral acts and the false appearance of domestic respectability. At times they collapse the space of the school entirely into the domestic space – making the home almost indistinguishable from the school. These stories anxiously comment on the ways in which schools produce the internal frontiers of the home and community.

The transformative power of school environments is captured in two types of accounts. The first of these are stories about the smuggling of other kinds of Indians into reserved places or scholarships. Whenever I discussed education Anglo-Indians of all ages would complain about the permeability of their community to infiltration by people pretending to be Anglo-Indians. Their greatest fear about this was not that it stopped them from getting places at the schools, but that these fake Anglo-Indians were indistinguishable from real Anglo-Indians to other Indians and that they lowered the tone and respectability of the community. This is a fear that initially appeared in colonial schemes of European education, but became that of Anglo-Indians during the campaigns of Gidney and Anthony for education as a community right. Gidney initially sought to limit European schools to Anglo-Indians rather than Indian Christians and people of other European backgrounds. Before independence the pages of the *Anglo-Indian Review* were full of concerns about people masquerading as Anglo-Indians to gain access to education. These anxieties continue to haunt people. In the more elaborate versions of these fears Muslims in particular intentionally contract second or third marriages with Anglo-Indian women solely in order to guarantee places for all of their children by all of their wives in English-medium schools. This is seen as outrageous because these children have no lineage right to these places, nor do they live an Anglo-Indian lifestyle. These accounts reflect a desire to assert that there is such a thing as an essential Anglo-Indian who deserves a particular kind of community right. Yet they also suggest that once people have been schooled to be Anglo-Indians they are almost indistinguishable from real ones.

These stories of 'infiltration' point anxiously to the central role of education in making Anglo-Indians. This is a matter of personal anxiety for Anglo-Indians, as is shown by the second kind of account of education they give. Education appears in the context of life histories as a guarantee of a particular kind of family origin. Often Anglo-Indians are without documentary proof of their lineage histories, so schooling is liberally used in conversation as an indication of European or British origins. For example note the following exchange with Esmi Stewart, a 50-year-old woman who lives in the railway colony at Kharagpur, when I asked her to tell me about her family history:

> My mummy was an orphan . . . Her father was a pure Englishman, six four in height, blue eyes. She studied in Stuart school in Cuttack.

Protestant School. Then it was run by a pure Englishman. Even Bishop
Westcott School, Ranchi, husband and wife English family was running
the School. My brother had an opportunity – he was in that school.
Eldest studied at St Vincent's, Asansol. My other sisters studied in St
Helen's, Darjeeling, and myself Cuttack.

Esmi is offering proof of her family origin through the medium of the
public institutions she and her relatives studied at. Similarly Trigger
Thompson, a 60-year-old retired train driver, insisted at one point in a discussion about what makes an Anglo-Indian

they speak English as a mother tongue. No matter how much education
an Indian has he cannot talk English to you. I'll tell you straight. You
can recognize an Anglo-Indian from an Indian any time only by the way
he talks. It's simple no matter how, no matter what qualifications. He
may be a professor, he may have any academic qualification, but they
can never talk English like us.

Yet in response to my next question: 'Were your parents very particular
about the way you spoke?' Trigger replied:

Oh yes, we were taught by English people. I went to the Bengal Nagpur
railway European School. Very proud it was and all the teachers and
masters were from England. They were all English teachers and our certificate was from England, Cambridge, but they abolished it. Now you
can buy any certificate.

In one breath a mother tongue that indicates origins becomes a facility
learnt in the space of a school in a way that retrospectively guarantees your
origin. These stories are full of an uncertainty about the stability of the categories of community that are in secular and in Hindu nationalism seen as
natural outgrowths from domestic lineage ties. This uncertainty is a product
of two things. The first of these is the historical experience of Anglo-Indians
of becoming European through education. The second is their current
experience of being a not quite authentic enough community to other
Indians. Their double position of being 'inauthentic' leads to their anxieties
about infiltration and uncertainties about inherited and acquired aspects of
being Anglo-Indian.

A third kind of account of education addresses the links between
domestic spaces and educational institutions. These school stories undermine the historical claim that European education creates moral selves and
corrects domestic disorders. They suggest instead that schools are part of and
enable family formation – in particular the formation of immoral or false
families. A characteristic version of this kind of school story was told to me
by Mercy Hastings, a 40-year-old widow and mother of four children

ranging in age from 18 to seven, who lives in a two-room shack on the out-skirts of the railway colony at Kharagpur. She was concerned to warn me about the character of other Anglo-Indians I knew. She began by telling me about Duncan Hall, who lives with two wives. His second wife was originally an orphan in St Thomas' boarding school in Calcutta. He convinced the nuns that her uncle had died and that he was now her legal guardian. They didn't bother to check his claim, and he took the girl home with him to be his wife. Mercy went on to tell me about another immoral family. She suggested that Emma Francis' family were not as respectable and European as they seemed. Her sister had married a Bengali and then left him. Their daughter was abandoned in St Thomas', Kidderpore. When Mercy asks Emma about her niece she denies all connections with her. In these stories schools, rather than being morally reforming institutions set apart from the domestic life of families, are an intimate part of family arrangements. Their existence helps to facilitate immoral behaviour and to create the false appearance of family respectability. School and home are tangled together in a way that reflects Anglo-Indians' historical experience of education. These stories also provide a muted counterpoint to the usual image of the Indian nation, in which education and the public sphere of civil society in general exist to serve communities that are ultimately rooted in domestic units.

Another variety of engagement with education among Anglo-Indians attempts to collapse the space of the school into the domestic space. This strategy seeks to secure the existence of community by an attempt to seal together domestic and school practices. Here there is no separation between family honour and reputation and that of the school and ultimately the community. The effort required to achieve this fusion is great, and often relies on the use of strict discipline. This strategy of attempting to fuse home and school is frequently fuelled by a lingering doubt about whether the family can live up to the standards set for being a member of the community of Anglo-Indians. Although there were many examples of this in Kharagpur and Calcutta, I will tell you about one family in which this strategy was particularly intense.

Kevin, a 38-year-old teacher at St James' School in Calcutta, grew up along with his three brothers and two sisters in the railway colony in Kharagpur. His father was an Anglo-Indian railway driver. His mother, an Indian Christian, mainly brought up the family and then taught in a local English-medium free school. Kevin began his education in the local railway school, where he remembered learning maypole dances from an English teacher. Then at the age of seven he went to boarding school at Loyola Jamshedpur. Here he was top in elocution, and he learnt discipline from the American priests. He then trained to be a teacher at Mount Hermon College, and has spent his adult life teaching in Calcutta English-medium schools. He now has three children with his wife Christine. Kevin sees his education as allowing him to escape the railway colony, where Anglo-Indians have only sunk into poverty and bad habits. He is highly critical of other Anglo-Indians, who, he feels, are letting down the community by not bothering to educate their children properly. But this simple story of self-improvement is not the only way Kevin understands education. He is very concerned that he and his family live up to the standards of dress, demeanour and self-discipline he learnt at Loyola and that he now teaches by example. He enforces this quite rigidly on his children, using a belt regularly to punish them if they defy his authority. His anxiety to do this is fuelled in part by his own sense that his mother's Indian Christian identity compromises in some way the Anglo-Indianness of himself and his family.

This fusing of the space of the school, home and personal identity came out particularly dramatically one evening. Kevin had invited family members to celebrate Narissa's birthday. These included Terence, an Indian Christian related to him by marriage, who is head of a Jewish school in Calcutta. Kevin and his family members had joked that he had become Jewish himself ever since working there. In this one remark they revealed their sense of the fusion of private and public identities associated with a school. As the party wore on into the night everyone began to discuss the various English-medium schools in Calcutta. Terence said that St James' was a hypocritical place, because they said they gave preference to Christian and Anglo-Indian children, but they didn't: for example, when he asked Kevin to get a place for his eldest son in St James', he couldn't do this. In response Kevin exploded in anger, saying that he had told Terence never to mention this in his house or to criticize his school in this house. Kevin added that he wouldn't have his school insulted and that he would defend its honour to all comers. He completed his outburst with the statement that the school's honour was his family honour.

This is a particularly intense example of the collapsing of the school into family and personal identity. It is revealing in its reversal of the assumption of both secular and Hindu nationalism that domestic practices naturally form the invisible ties of community, and that community identity is merely expressed in schools and in the wider public sphere of the encompassing nation-state. So intimate are these public spaces for Kevin that their honour is his family's honour. This is of course in part because he is a teacher; but it also reflects, as do the other examples I have given here, the intimate power of educational institutions for Anglo-Indians.

Finding a way to be a citizen-subject: self-actualization, school discipline and being Indian

The next series of Anglo-Indian school stories address a different issue – how to be a citizen-subject or someone who is self-determining and at the same time bound by obligations to the transcendent entities of the community and the nation. For Anglo-Indians this common theme of school stories takes specific forms related to the history of English-medium education and their present predicament of being a 'minority' within the nation. They often concentrate on the disjunctures between being your own self, the self imposed by education, and being Indian. In trying to think through these disjunctures the stories often return to sites and acts of discipline – so that the drama of being a citizen-subject is condensed into encounters with specific agents and events of disciplining.

A characteristic narrative of self-determination was that told to me by Trevor Gomes. He is a 45-year-old Anglo-Indian who is married to a Bengali woman and has one 14-year-old child. He works in middle management in a bank, and has been successful educationally and financially. When I asked him about his life and his decision to marry a Bengali, he joined the following themes together. First, he said that if he was going to write a book about his experiences he would never do it in English – Bengali would be his choice. English couldn't express the non-Anglo-Indian parts of his self. Besides, he associated English with his father, who forced them to read Dickens, and with his Catholic boarding school. The headmaster there was brutal. Because he was an Anglo-Indian himself, he gave terrible punishment to any Anglo-Indian boy who stepped out of line. One Anglo-Indian boy who had squeezed his toothpaste too hard had been caned in front of the school, while the headmaster said over him 'You're useless, wasteful, ungrateful, like all of your kind'. Trevor went on to add that this was really why he had married a Bengali and didn't want to be part of Anglo-Indian society – that it had made him try to be as Indian as possible ever since. Trevor leapt from attempting to find a way to tell an authentic story of himself as a Bengali to an account of the dramas of discipline he experienced at school. Ultimately it is these dramas against which he feels his life-choices to be Indian rather than Anglo-Indian have been made. The long history of colonial and postcolonial education for Anglo-Indians has made this site a particularly resonant one for Trevor. It is to a story of school that he returns in order to work out how to be authentic both to himself as an agent and to the transcendent entity of India.

Many Anglo-Indian school stories take up the theme of self-actualization and discipline in the particular context of sports. In both colonial and post-colonial schooling, drills and competitive events are intended as lessons in loyalty and effort for larger public institutions. However, in Anglo-Indian school stories sports play a different role from this intention. Sports create a sense of liberation from origins and a degree of autonomy achieved through replacing public disciplining in schools with private discipline and natural physical prowess. Sport also allows Anglo-Indians to weave together a sense of becoming Indian through their own efforts. A short example is the account offered by Mr Manook, a 60-year-old man, when I asked him to tell me about his life. Mr Manook told me that he started life in Iran, where his Armenian father and English mother had a farm. His mother died when he was five years old. So his father sent him and his three brothers to boarding school in Calcutta. They only saw him once or twice after that. The school was very strict. Mr Manook was scalded by boiling water from a samovar in

Iran when he was young. This affected his physical prowess, and he couldn't stand straight. The principal of the school, Mr Clark, was from England and was very strict, and used to tell him off all the time about his posture and physical weakness, saying, according to Mr Manook, 'You're not in Iran now'. But Mr Manook proved him wrong by taking up boxing and training himself in this. It was this skill that got him a job on the railways at the age of 14, which meant that he was free of the school he hated. He loved to compete for the Indian railways, and did so all his life. Mr Manook in this account overcomes the apparent handicap of his origins in Iran, which were stigmatized by his strict English headmaster, through his own physical discipline. His self-actualization is framed against the unfairness of school discipline.

A particularly strong example of self-fashioning through sport was the account offered by Donna Raffiq. Donna, an Anglo-Indian, had taught in the railway primary school at Kharagpur most of her life, and her husband, a Muslim, worked in the railways, running the sports club and as a workshop foreman. Here is how Donna told the story of her life and marriage. Donna was born at her uncle's house in Jamuria, in the middle of the coalfields. As soon as her father saw Donna's blond hair and strong limbs he started to call her his own dear *Koila* cat, meaning his coal-black cat. The joke of this name came from the fact that she was born in a coalfield, and she had the fire that coal has, and the speed and wickedness of a cat; and yet she had such fair skin. When Donna was three days old she was left alone on a bed. A monkey came in through the window and grabbed Donna and was sitting with her in its arms when her father returned to the bedroom. After sometime the monkey put her down. Donna added at this point in the story:

> Say what you like, they say now, the Hindus, Hanuman is the monkey-god and Hanuman is also the god of strength, massive strength like that; and so massive strength I had from when I was very young, god-gifted. I didn't have to build up strength in school. I was Hanuman's child. A natural sportswoman. I didn't ever need any training or discipline from the teachers. I didn't focus also on the lessons: I was very naughty, and the teachers scolded me; I just did the sports.

Donna's innate strength augmented by the blessing of Hanuman meant that while at school she represented Orissa in the national school games. Then she represented Bengal, followed by the South-Eastern Railway team, the Rangers Club and finally Mohameddan Sporting. Once she returned to Jamuria, where she was born. Here the contradictions between her own now established sense of Indianness conflicted with those of other Indians. She told me that:

> When I went out to a national competition in Jamuria, my father was very proud because I was racing for India on the soil where I was born.

But the crowd who came to watch and the journalists reporting didn't know I was representing the Indian team. There was a photo of me, and it says 'Russian girl wins', they thought I was pure Russian. When I was doing the march past, the crowd kept saying, 'There goes the Russian girl', and very close photo they took while I was doing the shot put and there they put on the photo, 'the Russian girl wins the day', big block black letters. It makes me so angry and all. They couldn't recognize I was Indian.

Donna met her husband Begum at a South-Eastern Railway tournament in which he was a participant, and they courted each other in secret from then on until they married. Here, as in many other stories about sport I heard from Anglo-Indians, it provides a medium for self-fashioning that takes them beyond their apparent origins and the limits of their minority schooling. In particular, it allows them to imagine themselves as active agents or citizens and to incorporate themselves as Indian rather than Anglo-Indian national subjects. It is these school stories more than any of the others I heard from Anglo-Indians that enable them for a moment to transcend the contradictions of their position as a very particular kind of citizen-subject of India. These stories represent attempts to create for themselves new kinds of internal frontiers that are made real not through the process of education, but by the natural prowess of the body.

Moving beyond issues of class and normalization: manufacturing citizens and the 'problems' of domestic, community and civic life

Anglo-Indian dispositions towards education have emerged from the contradictions of a particular colonial history of attempts to manufacture 'European' citizens. Yet it is important to note that the dilemmas that are revealed in their school stories are an acute version of issues that arise in a wide range of projects of education in India. The problem of creating citizens has in all contexts been posed as an issue of working out how to combine domestic, community and civic sentiments. Actual educational projects have found different ways of resolving this apparent problem, but they have all started from the assumption that it is a problem. Since the 1840s colonial and nationalist projects of education perceived domestic and community sentiments as impediments to national political life. As Kumar (1991) and Srivastava (1998) point out, both colonial and nationalist educationalists aimed to remove 'degenerate' domestic practices of language and religion in order to equip pupils to be rational members of civil society. Pupils were encouraged to overcome the 'Indianness', irrationality and narrow loyalties of their home in order to achieve the status of self-determining publicly minded adults. From the 1870s onwards, at the same time as schools were set up for Europeans and Eurasians as part of a programme of moral and national rearmament, Indian nationalists opened schools and colleges that taught in the vernacular. In a manner strikingly similar to the colonial state's plans for the education of Europeans and Eurasians, nationalists argued that this education should be reformist and moral. It would inculcate a spirit of Western rationality in order to counteract problematic narrow loyalties learnt in the home. It would also be suffused with a Hindu essence of spirituality similar to the Christian spirit of schools for Europeans and Eurasians. These too were projects of moral rearmament that created a problematic relationship between domestic, community and civic life, and marked the public sphere as permeated with a particular religious temper. The only difference of the Anglo-Indian experience of educational projects was that moral rearmament in their case involved the prescription and ascription of intimate lineage identities, so that their loyalties could be tied to the colonial state and the national/racial identity of being 'British/ European'.

Anglo-Indian experiences also speak of another kind of widely diffused educational project. This had as its goal not the sustenance of a shared civic life, but the revival and purification of communities bound by religion, language and sometimes genealogical ties. The assumption was that these entities would then take part in civil society as unified agents. This category of educational projects includes the Hindu revivalist schools created in the 1890s in North India and the Hindi vernacular schools set up by the Arya Samaj and the RSS from the 1930s (K. Kumar 1992; N. Kumar 1996). These schools, like the schemes for European and Eurasian education, naturalized differences of community, marked some people as more part of the state and civil society than others, and encouraged pupils to construct internal frontiers of morality and to transform their domestic practices. Strikingly, colonial, nationalist and reformist projects of education, whatever social groups they targeted, all made community connections and domestic behaviour relevant to political and national sentiments. They placed a recurrent issue on the agenda of education in India – are some community and domestic sentiments more pliable to transference into loyalty to the nation than others? They also made community a recurrent issue for debate in the field of post-independence education. Anglo-Indian experiences of education are only unusual in relation to this project of forging communities in that other Indians do not recognize Anglo-Indians as a genuine Indian community. This is because their collective identity lacks the rooting in place and particular domestic practices separate from those associated with the public sphere that gives most other community identities their naturalizing underpinnings. Other collective identities, such as Hindu or Bengali, appear to have a greater degree of authenticity, because these underpinnings distract from the long historical interaction between public institutions such as schools and the family. The difference in being Anglo-Indian is that it is more difficult to suture together ideas of community, family, nation and cultural inheritance.

Anglo-Indian experiences are not just relevant to wider Indian issues. They also reveal two aspects of the manufacturing of citizens through schooling that have remained underplayed in accounts of the history of mass education in Europe. The first is the connections between family and school and domestic and civic emotions. The second is the ways in which schooling naturalizes differences of community and marks some citizens as more part of the state and civil society than others. This Indian example, like those of other colonial and postcolonial states, speaks not only of class formation and class fears, but also of permeable domestic–civic boundaries, public moralities based on religious values, and notions of citizenship that rely on exclusion. It is not that these have not been and are not issues in European settings. We only have to consider current contentious debates in Britain about the place of state-funded community and religious schools in the national education system to demonstrate resonances across contexts. Instead, school stories from India illuminate aspects of European situations that have remained obscured. They do this quite simply because, as Stoler (1995) and Van der Veer (2001) have argued, colonial and postcolonial situations contain fragments of shared histories that have been forgotten in the metropoles of Europe. Projects of education and citizenship were often forged across these two apparently separate geographical domains by the same institutions and individuals. The problem of creating European citizens in colonial settings was for the officials designing the schemes just a more acute version of that of creating citizens in the metropole. It is therefore important that we place side by side these colonial and metropolitan histories. At the theoretical level Anglo-Indian stories alert us to the fact that in all European contexts we need to pay more attention to: how the domestic and civic are fused together in schooling; and how community loyalties are posed as relevant or dangerous to the education of citizens and to education as a project of exclusion as well as of normalization.

At a more general level this chapter has been an experiment in taking school stories seriously. Perhaps one of the most methodologically difficult aspects of analysing education is the problem of specifying its effects on children or on people through the course of their lives. One way of addressing the afterlife of education is to take note of how people themselves incorporate their experiences of schooling into their life histories and domestic practices. These narratives will of course change throughout life; but whenever they are told they make educational experiences a mobile and influential field for defining agency. They provide an invaluable insight into how the institutions and practices of schooling are internalized as part of the existential dilemma of being a citizen-subject.

My emphasis in this chapter on the internal frontiers produced in schooling and the existential project of citizenship leads to one final point. In spite of a deep history of sociological debate it seems to me that we still know very little about the content of the moral projects of becoming a citizen as they are practised by people. Durkheim and Mauss long ago argued that the modern moral individual grew out of, but transcended, Christianity. Durkheim, of course, spent much of his life designing educational forms that would produce this new rational citizen with a sense of duty and obligation to others. Critiques of Durkheim and Mauss are well established too. Perhaps two of the most useful are those of Balibar and Foucault, who suggest that the subjectivity of the citizen consists of little more than an illusion of individual agency and freedom. Both of these sociological positions rest on a somewhat abstract, institutional and legalistic sense of what the modern subject is. The idea of an internal frontier developed from Balibar, Foucault and Stoler's work can lead us beyond this to pay attention to the substance and dilemmas of being a citizen. We can take into our theoretical view not only the legalistic and educational schemes designed to produce subjects, but also the other senses of self that are fused with top-down administrative measures and the creative acts of people attempting to become citizens. This is more than an issue of expanding empirical knowledge, because an attempt to trace internal frontiers has the potential to affect our understanding of what modern subjectivity is. For example, listening to the accounts of Anglo-Indians and tracing the history of their education reminds us of two important things about the modern subject of nation-states. The first of these is that their public morality never becomes disconnected from a religious range of references. The second is that the ability to act as a citizen is always restricted or enabled by personal lineages, community connections and domestic life. So, to end, by exploring the internal frontiers of citizenship as an ethical project practised by people we can both question the existential illusion of individualism and freedom carried in this political idea and explore the creative agency of people as they make themselves into citizens.

Notes

1 Although Stoler uses 'interior', here, as suggested by Véronique Bénéï, I have chosen 'internal'. This latter usage highlights the process of internalization and leaves open the issue of what kinds of subjectivity are produced by projects of citizenship. These may all involve a process of internalization, but may not always emphasize the interior of the self. See the concluding section for more on this.

2 In this chapter I use the chronologically appropriate terms for Anglo-Indians. Until 1919 in the Montagu–Chelmsford electoral reforms the term 'Eurasian' was used for people of mixed parentage in India. After this date 'Anglo-Indian' was more widely used, and was legally defined as people of mixed parentage who had a European ancestor in their male line of inheritance. This is, in fact, how the Indian constitution defines them. The legal boundaries of this group, of course, shifted according to the colonial state's creation of institutions to regulate their identity, as did the names for them.

3 'Structure of feeling' is, of course, Raymond Williams' phrase. It is intended to capture the idea that private sentiments are in part a collective phenomenon produced by social changes.

4 Archbishop Bayly, 'Suggestions for Supplying the Educational Requirements of

East Indians and Europeans of the Working Class in India', File 70-68/69 *Bengal Proceedings: Education Department*, June 1875.

5 Richard Temple, 'Minute by the Lieutenant-Governor of Bengal 25 February 1875 on the Educational Means for the Poorest Classes of Europeans and East Indians', File 70-18, *Bengal Proceedings: Education Department*, March 1875.

6 G. N. Barlow, Officiating Commissioner of Bhagulpore Division to Secretary to the Government of Bengal, No 190G 13 March, File 70-38, *Bengal Proceedings: Education*, June 1875.

7 'Feringhees' or 'Firinghees' was a term used by British officials to refer to 'Indianized' people of Portuguese extraction.

8 Sir Ashley Eden, referred to in A. W. Croft to Secretary to the Government of Bengal, 4 September, File 26-42, 'Schools for Europeans and Eurasians', *Bengal Proceedings: Education*, November 1880.

9 Minute by Lord Lytton, 25 March 1879, quoted in full in appendix to *Committee on the Financial Condition of Hill Schools for Europeans in Northern India*, Simla: Government of India Press, 1904.

10 R. Roberts, Acting Agent East Indian Railway Company, No. 201G, 23 March, File 26-82/98, *Bengal Proceedings Education*: September 1876.

11 Oman (1877), OIOCL PWD/5/7, Coll. 35.

12 Inspector of European Schools in Bengal to the Director of Public Instruction in Bengal, *Official Meetings of the East Indian Railway Board*, No. 375, Calcutta 10 October 1884.

13 *Committee on the Financial Condition of Hill Schools for Europeans in Northern India* (1904).

14 Agent's No. 134 of 1903 on 'The Unsatisfactory Financial Position of Oak Grove Hill School', *Agent of the East Indian Railway Letters*, 3 September 1903.

15 Henry Gidney, 11th Annual General Meeting of the Anglo-Indian Association Calcutta, *The Anglo-Indian Review*, February 1938.

16 Articles 29(1) and 30(1) of the Constitution of India 1950.

17 Justice Kirpal, quoted ibid.

References

Primary sources

Agent of the East Indian Railway Letters (1903), Eastern Railway Library, Calcutta.

Bengal Proceedings: Education (1861), (1875), (1876), (1879), (1880), India Office Library.

Committee on the Financial Condition of Hill Schools for Europeans in Northern India (1904), Vol. 11: Oral Evidence, India Office Library.

East Indian Railway Report on Oak-Grove School (1915), National Library, Calcutta.

Official Meetings of the East Indian Railway Board (1885), Agent's Record Room, Eastern Railway, Calcutta.

Oman, J. C. (1877), 'On Training and Industrial Schools for Children of Railway Employees', *Proceedings of the Railway Conference*, OIOCL/PWD/5/7, India Office Library.

Report on the East India Railway Aided Schools (1906), National Library, Calcutta.

The Anglo-Indian Review, Anglo-Indian Association Headquarters, Calcutta.

Modern sources

Arnold, David (1979), 'European Orphans and Vagrants in India in the Nineteenth Century', *Journal of Imperial and Commonwealth History* 7: 2, 104–27.

Bayly, C. (1996), 'Colonial Rule and the Informational Order in South Asia', in N. Crook (ed.) *The Transmission of Knowledge in South Asia: Essays on Education, Religion, History and Politics*, Delhi: Oxford University Press.

Bear, Laura (1994), 'Miscegenations of Modernity: Constructing European Respectability and Race in the Indian Railway Colony, 1857–1931', *Women's History Review* 3: 4, 531–48.

Bear, Laura (2001), 'Public Genealogies: Nations, Documents and Bodies in Anglo-Indian Railway Family Histories', *Contributions to Indian Sociology* 35: 3.

Kennedy, Dane (1996), *The Magic Mountains: Hill Stations and the British Raj*, Berkeley, CA: University of California Press.

Kumar, Krishna (1991), *Political Agenda of Education: A Study of Colonial and Nationalist Ideas*, New Delhi: Sage.

Kumar, Krishna (1992), 'Hindu Revivalism and Education in North India', in M. Marty and R. Appleby (eds) *Fundamentalisms and Society: Reclaiming the Sciences, the Family and Education*, Chicago, IL: Chicago University Press.

Kumar, Nita (1996), 'Religion and Ritual in Indian Schools: Banares 1880–1940', in N. Crook (ed.) *The Transmission of Knowledge in South Asia: Essays on Education, Religion, History and Politics*, Delhi: Oxford University Press.

Shahidullah, K. (1996), 'The Purpose and Impact of Government Policy on Pathshala Guru Mahashoys in 19th Century Bengal', in N. Crook (ed.) *The Transmission of Knowledge in South Asia: Essays on Education, Religion, History and Politics*, Delhi: Oxford University Press.

Srivastava, Sanjay (1998), *Constructing 'Post-Colonial' India: National Character and the Doon School*, New York: Routledge.

Stoler, Ann (1989), 'Making Empire Respectable: The Politics of Race and Sexual Morality in 20th-Century Colonial Cultures', *American Ethnologist* 16: 4, 634–59.

Stoler, Ann (1992), 'Sexual Affronts and Racial Frontiers: European Identities and the Cultural Politics of Exclusion in Colonial Southeast Asia', *Comparative Studies in Society and History* 34: 3, 524–51.

Stoler, Ann (1995), *Race and the Education of Desire: Foucault's 'History of Sexuality' and the Colonial Order of Things*, Durham, NC: Duke University Press.

Van Der Veer, Peter (2001), *Imperial Encounters: Religion and Modernity in India and Britain*, Princeton, NJ: Princeton University Press.

Weston, C. N. (1938), *Anglo-Indian Revolutionaries of the Methodist Episcopal Church*, Bangalore: Scripture Literature Press.

Index

affirmative action programmes in favour of Chinese minorities 216

All Nepal National Free Students Union (Revolutionary) (ANNFSU(R)) 96

Altan Khan, leader of the Tumed Mongols 231n8

'amoral familism' in southern Italy 171

'Anatolian Question' (of the political future of the peoples of Anatolia) 110, 116

Anglo-Indian Association 245–6

Anglo-Indian education: reaction against rigidity causes some Anglo-Indians to attempt to become more Indian 254

Anglo-Indian teachers, and honour of institution where they teach 252–3

Anglo-Indians ('Eurasians') 23, 237–60; and ability to speak English as indications of personal provenance 250–1; and access to an English-medium education 250; legal definition of 259n2

Anthony, Frank, and right to European education 246–7, 250

anthropology and citizenship 4

antimafia activity: Antimafia Commission 175; education 175–83; events 183–4; as an indigenous Sicilian movement rather than a northern import 187; movement (*movimento antimafia*) 21, 172–7; 'new' antimafia of the 1980s and 1990s 174–5; 'old' antimafia of the 1950s and 1960s 174–5; working-class reactions to 184–7

antiracism 205–6

archbishop of Cyprus, control over Greek Orthodox education in Cyprus 107

army, role of in Pakistani textbooks 150

Arnold, Thomas 55n7

Aryans *see* RSS school textbooks

Ataturk ('father of the Turks') (Mustapha Kemal Pasa) 116; credited with freeing women from religious backwardness 119; as *gazi* (religious warrior) and ethnic father 116; reforms rapidly adopted in

Cyprus 116; referred to with capitalized third-person pronoun 116; as 'second prophet' and 'saviour' of the Turks 119

Aurangzeb (Mughal emperor) as portrayed in Indian and Pakistani textbooks 154–5

aydinlar ('lights', 'enlightened ones') (Turkish Cypriot intellectuals) 117

aydinlatmak ('enlightenment'), perceived need for among Turkish Cypriots 119–20

Ayodhya (site of the Babri Mosque and the alleged birthplace of the god Ram(a)) 159; *see also* NCERT textbook

Balibar, Etienne 259

Bangladesh 165–6n5

Bayly, Archbishop: provision of education for Eurasians and working-class Europeans in India 241, 259n4

beef-eating by Brahmins in ancient India *see* NCERT textbook

Bharatiya Janata Party (BJP) (Hindu nationalist) 156, 157, 158–9, 160, 164, 165, 166n17, n18, 248

bikas (development) in Nepal 78

Bildung/paideia/formation acquise 40, 55n7, 109–10

Borsellino, Paolo, antimafia magistrate, 174, 183

Bossi, Umberto, founder of the *Lega Nord* 171

Boxer Movement (*yi he quan*) and Boxer War 130, 140

'Brahmanization' *see* upper castes

Britain 22, 196–207

British colonial government, inability to control education content in Cypriot schools 106–10

British government of India's concern to raise educational standards of European and Eurasian supervisory workers 243–4